"OUR CROWD"

THE
GREAT JEWISH FAMILIES
OF NEW YORK

Stephen Birmingham

SYRACUSE UNIVERSITY PRESS

For the children
Mark, Harriet, Carey

Grateful acknowledgment is made to the following for permission to use the material described below: Mrs. Richard J. Bernhard and Mrs. Joan L. Simon for quotations from the unpublished autobiography of Adolph Lewisohn; Harvard University Press for a poem by Minnie Louis published in *The Promised City* by Moses Rischin, copyright © 1962 by the President and Fellows of Harvard College; Geoffrey T. Hellman for excerpts from a letter of his grandmother, Frances Seligman Hellman, to her brother, Edwin Seligman, dated May 2, 1880; Mrs. Herbert H. Lehman for excerpts from a letter which appeared in *Herbert H. Lehman and His Era* by Allen Nevins, Charles Scribner's Sons, 1963; The Macmillan Company for the letters of Otto Kahn which appeared in *The Many Lives of Otto Kahn* by Mary Jane Matz, copyright © 1963 by Margaret D. Ryan; Presses de la Cité, Paris, for a quotation from *D'Un Siècle à l'Autre* by Prince Poniatowsky, 1948. The translation of this material by Geoffrey T. Hellman appeared in "Sorting Out the Seligmans" in the October 30, 1954, issue of *The New Yorker;* J. & W. Seligman & Company for the letters of Joseph, Henry, William, and Isaac Seligman, a letter by Secretary Thompson, and portions of a speech by Jesse Seligman which appeared in *Over the Long Term: The Story of J. & W. Seligman & Co.* by Ross L. Muir and Carl J. White, copyright © 1964 by J. & W. Seligman & Co.; John M. Schiff for extracts from *Our Journey to Japan*, by Jacob H. Schiff, and two letters of Jacob Schiff which appeared in *Jacob H. Schiff: His Life and Letters* by Cyrus Adler, Doubleday Doran, 1928, Vol. I; Frederick M. Warburg for excerpts from "Reminiscences of a Long Life," by Frieda Schiff Warburg.

The genealogical chart is based on one which originally appeared in "A Business Elite: German-Jewish Financiers in Nineteenth-Century New York," by Barry E. Supple, *Business History Review,* Vol. 31, No. 2. The adapted and modified version which appears in this book has been redrawn and appears through the courtesy of the *Business History Review.*

Originally published in 1967 by Harper & Row, Publishers, Incorporated.

The paper used in this publication meets the minimum requirements of American National Standard for Information Sciences-Permanence of Paper for Printed Library Materials, ANSI Z39.48-1984. ∞™

Library of Congress Cataloging-in-Publication Data

Birmingham, Stephen.
Our crowd : the great Jewish families of New York / Stephen
Birmingham.
p.   cm. — (Modern Jewish history)
Originally published: New York : Harper & Row, 1967.
Includes index.
ISBN 0-8156-0411-4 (pbk. : alk. paper)
1. Jews—New York (State)—New York—Social life and customs.
2. Jewish bankers—New York (State)—New York. 3. Upper class—New
York (State)—New York. 4. New York (N.Y.)—Ethnic relations.
I. Title. II. Series.
F128.9.J5B5 1996
974.7'004924—dc20   96-32954

Manufactured in the United States of America

"OUR CROWD"

Modern Jewish History

Henry L. Feingold, *Series Editor*

Contents

PART IV THE AGE OF SCHIFF

PART V NEW YORK 21, N.Y.

ILLUSTRATIONS FOLLOW PAGE 244

Preface

It was my intention, when I undertook to write this book, *not* to write a book that would be simply "about rich people."

To be sure, none of the families here portrayed is needy. Far from it. But—to me, at least—their accomplishments and their contributions to the special spirit and *élan,* as well as to the physical appearance, of New York City make the fact of their wealth seem secondary. It was my feeling, when I considered this book, that such names as Lehman, Lewisohn, Schiff, Loeb, Warburg, Guggenheim, Seligman, Kahn, Straus, Goldman, and Sachs are nationally, and in most cases internationally, known. They stand for banking and industrial efficiency, government service, philanthropy, and vast patronage of the arts, science, and education. And yet, due to a persistent reticence and unwillingness to boast—which in themselves are noble attributes—the men and women who made these names celebrated are little understood as human beings. It was my hunch that behind the marble façades lived people with as much capacity for folly, and grandeur, as human beings everywhere. It should come as no surprise that this turned out to be the case.

As a novelist, my interest has always been in the romance of people, and I suppose I am always a bit more concerned with what people *are* than what they do. And so one question may call for an answer: What is particularly significant about these German Jewish banking families? As a reader, I am an habitual peeker-ahead at endings, and so I shall open the book with the same thought as the one I close it with: These German Jewish families are more than a collective American success story. At the point in time when they were a cohesive, knit, and recognizably distinct part of New York society, they were also the closest thing to Aristocracy—Aristocracy in the best sense—that the city, and perhaps the country, had seen.

Obviously, it was not possible to take up each of the hundreds of people who composed, and compose, "our crowd." I have tried only to write about those men and women who to me seemed either the most exceptional, or the most representative, of their day.

I want to thank a number of people who have been particularly helpful with information, guidance, and suggestions in the preparation of this book.

I am indebted to Geoffrey T. Hellman for permission to quote from his published material, for supplying me with documents, manuscripts, letters, photographs, and personal reminiscences of his family, the Seligmans, as well as for magically unearthing the unpublished autobiography of Adolph Lewisohn, which neither Mr. Lewisohn's children nor grandchildren knew existed. I am grateful to Mrs. Joseph L. Seligman of New York for further material on her husband's family; to Mrs. Carola Warburg Rothschild for similarly kind and gracious assistance with memories and family papers pertaining to the Warburgs, "old" Loebs, and Schiffs, and for giving me access to the memoirs of her mother, the late Frieda Schiff Warburg. I also thank Mrs. Dorothy Lehman Bernhard, and her sons Robert A. and William L. Bernhard, for insights into the Lehman clan; Mrs. Phyllis Goodhart Gordan, for data concerning the Goodharts and Walters; Mr. Frank Lewisohn and Mrs. Joan Lewisohn Simon, for their help with Lewisohn recollections.

I am deeply grateful to Mrs. August Philips (Emanie Arling) for permission to quote from her novel, *Red Damask* (which she wrote under the name Emanie Sachs), for her spirited recollections of the days when she herself was a part of "the crowd," and for her enthusiastic interest in my project. To Mr. Walter E. Sachs, I am indebted for Sachs and Goldman family and business reminiscences, as well as for access to his own unpublished autobiography. I would like to thank Messrs. Lee Klingenstein of Lehman Brothers, Carl J. White of J. & W. Seligman & Co., John L. Loeb, Jr., of Carl M. Loeb, Rhoades, Inc., David L. Mitchell of S. G. Warburg & Company, Ltd., and Professor Oscar Handlin of Harvard for their suggestions and pointers during various stages of the book, and Beverley Gasner, who read the book's first draft with an especially finicky eye.

This is the moment, too, to say a special word of thanks to Mrs. Mireille Gerould, who took on the job of financial researcher for the book with cheerful vigor, despite the fact that her research took her through periods of banking history when records, if kept at all, were kept most sketchily.

Though each of the people above has contributed to the book, I alone must be held responsible for its shortcomings.

I would also like to thank my friend and agent, Carol Brandt, for her coolheaded guidance of the project from the beginning, and to say a special word of praise to my friend and *wife,* Janet Tillson Birmingham, whose typing endurance is supreme and whose editorial hunches and suggestions are unerringly right. At Harper & Row, for their enthusiasm and moral support, I am grateful to Cass Canfield and the Misses Genevieve Young and Judith Sklar and, last but hardly least, to my editor, Roger H. Klein, who was first to propose that this was a book worth writing, and whose intelligence and taste have, in the process, affected nearly every page.

S.B.

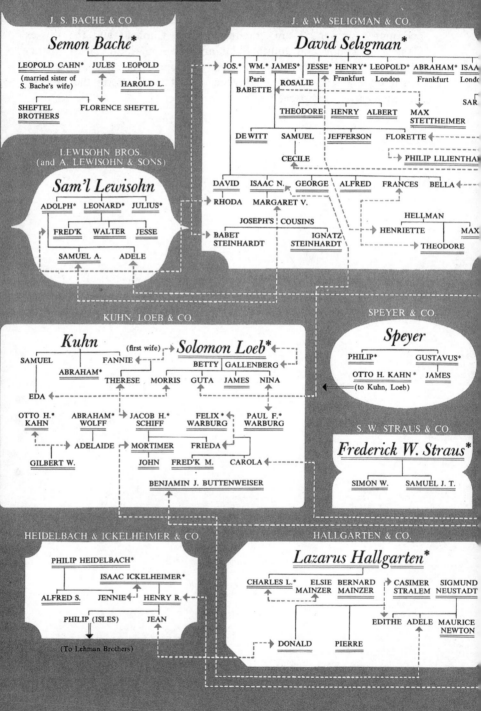

J. S. BACHE & CO.

Semon Bache*

LEOPOLD CAHN* — JULES — LEOPOLD
(married sister of S. Bache's wife)
HAROLD L.

SHEFTEL BROTHERS — FLORENCE SHEFTEL

LEWISOHN BROS. (and A. LEWISOHN & SONS)

Sam'l Lewisohn

ADOLPH* — LEONARD* — JULIUS*

FRED'K — WALTER — JESSE

SAMUEL A. — ADELE

J. & W. SELIGMAN & CO.

David Seligman*

JOS.* — WM.* — JAMES* — JESSE* — HENRY* — LEOPOLD* — ABRAHAM* — ISAA
Paris — ROSALIE — Frankfurt — London — Frankfurt — Londo
BABETTE — SAR

THEODORE — HENRY — ALBERT — MAX STETTHEIMER

DE WITT — SAMUEL — JEFFERSON — FLORETTE

CECILE — PHILIP LILIENTHA

DAVID — ISAAC N. — GEORGE — ALFRED — FRANCES — BELLA

RHODA — MARGARET V.

JOSEPH'S COUSINS — HENRIETTE — HELLMAN — MAX

BABET STEINHARDT — IGNATZ STEINHARDT — THEODORE

KUHN, LOEB & CO.

Kuhn — (first wife) — **Solomon Loeb***

SAMUEL — FANNIE — BETTY — GALLENBERG
ABRAHAM* — THERESE — MORRIS — GUTA — JAMES — NINA
EDA

OTTO H.* KAHN — ABRAHAM* WOLFF — JACOB H.* SCHIFF — FELIX* WARBURG — PAUL F.* WARBURG

ADELAIDE — MORTIMER — FRIEDA

GILBERT W. — JOHN — FRED'K M. — CAROLA

BENJAMIN J. BUTTENWEISER

SPEYER & CO.

Speyer

PHILIP* — GUSTAVUS*

OTTO H. KAHN* — JAMES
(to Kuhn, Loeb)

S. W. STRAUS & CO.

Frederick W. Straus*

SIMON W. — SAMUEL J. T.

HEIDELBACH & ICKELHEIMER & CO.

PHILIP HEIDELBACH*

ISAAC ICKELHEIMER*

ALFRED S. — JENNIE — HENRY R.

PHILIP (ISLES) — JEAN

(To Lehman Brothers)

HALLGARTEN & CO.

Lazarus Hallgarten*

CHARLES L.* — ELSIE BERNARD — CASIMER — SIGMUND
MAINZER MAINZER — STRALEM — NEUSTADT

EDITHE — ADELE — MAURICE NEWTON

DONALD — PIERRE

H. CARTER

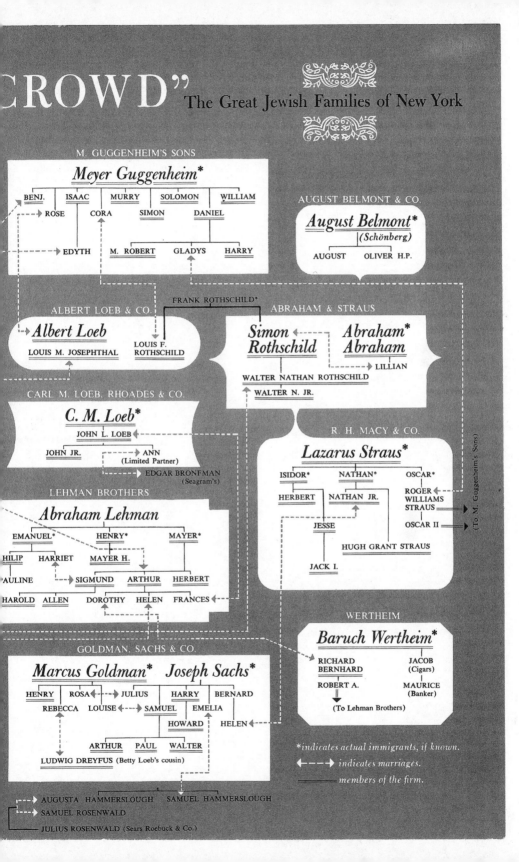

CROWD" The Great Jewish Families of New York

M. GUGGENHEIM'S SONS
Meyer Guggenheim*
BENJ. ISAAC MURRY SOLOMON WILLIAM
ROSE CORA SIMON DANIEL
EDYTH M. ROBERT GLADYS HARRY

AUGUST BELMONT & CO.
August Belmont*
(Schönberg)
AUGUST OLIVER H.P.

ALBERT LOEB & CO. FRANK ROTHSCHILD* ABRAHAM & STRAUS
Albert Loeb
LOUIS M. JOSEPHTHAL
LOUIS F. ROTHSCHILD
Simon Rothschild ← Abraham* Abraham
LILLIAN
WALTER NATHAN ROTHSCHILD
WALTER N. JR.

CARL M. LOEB, RHOADES & CO.
C. M. Loeb*
JOHN L. LOEB
JOHN JR. ANN (Limited Partner)
EDGAR BRONFMAN (Seagram's)

R. H. MACY & CO.
Lazarus Straus*
ISIDOR* NATHAN* OSCAR*
HERBERT NATHAN JR. ROGER WILLIAMS STRAUS
JESSE OSCAR II
HUGH GRANT STRAUS
JACK I.
(To M. Guggenheim's Sons)

LEHMAN BROTHERS
Abraham Lehman
EMANUEL* HENRY* MAYER*
HILIP HARRIET MAYER H.
AULINE SIGMUND ARTHUR HERBERT
HAROLD ALLEN DOROTHY HELEN FRANCES

WERTHEIM
Baruch Wertheim*
RICHARD BERNHARD JACOB (Cigars)
ROBERT A. MAURICE (Banker)
(To Lehman Brothers)

GOLDMAN, SACHS & CO.
Marcus Goldman* Joseph Sachs*
HENRY ROSA ← JULIUS HARRY BERNARD
REBECCA LOUISE ← SAMUEL EMELIA
HOWARD HELEN
ARTHUR PAUL WALTER
LUDWIG DREYFUS (Betty Loeb's cousin)

*indicates actual immigrants, if known.
←---→ indicates marriages.
═══ members of the firm.

AUGUSTA HAMMERSLOUGH SAMUEL HAMMERSLOUGH
SAMUEL ROSENWALD
JULIUS ROSENWALD (Sears Roebuck & Co.)

PART I

A PARTICULAR PRINCIPALITY

"PEOPLE WE VISIT"

By the late 1930's the world of Mrs. Philip J. Goodhart had become one of clearly defined, fixed, and immutable values. There were two kinds of people. There were "people we visit" and "people we wouldn't visit." She was not interested in "people we wouldn't visit." When a new name came into the conversation, Mrs. Goodhart would want to know, "Is it someone we would visit? Would visit?" She had an odd little habit of repeating phrases. If one of her granddaughters brought a young suitor home, she would inquire, "There are some Cohens in Baltimore. We visit them. Are you one of them? One of them?"

Granny Goodhart's rules were simple and few. One's silver should be of the very heaviest, yet it should never "look heavy." One's clothes should be of the very best fabrics and make, but should never be highly styled, of bright colors, or new-looking. Mink coats were for women over forty. Good jewels should be worn sparingly. One hung good paintings on one's walls, of course. But that anyone outside the family and the "people we visit" should ever see them was unthinkable. (House and art tours for charity, where one's collection could be viewed by the general public, had not yet come into fashion in New York; if they had, Mrs. Goodhart would have considered it a dangerous trend.) She believed that little girls should wear round sailor hats and white gloves, and that boys should concentrate on Harvard or Columbia, not Princeton. Princeton had graduated too many people she did not visit.

She believed that good upholstery improved, like good pearls, with wearing. She did not care for Democrats because she had found most of them "not gentlemen." It was hard to reconcile this with the fact that her own brother, Herbert Lehman, was Democratic Governor of New York State and was associating with "people like Roosevelt." She had never visited the Roosevelts, and wouldn't if she had been asked. As a Lehman, she belonged to one of New York's most venerable Jewish families (her husband's family, the Goodharts, were not to be sneezed at either), and she was entitled to her views. And, since most of the people she visited, and who visited her, lived much as she did and felt as she did about most matters, she was able to move through her dowager years in an atmosphere of perpetual reassurance.

She was concerned with her friends' health in general and with her husband's in particular. She worried about his tendency to overweight. "Now I think, Philip, you will not have the fish soufflé, the soufflé," she would say to him as the dish was passed to him. (But her maid, Frances, was on Mr. Goodhart's side; she always managed to slip a little on his plate.) Her husband often used the *Wall Street Journal* as a screen at the dinner table, and ate behind it.

There were few ripples in the pattern of her life. Once her cook broke her leg, and Granny Goodhart took to nursing the poor woman, who was well on in years herself and had been in the family "forever." Each night, at table, Mrs. Goodhart would deliver a report on the broken leg's progress. One night her husband said sharply, "Damn it, Hattie! You mustn't sympathize with her or she'll never learn!" Hattie Goodhart went right on sympathizing, of course, but stopped talking about it.

There were occasional other unsettling experiences. She and her friends did not believe in "making a point" of being Jewish, or of being anything, and sometimes this led to confusion. One of her Lehman sisters-in-law, a prominent Jewess like herself, was turned away from a hotel in the Adirondacks because, of all things, the hotel politely said it had a policy and did not accept gentiles! Then there was the visit from the young California psychologist. He was connected with the Institute of Behavioral Sciences, and had been conducting Rorschach tests with college students to determine their reactions to Adolf Hitler's anti-Jewish policies in Europe. Granny Goodhart met the young man in New York at the home of her daughter, Mrs. Frank Altschul. Everyone there was talking about what the young man was doing, and, after dinner, he offered to perform a few of his tests on the group. Granny took the Rorschach test, and—to the astonishment of everybody—it turned out that Granny was an anti-Semite!

Still, as one of the *grandes dames* of German Jewish society, Granny was admired and much loved by her friends. To her grandchildren she was a round little person smelling of wool and Evening in Paris who greeted them at the door with outstretched arms and peppermint candies clutched in both hands, and gathered them in. She may have had her ways, but at least she was true to them.

And, watching this doughty little lady walking slowly through the rooms of her house, it was possible—*almost* possible—to believe that Granny Goodhart's ways were eternal ways, and that hers was a world that had always been and would always be.

Most of the people Granny Goodhart visited lived within a clearly defined area—those blocks of prime Manhattan real estate between East Sixtieth and East Eightieth streets, bordered by Fifth Avenue, known in pre–Zip Code days as New York 21, N.Y.—in houses served, in the days before all-digit dialing, by Manhattan's "great" telephone exchanges: TEmpleton 8, REgent 2, RHinelander 4. It was a world of quietly ticking clocks, of the throb of private elevators, of slippered servants' feet, of fires laid behind paper fans, of sofas covered in silver satin. It was a world of probity and duty to such institutions as Temple Emanu-El (a bit more duty than devotion, some might say), that stronghold of Reform Judaism, and its rabbi, Dr. Gustav Gottheil, and duty to such causes as Montefiore and Mount Sinai hospitals, the Henry Street Settlement, and the New York Association for the Blind, whose annual ball is one of the great fixtures in the life of the Jewish upper class. For the children, it was a world of discipline and ritual—social as much as religious—of little boys in dark blue suits and fresh white gloves, little girls in dresses of fuchsia satin, learning to bow from the waist and curtsy at Miss Viola Wolff's dancing classes, the Jewish answer to Willie De Rham's. It was a world of heavily encrusted calling cards and invitations—to teas, coming-out parties, weddings—but all within the group, among the people Granny Goodhart visited, a city within a city.

It was a world of curious contradictions. It held its share of decidedly middle-class notions (dry-cleaning did not really clean a dress, no matter what the advertisements said—every young girl was taught this), and yet it was also a world of imposing wealth. Granny Goodhart's lifetime spanned an era, from the Civil War days into the 1930's, when wealth was the single, most important product of New York City. It was an era when Fifth Avenue was still a street of private houses, and the great mansions to which everyone was periodically invited included Otto Kahn's sprawling palace, Jacob Schiff's castle, the Felix Warburgs' fairy-tale house of Gothic spires. It was a world where sixty for dinner was commonplace (it was Otto Kahn's favorite number), and where six hundred could gather in a private ballroom without crowding. It was a world that moved seasonally—to the vast "camps" in the Adirondacks (not the Catskills), to the Jersey Shore (not Newport), and to Palm Beach (not Miami)—in private railway cars. A total of five such cars was needed to carry Jacob Schiff and his party to California. Chefs, stewards, butlers, valets, and maids traveled with their masters and mistresses, and a nurse for each child was considered essential. Every two years there was a ritual steamer-crossing to Europe and a ritual tour of spas.

Yet it was not particularly a world of fashion. One would find *The Economist, Barron's,* and the *Atlantic Monthly* on the coffee table more often than *Vogue* or *Town and Country.* One would expect to find a collection of Impressionist paintings, or of fine books, rather than elaborate furs or jewels. One worried about being "showy," and spared no expense to be inconspicuous. Granny Goodhart's sister-in-law was the daughter of Adolph Lewisohn, a man who spent $300 a month for shaves alone. To keep his Westchester estate from being an eyesore to his neighbors, he employed thirty full-time gardeners to manicure his acreage and nurse his fourteen hothouses. He was so determined that his parties be in the best of taste—for years his New Year's Eve ball in his Fifth Avenue house was one of the largest in the city—that, to keep his cellars supplied with the best wine and spirits, he ran up an average bill of $10,000 a month. And yet, at the same time, he had become inter-ested in prison reform. When not giving dinner parties for his friends, he could be found at Sing Sing, dining with this or that condemned man in Death Row. He gave the stadium that bears his name to City College because, as he put it, "They asked me to."

Mr. Lewisohn's friend and neighbor, Felix Warburg, had a squash court in his city house, another in his country house—which also had a polo field—a yacht, a set of four Stradivarius violins, and a set of black harness horses identically marked with white stars on their foreheads. When Mr. Warburg was depressed, he had a gardener build him a platform high in a tree; from there, Warburg would consider the possi-bility of clearing another of his famous "vistas" from the surrounding woods. Yet he was so inordinately domestic that, upon checking into a hotel room in a foreign city, the first thing he did was to rearrange the furniture into the coziest possible "conversational groupings." He liked to give away a million dollars at a clip to a list of some fifty-seven different charities, and yet when his children asked their father how much money he had, he would make a zero with his thumb and fore-finger. It was a world, in other words, that gave equal weight to modesty and dignity as to pomp, comfort, and splendor. Jacob Schiff, for whom one private Pullman was seldom ample, could therefore send his son home from a party because the boy's suit was too "flashy."

Mr. Willie Walter, whose son was married to Granny Goodhart's daughter, owned a custom-built Pierce-Arrow which he kept constantly replenished with new Packard engines. An astonishing piece of machinery, it was tall enough for a man to stand in. Mr. Walter suffered from glaucoma, and believed that it was the result of striking his head on the ceiling of a low car. There was, therefore, a practical reason for the automobile's imposing proportions. The tallest car in New York was always driven with its window shades down, and, both inside and out, its decor was restrained; every bit of chrome was oxidized so that it would have no glare, out of consideration for Mr. Walter's sensitive eyes. Though the Pierce-Arrow could be seen coming from blocks away, its head high above the heads of others, Mr. Walter also believed that toning down the car's trimmings made it less "conspicuous." (After Willie Walter's death, his heirs sold the Pierce-Arrow to James Melton, a classic-car enthusiast; Melton painted it, polished it, added all sorts of shiny gadgetry, and sold it to Winthrop Rockefeller, who added even more. You should see it now.)

To the city outside, this world seemed exotic and remote. It was envied, misunderstood, resented, but more often than not it was simply ignored, which was exactly what members of the Jewish upper class preferred. Overlooked, the group flourished and grew. It developed an outer shell that was opaque and impervious to prying. Within, a territory existed as intricately designed and convoluted as a chambered nautilus, a particular principality cloistered inside the world of the very rich. To those who lived there, it was all there was. It was New York's *other* Society—a citadel of privilege, power, philanthropy, and family pride. What was *not* so apparent was that it was also a citadel of uncertainty and fear. Under the seemliness there was bitterness, jealousy, warfare—no more and no less than in any society. One had to be brought up in the castle to realize that. For even murder, when it occurred, was politely kept "within the family."

Among the people Granny Goodhart visited were the Loebs, Sachses, Guggenheims, Schiffs, Seligmans, Speyers, Strauses, Warburgs, Lewisohns, and of course other Lehmans and Goodharts. There were also the Baches, the Altschuls, the Bernheimers, Hallgartens, Heidel-bachs, Ickelheimers, Kahns, Kuhns, Thalmanns, Ladenburgs, Wertheims, Cahns, Bernhards, Sheftels, Mainzers, Stralems, Neustadts,

Buttenweisers, Josephthals, Hellmans, Hammersloughs, Lilienthals, Morgenthaus, Roṣenwalds, Walters, and Wolffs. With the exception of the Guggenheims—who came from German-speaking Switzerland—all these families trace their origins to Germany (a surprising number to Bavaria). They have referred to themselves as "the One Hundred," as opposed to "the Four Hundred." They have been called the "Jewish Grand Dukes." But most often they have simply called themselves "our crowd."

The men of our crowd made their fortunes as merchants or bankers or—in the now somewhat antique phrase—as "merchant bankers." Their business monuments include R. H. Macy & Company (Strauses), Abraham & Straus (Abrahams, Strauses, and Rothschilds—"the Brooklyn branch" of the European Rothschilds), and a number of celebrated investment and banking houses in Wall Street, including Lehman Brothers; Hallgarten & Company; Speyer & Company; Kuhn, Loeb & Company; Goldman, Sachs & Company; J. & W. Seligman & Company; J. S. Bache & Company; and Carl M. Loeb, Rhoades & Company. Families such as the Lewisohns and Guggenheims, whose fortunes are usually associated with mining and smelting, also maintained banking houses downtown. Some families, such as the Wertheims, moved from manufacturing (cigars) into banking (Wertheim & Company).

For a long time you either belonged to "our crowd" or you didn't. For several generations the crowd was strikingly intramural when it came to marriage, making the crowd—to the larger crowd outside it—seem so cohesive and tight-knit as to be impenetrable. The "people we visit" became also the people we married. In the first American generation, a number of founding fathers married their own close relatives. Joseph Seligman and his wife were first cousins, and in the next generation Joseph's brother's daughter married Joseph's sister's son. Meyer Guggenheim married his stepsister, and a Lewisohn married his own niece— and had to go to Europe to do it since such a union was, at that time, against the law in the United States—and as a result of this match he became a great-uncle to his children and his brother's son-in-law. Three Seligman brothers married three sisters named Levi; several other Seligmans married Walters, and several married Beers. The Seligmans also followed the Jewish practice of offering widows in the family to the next unmarried son, by which process several women became double Seligmans. Double cousinships abound. Seligmans have also married Hellmans, Loebs, Lewisohns, Lilienthals, Guggenheims and Lehmans; Lehmans, who have married first-cousin Lehmans, have in addition married Lewisohns, Buttenweisers, and Ickelheimers; Ickelheimers have married Stralems; Stralems have married Neustadts; Neustadts have married Schiffs; Schiffs have married Loebs and Warburgs; Warburgs have married Loebs, who, of course, have married Seligmans.

Today the intermarriage within the crowd presents a design of mind-reeling complexity. But envision a dewy cobweb in the early morning on a patch of grass. Each drop of dew represents a great private banking house; the radii that fan out are sons and daughters, grandsons and granddaughters, and the lacy filaments that tie the whole together are marriages. Kuhn, Loeb & Company was originally composed of a particularly tight network of love—with Kuhn and Loeb (who were brothers-in-law) both related to Abraham Wolff, another K-L partner whose daughter married yet another partner, Otto Kahn. A Loeb son married a Kuhn daughter, and another Loeb daughter married another partner, Paul Warburg, while Jacob Schiff's daughter Frieda married Paul Warburg's brother Felix (a partner too). This turned an aunt and her niece into sisters-in-law, and made Paul his brother's uncle.

At Goldman, Sachs, two Sachs boys married Goldman girls, and another Goldman girl married Ludwig Dreyfus (a G-S partner), who was related by marriage to the above-mentioned Loebs, and a Sachs daughter married a Macy's Straus, while another Sachs daughter married a Hammerslough whose sister was married to a Rosenwald of Sears, Roebuck & Company. (Not surprisingly, when Sears puts a new stock issue on the market this is done by Goldman, Sachs & Company.)

The two founding fathers of J. S. Bache & Company, Leopold Cahn and Semon Bache, were linked in marriage as well as business, with Leopold married to Semon's wife's sister. Semon's son, Jules, married Florence Sheftel, the sister of another Bache partner. At Hallgarten & Company four principal partners—Charles Hallgarten, Bernard Mainzer, Casimer Stralem, and Sigmund Neustadt—were similarly intertwined: Hallgarten married to Mainzer's sister, and Stralem married to Neustadt's daughters. Heidelbach, Ickelheimer & Company was founded, in 1876, as the result of a marriage, when Isaac Ickelheimer married Philip Heidelbach's daughter. At a Westchester party recently, a Klingenstein, related to Lehmans, and a Kempner, related to Loebs, were asked if they weren't also related to each other. "I suppose so" was the reply.

For many years Wall Street firms such as these obeyed a kind of Salic law, with partnerships descending only to sons and sons-in-law. This discouraged outsiders and encouraged intermarriage. "In the old days on the Street," says one stockbroker, "your relatives were the only people you could trust." There was another reason. In the old days, if you were a Jewish immigrant, the only person you could turn to if you needed money was a relative. For forty-four years after its founding in 1867, Kuhn, Loeb & Company had no partners who were not related by blood or marriage to the Loeb-Kuhn-Wolff family complex. For nearly fifty years after Goldman, Sachs was founded, all partners were members of the intermarried Goldman and Sachs families. The Lehmans hardly seemed to need intermarriage at all; until 1924, nearly seventy-five years after the firm was founded, all the partners were named Lehman.

Two firms one might suppose had sprung from the same forebears—Kuhn, Loeb and Carl M. Loeb, Rhoades—did not. The Loebs of Kuhn, Loeb are no kin to the Loebs of Loeb, Rhoades, who are no kin to Harold Loeb and no kin to Gerald Loeb, the financial writer who works for E. F. Hutton & Company, nor to Leopold and Loeb who were a thrill-killing team from Chicago. The two New York banking families are always getting mixed up, even by the *New York Times,* which is usually most careful about such matters, but the descendants of Solomon (Kuhn, Loeb) Loeb, an earlier immigrant and founder of the more venerable house, are known in the crowd as "the *real* Loebs." Presumably, the descendants of Carl M. (Loeb, Rhoades) Loeb are unreal Loebs. The Rhoades name came in as a result of a nonmarital merger. Nobody knows quite why the name is retained (there are no Rhoadeses in the firm), unless for its overtones of Scholars and the Colossus of almost the same name. But by taking a tortuous route through Lehmans and Seligmans, it is possible to get these two Loeb families related to each other, by marriage.

The pattern of intermarriage has not always been strictly adhered to. Whenever someone marries "outside the crowd," someone is bound to comment that German Jewish society isn't a knit thing any more, that the structure is falling apart. Mixed marriages, anti-Semitism, and conversion are three linked themes that reappear often in the fugue of German Jewish life in New York. The Contents, for example, are a family of Dutch Jewish origin who were in New York long before the first Germans arrived. A number of German families have married Contents, and, as a result, Mrs. John D. Gordan,* a scholarly Bryn Mawr trustee—a granddaughter of Granny Goodhart—fell heir to two handsome Content family portraits. Painted in 1833, they are of Simon Content and his wife, Angeline, and each contains a mysterious detail. By Simon's hand rests the Hebrew prayer book; by Angeline's is the Book of Common Prayer. Willie Walter, Mrs. Gordan's grandfather, used to frown at the pictures when he entered the room and mutter, "It was not a mixed marriage. It was *not!"*

By strict crowd standards, one does not have to marry out of the faith to enter into a *mésalliance.* Years ago, Samuel Sachs's daughter, Ella, married a man named Harry Plotz, who was Polish, and there was a terrible fuss. It was not that young Plotz talked Socialism, but he talked Socialism so *loudly.* At about the same time, when Alva Bernheimer, who was definitely in the crowd, married the late Bernard Gimbel, who was not, this was considered an unfortunate match. The crowd con-

* Whose own marriage is a mixed one.

sidered the Gimbels "storekeepers." Someone said, "One department store family is enough," meaning the Strauses. Needless to say, with Gimbel's and Macy's the great Herald Square rivals, no Gimbel ever married a Straus.

When Gerald Warburg married Natica Nast, the daughter of Condé Nast, the crowd was just as startled. For a long time Natica was referred to as "a little Huguenot girl," and, by her mother-in-law, as "a girl of French extraction." The crowd still seemed unprepared, a generation later in 1950, for Felicia Warburg's marriage to Robert W. Sarnoff— whom one member of the crowd explained was "the son of that Russian radio man," Brigadier General David Sarnoff, chairman of the board of RCA. People had also sniffed in the 1920's when it was announced that John L. Loeb, son of Carl M., was engaged to marry the Arthur Lehmans' youngest daughter, Frances. At the Seligmans' Fishrock Camp in the Adirondacks someone said, "But those Loebs aren't *the* Loebs!"

But when R. Peter Straus married Ellen Sulzberger, the crowd was pleased to note that some people, at least, were doing the traditional—if increasingly rare—thing by marrying "within the crowd."

As happens in any social group, the German Jewish crowd in New York has become stratified, and a certain pecking order has evolved based on seniority. There is an Old Guard—families who migrated to America between 1837 and 1860—which would include the Seligmans, Lehmans, Strauses, Sachses, Goldmans, and "perhaps" the Guggenheims. The Guggenheims are a problem because, though they arrived in America relatively early (but not so early as the Seligmans and Lehmans), they did not become staggeringly rich until relatively late, and did not arrive on the New York scene until 1888, at which point the other German Jewish families had already coalesced into a fixed group. It took the crowd a while to get used to the explosive presence of the Guggenheims. As Peggy Guggenheim (whose mother was a Seligman) says of her two grandfathers, "Mr. Guggenheim far surpassed Mr. Seligman in amassing an enormous fortune and buying up most of the copper mines in the world, but he never succeeded in attaining Mr. Seligman's social distinction." In fact, the Seligmans were upset when Peggy's mother consented to marry Mr. Guggenheim. They dispatched a curt wire to Paris relatives saying, "Florette engaged to Benjamin Guggenheim, smelter." Everyone chuckled at the droll way the message became garbled crossing the Atlantic. It read, "Florette engaged. Benjamin Guggenheim smelt her." Also Old Guard are the descendants of Solomon Loeb (of Kuhn, Loeb), though he was a somewhat younger man than the progenitor Seligmans and Lehmans, and did not move from Cincinnati to New York until 1865.

Another member of this first generation of German Jewish immigrants—though he was never a part of the Old Guard "crowd"—was
August Belmont. As German Jewish life became fuguelike, his influence
provided an odd and troubling counterpoint.

Such names as Lewisohn, Schiff, and Thalmann belong to a younger
generation who migrated to New York soon after the Civil War. The
Warburgs and Otto Kahn belong to a third, still younger group who
came in the 1890's. Kahn, Schiff, and the Warburg brothers became
imposingly rich, and all three names became polarized around Kuhn,
Loeb & Company. There is a general feeling that these youngsters did
not have to work quite so hard for their money as the Old Guard did. A
split began to develop within the crowd, between the bright, young, very
rich "new group" and the settled, established, not-quite-so-rich "older
group." It was not only a difference in ages, but a difference in how the
two groups "did things." Though they all saw each other and entertained
each other, there were—emotionally, at least—two crowds.

The Warburgs like to point out that the Warburg family were well-to-
do bankers in Germany long before any of the Seligmans or Lehmans,
who were poor, even dreamed of coming to America. The Lehman-
Seligman camp is apt to say, "The Warburgs weren't anybody until they
married into the Schiffs, and Schiff wasn't anybody until he married into
the Loebs, so there you are." The Warburgs say loftily, "We came to
America and showed all the others how to do it." To this, one of the
Lehmans has replied sharply, "They tried to *tell* everybody how to do it,
is what they mean. *Our* family never had much to do with that Schiff-
Warburg group. We considered them terribly bossy. Of course there
were some people who tried to play their game. It was called 'Keeping
up with the Schiffs.' " "It must be terrible," Lord Lionel Rothschild is
supposed to have said, "to be a Jew and not be named Rothschild."
Clearly he was unaware of what was going on across the Atlantic in
New York.

Today in New York, when members of the crowd get together, long
hours can be spent arguing about which of the great German Jewish
families is the greatest, or grandest, or has accomplished the most, or
contributed the most. Which is the grandest of the families Cleveland
Amory has labeled "The Jewish Grand Dukes"? Several think the
Schiffs and the Warburgs, on the basis of their philanthropies alone,
should receive the palm. Others champion the Strauses, who, though
their money was made "in trade" (some Strauses branched out into
banking), have not been idle as philanthropists either, and have also
contributed notable figures to the worlds of American diplomacy,
publishing, and public service. Others argue that, if one is going to talk
about public service and government, one must give first place to the

Lehmans, who have contributed a New York Governor and U.S. Senator (Herbert), a prominent jurist (Irving), a major American art collector (Robert), and a promising young politician in the fourth generation (Orin).

But there are always the Seligmans. With their "social distinction," they set the tone of German Jewish society in New York for many years. They occupy an anchoring position in the crowd. Without them it is possible that there might have been no crowd at all.

PART II

OUT OF THE WILDERNESS

1837-1865

"MOUNT SELIGMAN"

In the late summer of 1964 a small item in the obituary page of the *New York Times* carried the news that "James Seligman, Stockbroker" had died at the age of seventy-four in his Park Avenue apartment, following a heart attack. A few perfunctory details followed. Mr. Seligman had been born in New York City, had graduated from Princeton, maintained an office downtown in Broad Street, and was survived by his wife and an elderly sister. No mention was made of the once great eminence of his family in financial circles, nor of the Seligmans' still considerable prestige. No note was taken that Mr. Seligman's grandfather, the first James Seligman, had been one of eight remarkable brothers who had composed J. & W. Seligman & Company, once an international banking house of vast importance and power. Nor was it noted that Mr. Seligman's great-uncle, Joseph Seligman, the firm's founder, had been a personification of the American success story. In slightly more than twenty years' time, he had risen from an immigrant foot peddler to a financial adviser to the President of the United States.

The news item, however, contained one note that may have struck readers who knew the Seligman story as ironic. The Seligmans had once been known as the leading Jewish family in America. They had been called "the American Rothschilds." The deceased's grandfather for

many years had been president of the board of trustees of New York's
Temple Emanu-El. (The office was supposed to be an annual one, but
every year the first James Seligman got to his feet and said, "Nomina-
tions for vice president are now in order.") Yet the obituary advised
that funeral services would be held at Christ Church, Methodist.

The Seligmans may not have started everything, exactly, but they
certainly started something. They also started early—proverbially an
auspicious time. Few great American fortunes, furthermore—and few
banking houses—have started from such unpromising beginnings. The
base of Mount Seligman was humble indeed.

Baiersdorf is so small that it does not appear on most maps of
Germany. It lies on the banks of the Regnitz River some twenty
kilometers north of Nürnberg, near the edge of the Bohemian Forest.
Old David Seligman was the village weaver. He was not technically
"old," but at twenty-nine he seemed so. A small, stooped, dour man, he
was given to complaining about his lot.

There had been Seligmans in Baiersdorf for over a century. Theirs
had been a family name long before Napoleon had decreed that
Germany's Jews no longer needed to be known as "sons" of their
fathers' names—Moses ben Israel, and so on. Seventeenth- and
eighteenth-century tombstones in Baiersdorf's Jewish cemetery recorded
the upright virtues of many of David's ancestors, all named Seligman
("Holy man" in German). To later generations in New York, this
would become a fact of some importance. Families such as the Seligmans did not just "come" from Bavaria. They had been established
there for many, many years.

None of the Baiersdorf Seligmans had been wealthy, but David
seemed the poorest, most discouraged of the lot. He enjoyed poor
health, made frequent trips to the cemetery, and from the words on
headstones of departed Seligmans drew a kind of solitary comfort. He
particularly admired one inscription from 1775:

HERE LIES BURIED

ABRAHAM SELIGMAN

IN RIPE OLD AGE, AN UPRIGHT MAN
HE WALKED THE WAY OF THE DOERS OF GOOD
JUST AND UPRIGHT HE ATTACHED HIS SOUL TO
RIGHTEOUSNESS
AND BUSIED HIMSELF WITH THE TEACHINGS OF
GOD AND WITH WORKS OF CHARITY
NIGHT AND DAY, FOREMOST AMONG MEN WHO
ARE BENEFACTORS

Such words did not apply to David. He was lonely and withdrawn. His boyhood friends were married and raising families, but David seemed resigned to bachelorhood. His little house in Baiersdorf's *Judengasse,* or "Jew Street," had begun to sag and leaned disconsolately against the next building. Business was terrible. Nevertheless, one morning in 1818, David returned from the neighboring village of Sulzbach with a plump, young girl named Fanny Steinhardt as his wife.

It was whispered on the *Judengasse* that David Seligman was incapable of fathering children. Fanny's condition during the next few months was watched with more than usual interest. One year after the marriage, Fanny bore David a son, Joseph. Over the next twenty years Fanny presented David with seven more sons and three daughters: William, James, Jesse, Henry, Leopold, Abraham, Isaac, Babette, Rosalie, and Sarah.

Child-bearing took its toll. Two years after the birth of her last child, at the age of forty-two, Fanny died. She had done her duty to the world. She had created the foundation of an international banking house.

But Fanny had given David more than eleven children. As her dowry, she had brought from Sulzbach a stock of dry goods—laces, ribbons, two feather beds, two dozen sheets, twenty pillowcases, and ten bolts of homespun cloth. These, she had cannily suspected, might appeal to the women of Baiersdorf. She had set up shop on the ground floor of David's house, and soon David, the weaver, had been able to call himself by the grander title of "woolen merchant," and had started a small side line selling sealing wax.

Joseph, her first-born, was Fanny's favorite child. As soon as he could see over the counter, he became his mother's assistant in her little shop. In the 1820's there was no German national monetary system. Coinage varied from region to region, and eight-year-old Joseph, at the cash drawer, was quick to notice this. As an accommodation to travelers passing through Baiersdorf, Joseph became a moneychanger—accepting out-of-town coins in exchange for local currency, and selling out-of-town money to men planning trips outside Bavaria. He made a small profit on each transaction. At the age of twelve he operated a miniature American Express Company. Foreign currency, including an occasional American dollar, passed through his hands. He was learning economics, arithmetic, and a bit of geography, his mother pointed out and patted him on the head approvingly.

Fanny was ambitious for all her children, but she focused her dreams on Joseph. At night mother and son would sit opposite each other at the wooden table in the sputtering light of a kitchen candle while she, bent over her mending, talked and the boy listened. Joseph remembered his mother's small, plump hands, and a gesture she had—placing her hand flat out on the table when she made a point. She told him of places better than Baiersdorf, and David reproved her for filling the boy's head with "grandiose ideas." He wanted Joseph for the woolen business.

But a Bavarian woolen business faced, in 1833, a gloomy future. Baiersdorf was a small town, and growing smaller. The Industrial Revolution was under way. Peasants, David's customers, were being forced from the land into industrial cities. Jobs and money in Baiersdorf were growing scarcer. The poor were faced with two choices, both involving further hardship: to move or struggle on where they were.

If the young German poor found themselves with little to look forward to, the outlook for young Jews was even more dismal. Jews were restricted on three sides—politically, economically, and socially. Forced to be peddlers, small shopkeepers, moneylenders—barred by law from dealing with goods that could not be carried with them—they were sequestered in the cramped *Judengassen* and trapped in a tightening strait jacket of regulations based on their religion. In the quarters where German laws forced them to live, they were permitted to own no property beyond the squares of land where their houses stood, and their right to even that much land was precarious. In Bavaria, where attitudes toward Jews were particularly reactionary, the number of Jewish marriages was limited by law in an attempt to keep the number of Jewish families constant. They were surrounded by a heavy network of special taxes, were obliged to pay the humiliating "Jew toll" whenever they traveled beyond the borders of the ghetto, were forced to pay a special fee for the privilege of not serving in the army—though it was an army that would not have accepted them had they tried to volunteer, because they were Jewish. Periodically, Jews were threatened with expulsion from their homes—and often were expelled—unless they paid an added tax for the privilege of remaining.

Three distinct currents of Jewish migration had begun in Europe. There was a migration from German villages in the south and east to northern cities, where Jews often found conditions somewhat worse than those they had faced before. (In 1816 the seven largest cities in Germany held only 7 percent of the Jewish population. A hundred years later over 50 percent of Germany's Jews lived in these seven cities.) There was a general east-to-west movement—out of Germany into England, Holland, and France. At the same time, there was a migratory wave *into* Germany from the east—from Czarist Russia and Poland. Some of these foreign Jews merely passed through Germany on their way to other lands, others stopped for a while, to rest. These latter had a further disruptive effect on the already shaky structure of Jewish communities. Some of these families paused long enough to pick up the German language and to take German names. (In future generations, in New York, it would become a matter of some importance whether such and such a Jewish family, with a German-sounding name, had been a true *native* German family, like the Seligmans, or a stranger from the east, passing through.) Swelled by immigrants from the east, the Jewish population in Western Europe more than tripled during the nineteenth century.

The final migratory move was also westward—across the Atlantic to the land of freedom and enlightenment, the land, moreover, of land and money. In 1819, the year Joseph Seligman was born, the American paddle-wheeler *Savannah* had been the first steam-driven vessel to cross the ocean. It made America seem wonderfully convenient. America fever swept through German villages, particularly in hard-pressed Bavaria. Already, from Baiersdorf, several bands of young men had taken off and were writing home of the wonders of the New World. Fanny Seligman wanted to get her children out of Germany, and she wanted Joseph to go armed with an education. She decided he would do something no Seligman had ever done. He would go to the university at Erlangen. He was just fourteen.

David Seligman protested that they could not afford it. But Fanny, in the best tradition of Jewish motherhood, is said to have gone to a dresser drawer, from which, carefully hidden behind a stack of linens, she withdrew a little knotted sack of gold and silver coins, her life's savings.

Joseph had pale blue, watery, heavy-lidded "Seligman eyes," which gave him an absent-minded, daydreamy look that was deceptive. His face was often set in a sleepy half-smile which gave strangers an impression that he was innocent, easygoing, even simple-minded. With a countrified accent and a changing voice, he loped around the University of Erlangen with his bag of books, a hayseed. Actually, Joseph was an extremely taut and sober-sided young man. He entered Erlangen with one determination—to get ahead. He avoided the social side of university life, and refused to be tempted by Erlangen's famous beer. He possessed another quality that would stand him in good stead in the future. He had a thick skin. The plumpish, solemn, standoffish boy was often taunted by his schoolmates; at times they baited him fiercely. If he was hurt by this, he hid it beneath a shell of indifference.

He was a brilliant student. He studied literature and the classics and, after two years, delivered his farewell oration to the university in Greek. He had also learned some English and some French. Along with the German, Yiddish, and Hebrew that he already knew, he now had six languages. None of these talents was designed to help him sell woolens or sealing wax. Joseph came home from the university with one thought in mind—to go to America.

Among Jewish families the feeling still ran strong that emigration was for the desperately poor. A departing boy was an advertisement to the whole community that a father could no longer afford to feed his son. David Seligman would have to wear his son's defection to America like a badge of shame, but there was an aspect of emigration that was even more alarming. From the land of freedom and enlightenment came rumors that young Jews in America were losing their religion.

It took Fanny a year to persuade David to let the boy go. Fanny made another trip to her little sack of coins—and got a secret loan from her Sulzbach relatives—for Joseph's passage money. David's final words to his son were a tearful entreaty to observe the Sabbath and the dietary laws. Fanny's final gesture was to sew one hundred American dollars into the seat of Joseph's pants.

In July, 1837, Joseph Seligman, seventeen years old, climbed on a horse-drawn wagon with eighteen other Baiersdorf boys. The trip to Bremen and the sea took them seventeen days. They camped along the roads at night. At Bremen Joseph bought passage on the schooner *Telegraph,* one of 142 steerage passengers. The price of a steerage ticket—forty dollars—included one meal a day, an unvarying diet of pork, beans, and a cup of water. Since Jewish law prohibited pork, Joseph Seligman was required to disregard his father's instructions from the beginning. Steerage was cramped, dark, and filthy—years later Joseph used to say of his first crossing, "The less said about it the better"—and Joseph's bed was a wooden plank. Crossing the Atlantic took nine weeks.

Joseph, considerably slimmer, arrived in New York in September in the middle of the great Panic of 1837—hardly a cheerful omen for a future financier. But he did not intend to stay in New York long. Fanny had a cousin in Mauch Chunk, Pennsylvania, and had urged Joseph to go to this unprepossessing outpost. Still with the hundred dollars sewn in his trousers, he started off on foot, a hike of just under a hundred miles.

The leading citizen in Mauch Chunk in those days was a man named Asa Packer, a native of Connecticut, who had established a yard where he built canal boats to haul coal from the local mines. Soon after arriving, Joseph presented himself to Mr. Packer, and the young Connecticut Yankee and the younger Bavarian Jew hit it off immediately. Joseph explained that he was good with figures, and Packer hired him as a cashier-clerk at the salary of $400 a year.

Joseph's quick friendship with Packer displayed what was to become an enduring Seligman habit—the lucky habit of getting to know, and to be liked, by the right people. In 1837 Packer was no more than a prosperous small-town businessman. But this bearded, craggy-faced man was to become a multimillionaire, a United States Congressman (from 1853 to 1857), the founder—with a check for one million dollars—of Lehigh University, the president of the Lehigh Valley Railroad, and a very good friend for a banker to have.

"MOUNT
BEAUTIFUL"

Young August Schönberg cannot have been called casual or "lucky" in his choice of friends; he chose them with too much care, not for their possible future helpfulness but for their present and specific use. Little is known about Schönberg's forebears for a simple reason. In later years he elaborately blurred, and eventually erased, his antecedents. It is known that he was born in 1816—three years before Joseph Seligman— in the Rhineland Palatinate in western Germany, not far from the French border, the son of Simon Schönberg, a poor merchant. (Later on he liked to create the impression that his parents were people of great wealth; all the evidence suggests the opposite.) He was not, as Joseph Seligman was, a dutiful son. He was a wild, unruly, often violent, undisciplined boy with a harsh tongue and cruel ways, who repeatedly flouted his father's authority—a cardinal sin in Jewish homes. Yet he had a razor-sharp mind and a biting wit.

A university, for an education or for polish, had no appeal for him whatever. He wanted to make money. At thirteen he went to Frankfurt—it is likely that he ran away from home—and went to work as an unpaid apprentice for the Rothschilds, the leading Jewish banking house in Europe. How he managed to get his toe in the Rothschild door is unclear.

There is evidence that the Rothschilds were appalled by Schönberg and yet fascinated by him. He was to exert this double effect on people throughout his life—aversion and, at the same time, attraction. He could be rough-spoken and abrupt, and he could be sweetly charming. One thing quickly became apparent to the Rothschilds—he was a financial genius. His first duties were sweeping floors, but he was soon admitted to discussions in the partners' room.

Yet as Schönberg's value grew, he became something of an embarrassment to the Frankfurt Rothschilds. He did not fit the aristocratic Rothschild "image," and so, still in his teens, he was transferred to Naples, where he became very Neapolitan and handled financial negotiations with the Papal Court. At the age of twenty-one, he was reassigned to Havana, where the news of the New York Panic of 1837 reached him. A panic, to Schönberg, suggested a use for his money-making talents. He wound up his Havana business quickly and hurried to New York, arriving the same month as Joseph Seligman, traveling, of course, first class. With Rothschild money, he began buying in a splendidly depressed market.

But some strange sea change had taken place. He was no longer August Schönberg but August Belmont, the French equivalent of Schönberg (meaning "beautiful mountain"). As August Belmont, furthermore, he was no longer a Jew but a gentile, and no longer German but, as people in New York began to say, "Some sort of Frenchman—we think."

New York City in 1837 seems in many ways to have been waiting for a man with August Belmont's talents and tastes to come along. Certainly it was an auspicious moment for a young man eager to make his fortune in banking to descend upon the city, and Belmont arrived with the tremendous influence and backing of the House of Rothschild behind him. The city's mood was up; it was the beginning of the so-called Golden Era, which would see New York change from a provincial port into a giant metropolis. The War of 1812 had given the country confidence in itself, had strengthened its credit abroad (up to then the Rothschilds had considered the United States too unprofitable an enterprise to merit an American agent), and the great age of railroads had begun. The railroads opened up outlying land and carried people there. Railroads carried products back to port cities like New York where, in turn, they were traded to pay for the European imports the newly opened country needed.

New York, by 1837, though it still resembled a steepled and gabled Dutch village sprouting from the Battery at the tip of Manhattan Island, had become the chief financial center of the nation and its major port, through which passed commerce to be financed, goods to be auctioned, and the inland producers' bills of exchange, drawn on British merchant banks, which, to provide cash, had to be discounted. New York, until then, had stood a poor third to Boston and Philadelphia. It had remained under the influence of the Dutch, whose chief economic interests had been limited to up-Hudson furs and their own vast estates outside the city. New York had not developed the tightly knit commercial and financial power groups of the older Eastern cities. There were not, as there were in Boston, such family complexes as the Cabot-Lowell-Lawrence group, which controlled and financed textile companies, or the Lee-Higginson-Jackson alliance, which dominated the money market. New York had not assumed the rigidity of Philadelphia, with its position as the seat of the only national banks the country had ever known. New York, in other words, was ready for the private banker—Pennsylvania in 1814 had passed a law outlawing private banking—it was a city for the entrepreneur, a city flexing its muscles and feeling young and big and strong. All this August Belmont was quick to sense.

New York was a merchant's city. It had become the chief wheat and flour market of the nation, shipping over a billion sacks of flour a year to Europe, and dispatching the major share of the country's cotton. It was also a gambler's city, and the young arriving immigrants—immigration itself was one of the biggest gambles of the day—only heightened the feeling of risk and speculation that was in the air. In the modern age of consumer goods, it is hard to imagine New York as a place where, though there was a great deal of money about, there was really very little to buy. But such was the case. In the absence of goods and luxuries in shops, New Yorkers spent their money gambling—buying and selling mortgages, bonds, IOU's and promissory notes. In 1792 the New York Stock Exchange—older even than London's—was formed under the famous buttonwood tree at the corner of Wall Street, and in 1817 it had been formally incorporated with a set of rules which, by today's standards, were delightfully lax, but which did require a listing of companies whose shares were being offered for trading. All over the country, people who wanted to gamble were turning to Wall Street. By the time of August Belmont's arrival, this casual bazaar was doing a volume of hundreds of millions of dollars a year. Farmers in the new Western lands were selling mortgages to buy stocks and bonds. Small manufacturers were both investing and offering their own shares for sale. Banking, though it had never had much order or logic or even rules, had had a certain predictability. Suddenly—almost overnight, it seemed—it became fast, frantic, and speculative.

The great pendulum pattern of boom followed by bust, which would dominate financial history for the next hundred years, had begun. The Panic of 1837, which would be followed by many more, was blamed on "the habit which all classes seem within the last few years to have contracted, of speculating beyond their means, of living beyond their income, of spending money before it was acquired, and of keeping up the appearance of men who had realized large fortunes while they were only in the act of accumulating them," according to the *Herald*. Before the panic, a speculating American public had invested over a hundred million dollars in canal bonds alone. In this competitive, win-or-lose business, a new kind of bank—and a new kind of banker—was needed. August Belmont saw this. He noticed that the old names which had dominated the early note-issuing commercial banks—names such as Hamilton, Morris, and Willing—were not moving rapidly enough, or skillfully enough, into the new field.

In the Panic of 1837 Belmont was able to perform a service which he would repeat in subsequent panics, and which helped make him a friend to bankers and to the United States Government. By negotiating large loans from the Rothschilds, he was able to shore up United States debtor banks. In other words, he was able, thanks to the hugeness of the Rothschild reservoir of capital, to start out in America operating his own Federal Reserve System.

Socially, New York was not at all the city in 1837 that Boston, Philadelphia, or Charleston was, and here again August Belmont found a niche waiting to be filled. New York society, according to members of the Morris family, consisted only of the Morrises, of Morrisania, their enormous estate north of the city in what is now one of the dreariest sections of the East Bronx. Colonel Lewis Morris once wrote of his city: "As New England, excepting some Families, was ye scum of ye old, so the greatest part of the English in the Province [New York] is ye scum of ye New." The Morrises were, in fact, the only New York family not "in trade." As for the other prosperous families of the city, they were all required to work for a living. The Roosevelts, Bayards, Van Cortlandts, and Rhinelanders were in the sugar-refining business. The Rhinelanders also sold crockery, and the Schuylers were importers. The Verplancks were traders, and Clarksons and Beekmans and Van Zandts were in the retail dry-goods business. Brevoorts and Goelets were ironmongers, and the Schermerhorns were ship chandlers.

Small, wistful newspaper advertisements of the period reveal how humbly the founding fathers of the great old New York families urged the public to buy their wares: Peter Goelet, from his shop in Hanover

Street, begs customers to buy his saddles and pewter spoons and announces that he has received "a consignment of playing cards." Jacob Astor—before he became John Jacob—offers "guitars, fifes and piano-fortes" from his shop in Queen Street, while Isaac Roosevelt extols the virtues of his "loaf, lump, and strained sugar and sugar-house treacle."

Such social life as existed among these folk depended largely on the weather, and when it was balmy and fair, New York society sat outside their front doors on wooden benches and nodded and chatted with their neighbors across the way. Picnics in the wooded hills of midtown Manhattan were also popular, as were boating jaunts to Brooklyn. There were hunting and fishing parties for well-connected young men on the banks of the Harlem River and, in winter, frequent skating parties for both sexes on a Hudson which, in those naïve days before pollutants, often froze from Manhattan to the New Jersey shore. When society entertained, it did so with seriousness. As Washington Irving humorously commented, "These fashionable parties were generally confined to the higher classes, or noblesse, that is to say, such as kept their own cows, and drove their own wagons. The company commonly assembled at three o'clock, and went away about six, unless it was in winter time, when the fashionable hours were a little earlier, that the ladies might get home before dark." Social life certainly seems to have been a barren and bleak affair. As Frederika Bremer wrote, "Here, where almost every person works for a living, one cannot properly speak of a working class, but quite correctly of people of small means and somewhat limited environment and circumstances—*a class which has not yet worked itself up.*"

To the people living in New York, it was something else again. Many New Yorkers actually considered themselves quite racy. In fusty Boston and austere Charleston, for instance, society never dined in public. But in New York society had discovered the restaurant, and the fashionable gathered at Niblo's and Delmonico's for dinners and even floor shows. The daring drank wine, and the less daring mixed a little wine with their milk.

In upstate New York such old patroon families as the Van Rensselaers—Stephen Van Rensselaer in 1838 was said to have an income of a million dollars a year—made periodic excursions to their city houses, leaving their stamp on social life. The Van Rensselaers, said James Silk Buckingham, "give a great gravity and decorum to the general tone of society here. There is less of show in houses, carriages, and horses; less of ceremony and etiquette in visiting; very early hours for meals; seven for breakfast, two for dinner, and six for tea; plainer and more simple fare." The plainness and the decorum, however, did not delight an English visitor of the period, Margaret Hunter, who wrote home after a dinner party at Mrs. Van Rensselaer's that she found all the guests "exceedingly commonplace," and was "amused with the motley company we meet here, Senators, lawyers, actors, editors of newspapers, one of them a Jew, all placed indiscriminately at table and all joining equally in the conversation." Still, such as it was, it was New York society, and August Belmont determined to join it and to help it "work itself up."

Though there was no explicit anti-Semitism in New York at the time, it was generally considered "better"—among such families as the Roosevelts, Van Rensselaers, Goelets, and Morrises—not to be Jewish. Yet there was, at the same time, a distinct Jewish upper class, composed of families who had been in the city even longer than some of the leading gentiles.

The first recorded Jewish settler in Manhattan was a man named Jacob Barsimson who arrived early in 1654. He was an Ashkenazic, or German, Jew. No one knows what happened to Mr. Barsimson, and his importance to history has been eclipsed by the arrival, somewhat later that same year, of twenty-three Jewish immigrants aboard the bark *St. Charles,* often called "the Jewish *Mayflower.*" The *St. Charles* had carried its passengers from Recife, Brazil, but actually the little band's journey had begun thousands of miles farther away and years before in fifteenth-century Spain and Portugal. There, after the violence of the Inquisition—and, by a prophetic coincidence, in the same year that Columbus discovered the New World—the Catholic monarchs had ordered all Jews to adopt Christianity or depart the Iberian Peninsula. Those who would not convert had fled and scattered—to Italy, Turkey, Hamburg, and to various Baltic ports. Many had been drawn to the tolerant atmosphere of the Netherlands, and when the Dutch conquered Recife in 1630 and urged settlers to go to the new possession and form colonies, many Jews had migrated to South America, where they found a few years' peace. But in 1654 Recife had been reconquered by the Portuguese, and Brazil was no longer safe for Jews. They fled once more. The *St. Charles* passengers were on the last stage of an exodus of the ancient Sephardic culture from medieval Spain.

In the unwritten hierarchy of world Jewry, the Sephardim are considered, and consider themselves, the most noble of all Jews because, as a culture, they claim the longest unbroken history of unity and suffering. The arrival of twenty-three Sephardim in New Amsterdam was not auspicious. When he discovered they were penniless, Governor Peter Stuyvesant threw the lot of them in prison. There they might have stayed, but, fortunately for them, many stockholders of the Dutch West India Company were Jewish and so Stuyvesant was persuaded to release the twenty-three on the condition that "the poor among them" be no burden and "be supported by their own nation." Within a year most had established themselves as merchants, trading in tobacco, fish, and furs, though they were not admitted as freemen until the next century. As a group, the Sephardim were proud, diligent, but an aloof and somewhat crusty people, and they were once labeled "the obstinate and immovable Jews."

The great Sephardic families of New York, many of them descended from the *St. Charles* arrivals, include the Hendrickses, the Cardozos, the Baruchs, the Lazaruses, the Nathans, the Solises, the Gomezes, the Lopezes, the Lindos, the Lombrosos, and the Seixases. By the beginning of the nineteenth century a number of the Sephardim had become quite wealthy. Old Harmon Hendricks, for instance, had a copper store in Mill Street (now South William Street) and a factory in New Jersey which was the first copper-rolling mill in the country. He died in the 1840's, according to one report, "immensely rich, leaving over three millions of dollars" and a great deal of valuable real estate. His daughter was married to Benjamin Nathan, a stockbroker in Wall Street, and, in fact, Hendricks copper shares were considered among the blue chips of the era. In *The Old Merchants of New York City,* published in the 1860's, Joseph A. Scoville reported that

> With all the revulsions [sic] in trade, the credit of the [Hendricks] house has never been questioned, either in this country or in Europe, and today in Wall Street, their obligations would sell quite as readily as government securities bearing the same rates of interest. No man stood higher in this community while he lived, and no man has left a memory more revered than Harmon Hendricks. When he died, the synagogue which he attended lost one of its best friends, and the rising generation of that numerous family could not have a better example.

Elsewhere the Jews were regarded with a similar admiration and respect and, because they were still relatively few in number,* with curious interest. In 1817, when a watchmaker named Joseph Jonas became the first Jew to settle in Cincinnati, one report says:

> He was a curiosity at first, as many in that part of the country had never seen a Jew before. Numbers of people came from the country round about to see him, and he related in his old age of an old Quakeress who said to him, "Art thou a Jew? Thou art one of God's chosen people. Wilt thou let me examine thee?" She turned him round and round, and at last exclaimed: "Well, thou art no different to other people."

In New York the Sephardic families and their synagogue, Shearith Israel, had a distinct and special status. Many of their men had fought on the side of the colonists in the American Revolution, and as merchants and

---

* There were probably less than one thousand Jews in America by the end of the eighteenth century.

bankers they had helped finance the war and provision and outfit its armies. Haym Solomon, who had come from Poland, worked closely with William Morris and the Continental Congress as a broker, and helped raise a particularly large sum for the Revolution. For his services he was given the official title of "Broker to the Office of Finance." Even earlier, Jewish bankers had lent money to Lord Bellamont, a particularly improvident eighteenth-century colonial Governor of New York, helping to keep the colony financially on its feet, and New York's first Lutheran church was built with money advanced by Jewish bankers— among them Isaac Moses, who helped establish the Bank of North America in 1781.

But by the beginning of the nineteenth century the complexion of the Jewish community in New York had begun to change. German Jews had begun to trickle in. At first, the Germans were taken into the established Sephardic congregation, intermarried with the Sephardim, and adopted the Sephardic ritual, which had already become quite Americanized. But, as the German migration grew, it became increasingly difficult for the Sephardim to accept the Germans. As Charles Bernheimer has said, "The small Sephardic communities, in defence of their own individuality, could not, and, by reason of their hidalgo pride would not, continue to absorb the new element. On the other hand, the prominent, useful individuals of the German section felt the propriety of devoting themselves to the needs of their countrymen." This was part of it. There was also a matter of "native American" versus "foreigner" and, more than anything, a matter of class. The Sephardim had become successful businessmen and—to their way of thinking, certainly—sophisticated and cultivated city dwellers. The Germans, on the other hand, particularly after the fall of Napoleon in 1815 and the beginning of European reaction, were for the most part poor, soiled-looking, and underfed. Most of them were arriving, like Joseph Seligman, in steerage. When they could manage the language at all, they spoke English with heavy and guttural accents. Most had had little education. They seemed uncultivated, and—because they were poor—aggressive. They were an embarrassment. The Sephardim were merchants and bankers; the Germans were going off as foot peddlers. And so by 1837 the doors of the Sephardim—and of Synagogue Shearith Israel—were closing to Germans. August Belmont, *né* Schönberg, may, with his usual acuity, have realized this also. His quick and complete apostasy—and his determination to climb into the gentile society of the Morrises and Mrs. Van Rensselaer —may be explained by the fact that the best class of Jews in New York would not have asked him to *their* picnics, hunts, and parties.

The first thing New York society noticed about August Belmont was that he had lots of money. It was Rothschild money, to be sure, but he used it lavishly. As a financier with the funds of the world's largest private bank at his fingertips, he was immediately important not only to American companies but to the United States Government, which was always running out of cash and whose credit needed constant infusions from bankers. August Belmont became a figure, both as a host and as a guest, at New York parties. He spoke some Italian, a little Spanish, a little French, and all three languages with an atrocious accent, but nobody in New York knew the difference. It was exciting to hear him drop phrases in foreign tongues, and he was admired for his hand-kissing "Continental manner." (New York society regarded anything European as synonymous with elegance.) August Belmont could by no means have been considered handsome. He was short and rather stout, with iron-colored side whiskers. His features were round and Germanic, but his eyes were arresting—small, but astonishingly black and bright. Yet they were evasive eyes, which never looked directly at a person and seemed forever focused on some object in the middle distance.*

For all this, there was something about him that caused women to have impure thoughts—a hard-to-define but vaguely titillating vulgarity. Meeting a woman, those jet-black eyes would fall to rest upon that curve below her throat and appear to be defrocking her, crinoline by crinoline, from that point downward. At the same time, his cynical manner and harsh, bitter tongue, along with his clear reluctance to reveal his past, made him a figure of mystery and glamour. It was whispered that he had insatiable sexual appetites, and was a cruel and demanding lover. It began to be rumored that the Rothschilds "had a reason" for wanting Belmont out of Europe. To what hideous Rothschild secret was he privy? There had to be something. Why, if he was their "representative," was his new banking house not called N. M. Rothschild & Sons rather than August Belmont & Company? The unfounded rumor started—and is still heard today—that Belmont was actually an illegitimate Rothschild son.

The men did not take to him quite so much as the ladies did. Still, they knew it was wise to listen to him, and so he went everywhere and met everyone. He announced himself to be an epicure, and was perhaps the first person in New York to make the serving of good food fashionable. His own dinner invitations to Delmonico's assumed priority over all others. In the early days, to be sure, no one quite knew where he lived. (Some said he slept in his office.) And men who had accepted his hospitality and eaten his food began to say to their wives afterward, "For God's sake, don't introduce that man Belmont to our daughters!"

But it would be to no avail. For the next fifty years New York society would dance to whatever tune August Belmont chose to play.

* An animator for the Disney studios in California told the author that he had modeled the character of the evil coachman in *Pinocchio* on a portrait of August Belmont.

– 4 –

ON

THE ROAD

There was no society in Mauch Chunk to distract Joseph Seligman, even if he had been able to afford its pleasures. Mauch Chunk isn't much of a town today, and it was less in 1837, when Joseph arrived.* But Joseph took to the town, and his work with Asa Packer, with gusto. Packer, a dozen years older than Joseph, became Joseph's tutor and protector.

The Yankee Packer's affection for Joseph was understandable. Jewish immigrants in the seventeenth and eighteenth centuries had found

---

* In 1954, hoping to improve its prospects, Mauch Chunk renamed itself Jim Thorpe, after the famous athlete. The improved prospects failed to materialize and, ten years later, Jim Thorpe decided to change its name back to Mauch Chunk. It never considered calling itself Joe Seligman, and the towns which did name themselves Seligman after Joseph and his kin have had no better luck than Mauch Chunk from tying in with a noted personage. Seligman, Missouri, had only 350 residents in 1880 when it stopped being Roller's Ridge and became Seligman, in honor of Joseph; its population is about 400 today. Seligman, Arizona, northwest of Phoenix, named after Jesse Seligman, is still an arid sheep-raising freight-division point on the Santa Fe, in the neighborhood of which live some 700 souls. A third Seligman, in White Pine County, Nevada, gave up long ago and no longer exists.

themselves treated with special friendliness by people from New England. New England Puritanism, with its literal interpretation of the Old Testament, was a sort of neo-Judaism—a Judaism translated into Anglo-Saxon terms. The Puritans coming to America had identified themselves with the Israelites in search of the Promised Land, and King George III was equated with the Pharoah. They called the new land Canaan and frequently referred to the Covenant they had made with God. Early in New England the Hebrew language became a major subject taught in colleges, and even secondary schools. To refer to a fellow New Englander as "a good Jew" was to pay him the highest compliment; it meant that he was pious and industrious; it had nothing to do with his blood or his religion. New England parents gave their children Old Testament names—Moses, Joshua, Abraham, and so on. New England Protestantism was considered an outgrowth, or extension, of Judaism, and New England preachers spoke continually of Zion and Jerusalem, of "the God of Israel" and "the God of Jacob."

The Puritans were also convinced that the second coming and final judgment were at hand, and knew, as an article of faith, that the conversion of the Jews would precede these cataclysmic events. It had become a New England tradition to cherish the people who would play such an important role in Puritan salvation, and to encourage their conversion. This lingering belief that Jews were worthy of special respect and honor would stand them in good stead when they began to enter the financial community of Wall Street, a world whose dominant figures were men whose roots extended back to Puritan New England.

At the end of the first year Packer wanted to raise Joseph's salary to $500 a year, but Joseph, who had managed to save $200, was anxious to go out on his own. Reluctantly, Packer let him go.

During his stay in Mauch Chunk Joseph had noticed that men and women from outlying farms made occasional, and laborious, wagon trips to market in the town. He had also made note of the things people bought. His theory was that for the convenience of having goods brought to their doors farm families would be willing to pay a bit more than the prices charged in town, miles away. With his savings, he bought some merchandise—small jewelry, some watches, rings, and knives—and, with a pack, set off on foot, peddling his wares through rural Pennsylvania. Within six months he had put aside $500, enough to send passage to his two next oldest brothers, William and James, who, back in Baiersdorf, itched to join him.

They were a strange-looking lot, the three Seligman brothers and peddlers like them—bearded, shaggy-headed, their faces dusty from the road, in long ill-fitting coats and baggy trousers, walking in mud-caked shoes, with a shuffling gait, stooped under their packs—but how they looked didn't matter to them. They carried sticks to ward off dogs, and they had to endure children who came running out after them crying, "Jew! Sheeny! Christ-killer!" Boys pelted them with handfuls of gravel, sticks, and green apples, and leaped at them to pull their beards or knock off their hats. They shuffled on with their dreams bottled inside them, driven by a furious singleness of purpose—to make money. At night they slept in open fields, under their coats, with a pack for a lumpy pillow. In return for a few chores a farmer might let a peddler sleep in his barn. A true bed was a luxury and baths were rare. Keeping the dietary laws was an impossibility. Yet the Seligman boys always assured old David, in their letters home, that the laws were being faithfully kept.

Joseph's selling theory was a simple one: "Sell anything that can be bought cheaply, sold quickly at a little profit, small enough to place inside a pack and light enough to carry." The boys sold bolts of woolen and cotton cloth, lace trimmings, velvet ribbons, thread, men's handker-chiefs and undershirts, women's shawls, sashes, tablecloths, napkins, pins, needles, bobbins, buttons, thimbles, shoehorns, and cheap spec-tacles. Their packs weighed from one to two hundred pounds.

If an item was needed in an area, the boys were willing to walk to a town where it was available, buy it, and bring it back. A local store had run out of tobacco. William Seligman walked twelve miles to another town where he traded a German silver ring, which he had bought for under a dollar, for a hundred penny cigars. He then walked twelve miles back and sold the cigars for four cents apiece. The 300 percent profit made it worth the walk. A peddlers' grapevine, composed of men like themselves, kept peddlers informed of conditions in surrounding areas.

Joseph learned that "Newcastle disease" had infected the poultry flocks of a nearby village. He traded two yards of cotton print for a pair of healthy laying hens, and carried them there, clucking and flapping, one under each arm. He sold them at a tidy profit. As he grew to know his territory and customers, Joseph was also able to initiate a practice that made him a popular peddler. He extended a bit of credit here and there, and this was appreciated.

But the plain fact was that the peddling Seligmans didn't care how they were treated (which would stand in contrast with their attitude in New York a few years later, when they would care very much). They took rebuffs and abuse on the road willingly because peddling was only a means to an end. By 1840 the three Seligman boys had realized part of this end: they had made enough money to rent a small building in Lancaster, which they used as headquarters for their peddling enter-prises. In the front they opened a shop to display their wares. In the back they had beds to sleep in. It gave them their first real business address in America. In 1841 they sent passage home for a fourth brother, fourteen-year-old Jesse, to help them peddle and tend the store.

MRS. RANKIN'S
GALOSHES

The store gave the Seligmans a warehouse for their goods. They could expand their line into larger, heavier, and more general merchandise—boots and overshoes, brooms, bustles, hardware, and bags of feed. They were graduating from foot peddlers to small-town merchants.

Joseph was a perfectionist, a stickler for rectitude, and had no patience with anything that smacked of wasted motion. He had the energy of an ox, and anyone less energetic infuriated him. But, as he became a businessman—with that important commodity, a place of business—a change began to come over him. He began to assume dignity. He acquired presence. He shaved his face smooth, and combed his fine head of silky, light-brown hair back in the slightest wave, revealing a fine, high forehead. He smelled of soap, pomade, and a better brand of cigars. As a ragged peddler, thrusting his goods with eager hands before skeptical farmers' wives, he had been a compulsive smiler. Now he smiled less, and his expression to the world at large became one of wise, fatherly tolerance. His presence did not inspire intimacy; it was not intended to. It was intended to inspire confidence and command respect.

William, next to Joseph in age, was a clever but overweight and rather lazy fellow. He loved to eat, and was—to Joseph's distinct displeasure—fond of wine. He also showed a penchant for young ladies; Joseph still considered women a waste of time and money. William fancied himself a wit, and was forever making jokes which left Joseph not amused. (None of William's famous "jokes" is recorded, and perhaps that is just as well; one prank, however, was to sneak up behind his brothers in the store and give them a playful kick in the pants.) As a businessman William was somewhat devil-may-care. Joseph examined William's accounts with more than the usual amount of scrutiny. In years to come this was to prove a wise practice.

The third brother, James, was not particularly good with figures. Little discrepancies—not through guile, but through oversight—turned up in James's accounts. But James was handsome, the best-looking of the boys, and affable—and a born salesman. He used to boast that he could sell umbrellas on the Gobi Desert, and though he kept a poor ledger, he loved the feel and jingle of money in his pockets. As a result, his peddling profits often topped the other boys'—even Joseph's own— which placed James high in Joseph's esteem. Though still a teen-ager (which Joseph considered too young for such interests), James had lady friends in Lancaster whom he squired around. Joseph scolded William for his interest in women, but forgave it in James.

Unlike James, Jesse *was* good with figures. Though barely fourteen, Jesse had the audacity to point out niggling errors in Joseph's bookkeeping. No matter how hard Joseph tried to shape his brothers into an efficient working unit, the four spent a certain amount of time wrangling and shouting at one another. Joseph, the worrier and account-keeper, often accused the other three of not taking the business, or themselves, as seriously as he did.

Soon after the Lancaster store was opened, young James came to Joseph with a selling idea. Pennsylvania was in danger of becoming overpeddled. James wanted money to buy a horse and wagon which could carry more goods and take him farther afield—to the South where, James had heard along the grapevine, things were considerably better, where people were crying "Cotton is King!" and a slave economy was making men wealthy.

Joseph, who tended automatically to resist suggestions from the younger boys, reportedly replied, "What do I say? I say *chutzpah!* Horse and wagon indeed! What are your feet for?"

James persisted. A horse and wagon, as he put it, would give the Seligmans "a traveling store."

Joseph was adamant. James might be a good salesman, but he still needed more experience in selling before embarking on such a venture. While he and Joseph were arguing, James later remembered, a certain Mrs. Rankin, the wife of a local grocer, came into the store. Mrs. Rankin's entrance was a pivotal event in the Seligmans' business history.

It was a warm and lovely summer day. James pulled Joseph aside and whispered, "If I can sell her a pair of winter galoshes, will you let me go?"

Joseph, who found it hard to refuse a wager, hesitated, then shrugged and nodded. James hurried out to wait on Mrs. Rankin, who was looking for a few yards of cotton print.

"Pretty bad storm coming, Mrs. Rankin," James said. "You'll need a pair of warm galoshes."

"Storm?" she asked. "Really, Jim? How can you tell?"

"I can feel it in my bones, Mrs. Rankin. My bones never lie. A bad storm—snow and sleet. You'll need galoshes."

"Snow and sleet? In June?" She laughed. "Oh, Jim, you're joking me!"

He gave her his best smile and said, "But you'll need some good galoshes when winter comes, won't you, Mrs. Rankin? Let me sell you a nice pair."

"Oh, all right!" she laughed. "Jim Seligman, you are a caution!"

"I'll have them for you within a week," he said.

After Mrs. Rankin left, Joseph was stern. "James," he said, "I want you to remember never to make misstatements in order to make a sale. What you did was clever and amusing, but don't go too far. We want to keep our reputation for honest dealings."

Years later, however, James Seligman would give this bit of advice to his sons and grandsons: "To sell something you have to someone who wants it—that is not business. But to sell something you don't have to someone who doesn't want it—*that* is business!"

As the first mobilized Seligman, James set off on a wide-swinging tour of the American South. In a surprisingly short time he was back, and spread his profits on the table before his brothers' wondering eyes—$1,000 or, as James remembered later, "more than either of my brothers had earned." Jesse, however, looking over the figures, noticed that James had forgotten to deduct the cost of the horse and wagon, which made the profit only about $800. Still, it was an imposing sum. As Jesse wrote later, "We concluded to take the advice of this purse-proud Nabob—that we would better our condition by removing to that section of the country."

In the fall of 1841 the four boys pulled up stakes in Lancaster and, with $5,000 worth of merchandise which took nearly all their joint capital, set out for New York, where they boarded a schooner for Mobile. The trip took them six weeks and almost cost them their lives. A storm hit the ship and nearly sank it—for several days it was officially reported as lost—but when the boys finally reached Mobile, they were in good enough health to set up an open-air tent to display their wares.

But soon they were quarreling again. James, pointing to the new profits, took a perhaps understandable attitude of I-told-you-so. Feeling that he had "discovered" the South, he began to argue that he should direct the Seligmans' Southern operations, which did not sit well with Joseph, who complained that the profits were not what he had expected. Joseph's little organization seemed on the verge of falling apart.

Then a letter arrived from Baiersdorf. The redoubtable Fanny had died. Mournfully, old David also said that his woolen business was in such a state that he could no longer afford to keep the seven motherless children in Germany.

Joseph quickly took charge. They must bring the remaining Seligmans to America. The boys pooled their resources and sent $2,000 to Baiersdorf, and early in 1842 a small band of Seligmans prepared to cross the Atlantic. Led by Babette, who was twenty, and Rosalie, fifteen, were ten-year-old Leopold, eight-year-old Abraham, seven-year-old Isaac, and baby Sarah, who was two. Old David, who had watched with dismay while his oldest sons left one by one, watched these six leave with resignation. He had chosen one last son, thirteen-year-old Henry, to remain as his helper. James headed North to meet his brothers and sisters in New York, to find rooms for them all in Grand Street, and to see that the younger ones were enrolled in school to learn English—a prerequisite for any American enterprise. When news came from Baiersdorf that old David's woolen business had failed completely, Joseph wrote back assuring his father's creditors that his debts would eventually be paid. The last Seligmans to arrive on these shores, in 1843, were old David and Henry.

David Seligman seemed dazed by the New World, confused by what his sons were doing. He tried to follow their far-off wanderings through tiny Alabama towns with queer names—Frisco City, Gosport, Suggsville, Gees Bend. It seemed clear to him that they had become hoboes or, even worse, beggars. Though the boys sent money regularly to New York, David could not believe that they were earning it honestly. David died in New York, barely two years after his arrival, certain the Baiersdorf Seligmans had come a long way down in the world.

Today David's bones reside in the Seligman mausoleum in the Salem Fields Cemetery of Temple Emanu-El, in Brooklyn. The mausoleum, a vast marble edifice in the Byzantine style, is now the home of over forty

Seligmans, whose names occupy places of varying luster in American financial, philanthropic, and social history; and who, though they may have had their differences, now lie united and presumably at peace. Nearby stands the Guggenheim mausoleum, which is larger (some say "showier"), but, as the Seligmans point out, the Seligman mausoleum commands the finer view. And, since these mausoleums are maintained by trusts which control considerable funds, the Seligmans say, "Our mausoleum usually does a little better on the market."

6

ON TO

THE CITY

The arrival of all those additional Seligmans turned out to be providential for the four peddling brothers. The extra mouths to feed not only made them peddle harder; the new arrivals also forced them to settle their differences. They were providers now, and, by remote control, householders. The boys in the South now had a strong emotional tie with New York. They began making frequent trips North—always to buy goods, but also to check on the group in Grand Street. If it had not been for the children, the brothers might have continued the profitable but humble business of wandering through Alabama, peddling, setting up shops by the side of the road, and moving on. The influx of children gave them a new sense of purpose.

In their earliest Alabama days their shops had been set up under tents or in the open air. In Birmingham an old spreading tree near the center of town is known as "the Seligman tree." Today no one knows why, but it is one of many trees under which the boys spread their goods. But soon after the children arrived, the boys rented three permanent buildings in villages outside Selma and opened dry-goods stores—one in Greensboro, one in Eutaw, and one in Clinton.* Now they were small chain-store operators. They hired their first clerks. They continued to peddle a bit, but now most of their time was spent buying. In New York Babette and Rosalie ran up pairs of men's work pants and rolled hems for handkerchiefs, and whenever a brother arrived in town, the girls presented him with armloads of handiwork for the Seligman stores.

As a peddler Joseph had been willing to take the jeers and slurs that went with the territory. But as a proprietor of three stores he was not. Selma apparently was no freer of bigotry in the 1840's than it is today, and when a Selma man made an anti-Semitic remark to Joseph, Joseph retaliated. Joseph was small-boned and short, and in the fight that ensued he got the worst of it. But he must have conducted himself well enough because the man pressed assault charges against him.

When the case came to trial, it became clear that the judge was also an anti-Semite. He made repeated references to Joseph as "this Jew," "this foreigner," and "this member of a so-called Chosen Race." He found Joseph guilty, and was about to pronounce a prison sentence. It was probably the bleakest moment in Joseph's life. Then a young man who had witnessed the fight, and knew its cause, stood up in the courtroom and spoke out for Joseph. The young man happened to be the son of an Alabama Supreme Court justice, and his words had weight. The judge reversed his decision, and Joseph was released. The Alabama jurist's son—one of a growing list of importantly placed men the Seligmans would have the good fortune to stumble upon—was to enter the Seligmans' lives at another crucial moment, later on.

In New York both Babette and Rosalie had met young men who now asked to marry them. Both were men of solid German Jewish stock— Babette's was Max Stettheimer, and Rosalie's was Morris Lehmaier (later changed to Lemaire). The girls excitedly wrote Joseph of these developments, but Joseph at first was not pleased. It seemed to him only another problem on top of all his others. Problems, in a family the size of the Seligmans, came several at a time. What would become of the other four children—Leopold, Abraham, Isaac, and baby Sarah? Joseph gave his consent only when the girls agreed to split the four smaller children between them. But when Babette's wedding, the first of the two

---

* For many years the Seligmans, and families like them, would show a preference for renting their places of business and their homes rather than buying them. This was not a reluctance to settle down. They remembered too well the futile attempts of Jews in Germany to buy land and the many instances where Jews had been summarily expelled from land they had thought they owned. The Seligmans would display this same reticence toward parcels of real estate when, not many years later, for an astonishingly low price that they could easily have afforded, they had a chance to buy one-sixth of Manhattan Island.

to occur, drew near, Joseph would send only one brother, James, North to attend it, and he gave James an additional assignment—to set up a New York store. James found a corner location in downtown Manhattan and rented it. "J. [for Joseph] Seligman & Brothers, Merchants" opened for business at No. 5 William Street in 1846.* At last the Seligmans were city folk, and right around the corner from Wall Street.

New York, at this time, was a town that still looked and sounded like a seaport. What is now the financial district was a long way from the maze of narrow, airless canyons between towers of granite and glass and steel that it is today. Instead, a fresh salt breeze blew across Bowling Green from the bay and the Atlantic beyond, and the horizon was hectic with the masts of sailing vessels from foreign ports, and the streets were noisy with horses and wagons and men unloading cargo. The spirit of oceangoing commerce was everywhere. And—what would be a rarity today—one could actually see and smell the products that were making their way into the port: the bales of hides and fleece and sacks of wheat and flour from the opening West; cotton from the South; bars of copper from the Great Lakes; crates of poultry from upstate and New England; meats, vegetables, eggs, fish, timbers for railroad ties. Very soon bars of gold would be unloaded on the streets from California. Everything was out in the open air. Stocks were traded on street corners along with diamonds and foreign currency. New York *was* trade—there was virtually no other business. In this zesty atmosphere it was impossible for a young man not to smell the money to be made.

Babette's marriage gave Joseph his first brother-in-law, and Joseph put him promptly to use. Along with William, Max Stettheimer was sent to Saint Louis, where W. Seligman & Company was opened at 166 North Main Street. With stores in New York and Saint Louis, in addition to Greensboro, Clinton, and Eutaw, things were looking up again. Max Stettheimer's father, Jacob, was taken in, placed in the New York store, and in a short space of time Abraham Seligman—now fifteen and ready to work†—was shipped to St. Louis to assist William; Max Stettheimer was shipped back to New York to help his father, where the firm name was changed to Seligman & Stettheimer, Dry Goods Importers; Jesse and Henry were shifted out of Alabama to upstate New York, where, in Watertown, their new firm was called J. & H. Seligman,

* On this corner, later renumbered One William Street, would eventually rise the ornate eleven-story headquarters of J. & W. Seligman & Company. This wedge-shaped building, topped by a Romanesque tower, is now a landmark of the financial district as—through the many ironies of financial fortune—the present home of Lehman Brothers.

† Where was Leopold, two years older than Abraham? Leopold was a slow-starting Seligman, and would prove to be something of a trial to Joseph as the years went by. Babette used to argue that Leopold was "artistic."

Dry Goods. (Jesse liked to say the "J." stood for Jesse, but anyone who knew Joseph knew that all J.'s really stood for Joseph.) In Watertown the Seligmans ran their first advertisement in the Watertown *Jeffersonian,* which announced:

SHAWLS! SHAWLS!!

200 ALL WOOL LONG SHAWLS of the Richest Colors and Latest Styles, just arrived and will be sold at prices which cannot fail to suit all purchasers. Brocha, Cashmere, and Silk Shawls we offer now at lower prices than ever heard of!

It was a chilly October morning, and the ladies came in droves.

In Watertown the Seligmans made another valuable friend. He was First Lieutenant Ulysses Simpson Grant of the 4th Infantry, who was stationed at Madison Barracks, eleven miles away, and who dropped into the Seligmans' store looking for "a bit of finery" for his new bride. Jesse waited on the sad-faced young Lieutenant and, as Jesse wrote later, "On our acquaintance we immediately became friends."

Probably Grant was looking for a new male friend his own age at that point. Most of his friends prior to that year had been made in taverns, and already his commanding officer had begun warning him about his drinking habits. His new wife was doing her best to steer him toward other forms of sociability. At her urging, he had helped form Rising Sun Division No. 210 of the Sons of Temperance Lodges in Watertown, had become presiding officer of the lodge, and often marched militantly in local temperance parades. In his off-duty, nontemperance-meeting hours, Grant began sitting around with pleasant, sober Jesse Seligman. The two played checkers, whist, and poker, chewed tobacco and smoked cigars. Grant hated to talk politics.

Rosalie was the sentimental Seligman sister. She doted on her husband and on married life in general, loving to perform such wifely tasks as polishing his shoes, brushing his hair, rubbing his back when he was weary, and nursing him when he was indisposed. She quickly became pregnant, bore him a daughter, wept that it wasn't the son he'd hoped for, and longed to be pregnant again. By the spring of 1848 Babette was pregnant, and Rosalie's world had become a rosy blur of cooking, house cleaning, medicines, motherhood, and obstetrics. She began to worry about her brothers' unmarried state—particularly Joseph, who was approaching thirty. Joseph, meanwhile, was busily making plans for his first trip back to Germany to buy more goods for his stores.

Rosalie began a secret correspondence with a Baiersdorf girl named Babet Steinhardt, who, Rosalie had decided, would be the perfect mate for Joseph. Babet was a first cousin—she was Fanny Seligman's brother's child—which made it seem all the cozier, and a match Fanny would certainly have approved. Rosalie filled her letters to Cousin Babet with rapturous details of Joseph's good looks, gentle nature, and money. And to Joseph Rosalie began dropping references to Babet's beauty, modesty, and housekeeping skills. She suggested that he combine his business trip to Germany with a *Brautshau* (bride search), and hinted that, in view of his rapidly expanding operations, a time would come when he could no longer count on brothers and brothers-in-law to help him out; he would need sons. Joseph got the point. But he was annoyed at Rosalie for hammering Babet's virtues so tirelessly, and accused her of wanting to collect a marriage broker's commission.

When he got to Germany, however, he made a trip to Baiersdorf. Word of his affluence had spread, and there was a sizable welcoming committee on hand to meet him. He sought out all his father's creditors, paid them, and insisted on adding accumulated interest. He visited his mother's grave. And he met Babet Steinhardt. She was just twenty, and, to his surprise, Joseph found her quite as advertised. He married her in a *gemütlich* village ceremony and in November, 1848, started home with her—the first Seligman to travel to America in other than steerage class.

7

MATTERS OF

STATUS

It would become a question of some importance, later on in New York when the German Jewish crowd had crystallized around such families as the Seligmans, Lehmans, Guggenheims, Goldmans, Sachses, and Loebs, whether one's immigrant ancestor had "started with a wagon" or started on foot. It was nearly, though not quite, as important as how far back one could trace one's family history in Germany.

Which means of "starting" transportation was actually "better" would become a debatable point. On the one hand, starting on foot showed a certain physical stamina. Starting with a wagon, on the other hand, might indicate superior business acumen. Most Lehmans feel strongly that the Lehmans started with a wagon. One thing is certain. By 1844, when Henry Lehman arrived in Mobile, the wagon had become the fashionable means of peddling. With his wagon, then, he started north along the Alabama River and within a year had worked his way successfully to Montgomery.

The capital of Alabama, however, in those days was a town not much bigger than Rimpar, Bavaria, where Henry had come from—four thousand population, to which Montgomery added two thousand slaves —but it was considerably less attractive. Montgomery was approached by planked roads which disintegrated into rutted, unpaved streets in the center of town. The streets turned into rivers of red mud in rainy weather, and the buildings were hastily erected frame affairs that leaned against each other and against a variety of livery stables. The livery-stable odor, and the swarms of flies it drew, pervaded Montgomery air, and between the buildings open sewers ran down to the river and its row of rickety piers, drawing more flies. Yellow fever was endemic. Rats the size of small dogs took charge of the streets at night. The only buildings of any consequence in Montgomery were three pretentious hotels—the Exchange Hotel, the Madison House, and the Dexter House—built by speculators whose faith in Montgomery's future as a cotton capital had been supreme. At the time of Henry Lehman's arrival these dreams had not yet materialized and the hotels stood largely empty.

For all its unappetizing appearance and unhealthy climate, Montgomery was a prospering town. Its location on the banks of the Alabama linked it to the ports of both Mobile and New Orleans, and made it a natural warehouse and trading center from which the flourishing cotton trade could radiate. Henry Lehman rented a small building in Commerce Street and spread his stock of merchandise on wooden shelves—crockery, glassware, tools, dry goods, bagging, and seeds. With a hand-painted shingle that read "H. Lehman," the Lehman name entered the annals of American enterprise. Henry lived in a room behind his shop, working late at night over his account books by the light of a whale-oil lamp, doing what Joseph Seligman had done, saving money to send home for more brothers. It was a lonely, celibate existence—in Montgomery Henry became known as "our little monk"—and in the quiet hours he began to fear for his own health. "There is money to be made here," he wrote to Germany, "if the Fever doesn't get me first." Within two years he was able to send for his next-younger brother, Emanuel, and by 1850 Mayer, the youngest, had joined him. The offices of the firm, now called Lehman Brothers, stood in Court Square in the heart of town, directly opposite Montgomery's main slave-auctioning block. The Lehmans were listed in the city directory as "grocers," but they advertised themselves as "Agents for the Sale of Leading Southern Domestics"—from which it should not be inferred that the Lehmans sold slaves (though they were eventually prosperous enough to buy a few). "Domestics," in the cotton business, referred to "osnaburgs, sheetings, shirtings, yarn, cotton rope, and ball thread." They were, in other words, cotton brokers.

The Guggenheims are proud to say that they started on foot and, so doing, amassed what may have been the greatest single fortune in

America. The only fortune that may outweigh the Guggenheims' is that
of John D. Rockefeller. It seems senseless to quibble. The Guggenheims
became immensely rich. But one of the great "problems" with the
Guggenheims, socially, in New York had less to do with their foot-borne
origins and their wealth than with their curious proclivity for surrounding themselves with scandal. Several Guggenheim men have had the
misfortune of dying on the doorsteps of strange ladies' houses, or of
becoming involved in spectacular breach-of-promise suits.

Records place Guggenheims in Lengnau in Canton Aargau in German-
speaking northern Switzerland, as early as 1696—a document of that
year refers to *"der Jud Maran Guggenheimb von Lengnau"*—and the
family had probably come to Lengnau from a German town called
Guggenheimb (now Jugenheim), near Heidelberg. Whether some controversy prompted the family's move from Germany to Switzerland is
unknown, but by the 1740's the Guggenheims of Lengnau were involved
in a scandal that shook the foundations of Jewish communities in two
countries.

It started with a visit to Lengnau by a young Swiss divine named
Johann Casper Ulrich, pastor of the Cathedral of the Holy Virgin in
Zurich, a Protestant cathedral despite its name. An earnest, scholarly
man, Ulrich had become interested in rabbinical studies and Jewish
culture while a seminary student. He had come to Lengnau (this town
and the neighboring village of Endingen were the ghettos of Switzerland) because he had heard of a certain Jakob Guggenheim, a *parnas,*
or elder of the synagogue, and a *lamden,* or scholar. Pastor Ulrich was a
great admirer of the Jews. (He later published a *Collection of Jewish
Narrative*s, one of the first books written by a Christian of the era which
portrayed Jewish life with sympathy.) The pastor met the *parnas,* and
the two got along very well. Jakob Guggenheim took the pastor into his
home, and the two spent long afternoons discussing Jewish history and
arguing religious theory. But it soon became apparent that Pastor
Ulrich's main interest in the Jews was in converting them.

Ulrich made no headway with Jakob Guggenheim, who took the
pastor's proselytizing efforts with good humor, but Ulrich noticed that
he had a more interested listener in Jakob's young son, Joseph.

Joseph was brilliant, sensitive, and high-strung. He had been educated
at a Talmudic academy, and loved theological debate. Ulrich knew that
in order to work on Joseph he would have to get him away from his
father, and so he persuaded Jakob—and the Swiss authorities—to let
Joseph come and live with him in Zurich, a city that was open to Jews
only during certain hours of the day. Why did the *parnas* let his son go?
Perhaps he was flattered by the pastor's interest. Surely he did not think
that his son was susceptible to conversion.

In Zurich, Ulrich flooded the boy with pamphlets from Halle, Germany, the center of Protestant missions to convert the Jews, and gave him a copy of the New Testament printed in Yiddish. As the boy began to waver, Ulrich's pressure upon him grew more intense. When the youth burst into tears, the pastor would fling him to his knees and try to force him into an ecstasy of prayer. The atmosphere of the Ulrich home had become hysterical when Joseph Guggenheim suddenly suffered a complete mental collapse. He recovered, then suffered another.

The Ulrich-Guggenheim conversion effort grew into one of the longest on record. It lasted sixteen years. Finally Joseph announced his decision—perhaps consent is the better word—to be baptized, and, amid much prayer and weeping by both pastor and convert, the ceremony was performed. The Christian faith had gained a soul but a sadly broken man.

It was agreed that Joseph's conversion should be kept a secret from the Jewish community at Lengnau, and for two years it was. Then it leaked out, and the Jews of Lengnau reacted violently. They accused their former pastor friend of conspiracy and of violating their hospitality, as, indeed, he had done. Ulrich retaliated with accusations of his own, claiming that Joseph's mental illness had been induced by the Jews as a tactic to prevent him from accepting Christianity, and charging that the Jews now "conspired to murder" Joseph, preferring a dead Christian to a live one. The battle over Joseph Guggenheim's soul erupted into all the Jewish and Christian journals of the day, spread across the Swiss border into Germany, where at least six rabbis issued blistering pronouncements against Ulrich. Two successive governors of Baden and nearly all the high officials of Zurich were drawn into the controversy. Eventually, the pastor was conceded to have won, and soon after that the disputed soul departed for the heaven of its choice. It must have been the Christian heaven. The name Joseph Guggenheim was expunged from the Guggenheim family tree.

Joseph's brother Isaac Guggenheim, meanwhile, was proving himself a more solid and less emotional sort. Isaac was a Lengnau moneylender, and he became quite rich. As an old man he was a patriarchal figure—grave, bearded, in kaftan and skullcap, surrounded by his hovering and attentive family, moving grandly through the streets or sitting in state in his house where he received petitioners for loans. An indication of his stern and frosty manner is the fact that old Isaac became known locally as "Old Icicle." From him, all the American Guggenheims descend. When "Old Icicle" died in 1807, his estate consisted of an enormous trunk. When this was ceremoniously opened, it was found to contain 830 gold and silver coins, plus all the articles Isaac had accepted, over the years, as collateral on loans: 72 plates, a mortar, a frying pan, two kneading pans, a Sabbath lamp, "a ewer with basin for washing hands," a brass coffee pot, 4 featherbeds, 19 sheets, 15 towels, 8 nightshirts, and a child's chamber pot. The valuation of this estate was placed at 25,000 florins, which was quite a nice sum.

"Old Icicle" Guggenheim had many children; his oldest son was named Meyer, who married and had eight children, four boys and four girls, and soon one of these sons, Samuel, was making a name for himself. The typewritten translation of the following news item, with its erratic spelling and mixed tenses, now hangs in the partners' room at Guggenheim Brothers in New York:

Samuel Guggenheim

On the 25th of July, 1818, fire broke out in Wyle, in the Canton of Zurich. A whole house soon enveloped in flames, and made the hurriedly arrived people shudder. But, oh! two peacefully sleeping children were still within the building. The cries of anguish of the congregated populace of the town and the cracking of the flames and smoke woke the little ones from their sweet slumber, apparently only to die the sleep of death. Who can command the flames? Who can save the little ones? A Hebrew, Samuel Guggenheim of Largan [Lengnau], Canton Aargan [Aargau], Switzerland, a man full of presence of mind and honest courage, rushed into the blazing house, graps [grabs? grasps?] both children and carries them triumphantly through the terrible heat and smoke to safety.

But, oh! Even more thrilling exploits would the Guggenheims carry out. Equal to their ability to stir up controversy is their love of drama.

Samuel's older brother was Simon. By Samuel's and Simon's generation, the considerable competence that Old Icicle had left behind him was spent and gone, and the Guggenheims were poor again. Simon was the village tailor, and hardly saw a florin enter his shop from one week to the next. With its maze of restrictions and special taxes, life for the ghetto Jew in Switzerland was onerous anyway, but for the poor man it was hideous. Households in the Lengnau-Endingen townships were limited by decree in 1776 to the then existing figure—108—and Jews were not permitted to enlarge or alter the exteriors of their houses. To escape the tax collector, families hid with other families. Householders received expulsion orders frequently, and the only way to avoid eviction was to renew—for a price—the "Safe-Conduct and Patronage Letter." As early as 1840 Simon Guggenheim, a small, thin, intense man with a haggard face and brooding eyes, had begun dreaming of escaping to America. But he had a wife and five children—a son, Meyer, and, disappointingly, four girls—and he simply could not afford it. Then his wife died.

Good fortune now stepped in. In 1846, when Simon was in his fifties, another death in Lengnau created a forty-one-year-old widow, Rachel Meyer. Rachel had seven children—three sons and four daughters—and she also had a little money. Simon married her, and late in 1847 the combined families—fourteen in all—set off for America. Their ship took the customary two months to cross the Atlantic, entered the mouth of the Delaware River in 1848, and deposited them all in Philadelphia. Simon was then fifty-six; his son Meyer was twenty. Father and son set off peddling into the anthracite country, as the Seligman brothers had done a decade before.

Meyer Guggenheim was short and slender, but well-knit and hand-some. That a shipboard romance could have blossomed under steerage conditions of filth, suffocation, and darkness seems strange, but it did. Crossing the ocean, Meyer had fallen in love with his stepmother's fifteen-year-old daughter, Barbara. She has been described in the family as a beauty with "unusually fair skin," "eyes that were brown in some lights and soft warm gray in others," and "auburn hair that burned in the sun." Barbara's auburn hair burned in young Meyer's mind as he peddled the dreary mining towns of northeastern Pennsylvania. He married his stepsister in 1852 in Philadelphia.

But as a peddler Meyer Guggenheim made a discovery which, in the beginning, eluded men like the Seligmans and Lehmans, and which turned his career in a different direction. He realized that for every dollar's worth of goods sold he was returning sixty to seventy cents to the manufacturer. In other words, he was working two-thirds of each peddling day for manufacturers and only one-third for himself. Meyer began to consider ways in which he could reverse this situation. "Obvi-ously," says Milton Lomask, a Guggenheim biographer, "he must put something of himself into one of his products. But which one?"

With considerable wisdom, he decided to concentrate on the one product about which he had received the most complaints. This was a certain brand of stove polish. Housewives had told him that the polish did a fine job on their stoves, but that it also soiled and burned their hands. Meyer took the polish to a chemist friend, asked him to analyze it and, if possible, to isolate the soiling and burning ingredient from the cleaning and polishing agent. The chemist analyzed the polish, suggested a new formula, and presently Guggenheim's stingless, stainless stove polish was offered to the ladies on Meyer's route. It was a success. Meyer's father, Simon, was now in his sixties and getting too old to peddle, and so Meyer took him off the peddling route and assigned him to the house to brew up vats of stove polish. The business ethics of taking an existing product, changing it slightly, and selling it under another label are best left to a patent attorney. There was no Better

Business Bureau in those days, anyway. By a similar process, Meyer soon added Guggenheim's bluing and Guggenheim's lye to his household-products line.

The two families who would compose Goldman, Sachs started not only on foot but, romantically enough, as runaways. Young Joseph Sachs was a scholarly son of a poor Bavarian saddlemaker who grew up in a village outside Würzburg. As a lad in his teens he was hired as tutor in the home of a wealthy Würzburg goldsmith named Baer to teach the Baers' beautiful young daughter, Sophia. In a fairy-tale way, the poor young tutor and the lovely young merchant princess fell in love. Naturally her parents disapproved. So the couple eloped to Rotterdam, were married there in 1848, and that same year boarded a boat for America, landing in Baltimore. Where the money came from that financed the elopement and the schooner crossing is not clear. Very likely Sophia, a practical girl, pocketed some of her father's gold before departing.

In that same pivotal year twenty-seven-year-old Marcus Goldman, a more down-to-earth sort, arrived in New York. He was also a Bavarian, born in a small village, Burgbrebac, near Schweinfurt, and he quickly set off for the area that, rightly or wrongly, young German Jewish immigrants had heard was the peddlers' paradise, the coal hills of Pennsylvania. In 1848 another girl from Bavaria, named Bertha Goldman—of another Goldman family—had arrived in America to join her already migrated relatives in Philadelphia. She was nineteen. In Philadelphia Miss Goldman and Mr. Goldman met, fell in love, and were married. The Goldman-Goldman union was to become remarkable in New York's German Jewish crowd for the fact that, try as they might through the years, Bertha and Marcus Goldman could never discover a way in which they were even remotely related.

Before Marcus married her, Bertha Goldman had had—and it was unusual for the 1840's—a career. She had supported herself quite nicely doing embroidery and fine needlework for Philadelphia society women. None other than Mrs. Wistar Morris wore a Bertha Goldman hat. Soon, with Bertha's help, Marcus Goldman was able to make the transition from dry-goods and notions peddler to respectable shopkeeper. He set up his own clothing store in Market Street, and rented a comfortable house in Green Street. But Bertha hated Philadelphia. She was urging her husband to take another step forward—to New York, where she had friends.

In 1849, if anyone had looked over the incoming steerage passengers with an eye to predicting which one seemed least likely to succeed,

Solomon Loeb might easily have been selected. He was a thin, sallow, fidgety boy with intense, frightened-looking, blue eyes. His hair had receded prematurely from his forehead, leaving a fluffy mound of curly black hair on either side of his head, creating an effect of furry horns. He had been a sickly child of an even sicklier family—of fifteen Loeb children, only six had lived to maturity—and he had developed an obsession about his health and had a pathological fear of germs which conditions in steerage did little to soothe. He had been violently seasick the entire journey, during which, he later swore, not a mouthful of food had passed his lips. Halfway across the Atlantic—traveling with his only pair of shoes strapped to his back—he had decided that he was going to die, and begged a fellow passenger to throw him overboard. The passenger demurred and wanted to know, "Why don't you throw yourself over? Why make me do it?" Weeping, Solomon said that he was too weak to lift himself up to the rail. "Just put me up on the rail so I can roll over," he said.

Loeb had come from the Rhineland city of Worms, where his father had been a poor wine merchant, as had several generations of Loebs before him. Still, Solomon's mother, Rosina, laid claim to a certain social standing. She was a contemporary of Kaiser Wilhelm I and liked to talk of *"Ich und der Kaiser,"* suggesting that she and the Kaiser had actually been friends. She could recall Napoleon and the time when the Rhineland was freed and Jews were first permitted to have surnames of their own. Rosina often left the impression that she herself had had something to do with this. Like Joseph Seligman's mother, Rosina Loeb had been accused of giving her son "grandiose ideas," and she had picked Solomon as her first boy to emigrate. She had also selected Cincinnati as Solomon's destination. The son of some cousins of hers named Kuhn had gone there a few years earlier and was reported to be prospering.

In the 1830's and '40's, many Germans—Jews and non-Jews—had settled in and around Philadelphia. (Earlier migrations had been attracted by the liberal policies of William Penn. Later, Germans went to Pennsylvania to be with other Germans.) Now the German movement was farther westward, to the bustling Ohio River port which was then the third largest city in the United States. In 1849 boatbuilding, shipping, and meat-packing were Cincinnati's main industries. As many as three hundred river boats steamed into the harbor a day, and over a quarter of the country's pork was packed there. The city had such a large German-speaking population that it was virtually bilingual, and German was taught in all public and parochial schools. The section of town north of the canal, where most of the Germans lived, was known as "Over the Rhine." Jews, of course, were not particularly attracted by the pork-packing industry and were drawn, instead, into the textile trade, which was also booming, and into cloak and suit manufacturing. Abraham Kuhn, who had started as a peddler, had opened a dry-goods shop and now operated a small factory where he made men's and boys' pants. He had made enough money to send home to Germany for his brothers and sisters. He was looking for another helper, and he took on Solomon.

Temperamentally, the two men balanced each other. Abe Kuhn was phlegmatic. Solomon was excitable. Abe had fallen in love with fabrics, their colors and textures. Solomon was color-blind and didn't know buckram from bombazine. But he understood money and knew how to sell. Abe Kuhn had been thinking of opening another outlet for his goods in New York, and Solomon's first job was to set this up. Soon he was back in New York and had opened a soft-goods shop at 31 Nassau Street, around the corner from the Seligmans. For several years, while Kuhn minded the shop and factory in Cincinnati, Loeb commuted back and forth between the two cities, carrying the pants from factory to store on the Erie Canal. Soon he was able to send back to Germany for his brothers and sisters, along with his mother and father, and settle them in Cincinnati. All the Kuhns and Loebs, plus some additional cousins named Netter and Wolff, worked in the Cincinnati business, and presently they began to marry one another. Solomon married Abe's sister Fanny, and Abe married Solomon's sister. The double brothers-in-law then changed the name of their operation to Kuhn, Loeb & Company, and they all, nine Loebs and four Kuhns, moved into one large house "Over the Rhine." Fanny bore Solomon his first child in this house, a daughter whom the couple named Therese. This large and happy and prosperous clan might never have left Cincinnati if Fanny had not become pregnant again and, along with her second baby, died in childbirth.

A family conference was called to decide what was to be done in this unhappy situation. Little Therese, the cousins said, needed a mother. There were no unmarried girls left in the family for Solomon. Obviously, seasick-prone or not, the thing for Solomon to do was to go back to Germany and find a new bride. In fact, the cousins had a candidate in mind—a Mannheim girl named Betty Gallenberg. That no young girl from the existing German Jewish stock in Cincinnati was considered may seem odd. The truth was that clans like the Loebs and Kuhns, to whom the family was the business and the business was the family, knew virtually no one in America outside the family group. A likely German Jewish girl might have lived right next door, but they would not have met her.

So, gritting his teeth, Solomon set off on his *Brautshau*. In Mannheim he called on Betty Gallenberg. She was plain as a pudding, plump, motherly, healthy, a good cook and housekeeper, and, since Solomon was considering her qualifications as a child's nurse more than as a wife, he put his proposition to her. She accepted it, they were married without further ado, and he fetched her back to Cincinnati.

It now began to be apparent that neither Solomon Loeb nor Abe Kuhn possessed Seligman-sized ambitions. Both had prospered and both were satisfied with the tidy little fortunes they had amassed. Kuhn had always been homesick for Germany and planned to take his wife and family home. Loeb agreed that he was ready to retire also, but he was fond of Cincinnati and would stay there. He explained this to his young wife, who, at that point, took the future of Kuhn, Loeb & Company into her own hands.

A few years earlier, Charles Dickens had visited Cincinnati; it was one of the few American cities he liked. Not so Betty Gallenberg Loeb. She hated "Porkopolis," as it had been nicknamed, from the moment she saw it. She considered it a crude, boring, uncivilized outpost. She was also apparently unprepared for the plethora of Loeb in-laws she found waiting to welcome her, and was irked by their tendency to patronize her and treat her like a housemaid. "They treat me as if they had bought me," she wrote angrily home to Germany. She referred to Cincinnati as "a city of pigs, a monster piggery," and it is likely that she included some of her husband's relatives in this category. She found her brothers- and sisters-in-law noisy and boorish, and, though her own background was no more genteel than theirs, she considered them common. One sister-in-law, she pointed out with disgust, had given her a dozen jars of homemade preserves as a wedding present. As for the men, she found "everyone talking about nothing but business, and how to get rich quickly." That being the case, she decided to find out just how rich her new husband was. She looked over his accounts and discovered that he was worth nearly half a million dollars. That was sufficient, she told him, to move her "out of the pigs" and into New York.

8

MATTERS OF STYLE

New York in the 1840's was changing—more rapidly, perhaps, than any city in the world has ever changed—from a picturesque seaport "city of masts and spires" into a noisy and competitive commercial capital. Society, too, was becoming more competitive as more rich newcomers strove to get in, and suddenly bookshops and news kiosks bristled with books and articles on how to be accepted, and what was "good form" and what was not. Still, though everyone both in society and out of it talked incessantly about what was "proper social usage" and about "etiquette" and *"comme il faut,"* things seem to have remained in a somewhat primitive state, to judge by some of the social "dos" and "don'ts" published in the period.

One etiquette writer, for instance, says reproachfully,"What an article is a spittoon as an appendage to a handsomely furnished drawing room!" and another advises guests at a dinner party against "shaking with your feet the chair of a neighbor," and suggests that "ladies should never dine with their gloves on unless their hands are not fit to be seen." If a lady should make "an unseemly digestive sound" at dinner or "raise an unmanageable portion to her mouth," one should "cease all conversation with her and look steadfastly into the opposite part of the room." While at table, says one writer, "all allusions to dyspepsia, indigestion, or any other disorders of the stomach, are vulgar and disgusting. The word 'stomach' should never be uttered at table," and the same writer cautions that "the fashion of wearing black silk mittens at breakfast is now obsolete." When traveling alone, ladies should "avoid saying anything to women in showy attire, with painted faces, and white kid gloves . . . you will derive no pleasure from making acquaintance with females who are evidently coarse and vulgar, even if you know that they are rich."

Men of the era seem to have been even slower to learn the rules of delicacy. One manual of the 1840's says: "The rising generation of young elegants in America are particularly requested to observe that, in polished society, it is not quite *comme il faut* for gentlemen to blow their noses with their fingers, especially when in the street." The gentlemen's habit of chewing tobacco created no end of special problems. "A lady on the second seat of a box at the theatre," writes a social critic of the day, "found, when she went home, the back of her pelisse entirely spoilt, by some man behind not having succeeded in trying to spit past her." And an English visitor was surprised to see John Jacob Astor remove his chewing tobacco from his mouth and absently begin tracing a watery design with it on a windowpane. Other European visitors were startled by what appears to have been a social custom exclusively New York's. On the horse-drawn Fifth Avenue omnibuses it was considered *de rigueur,* when these vehicles became crowded, for seated gentlemen to let ladies perch on their knees.

Though much of the criticism of New York's bad manners came from Europeans, it does appear to have been largely justified. In 1848 the New York *Herald* took New York society to task for "loud talking at table, impertinent staring at strangers, brusqueness of manners among the ladies, laughable attempts at courtly ease and self-possession among the men—the secret of all this vulgarity in Society is that wealth, or the reputation of wealth, constitutes the open sesame to its delectable precincts."

Very much a precinct leader was August Belmont. His passionate interest in high society was perhaps peculiar for men of his day (editors and cartoonists of the nineteenth century usually depicted social climbing as a woman's occupation), but at least it was consistent. Perhaps his glimpse of Rothschild grandeur had given him his abiding urge to be a social potentate. In any case, three years after his arrival in America, we find him dashingly in Elkton, Maryland, and, "over a subject too trite to be mentioned," fighting a duel.

Dueling was an established social-climbing technique, and August

Belmont seems to have chosen his opponent more for his publicity value than anything else. It was Edward Heyward, "one of the exquisite sons of Mr. Wm. Heyward," a member of the ancient and noted Heyward family of Charleston. No one was killed in the duel, but both men were injured, and Belmont, who was shot in the thigh, declared his honor satisfied. And, by having chosen a Heyward as a dueling partner, he established himself with the press and the public as a gentleman of Heyward quality. The duel, in fact, did more than anything else to register the Belmont name in the annals of American society.

What the quarrel, which took place at Niblo's restaurant in New York, was really about is now uncertain. Belmont, naturally, always liked to leave the impression that Heyward had made some ungallant allusion to a lady in Belmont's party. But there is also a story that Heyward had made a veiled reference to Belmont's Jewishness—a particularly touchy subject.

Belmont was always sorry that his dueling scar appeared in such an ignominious spot, and the wound gave him a pronounced limp which would be a permanent affliction. The wound and the limp seemed to increase his bitterness. His rolling gait heightened his threatening appearance as he entered doorways of salons. The duel and the scar seemed to add to his sinister allure, and through New York drawing rooms rumors began to circulate of certain society ladies who, for one reason or another, had been permitted to see that scar.

In the years since his arrival Belmont had been so successful at channeling Rothschild funds into the United States Treasury in return for government securities that he was rewarded, in 1844, by being appointed United States Consul General to Austria—a move designed not only to provide Mr. Belmont with prestige but also to place him close to the Vienna House of Rothschild where he could be of further usefulness. Things, of course, did not always go smoothly. When the state of Pennsylvania defaulted on $35 million worth of state bonds held by British investors, including the Rothschilds, Belmont, in Paris trying to place another U.S. Federal Government loan, was icily told by Baron de Rothschild, "Tell them you have seen the man who is at the head of the finances of Europe, and that he has told you that they cannot borrow a dollar. Not a dollar." Still, the United States was too good a customer of Europe's—buying such items as railroad ties, which lack of American know-how still made difficult to produce here, in return for American cotton and wheat—for the Rothschilds to remain angry for long. Also, Belmont was too canny a trader to let such upsets damage his friendships on both sides of the Atlantic.

In New York he was very much a man about town. He had made himself, à la the Rothschilds, a connoisseur of horseflesh and had, with his friend Leonard Jerome, founded Jerome Park Racetrack. But he had never been invited to join the Union Club, considered the best men's club in town. He also seems to have invented a social attitude which was soon being widely copied—the attitude of indifference. When invited for dinner at eight, August Belmont rarely appeared before ten or eleven. Punctuality, he seemed to be saying, was the courtesy of peasants. It seemed very chic and "very European" to arrive at dinner with the finger bowls, and this affectation—which is still to be encountered in New York, to the bafflement of Europeans—may be blamed on August Belmont.

Belmont did not do particularly well when it came to cultivating such old patroon families as the Van Rensselaers, nor was he admired by the Astors, the fur-trading family which, in the 1840's, was probably the richest family in New York. He did, on the other hand, get along nicely with such Old Guard families as the Costers and the Morrises, and he was also a friend of an ex-ferryboat captain, now a millionaire, named "Commodore" Cornelius Vanderbilt. New York society was giving up picnics and skating parties and turning to large formal subscription balls—always given in hotels or restaurants since there were still no private homes big enough to contain them—and it irked August Belmont that he was not invited to every one. There was, for instance, the great City Ball of January, 1841, so called because it was held at the old City Hotel. Eight hundred guests danced in a ballroom lighted with two thousand tapers, but August Belmont was not among them. Soon a series of Assembly balls was organized to be held at Delmonico's, and, to make certain that he was asked, Belmont took decisive action.

In a story told by the Van Rensselaers, Belmont went to the invitation committee and said, "I have been investigating the accounts of you gentlemen on the Street. I can assure you that either I get an invitation to the Assembly this year or else the day after the Assembly each of you will be a ruined man." It was one of the most telling examples of the kind of power that could be wielded by one man ("a Wall Street banker, not even a native American") in nineteenth-century New York. Belmont got his invitation, but—according to a story that sounds much more like wishful thinking than the truth—arrived at the Assembly to find himself the only person there.

Belmont, on the other hand, though there was still some uncertainty about where he actually *lived* (he seemed to inhabit a series of hotels) could and did give balls of his own. Fancy-dress balls were his favorites, and he loved to put on a powdered wig and ruffled collar and appear as Louis XV or, with a tricorn hat and sword, as Napoleon. (Once, when he learned that another guest was planning to come as Louis XV, Belmont appeared in a full suit of steel armor inlaid with gold which had cost him $10,000, causing a bemused reported from the London *Chronicle* to ask, "Were all the costumes ticketed with the price?") In some ways Belmont seemed consciously trying to outdo the Astors. In 1846 John Jacob Astor, Jr. married the daughter of Thomas L. Gibbes, a South Carolina aristocrat, and the marriage was the occasion of a great reception. The Astors' "spacious mansion in Lafayette Place was open from cellar to garret, blazing with a thousand lights," but August Belmont once more was not invited. Then, in 1847, he made a move that forever removed doubts about his social position. He proposed to, and was accepted by, Caroline Slidell Perry.

He had chosen her as carefully and cynically as he chose his wines, his dueling opponents, the stocks for his portfolio, his name, and his religion. The Perrys were not imposingly rich, but they had all the social cachet that Belmont wanted and needed, more than he needed money. Caroline was the daughter of Commodore Matthew Calbraith Perry, hero of the Mexican War and the officer later credited with having "opened Japan to the West," and her uncle was another naval commander, Oliver Hazard Perry, hero of the War of 1812 and the Battle of Lake Erie. Caroline, furthermore, was wan, pale, and dreamily beautiful, an exquisite creature who wept bitterly when she was told that families "of wretched poor" lived south of Canal Street, which was why her coachman would not drive her there. In 1848 the elder John Jacob Astor died leaving a fortune of twenty million dollars, and was accorded a great funeral conducted by "six Episcopal clergymen." The Belmont-Perry nuptials of that same year had only one clergyman officiating, but they were of course Episcopal. The wedding was at Grace Church, and it was an even more glittering social event than the Astor funeral. There were at the reception—in addition to a complement of Morrises, Vanderbilts, Costers, Goelets (no Van Rensselaers), Webbs, and Winthrops—even a few Astors, come out of mourning. Even more important, as far as August Belmont was concerned, was the fact that a few weeks before his wedding he was invited to join the Union Club.

Lower Fifth Avenue and Washington Square were already sprouting palaces of brownstone and marble. Though there was still no Central Park to give Fifth Avenue a garden view for much of its length, that wide thoroughfare running up the spine of Manhattan was already becoming the city's best residential address. Soon after their marriage, the young Belmonts established themselves in a lower Fifth Avenue house that was grander than anything that existed in New York. It was, among other things, the first private house in the city to have its own ballroom—a room designed for nothing but the annual Belmont ball and which, as Edith Wharton commented later, "was left for three hundred and sixty-four days of the year to shuttered darkness, with its gilt chairs stacked in a corner and its chandelier in a bag." The Belmonts were also the first to own their own red carpet, to be rolled down the marble front steps and across the sidewalk for parties, instead of renting one, along with the chairs, from a caterer.

The Belmont house awed New York society. It was much more magnificent than the Astors' old house in Lafayette Place, and it made everybody feel that they had been doing everything very provincially until August Belmont came along from—well, where *was* he from actually? people asked. The Belmont mansion was one that New Yorkers pointed out to visiting friends from other cities. When the visitors expressed curiosity about what lay within it, New Yorkers said, "We shall see whether we can get you an invitation." And so August Belmont, the archetype social climber, had made his house the goal of every climber's dreams. Belmont's relationship to New York society became, according to one observer, "like a man on the back of a donkey holding out, to make the donkey move, a carrot on a stick. He manages to lead the donkey forward and yet, at the same time, the beast is obliged to bear his weight."

To be sure, he was guilty of some rather odd gaffes, such as having his portrait painted with his hat on. And there was no uncertainty about his father-in-law's position in the Belmont household. Belmont used the Commodore as his butler. "There's a good fellow," he would say to the old gentleman, "run down to the cellar and see if there are six more bottles of the *Rapid* Madeira." And, as the Commodore scurried off, Belmont would call after him, "And try not to shake them on the stairs!" But the Belmonts' was the first house in New York to have its art gallery lighted from a skylight in the roof, and the collection of art itself was remarkable—including Madrazo, Meyer, Rosa Bonheur, Meissonier, Munkácsy, Vibert, and, to scandalize New York society, a number of the voluptuous nudes of William Bouguereau. One of the most scandalized was Belmont's neighbor, James Lenox, who lived directly opposite him on Fifth Avenue. Lenox disapproved of nearly everything about Belmont, but the Bouguereau nudes he considered downright immoral. Belmont, learning this, hung the largest and the nudest Bouguereau in his front foyer, where it confronted the Lenox house every time the Belmont door was opened—which, with the Belmont entertaining schedule, was often. Lenox, a miserly sort, became obsessive on the subject of Belmont's extravagance, and, according to Lucius Beebe, when Lenox was told that August Belmont spent $20,000 a month on wine alone, he collapsed of a heart attack and died.

It was August Belmont's reputation as a host that gave his parties priority over almost anyone's in New York. His chef had been trained by the legendary Carême, and was given regular refresher lessons by such restaurateurs as Lorenzo Delmonico. Singlehanded, Belmont introduced gourmet food to the New York private home, which up to then had been very much on a corned-beef-and-potatoes diet. Two hundred guests could sit down at a table set with the Belmont gold service. They were waited on by an equal number of footmen, who presented them with such delicacies as *aspic de canvasback* and truffled ice cream. Of course it was rumored that he had not only supervised the design and interior decoration of his brownstone palace, selected all the paintings, porcelains, statuary, and *objets d'art,* but also interviewed and trained all the servants, did the ordering, told his gardeners what hothouse flowers to grow for the dinner table, oversaw the flower arrangements, selected the guests, planned the menus, checked the place cards, and taught his chef new dishes. He was once overheard saying that the secret of *pâté de foie gras de canard de Toulouse* was: "Never lift the lid of the casserole while it's simmering."

It was also said that he dictated the notes his wife wrote, personally picked out all her gowns and jewelry, and could sometimes be found going over the marble table tops with a dustcloth. These details seemed odd, a little out of keeping, and not quite *comme il faut.* But then everyone had to admit that Caroline Perry Belmont wasn't exactly clever. And at least he was gallant. He always gave her credit. As his guests entered his drawing room to be received by his slim, pale confection of a wife, he would murmur, "Isn't my wife a marvel? Who but she would have the courage to wear pink this season?"

To immigrants who were his contemporaries, such as the Seligman brothers, August Belmont became a kind of symbol of what a poor German Jew could do, with any luck at all, in the New World.

TO THE
GOLD FIELDS

In 1850 the Seligman enterprises were scattered across the East, and the brothers themselves were still, to a certain extent, nomadic. Though the boys were prospering, living was sparse and frugal. Joseph insisted on this. Joseph wanted his brothers to be able to pack up and move on a moment's notice, whenever a new business opportunity presented itself. The boys lived in rooming houses in their respective cities, and Joseph —still the only married brother—occupied quarters that were equally unprepossessing, a two-room flat in downtown Manhattan, off Broadway. He was very much in charge of the family's farflung operations, and made frequent trips to Watertown and St. Louis to check on things. William, the brother Joseph trusted the least, required the greatest attention, and there is evidence that the entrance of all the Stettheimers into the family—Max not only had a father but several brothers who needed jobs—was becoming a problem.

At the same time, the general disorder affecting America had been correctly diagnosed as "gold fever," and the first Seligman to succumb to the new disease was twenty-three-year-old Jesse in Watertown. At first, Jesse toyed with the idea of buying his own pick and shovel and going directly to the California hills to dig. Joseph, however, opposed this. Seligmans, he pointed out, knew nothing about digging. What they did know about was stores. He suggested that Jesse consider opening a Seligman store somewhere in the vicinity of where gold was being spent. Jesse agreed, and asked permission to go.

Joseph was reluctant to have Jesse leave the profitable business in Watertown, but he had also been worried about "artistic" Leopold, the dreamy-eyed brother who had reached the advanced age of nineteen without contributing anything to the Seligman fortunes beyond pencil sketches. Joseph decided that Jesse should take Leopold with him to San Francisco and teach him storekeeping. Henry would be left in charge of Watertown, and could, in addition, take over Jesse's old duties of playing cards and checkers with a teetotaling Lieutenant Grant.

Jesse and Leopold had originally planned to travel overland to San Francisco, but Joseph's wife, Babet, made such a fuss—wailing, "But the Indians! The terrible Indians!"—that plans were changed and the boys booked steamer passage. It was a route that would take them through the Caribbean to Colón, Panama, over the Isthmus on mule-back, and then upward along the Mexican and California coast. Onto the ship with them went a staggering amount of small merchandise—$20,000 worth—which took nearly all the capital the Seligman brothers had on hand at the time. But, the boys figured, California prices, spurred by the gold rush, were bound to be inflated.

Debarking at Colón, the two loaded their stock of goods on mules and started across the Isthmus. Soon others from the boat were ill and dying from Panama fever, but the two boys with their important cargo pushed on through the jungle. Midway across, at Gorgona, the supply of mules ran short; there were not enough to carry the Seligmans' goods, and the boys were forced to stop. Here, young Leopold came down with fever. Two weeks later mules arrived, and Leopold had to be lashed to the back of Jesse's mule. When they reached Panama City and the Pacific, they had missed the steamer to San Francisco. Leopold, delirious, was carried aboard the wooden side-wheeler *Northerner* on a stretcher. It was not until the boat reached Acapulco that he was out of danger.

Looking over San Francisco in 1850, Jesse wrote in his ledger: "Very high winds prevail at times—there is a scarcity of water . . . the houses are frame structures, a few of iron." And he saw "Great danger of a conflagration." Fire was a major threat to a dry-goods merchant, and Jesse knew this from sorry experience. A year before, a fire in his Watertown building had destroyed $6,500 worth of merchandise, of which only $4,500 was insured. Prudently turning down several "frame structures," Jesse managed to rent one of the few brick buildings in San

Francisco, which stood next to "the gay and fashionable Tehama House, kept by a Captain Jones" at the corner of California and Sansome streets.

Jesse was right about gold-crazy prices. San Francisco bootblacks were earning twenty dollars a day. To launder a dozen shirts cost ten dollars. Coins smaller than half-dollars were considered worthless and were not accepted by tradesmen. In his new store Jesse's markup was what the market would bear, and it was soon apparent that it would bear quite a bit. Tin cups and pans for which he had paid pennies in the East were sold for five and ten dollars apiece. He sold five-dollar blankets for forty dollars, and wine and whiskey for twenty to thirty dollars a quart (though Seligmans today don't like to remember that they were once in the liquor business). Through it all he tried to teach Leopold the rudiments of storekeeping. But Leopold, having recovered from Panama fever, now succumbed to agonies of homesickness, and was a slow learner.

San Francisco was a wide-open, rip-roaring gambling town. Men were shot down in the streets at the slightest provocation—one day a stray bullet out of nowhere tore through Jesse's hat—and law enforcement was a casual affair at best. Jesse was careful to avoid the temptations of San Francisco, and was even more careful to see that Leopold avoided them. This wasn't always easy, since some of the most tempting goings on were next door in Captain Jones's Tehama House Hotel. In a letter home, Jesse observed that one of the best-paid professions in San Francisco was "probably the world's oldest," and ladies of Tehama House quality charged three or four hundred dollars for an evening's entertainment. In less fashionable parts of town the streets teemed with American, German, Mexican, Chinese, and Kanaka women from the Sandwich Islands who were willing to oblige for less pay. "We are," Jesse assured a worrying Joseph, "careful to eschew such pleasures, you may be sure." (But once young Leopold wistfully made a little list of some of the most popular ladies' names: "Madame St. Armand, Helene, Angele, Emilie. . . .") To while away their San Francisco evenings, Jesse played his flute and Leopold worked at his sketch pad, trying to ignore the squeals and giggles and occasional bursts of gunfire from the Tehama House. In view of the prices charged by laundries and boot-blacks, the boys also washed and ironed their own shirts and shined their shoes. In another prudent move, Jesse joined Howard Engine Company No. 3 of the San Francisco Fire Department.

On the morning of May 3, 1851, fire broke out. Within hours the business section of the city was in flames. Empty air spaces under the planked streets became great blowpipes to spread the fire from block to block. Jesse helped fight the fire in the center of the city until it was declared out of control, then hurried back to his store. Next door, he found Captain Jones and his staff of waiters, bellboys, croupiers, and "actresses" on the roof of the Tehama House stretching water-soaked blankets across the gables and standing by with buckets and brooms.

"You've got a frame building!" Jesse called up to the Captain. "What good do you think those wet blankets are going to do?"

"I'll take care of my building and you take care of yours," said the Captain.

"But don't you see?" said Jesse. "The fire will reach my building first. If we can save my brick building, we can save yours as well."

The Captain shouted, "By God, Seligman, I think you're right!" Immediately he dispatched all the bellboys, waiters, croupiers, and actresses, with their blankets and their buckets, to the roof of Jesse's store. Then Jesse diverted Howard Engine Company No. 3 to service in his block. Seldom was a job of Seligman salesmanship to prove so profitable. Of all the buildings in the area, only two were completely spared—Jesse's store and the Tehama House. After the fire Jesse found himself the proprietor of the only general store left standing in San Francisco. Frantically, he wrote home to Joseph for more merchandise.

In later years Jesse used to say proudly that, though he was certainly in a position to, he never took advantage of the disaster by raising any of his prices by so much as a penny in the months after the fire. But he didn't lower them, either. After all, Jesse's prices, by standards elsewhere in the country, were already outrageous. As San Francisco's only postfire merchant, he made what can only be described as a bundle. Soon profits from San Francisco were accounting for such a large share of the Seligmans' income that the Watertown store was closed and Henry hurried to San Francisco to help Jesse, who had been getting precious little help from Leopold. (Coincidentally, Grant's 4th Infantry was ordered out of Madison Barracks that same year and was dispatched to the Pacific Coast.)

The Seligmans' importing-retailing days were almost over. In New York their most profitable import had become gold from California. From New York, gold that was not traded on the market traveled on to Europe to purchase new supplies for the Seligman stores. The Seligmans still dealt in dry goods, cotton, hides, boots, shoes, pots, pans, cigars, undershirts, and whiskey, but as buyers and sellers of bullion they found themselves, almost before they knew what had happened to them, in the banking business. By 1857 over $500 million worth of gold had made its way eastward from the California hills, a good deal of it passing through the hands of the Seligmans.

To become a banker in those naïve days was almost as simple a matter as saying, "I am a banker." A National Banking Act did not

exist until after the Civil War, and banks—particularly private banks—
were organized with startling informality. Everybody in New York, it
seemed, was involved in one way or another with the money trade, and
it was said, in fact, that to be a banker all one needed was to dress like
one. Joseph Seligman and his brothers had already learned many
banking fundamentals. The Seligman stores had sold goods on credit,
loaned money, bought and sold IOU's, and even carried deposit accounts. "Stay liquid," Joseph was writing his brothers. "Never invest in
property, or give a mortgage loan." Joseph had made an important
discovery. There was a considerable difference between buying and
selling undershirts and buying and selling funds and credit. Undershirts
could earn profits for the merchant only during the hours his store was
open; otherwise it stood idle, a liability. But money stayed active around
the clock. Credits were not subject to opening hours. When money was
put to work, it worked twenty-four hours a day, seven days a week,
three hundred and sixty-five days a year, and stopped for no holidays,
Jewish or gentile. "Money," said Joseph solemnly to his brothers, "earns
money even while you sleep."

By 1852 Joseph Seligman, trading his bullion from California on the
gold market, was a familiar figure in the New York financial community.
His name and his credit were known by the big commercial banks. He
was making the logical, almost inevitable transition from merchant to
banker. It was a progression that other immigrant merchants would
soon make, but the Seligmans, of the German Jewish group, were
making it first. (Later on, in Jewish society, there would be a point of
social distinction between families such as the Seligmans who evolved
from storekeeping into banking and such families as the Strauses of
Macy's who had "stayed behind" in retailing.)

Through the early 1850's the American economy spun upward in a
giddy spiral. Led by the flood of gold from California, stocks on the
New York Stock Exchange climbed higher and higher. The boom was
on in Western lands and railroads, and shares in these companies were
used as collateral for loans, which were used to buy more shares, which
were used as collateral for loans—and on and on. The Bank of England
was expanding, tariffs were rising, and New York's commercial banks
kept easing credit and then easing it some more. The stock market
seemed to know no top. Never before had New York women been so
extravagantly dressed. Gambling at large private parties suddenly became a factor in New York social life, and everyone gossiped about this
or that great fortune that had been lost, or won, at whist, poker, or
roulette. Mansions marched up the side of Murray Hill, and newspapers
fretted about parties of the newly rich which turned into "orgies of
Pompeiian license." The stock of a railroad company, meanwhile, that

existed nowhere but in a promoter's mind climbed from twenty-five cents a share on Monday to $4,000 a share on Friday. These were busy days for the Seligmans.

One bright morning in 1857, however, Joseph, on his trading rounds, overheard the cashier of one of New York's commercial banks speak of a distressing shortage of cash. The bank was going to begin to call in loans. Joseph moved quickly. He ordered his brothers to "liquidate all but prime securities." When the bubble burst, the Seligman silver and gold were packed in strongboxes and stuffed for safekeeping under Joseph's and Babet's bed. In the course of the Panic of 1857 every commercial bank in New York closed its doors but one. The Seligman brothers went through it unscathed, and that venerable Wall Street epithet, "the Midas touch," which would be applied, rightly or wrongly, to so many financial figures in years to come, was now applied to them. The recovery from the Panic of 1857 was as spectacular as the panic itself. The bubble had no sooner burst than it began to reinflate. So much gold was pouring into New York from California that gold held in New York banks climbed from eight million dollars' worth in October to twenty-eight million two months later, and a ten-million-dollar loan from the Rothschilds made, via August Belmont, to bolster the credit of U.S. banks was repaid the same day. But in this new upsurge the Seligmans again had the advantage of a head start.

In 1857 Joseph established himself in his first Manhattan brownstone—rented, of course, for he would not be tied down with real estate—on Murray Hill, the city's best address, and a year later he rented himself a summer place from A. A. Low, a wealthy merchant, on then fashionable Staten Island. A multiple-residence pattern for German Jewish society was thus indelibly established. Each year since their marriage Babet had borne him a child—already there were five—and the multiple-baby pattern for Seligmans was thus preserved. Joseph, a success as a provider, husband, and father, was beginning to believe his own myth. He had begun to think it was time he had his portrait painted. (Two years later he did; in it he looks most dignified.) From a peddler Joseph Seligman was turning into a Personage.

He had begun to take careful notice of the behavior of August Belmont. "He is a Jew," Joseph commented, "yet he goes everywhere, meets everyone, and 'Society' swirls about him." Joseph was a little uneasy about "swirling" with society, but he would not have minded doing business with same. He was not a toady, though, and would not fawn or flatter his way into gentile drawing rooms. If those in society wanted him, they would have to come to him.

Meanwhile, he had the satisfaction of suspecting that only August Belmont stood in the path of his ambition to become the most important Jewish banker in New York.

And as for social life he had his brothers and his sisters, who were becoming quite a crowd in themselves. By now, four more of Joseph's brothers were solidly married to solidly Jewish girls—party-loving William to Regine Wedeles, handsome James (his was considered the most auspicious marriage of all) to Rosa Content of the pre-Revolutionary family, Jesse to a girl from Germany named Henriette Hellman (Henriette claimed she could trace her ancestry back to King Solomon and the Queen of Sheba), and Henry to Regine Levi, who had two younger sisters whom two more Seligman boys, Leopold and Abraham, would soon marry, drawing the complex of family and money still tighter together. Family Sunday dinners at Joseph's house were now introduced. "Sunday evenings at the Seligmans," in fact, would continue as an institution, as an almost classic fixture of German Jewish social life in New York, for nearly eighty years.

During this period, the Lehmans of Montgomery, Alabama, had become very Southern—slaveowning, Southern-accented, and devotees of Southern cooking, even of the pork. Cotton, still king, was doing for the Lehmans approximately what gold was doing for the Seligmans, and the living was easy. The three brothers were still cotton brokers, and their customers were buyers and manufacturers in the American North and in England. Payments for cotton took the form of four-month drafts on New York banks and sixty-day sterling bills on London banks, and these bills of exchange—promissory notes representing goods in transit —were negotiable. In the South they were one of the most popular forms of currency, and in New York these cotton bills could be sold for cash, at a discount. New York, then, was the true center of the South's cotton economy, and frequent trips to New York were necessary. Emanuel Lehman was usually assigned to the New York money run, while Henry and Mayer carried on in Montgomery.

In the fall of 1855 Montgomery had another of its periodic yellow fever epidemics. Henry Lehman had always feared the disease, and the new epidemic was savage. At his brothers' urging, Henry traveled to New Orleans, which was considered safer. There, the founder of Lehman Brothers came down with yellow fever, and died at the age of thirty-three. The surviving brothers, twenty-nine and twenty-six respectively, were left to carry on.

By 1858 it had become mandatory that the Lehmans have a permanent New York office, and so Emanuel, who had had the money-market experience, headed North to establish himself at 119 Liberty Street, hard by the Seligmans. While Joseph Seligman was observing the habits of August Belmont, Emanuel Lehman began observing the habits of Joseph Seligman. That same year Emanuel married a New York girl named Pauline Sondheim, and the Lehmans rented a Murray Hill brownstone—also hard by the Seligmans. Mayer, who got along well with the planters and farmers, remained in Montgomery and married a New Orleans girl, herself an immigrant from Würzburg, named Babette Newgass.*

From a tactical standpoint, this deployment of cotton-trading Lehmans was brilliant. But thus deployed on opposite sides of the Mason-Dixon Line, the Civil War—the war the whole South had been talking about but that the Lehmans had never believed could actually happen—found them and disunited them. In April, 1861, President Lincoln imposed the blockade. Mayer, in Montgomery, was cut off from his Northern manufacturers and his Northern money. Emanuel, in the North, was cut off from his Southern supply of cotton. It was a staggering blow. *"Alles ist endet!"* Emanuel scrawled despairingly on a pad in his New York office.

If buildings in the financial district had been tall enough to make a suicidal leap productive, Emanuel might have leaped—thereby depriving New York of what is now the largest investment banking house in Wall Street.

---

* There are very nearly as many Babettes and Babets in the trees of German Jewish families as there are Mayers and Meyers. From a business standpoint Mayer Lehman's marriage to Miss Newgass seemed particularly prudent. Her sister was married to Isaias Hellman, one of the San Francisco Hellmans, and founder of the first bank in Los Angeles; he later became president of the Wells Fargo–Nevada Bank in San Francisco. Babette also had a brother, Benjamin Newgass, who lived in England and served as the Lehmans' representative in the manufacturing British Midlands.

10

"THIS UNHOLY REBELLION"

William Seligman liked to say that he had predicted the Civil War, and implied that the nice position the Seligmans found themselves in as a result of the war was largely his doing. William exaggerated. On the other hand, William, already expanding in girth from seven-course dinners with nine wines (*two* sherries with the soup, no less!), did make a business move just before the war's outbreak. It turned out to be such a lucky one that Joseph rewarded William with his very own initial—next to Joseph's—in the ultimate firm name, J. & W. Seligman & Company. William had parted company with his brother-in-law, Max Stettheimer, in St. Louis (the Stettheimer-Seligman alliance was increasingly uneasy) and had come to New York to join Joseph. There, in 1860, William decided, since the Seligman stores sold such items as undershirts and pants, to buy a factory that made undershirts and pants. It was not so imaginative a move as Guggenheim's stove polish, but it was most fortuitous.

The cannon that exploded over Fort Sumter had barely ceased to echo when William and Joseph had devised a strategy by which to woo government uniform contracts out of Washington for the new factory—which, it turned out, was the fourteenth-largest clothing house in those of the United States which had not seceded.

The Seligman strategy was this. First, the brothers made several generous personal "contributions" to the Union cause. These money gifts were gratefully accepted. Next, they contacted one of the few friends they had in the capital, a fellow German immigrant named Henry Gitterman. Gitterman's position in Washington was not lofty, but, for the Seligmans' purposes, it was crucial. He was an army sutler, or provisions agent. In a beautifully worded, apple-polishing letter to Mr. Gitterman, full of patriotic zeal and suggestions of shared calamity, Joseph offered to join hands with Gitterman and help him "in any way possible during the great crisis facing our Nation." Joseph further volunteered to send an able-bodied Seligman to Washington—young Isaac—to help Gitterman with his "multitudinous, onerous, and vitally important" chores (i.e., to help Gitterman buy uniforms). Gitterman, in an equally flowery reply, was overwhelmed at Joseph's selflessness, loyalty, and high sense of duty—and accepted Isaac.

Isaac was a crotchety Seligman, with an individualistic approach to business. He had not joined his brothers in their New York and San Francisco operations. He had preferred to run his own lace and embroidery shop, removed from the others, in Cedar Street. His brothers had invited him to come in with them several times, but Isaac had declined. Isaac was a temperamental Seligman, with a sharp tongue and a quick temper, and had a reputation for barbed invective whenever business did not go exactly as he wished. But he was spunky, with great temerity and gall. The Washington assignment appealed to him. After all, he did not expect the embroidery and trimmings business to be particularly profitable in wartime. And so Isaac became what Joseph, during the early days of the war, referred to meaningfully as "our man in Washington."

Isaac's first discovery was that, strategy or no strategy, the Seligmans would have no trouble at all getting government contracts for army uniforms. The reason was dismal and simple. Larger, older-established Northern clothing manufacturers wanted nothing to do with government contracts. At the outbreak of the war the United States Treasury was in greater shambles than Fort Sumter. Southern banks had been quietly withdrawing large amounts of funds on deposit in the North. When Lincoln took office, he found his Treasury almost empty. The Federal debt was increasing, and American credit abroad was disappearing. Conservative businessmen wanted no deals whatever with the government. They considered it far too risky.

But risk was a stimulant to Isaac. As Gitterman's assistant, he was soon assisting Gitterman to assist the Seligmans. Their first army order came through—for 200 sergeant majors' chevrons and 200 quartermaster sergeants' chevrons, at thirty cents apiece, a total order of $120. It wasn't much, but it was a toe in the door, and presently the Seligmans were asked to outfit New York's 7th Regiment for active service—for a considerably larger figure.

Isaac busily got to know as many influential people in Washington as possible. Mr. Gitterman brought Isaac along to a large reception at the White House, where Isaac was introduced to a particularly important contact—President Lincoln. Isaac was surprised at the informality of White House receptions and was shocked to see "men appearing in their shirt sleeves! What would be thought of such an occurrence at a Court reception in London?" Gitterman was equally startled to hear young Isaac make this sartorial point to the President. The Seligmans, Isaac explained to Lincoln, were in the clothing business and could certainly outfit these improperly dressed gentlemen in nice-fitting suits and jackets. "We also make very nice uniforms, sir," said Isaac. "The pride of any army!" Lincoln looked briefly confused, then smiled, and promised to make a note of this.

Sure enough, the size and number of the Seligmans' uniform contracts speedily mounted. Their clothing mills were put on a seven-day-week basis. But soon the hazards that went with accepting these orders became painfully apparent. In a letter to Gitterman in Washington, eight months after the Seligmans' first contract, Joseph wrote:

> Your note just received, informing me that the appropriation for the clothing of the Army is exhausted, is startling and an alarming announcement to me, for the United States are indebted to my firm a million of dollars! Under the severe pressure of this burden we authorized you to make an arrangement for the payment of 400,000 of this sum in 3 year Treasury 7.30 Bonds. . . . I brought to Washington vouchers for this amount. . . . I had pledged to Banks in New York for 150,000 for which sum we gave our checks payable next week. If I am unable to realize this sum very promptly I see no alternative but the suspension of our house, which will drag down 20 other houses, and throw 400 operatives out of employ.
>
> Do my dear sir, for God's sake see if you cannot make some arrangement with the Secretary, by which this dreadful catastrophe may be avoided.
>
> This is really a question of life and death with me and I beg your earnest and prompt attention to it.

Apparently, Joseph got his money, for the records show $1,437,-483.61 paid to the Seligmans by the government in the twelve-month period following August 1, 1861. It is also clear that Joseph had to work for every penny of it. As part of his payment, he had been forced to accept, quite against his better judgment, hundreds of thousands of dollars' worth of the "3 year Treasury 7.30 Bonds." Joseph, in his passionate belief in—and, at that point, need for—liquidity, was then obliged to try to sell these bonds. But the Union armies had suffered serious losses, and public faith in the North's ability to win the war was slipping. Pro-South and antidraft demonstrations were taking place in New York, and there were reports of "wealthy ladies in the North wearing Rebel cockades." Union bonds were unsalable. In desperation, Joseph boarded a ship for Europe.

There he found that news of the Union's finances had preceded him. The "7.30" bonds were designed to yield 7.3 percent interest, payable semiannually. In Europe such a high rate of interest was taken as a sign of panic in Washington—as indeed it was. Joseph was able to dispose of some of his bonds, but it was a slow and uphill process. Meanwhile, to pay for its uniforms, the Treasury was dumping more and more of its bonds into Joseph's unwilling hands. Joseph found himself in the agonizing position of having to sell Union shares, so that the Union could be supplied with money, so that the Union could pay his own bills with more shares, etc., etc., into what must have seemed a whirlpool of unsupported credit.

In later years, Joseph Seligman's bond-selling efforts in Europe during this period became one of the most highly debated points in the Seligmans' career. According to Linton Wells, "In March, 1862, Joseph went to Washington and consulted President Lincoln and Secretary of the Treasury Chase regarding the placing of [Union] bonds in Frankfurt and Amsterdam."* Then, says Mr. Wells, Joseph left for Europe with a clutch of Union bonds and "achieved success far beyond his dreams. Not only did he dispose of substantial quantities of government bonds and treasury notes, but he was able to arouse considerable sympathy for the Union cause . . . and did more than anyone else on record to establish and maintain its credit abroad. . . . He . . . placed enormous quantities of bonds in Frankfurt, Munich, Berlin, and Amsterdam . . . a small amount in Paris . . . a fair market for them in England." Wells winds up saying that of the $510 million worth of bonds placed between February, 1862, and June, 1864, "more than $250,000,000 were placed abroad, and the Seligmans disposed of more than half this amount, contributing to the sale of a major portion of the

* In 1931 Wells, a former Seligman staff member, completed a thousand-page manuscript, "The Story of the House of Seligman." Never published, it reposes in the New-York Historical Society Library.

other half by their incessant propaganda in favor of the Union cause." This account has become further inflated by another historian, W. E. Dodd, who has called Joseph's bond-selling "equal perhaps to the service of the general who stopped Lee at Gettysburg."

Linton Wells has also written that Joseph Seligman, during a visit with President Lincoln, "persuaded" Lincoln to put Grant in charge of the Union forces, which Lincoln of course did.

These constitute sizable claims, and subsequent Seligman generations have cooperated with Messrs. Wells and Dodd in carrying on the legend that Joseph Seligman won the Civil War by paying for it. Unfortunately, no records exist which quite bear out these claims. Treasury records for the Civil War period are incomplete, and Seligman records on this score are now lost. Joseph did visit Lincoln and Chase in 1862, but the subject and outcome of their conversation were not recorded. (Joseph may very well have gone to beg them to *stop* paying him with Union bonds.) Joseph *was* in Europe during the months following, but if he was achieving success "beyond his dreams," his letters home don't show it. He hardly mentions Union bonds at all. He seems much more interested in an idea that had been growing in his mind—to set up an international Seligman banking house, a house designed along the lines of the House of Rothschild, a house whose style was represented in America only by August Belmont. But first Joseph would have to wait out the war. In January, 1864, he wrote: "Should we conclude to go into Banking, my presence in Europe during this summer and winter may be necessary to put things into train for the Banking business. The fact that I have done little or nothing up to this time is no proof of my inability to effect something, but arose out of our cautiousness not to enter into anything during war time." ("Up to this time," of course, includes the time Joseph supposedly had sold Union bonds in the hundreds of millions' worth, yet Joseph seems apologetic, almost defensive, about having done "little or nothing.")

For a great propagandist of the Union cause, Joseph's letters during the early war years are oddly gloomy and pessimistic about the Union's chances of winning. In 1863 he confided to his friend Wolf Goodhart that he didn't much care which side won the war; he simply wanted it to be over, so he could set up his banking house. As a booster of American credit abroad, he took this stand in a letter to his brother William: "As I have so often said, the wealth of the country is being decimated and people are rich in imagination only. Calif. is the only exception up to this time. Query, how long will it last even there?" (To bolster his sagging morale, William Seligman wrote hurriedly back: "The Cal. capital has swelled to $900,000.")

At one optimistic point, Joseph bought some Union bonds for his own portfolio, then quickly became discouraged about their prospects and wrote: "I am almost tempted to resell the U.S. Stock which I bought and keep my hands clear of the present degenerated American race." His brother James was more hopeful and wrote suggesting that the brothers buy $100,000 worth of Union securities for their own accounts. Joseph turned him down. "Do not be afraid," he answered, "that the Government will want no more money after the 1 June—even if the South should have been whipped so badly as to offer to make peace, the Gov't will need hundreds if not thousands of millions yet, to pay for claims of all description and for the purpose of emancipating the Negro."

From money, Joseph's Civil War letters turn to homely family matters: "Hope Bro. Wm's Ida has entirely recovered from her indisposition. . . . Hope Bro. Abrm has safely reached N.Y. and if he finds no suitable match I will go with him on a *Brautshau* in Germany. I have so far not found the proper article yet."

Of Grant he makes almost no mention. True, Grant was Jesse's and Henry's friend more than he was Joseph's. And Joseph was significantly silent on one piece of news that must have reached him from America— Grant's famous Order No. 11, which expelled Jews from behind the Union lines, an action that has never been satisfactorily explained. In 1863, however, when some Republicans were opposing Lincoln's reelection and were offering Grant as a substitute, Joseph commented angrily: "I see the d——d Herald nominates Grant. This is probably done to cause a split between Lincoln and Grant."

This much, however, of Joseph's Union bond-selling is known. Early in Lincoln's *second* administration, in 1865, William Fessenden, who succeeded Chase as Secretary of the Treasury, announced a $400 million issue of new government notes. Joseph Seligman headed a group of German bankers in New York who wished to underwrite $50 million worth of these notes, but the Secretary would not accept the terms of the syndicate. Thereupon, the Seligman brothers took an active part in selling these Federal securities themselves, and it is recorded that they sold over $60 million worth.

But this, of course, was in another part of the Civil War forest: the tide of the war had already turned against the South; the Union's financial climate had brightened both in the North and in Europe; and it was a different bond issue.

For Mayer, the Montgomery-based Lehman, the war meant that his cotton business would have to be modified if it was to survive. Some cotton could still be shipped North. Chinks in the blockade appeared periodically, and small shipments could be sneaked through. Cotton could also be sent to New York, expensively, via England. But the main need was for warehouses where Southern cotton could be stored for the duration of the war. Mayer approached a merchant named John Wesley Durr, a partner in a firm which owned the Alabama Warehouse. Mayer and Durr formed a partnership called Lehman, Durr & Company, and bought the Alabama Warehouse.

Among Mayer Lehman's close friends were such Confederate celebrities as Thomas Hill Watts, wartime Governor of Alabama and, for a time, Attorney General under President Jefferson Davis (Watts called Mayer Lehman "one of the best Southern patriots"). Another friend was the Confederate political leader, Hilary A. Herbert (after whom Mayer would name his youngest son, Herbert H. Lehman). As Joseph Seligman had done in the North, Mayer offered his services to the Confederacy "to assist in every way possible."

In 1864 the South was agitated by reports that captured soldiers were being starved and brutalized in Union prisons (similar rumors about Confederate barbarity were stirring up the North), and the Alabama Legislature authorized Governor Watts to spend half a million dollars for the relief of Alabama captives. A plan was devised. A shipment of cotton would be sent through enemy lines to New York, accompanied by an agent. In New York the cotton would be sold and the agent, after deducting his commission, would buy and distribute blankets, medicines, and provisions to the prisoners from the proceeds. Mayer Lehman, who was eager to see how his brother in the North was faring, offered to be this agent, despite the "extreme hazard" of the operation. Watts agreed, and wrote to President Davis, saying of Mayer: "He is a foreigner, but has been here fifteen years and is thoroughly identified with us. It will be necessary for him to go through the lines. I ask that he may be furnished with the proper passports and indorsed by you as the Agent of the State of Alabama." Jefferson Davis complied, drew up the requested papers, and some fifteen hundred bales of cotton were actually shipped to Mobile to await Union permission for their transportation, along with Mayer, through the lines.

That this plan—which, today, seems to have been conceived in wonderful innocence—should have failed is no surprise. Still, in January, 1865, we find Mayer Lehman writing a polite letter to the Commander of the Union Armies, General Grant, requesting safe conduct through the battle lines and saying: "We well know what a gallant soldier must feel for those brave men, who by the fortunes of war are held prisoners exposed to the rigors of climate to which they are not accustomed, the severities of which are augmented by the privations necessarily attendant upon their condition." The letter could not have been more diplomatic. But Grant must have thought the whole scheme utterly dotty—or perhaps fishy. Why should Mayer Lehman, one of the South's leading cotton merchants, be concerned with shivering prisoners and Northern weather? As far as Grant could see, all Lehman wanted to do was sell his cotton in the Northern market. In any case, Grant did not answer Mayer's letter. Two weeks later, Mayer wrote again, enclosing a copy of the original communication. This was not answered, either.

Washington in the meantime, which Mayer had no way of knowing, had embarked upon a tough policy of attrition against the South, designed to wear the rebels down and end the war quickly. In April came Lee's surrender, and before the Federal troops moved into Montgomery over 88,000 bales of cotton were set to the torch, including the entire inventory of the Alabama Warehouse Company.

Emanuel Lehman in the North, after the initial blow of Lincoln's blockade, was able to carry on his business through the war, in a limited way. He sold what cotton made its way through the blockade from Mayer, and agented shipments that came by way of England, which he visited several times. In London he found an atmosphere more cordial to his Southern sympathies than in New York. Mayer wrote to him there suggesting that, through connections with men like Watts and Herbert, Emanuel might like to be an agent for the sale of Confederate bonds. Emanuel found the European market for Southern securities—during the early stages of the war, at least—considerably better than for Northern ones.

In London, Emanuel Lehman and Joseph Seligman encountered one another, each with his supply of bonds, two salesmen for two warring powers. Their manner toward each other was cool, reserved. Though both men were loyal to their respective causes in the "unholy rebellion," as it was called, they were not really in the business of fighting a war. They were in the business of making money.

Up to the outbreak of the war, August Belmont had been financial adviser to the President of the United States. During the war's first months, Lincoln leaned on Belmont for Rothschild money as heavily as Gitterman and the Quartermaster Corps leaned on the Seligmans for uniforms. This placed Belmont in an awkward position. Reflecting the general frame of mind in Europe, the Rothschilds had grave doubts about the North's chances of winning, and gave Belmont and the United States Treasury only lukewarm and hesitant support. Lincoln's fundraisers were forced to look for new sources of supply, and found them in the bond-selling efforts of such men as Joseph Seligman. As the war progressed, affection for Belmont in Washington declined and esteem for Seligman grew. By the war's end, though he may not have actually "won the war," Joseph Seligman was very dear to Washington's heart.

Obviously, this was the moment for Joseph to put his great plan to work. Within hours of Lee's surrender, Joseph had summoned his brothers together to organize the international banking House of Seligman. The house would span the American continent and sweep across the face of Europe. Each brother would be given an assignment suitable to his temperament and talents. William Seligman, who had bought the portentous clothing factory and who loved good food and wine, would be placed in charge of Paris. Henry, who had remained in Germany longest of all the brothers, was given Frankfurt. Isaac, the first Seligman to meet a President, was assigned to London and told to do everything possible to meet the Rothschilds. Joseph, James, and Jesse—whose old friend Grant was the American hero of the day—would remain in New York. Abraham and Leopold, whom Joseph by now knew to be the least competent of his brothers, were assigned to San Francisco, a city, now that the great gold wave was subsiding, that had become of less importance. The House of Seligman was a frank copy of the House of Rothschild, and Joseph admitted it. After all, what other models were there?

J. & W. Seligman & Company, World Bankers, was officially born. But an even more meaningful moment occurred a few days later when Joseph was walking down Nassau Street. Coming from the opposite direction, with the patrician limp from the old dueling wound that had become his trademark, was none other than the great man himself, August Belmont. As Belmont approached, he looked at Joseph, smiled slightly, touched his silk hat, said, "Hullo, Seligman," and limped on. Joseph knew that he had arrived.

That evening Joseph bought his wife a present. It must be remembered that the 1860's were not a period of great taste. It was the era of the whatnot, the figurine, the antimacassar, the rubber plant, and the piano sweltering beneath a Spanish shawl. Joseph's gift to Babet was considered one of the decorative "musts" of the day—a gold-plated rolling pin, designed to show that its owner "no longer made her own bread, but was financially able to endure the strain of purchasing ready-made loaves at the grocer's."

The war was over. The boom was on. In the South the cotton market was reviving, and soon the Seligmans opened another office in New Orleans. It was there that Joseph Seligman achieved a remarkable feat of postwar diplomacy. He invited General Ulysses S. Grant, former Commander of the Northern Forces, and Brigadier General Pierre Gustave Beauregard, former Commander of the Southern Army of the Potomac, the man who directed the firing on Fort Sumter, to dinner.

Certainly it is one of the great tragedies in Civil War history that the dinner-table conversation *chez* Seligman was not recorded. But it is known that dinner started with "delicious little prawns from the gulf," and that the two generals "chatted amiably." Grant drank rather a lot of Alsatian wine and, at one point, wanted to sing. After dinner the two generals played snooker in the billiard room. Grant lost, then the two old enemies went for a brief stroll, arm in arm, through the starlit garden while Joseph Seligman smiled benignly on.

PART III

INTO
THE MAINSTREAM
1866 - 1899

11

PEDDLERS IN
TOP HATS

James Truslow Adams calls the years following the Civil War "The Age
of the Dinosaurs." In it, fortunes would amass in America on a scale
never before imagined. Twenty years earlier there had not been five men
in the United States worth as much as five million dollars, and there
were less than twenty worth one million. Soon a New York newspaper
would report that there were several hundred men in the city of New
York alone who were worth at least a million, and some who were
worth more than twenty million. The fortunes, furthermore, were being
made in ways never before heard of—from steel mills, steam engines,
and oil from the Pennsylvania hills. Telegraph lines were stretching
across the country, the Cattle Kingdom was opening in the West, railroads were being built furiously and recklessly—parallel to each other
and at cross-purposes with each other—to tie the sources of wealth
together, and entrepreneurs from all over America were descending on
New York to tap the money market.

83

To Old Guard New York, the situation was alarming. George Templeton Strong, a diarist of the period, bemoaned the "oil-rich shoddy-ites" from out of town who invaded the city,* and wrote:

> How New York has fallen off during the last forty years! Its intellect and culture have been diluted and swamped by a great flood-tide of material wealth . . . men whose bank accounts are all they rely on for social position and influence. As for their ladies, not a few who were driven in the most sumptuous turnouts, with liveried servants, looked as if they might have been cooks or chambermaids a few years ago.

The ladies in their snappy turnouts and the men with their expanding bank accounts appeared to care nothing about the things that mattered to people like Mr. Strong. They seemed to consider "background" unnecessary. As a character called Mrs. Tiffany in the play *Fashion,* an ex-milliner whose husband had struck oil, commented, "Forget what we *have* been, it is enough to remember that we *are* of the *upper ten thousand.*"

Central Park had been carved out of the middle of Manhattan in 1856; if this move had been delayed for as little as ten years, there probably would have been no park at all; the land would have become too precious. Now the winding roads through the park became avenues where ladies paraded ritually every afternoon for the world to envy and admire. The park's bridle paths made riding fashionable, though a Miss King complained that she received "disapproving glares" from the windows of the Union Club when she drove by, behind her own little pony phaeton. Men such as Roosevelt Roosevelt and DeLancey Kane used the park to show off their dashing four-in-hand coaches.

Society still lived well below the park, on lower Fifth Avenue, and Ward McAllister had announced that he really could not bother "to run society" north of Fiftieth Street (the park began at Fifty-ninth). Along lower Fifth, however, the mansions of Astors, Vanderbilts, Webbs, Jays, Roosevelts, Morgans, Morrises, Newbolds, and Rhinelanders were a marvelous fairyland of spired, turreted, gabled, and minareted castles in styles borrowed from every place and period imaginable. It all added up to "New York aesthetic," and the street dazzled visitors. In New York drawing rooms Eastlake furniture with its cut-out gilt designs was being replaced by Venetian Gothic. Stylish decorative touches included elaborate vases filled with cattails, Japanese fans, and medieval suits of armor. Embroidery was fashionable, and heavy embroidered "throws" were draped languidly across velvet chairs and sofas. In the rich suburbs—Westchester County led in chic—it was the era of the cast-

---

* Mr. Strong himself, however, owned ten thousand shares of Kenzula Petroleum.

iron lawn animal—the deer, the elk, and the Saint Bernard dog being the beasts most favored.

It was an era when a display of wealth was considered perfectly proper. A fashion note was the "peek-a-boo" ladies' shirtwaist, which allowed the wealthy lady to display a bit of herself along with her costly clothes. A great deal of formality, even stiffness, characterized all social occasions. Society families dressed for dinner even when dining alone. Food was heavy, plentiful, but unimaginative—August Belmont's meals were an exception—and eight-course family dinners were no surprise. It was an era so well tended that guests, arriving at the Frank Vanderlips for dinner on the wrong evening, were, to spare them embarrassment, not advised of their mistake, and were simply ushered in to a customary eight-courser. The calling-card ritual became so elaborate that only a few people could remember all its rules, and most women had to keep the little manual in their reticules to look up which corner of which the card should be turned down for which occasion and so on. Symbolic of the heaviness of the period was the moment at the ball given for the visiting Prince of Wales in 1860 when the ballroom floor started to collapse from the weight of the gathering and had to be hastily shored up from beneath.

It was a society also that was eager to classify itself, to decide who was who, who "mattered" and who didn't. The personality of Ward McAllister suited this new attitude perfectly—he may even have invented it. McAllister had decided that there were two elements of importance in New York—the "nobs," as he called them, or the old families who had more position than money, and the "swells," a newer-rich group who "had to entertain and be smart" in order to hold their own. A Morris or Van Rensselaer, in other words, was a nob. A Vanderbilt was a swell. McAllister decided that a coalition society should be formed out of these two groups, in order to form "a fixed upper class" that would resist the invasions of "profiteers, boorish people, people with only money." McAllister did not say that this included people like the Seligmans, but the implication was clear.

McAllister's formula was as good as any, and, since society needed formulas to reassure itself of its importance, it was adopted. There were no Jews at all in McAllister's combined group,* and the unspoken sentiment began to be felt that, though Jewish bankers would be tolerated in the financial community of Wall Street, they would not be welcomed on Fifth Avenue. New York's patrician Sephardic families

---

* Unless, of course, a persistent bit of gossip one still hears in New York is true—that the Astors themselves were originally Jewish. There is also a little band of old New York families who make the same assertion about the Vanderbilts.

quickly noticed that their names were not included in McAllister's collection either. Some Sephardim expressed relief at this. But others resented it. They blamed the new exclusivity on the behavior of the "loud, aggressive, new-rich Germans." To the Sephardim, the Germans had become the toplofty, arrogant "Mrs. Tiffanys."

Society might be able to overlook the German Jews, but the business community no longer could. The Seligmans were a fact of Wall Street life, and now the Lehmans began to emerge. Despite the setbacks of the war, the Lehmans had quickly revived their cotton business. Emanuel re-established himself in Fulton Street, and Mayer—with his Southern partner, Mr. Durr—reassembled Lehman, Durr & Company in Montgomery, and simultaneously opened Lehman, Newgass & Company in New Orleans (with his brother-in-law, Benjamin Newgass), once again around the corner from the Seligmans. Montgomery was the center of the Alabama-Georgia-Piedmont cotton trade, while New Orleans served the rich Mississippi-Louisiana area. In 1866 nearly a third of the cotton shipped from American ports passed through the port of New Orleans, and in the inflationary postwar period cotton soared to the unprecedented price of fifty cents a pound. But New York was still the money capital of cotton, and in 1868 Mayer Lehman decided to join his brother, leaving Newgass and Durr to handle affairs in the South. Lehman Brothers took new offices in Pearl Street, just off Hanover Square, center of the cotton trade.

One thing was noticed that had not been apparent before: the two brothers looked almost exactly alike, with bright eyes, full beards, and high foreheads. The effect of twinship created the impression of one Lehman being several places at once, and their attitudes of bounce, ebullience, and good nature soon earned them the quaint nickname of "the Cheeryble Brothers." (In their portraits which hang in the partners' room at Lehman Brothers, they do not look very Cheeryble; they look properly bankerly and stern, but doubtless being together after a long separation made them Cheeryble in 1868. At Lehman Brothers the bearded faces in the partners' room are called "the Smith Brothers," since there is a certain resemblance to the cough drop pair.)

But appearances can be deceptive. Temperamentally, the brothers were quite different, Emanuel the "inside" money man, Mayer the outgoing contact-maker. Emanuel was conservative and cautious, Mayer speculative and bold. Members of the family have said that Emanuel would study the financial picture and say, "It's a good time to sell." Mayer would look at the same evidence and say, "It's a good time to buy." Once, at the height of a panic on the Cotton Exchange, Mayer was seen striding out of his office in silk hat, frock coat, and striped trousers, with his heavy gold watch fob swinging at his waist, wielding his gold-handled stick and wearing a smile on his face and a general air of confidence. A young associate ran up to him and said, "Mr. Lehman, aren't you *worried?*" Mayer replied, "My dear young man, I see you have had no experience with a falling market," and strode on. Others in the family summed up their differences, saying, "Mayer makes the money and Emanuel conserves it." (In the portraits, one notices that Emanuel wears a dark and sober cravat; optimistic Mayer wears a jaunty, Cheeryble bow tie.)

Nor were the Seligmans and Lehmans the only immigrants in New York who were making the great transition from peddling and store-keeping in the provinces to banking in the big city. Now, in 1867, the downtown financial district noticed a new firm called Kuhn, Loeb & Company, and its top-hatted little proprietor, Solomon Loeb. At his wife's insistence, Loeb had moved from Cincinnati—the "Porkopolis" she hated—had bought a brownstone in East Thirty-eighth Street (though he was warned that it was "too far uptown" and was "sure to be a bad investment"), and had opened his private banking offices in Nassau Street. The firm had a starting capital of $500,000, and the original Kuhn, Loeb partners were listed as "A. Kuhn, J. Netter, S. Kuhn, S. Loeb, S. Wolff"—all relatives. (Loeb's original partner in the Cincinnati clothing business, Abraham Kuhn, soon retired from the firm and returned permanently to Germany.)

Marcus Goldman, another cloak-and-suiter, also yielded to his wife, and removed her from the city *she* disliked so much, which was Philadelphia. In New York, Goldman hung out a shingle in Pine Street announcing that he was now "Marcus Goldman, Banker and Broker." The Goldmans entered the brownstone world of Murray Hill, and joined the group of families whose spiritual center was Temple Emanu-El, and whose acknowledged social leaders were named Seligman.

Marcus Goldman's downtown "office," like those of most fledgling bankers of the day, was in sharp contrast to the way he lived uptown (around the corner from the Astors) and the way he dressed. Sumptuous downtown offices were still a long way off, and Marcus' was a cellar room next to a coal chute. In these dim quarters he installed a stool, a desk, and a wizened part-time bookkeeper (who worked afternoons for a funeral parlor).

In what was the standard banker's uniform—tall silk hat and Prince Albert frock coat—Marcus Goldman started off each morning to visit his friends and acquaintances among the wholesale jewelers in Maiden Lane, and in the "Swamp," where the hide and leather merchants were located. Marcus carried his business in his hat. He knew a merchant's chief need: cash. Since rates on loans from commercial banks were high, one means New York's small merchants had of obtaining cash was to sell their promissory notes or commercial paper* to men like Marcus at a discount. Commercial paper was then being discounted at 8 to 9 percent, and Marcus purchased these notes in amounts ranging from $2,500 to $5,000 and tucked the valuable bits of paper inside the inner band of his hat for safekeeping. As his morning progressed, his hat sat higher and higher above his forehead.

Then, in the afternoon, he would head uptown to the commercial banks. He would call on the Commercial Bank in Chambers Street, the Importers & Traders in Warren Street, or the National Park Bank in John Street. He would see the cashier, or perhaps the president, deferentially remove his hat, and they would begin to dicker.

Marcus was doing what Solomon Loeb was doing, what the Lehmans were doing with their cotton bills, and what the Seligmans were doing on a somewhat grander scale with their bonds (which in essence are simply government, or industry, promises to pay). Marcus, however, didn't seem to need partners. From the very beginning, he was able to sell as much as five million dollars' worth of commercial paper a year.

Bertha Goldman was able to afford, in 1869, one of the "sumptuous turnouts with liveried servants" described by Mr. Strong to take her on her morning rounds of shopping and errands. But Marcus chose to walk. So did Solomon Loeb. So did the Lehmans and the Seligmans. "Trading on the Street" meant just that. As the pedestrian bankers met each other, they bowed to each other solemnly. On their daily tours they appraised the altitudes of each other's hats.

Walking was becoming a tradition among the Jewish bankers. They all had wives who believed in feeding their husbands hearty breakfasts, enormous midday meals, and Lucullan dinners. Walking countered some of the effects of these. There was a point of dignity, too. Carriages were for lazy men and men of little consequence. The splendor of the conveyance could dim the splendor of the passenger folded up within. Walking toughened the physical and moral fiber, but it was also a social form of locomotion. Walking, a man could meet his friends. Afoot, he could keep abreast of what the competition was doing. One did business while one walked, and one walked even when one sailed. In a few years' time, Jacob Schiff—who would tower above every financial figure in Wall Street—would be able to boast that he had made a million dollars while doing his morning constitutional about the deck of the *Berengeria*.

---

* One way to visualize a piece of "commercial paper" is to think of a postdated check. If, today, you drew a check for $100 dated six months from now, based on funds you expected to have by then, you would find few people who would give you a full $100 for that piece of paper. But you might find someone willing to pay you $90, and that person, in turn, might find a more affluent source willing to buy it from him for $95. It is illegal to trade personal checks this way, but commercially it is quite a legal operation.

(The Jewish bankers were remarkable among nineteenth-century travelers because they *talked* to people; gentile society of the period was antisocial when it traveled, afraid of strangers, foreigners, parvenus, and other dangerous shipboard alliances.)

Of course it also may have been true that the bankers walked out of habit. The grandiose phrase for men like Marcus Goldman, Solomon Loeb, and the Seligmans was "merchant bankers." But they were, in many ways, still peddlers covering their routes, only now they were peddling IOU's.

THE

"OUR DEAR BABETTE"
SYNDROME

By the war's end Joseph Seligman's wife had presented him with a total of nine children, five boys and four girls. Joseph's brothers and sisters, and their wives and husbands, were following Joseph's prolific example, and having seven, eight, nine, even thirteen children apiece. From the original eleven immigrant Seligmans, the combined Seligman family—husbands, wives, and children—had swollen to number 104, or, as Joseph reminded his brothers, a profit in people of 845 percent.

Dynastic Joseph mother-henned all the pregnancies in the family, which was quite a job since there were often several at once. Naturally he preferred male children to female, and he seems very nearly to have gotten his way. Of eighty-two Seligman children, forty-four were boys. The Seligman children also defied infant-mortality rates of the period. Of the four score plus who composed the second generation, only two did not live to maturity. This healthy and numerous tribe would, one might think, provide personnel to staff an operation of almost any size.

There was only one trouble, one which affects all dynasties, and one which New York German Jewish families, who drew an equation between the family and the business, would all encounter. Joseph encountered it early, long before he was required to tackle the job of fitting sons, sons-in-law, nephews, and nephews-in-law into the slots he had ordained for them. No sooner had he got his transatlantic and transcontinental table of organization set up, with each brother-in-law and brother in his appointed place, than he discovered he had men who were unhappy at, or unequal to, their duties. There was Max Stettheimer, for instance, Joseph's sister Babette's husband.

The position of a Seligman sister was a difficult one to begin with. She was totally dependent on her brothers for money, and though they were generous, it was in a high-handed way which left the girls in the dark as to how wealthy the family really was. Monetary matters were considered damaging to a woman's brain, and so the Seligman brothers spared their womenfolk all financial details that they believed were beyond their grasp. Whenever business went badly, the women's allowances would be cut, but never with an explanation. The women resented this, but there was nothing they could do. The men were making the money, and were their benefactors.

Babette's position was particularly unhappy. Max Stettheimer was a stolid but colorless man, moody and uncommunicative, and such life as they had together was passed in a kind of upholstered silence. Max, apparently, was fond of sitting. In letters of the time, whenever reference is made to Max—and there are very few—it is with the comment, "Max sat there." There is a possibility that he was not very bright. Max and his father were importers by training and tradition. Buying and selling goods was a process Max understood. But the intricacies of finance—factoring, bond-selling, moneylending—eluded him. Early in his marriage to Babette, Joseph had placed Max in the St. Louis store, where he had worked with William. But now, nearly twenty years later, when Joseph was ready to abandon storekeeping altogether and go into international banking, Max dug in his heels. Joseph's plan was to send Max to Paris with William. But Max did not want to go to Paris, or into banking, or to work with William.

Taking Max's side was Max's father, Jacob Stettheimer, who had joined the Seligman enterprises when his son married into the clan, and adding her support to the Stettheimer faction was Jacob Stettheimer's wife. The senior Mrs. Stettheimer was jealous of the Seligmans, and disapproved of the way Babette was raising her children. And so Joseph tried to move forward with his grand design, while all the Stettheimers lined up against all the Seligmans.

The situation grew stickier daily. At home Max complained to Babette that her brother was "against" him, was trying to "lord it" over him, and "wants to push me around." Babette tried to intercede with Joseph on her husband's behalf, and Joseph explained to Babette that if she had any loyalty to her family she would get Max—and Max's father—to do as they were told. "After all, we have made Max a rich man," he reminded his sister.

Unwisely, Babette carried this message back to Max, who thereupon presented Joseph with an ultimatum. If he and his father were not allowed to continue their importing business unhampered by Joseph, they would leave Joseph's organization altogether. Max then told Babette that if he and the Seligmans parted company he would never permit her to see any of her brothers and sisters—who were her whole life—again. In desperation, Joseph turned to William for help, writing:

> Max insists that we go into importing again. And if we do not enter into it as largely as of old he will get other partners. Nothing would please me more, were it not for our dear Babette who says as soon as Max ceases business connections with us, she will face a life more insupportable than hitherto, and begs of me to try to keep him in. If only for her sake I deem it my duty, provided I cannot place him in Paris or Frankfurt as I would prefer, to commence importing again.

William had a practical suggestion. The dispute, he hinted, might be settled in some other area—specifically the money area. Sure enough, Max had his price, and so did Jacob. A sum was given to Jacob—enough to establish him in an importing business of his own. Another sum, in the form of a larger share of the business, went to Max, who, in turn, agreed to join Henry in Frankfurt. As another concession to Max, and to please Babette, Joseph agreed to change the name of the Frankfurt house to Seligman & Stettheimer and to let Max engage in importing and exporting on the side. It would not be true, of course, to say that this made everybody happy. It was a makeshift arrangement, costly to Joseph and one which Max had accepted only grumblingly.

At the same time, Joseph was trying to cope with a different family problem in San Francisco. He had long realized that artistic Leopold needed a firm hand to guide him. He had assumed that in the West Coast office Abraham would provide this. But it soon turned out that this was not to be the case. Neither Abraham nor Leopold seemed to know what he was doing. While Leopold daydreamed over his sketch pad, Abraham—who at least undertook every project with great enthusiasm—embarked upon a long series of bungling, lightheaded, and expensive mistakes. An incompetent brother-in-law was bad enough, but to have two blood brothers who were no good at banking was inconceivable.

To Joseph, everything was a question of learning, as he himself had learned, and so, patiently, he began trying to teach Abraham banking by mail. "You are, of course, green yet in the banking business, as we were a few years ago," Joseph wrote from New York, "and it is only through extraordinary caution, trusting no one, except we knew from our knowledge that he was safe *beyond all doubt,* that we got along without making heavy losses." But Abraham and Leopold apparently trusted everybody, and Joseph kept having to spell things out for them: "The main thing in a banker is safety, with ability to reach his money at a moment's call. . . . The subject of taking deposits is rather a risky one, inasmuch as depositors can (and will, in times of panics) call for all their deposits, which is enough to break any but the very strongest banks. You will at first not take deposits on call from anyone." He outlined his creed, which was to stay, at all times, as financially liquid as possible: "Never lend money without a security which you can sell at any time. *Never endorse or go security for a living man."* (By this, of course, Joseph did not mean that his brothers should endorse dead men; he meant that they should back *businesses,* not people, since human beings are seldom negotiable.) On and on Joseph went, explaining the rudiments of banking, trying to put the obvious in the clearest possible terms. But the two brothers never seemed quite to grasp what Joseph was talking about. They were not helped, either, by being married to the socially ambitious Levi sisters, who conspired to keep their husbands' heads turned toward affairs other than business.

When Abraham Seligman should have been buying, he sold. When he should have sold, he bought. Finally a despairing Joseph wrote to him:

> I am afraid, dear Abe, you are not smart enough for the California bankers and brokers, for whenever gold goes up you appear to get stuck with currency, and whenever it goes down you "cannot get much." You must be wide awake and if you don't get correct quotations daily from here we will telegraph you daily or whenever a change directs.

But apparently even the daily telegrams did not help. In the summer of 1867 Joseph decided to trim the San Francisco operation, and wrote, still hoping somehow to make at least Leopold a banker: "After collecting up, we may probably get Brother Leopold to take hold of some other branch of our banking business," and, a few days later, added gloomily:

> Brother Abe will join Brother Leopold in endeavoring to collect up all that is due us, getting everything which cannot be collected in good shape, but expect you to grant no unnecessary indulgence, so that we do not lose much interest, as we already lose enough on selling the stock . . . $500,000 worth of goods is alone a loss of $100,000. There-

fore, I trust there will be no interest lost on debts and everything collected up close.

Joseph then shipped Abraham to Frankfurt to join Henry and Max, and Leopold to London to join Isaac. It was hardly the arrangement Joseph wanted. He now had two ineffectual operatives, Abraham and Max, in his Frankfurt office. Who to handle Seligman affairs in the American West would be a continuing problem. And the whole Abraham-Leopold adventure in San Francisco had been far more expensive than mollifying Max and "our dear Babette." Furthermore, the "our dear Babette" syndrome—Joseph's feeling that it was his duty to provide places for relatives in his business no matter how meager their talents were—would go on plaguing him for years to come. Bankers, it seems, are born, not made.

13

"GETTING
OUR FEET WET"

Men were getting rich, but the American Government's financial state remained precarious during the early Reconstruction period. In 1866 there was less than a hundred million dollars in the U.S. Treasury, yet the public debt was edging rapidly toward the three-thousand-million mark. Hugh McCulloch, Secretary of the Treasury under both Lincoln and Johnson, was an experienced financier (he had served as Comptroller of Currency during the war) who understood bankers, and bankers understood him. His postwar plans for the economy included payment of short-term government obligations by issuing and selling long-term bonds, payable in ten to forty years. The Seligmans, for their bond-selling efforts during the war, were offered a large share of McCulloch's new bonds to sell. "Patriotism directs that we accept this assignment," Joseph wrote his brothers. There was also a commission to be earned from selling bonds, though it was a small one.

Joseph took the assignment, and the bonds sold well, but in the meantime he looked around for more exciting ways to make money.

One piece of business floating around New York in 1867 was $450,000 worth of stock in the New York Mutual Gas Light Company, an early ancestor of the Consolidated Edison Company. Nobody thought much of this stock, which sold for pennies a share. Shares were traded for drinks at local saloons. But two men thought the stock had promise. One was Cornelius Vanderbilt, Sr. The other was Joseph Seligman. Joseph began buying up New York Mutual shares from bartenders as he made teetotaling rounds about the city. Presently the company was laying twenty-four-inch gas mains under the city streets. The value of the stock climbed to five million dollars and was selling for $100 a share. The Seligmans and "Old Vanderbilt," as Joseph affectionately called him, made a tidy million dollars each.

It wasn't any special "shrewdness" that made Joseph invest in issues like this. It was more like beginner's luck. Indeed, it is one of the phenomena of the Stock Market that some men seem naturally to be lucky in it while others simply are not. Joseph's heirs and assigns today wince at mention of the far more lucrative opportunities he turned down. Just prior to the New York Mutual Gas bonanza, Joseph was advised that all the land north of Sixtieth Street and west of Broadway—up to 121st Street, where Grant's Tomb now stands, and including most of what is now West End Avenue and Riverside Drive—was for sale. The price for this tract was $450,000—more than three square miles of Manhattan for a fraction of what a single city block would cost now. It was perhaps the best bargain since Peter Minuit's original purchase of the island from the Indians. Joseph had the money, but said no. "It is a bad investment." Had he felt otherwise, the Seligmans today would easily be the richest family in the world. Again he was showing his distaste for tying up money in anything that could not be sold quickly and his distrust of real estate. (In closing his San Francisco store, he had simply given the land to the city rather than go to the trouble of trying to sell it.)

From the beginning, the German Jewish bankers backed the riskier issues, but this was not because they preferred them to issues with less risk. Each issue that came into their hands had a little extra risk built in. The older-established, more conservative New England-bred bankers had Old School ties with the older-established, more conservative, less risky companies. They shied away from newer and more speculative ventures and, for reasons of prestige, avoided all cheap stocks. "Let the Jews have that one" was the saying on the Street. This was not anti-Semitism exactly. "Old Vanderbilt," though he wasn't Jewish, was equally a parvenu in the 1860's and was in the same position as the Jews. It was simply that the older houses could pick and choose, and the newer bankers pawed through the leftovers like ladies at a bargain sale.

"Do not worry, as we are still getting our feet wet," Joseph Seligman reassured his brothers when things went wrong—as happened frequently.

The New Orleans operation, under brother-in-law Max Hellman, was doing particularly well, thanks to the resumption of cotton trade. "The financing of imports in a period of reconstruction, the discounting of cotton bills—what an opportunity for addition to the Seligman fortune!" Joseph had written in 1865. By 1867 the prediction was coming true. Max Hellman was a stern-faced, square-jawed young man with a bristling mustache and heavy eyebrows. He had been born in Munich. "Max," Joseph wrote of Henriette Seligman's brother, "is a selfish man in some ways"—but selfishness is not always a negative quality in a trader. On the plus side, Joseph said, "Max has the kind of manners that will be liked in Southern Society." This seemed to be true also. Max did such a brisk business in buying and discounting cotton exchange bills that Joseph wrote him proudly: "We would say that, with the exception of Brown* and you, *we have reason to know* that every other banker *has lost money* this season in purchasing bills in New Orleans."

But Max made mistakes. Gold bullion was still making its way from California to the Southern port, then to New York, and then to Europe, where it was again resold. And, in February, 1868, Joseph wrote to Max to say: "We received yesterday some 23 large bars, which you state to be gold and which the U.S. Assay Office returns to us as being *pure brass!* Had they been gold they would have been worth about ¼ million dollars to judge by the weight. We are glad you made no advance on them, but we had to pay freight to New York and also $5.00 to the U.S. Assay Office for their trouble." Joseph added: "Please be more careful in the future."

In the fall of that year, Joseph decided that Max needed a change of air. He transferred Max to Paris to work with William, and specifically asked Max to keep an eye on William, who was being less than careful in the rendering of his accounts. The Jewish practice of making up a marriage purse for each daughter in the family when she became engaged had been instituted by Joseph, who imposed a levy on each brother based on the size of his most recent profit statement. Joseph's oldest daughter, Helene, had become engaged that year in New York, and William had submitted a particularly impressive statement from Paris. Joseph wrote him that his share-of-purse would therefore be considerable. William, red-faced, was forced to reply that he had lied about his profits on that statement "to save you, dear Joe, from worry in

---

* Probably one of the Browns of Brown Brothers, later Brown Brothers, Harriman, Inc.

New York." Of course William knew immediately why Joseph was sending Max to Paris, and was furious.

To replace Max in New Orleans, Joseph picked Max's younger brother, Theodore Hellman (who later married Joseph's daughter Frances, thereby becoming a Seligman brother-in-law and son-in-law, and weaving the Seligman-Hellman families into an even tighter web; but when he went to New Orleans he was still a bachelor of twenty-four). Theodore was tall and slender and handsome, with curly dark sideburns and a Grecian profile. If Southern society liked Max's manners, it liked Theodore's even more. His good looks helped outweigh the fact that he was, to all intents and purposes, just another Northern carpetbagger (he rather resembled Clark Gable as Rhett Butler), and he was soon a fixture in the New Orleans party circuit.

Theodore was a believer in miracles, and was responsible for some Seligman miracles—even though, as happens with miracle workers, his miracles had a way of backfiring on him. He was superstitious. A black cat crossing his path in the morning would keep him away from the Cotton Exchange all day, and he had a phobia about the number 13. He would not sit down at a table where there were thirteen for dinner, and would not buy notes in which the number 13 appeared. He had a mystical belief in the number 24—perhaps because it was in his twenty-fourth year that he was first given a position of responsibility with the Seligmans. But, in buying only bills which contained the number 24 and refusing those that contained the number 13, he forgot that the point of it all was to buy bills in the South, at a discount, that could be sold in the North or in England at a profit. Particularly critical of Theodore's methods was quick-tempered Isaac Seligman, who had the task of trying to sell Theodore's bills in London. Isaac wrote to Joseph: "I daresay the difficulty [in New Orleans] to obtain proper bills is very great, but the difficulty here to get rid of them . . . is still greater. . . . If Theodore cannot send us only *A-One* bills, you must find some other occupation for him!" (Theodore's behavior almost drove Isaac to a nervous breakdown, and Isaac wrote that he had "to give up walking home of an evening along the Thames Embankment for fear of taking a sudden plunge into the river, thus ending my career.")

One night in a dream, Theodore saw two numbers recur repeatedly. Waking, he wrote them down. It was the time of the great California lottery, and, assuming that these numbers represented a message from the Beyond, or at least from the West Coast, he went first thing in the morning to the lottery agency and bought the two numbers. Both were in line for the largest prizes, and cost him twenty dollars apiece. Later in the day a gentleman came to see Theodore on business and, told of the dream, persuaded Theodore to sell him one of the numbers—for twenty dollars. That number won a $15,000 prize. But the number Theodore kept for himself, 154077 (its digits added up to 24), won the largest prize of all—$100,000. Theodore immediately sent this sum North for the Seligmans to invest. The Seligmans were beginning to dip their toes into new railroad ventures, and Theodore's money was used to buy bonds in railroads that rather quickly went into receivership. Theodore's bonds were sold for a mere $8,000. As far as is known, the Seligmans never apologized to poor Theodore for losing his little windfall so rapidly, and instead went right on scolding him for his "lack of sound business methods."

Actually, Northern money was so much in demand in the South that it was hard for a firm such as Seligman, Hellman & Company to lose money during the Reconstruction era. But ultimately, in 1881, Theodore, whose real problem was perhaps that he was too eager to be liked and too quick to say yes, did involve the firm in a loss when a borrower he trusted failed to repay $20,000. He had broken one of Joseph's cardinal rules ("Never go security for a living man"). It was a small loss, but 1881 had to be Theodore's unlucky year. It was his thirteenth in New Orleans.

Joseph, however, did not always follow his own rules. In 1866 a certain S. H. Bohm of Helena operated a business that involved the appraisal, buying, and shipping of gold out of the Montana Territory. Abraham Seligman had heard of Bohm, and wrote Joseph urging him to enter into a partnership with the man. Joseph indignantly wrote back: "No profit would induce me to lend my name to anyone where I, or a brother of mine, were not present to watch!" But anyone dealing in gold interested Joseph, and Abraham's suggestion lurked in his mind. Soon he had contacted Bohm, and was writing to him cozily: "We would in order to facilitate your business and to give your house an A-1 reputation, go in as special partners with a certain amount of capital." In New York, Joseph began referring to the Bohm-Seligman enterprise as "our Montana house."

But Joseph's first hunch had been prophetic. Bohm needed watching. He began loaning the Seligmans' money without their knowledge and overdrawing on the firm's account. Joseph sent an aide, F. A. Benjamin, to Helena to look into things and was soon writing to him: "Bro. Abm telegraphs that you had discovered an additional indebtedness of $30,000. Now I am astonished at this discovery. I have lost all confidence in Bohm. . . . Now you must stop this game . . . if not we must try to find places behind keys and locks for all these chaps . . . these bad eggs." More embezzlements were uncovered, and in a later letter a dazed Joseph wrote wondering, "By what process have they made away with ¼ million of dollars in so small a place as Helena?"

If there was one thing that Joseph disliked more than losing money, it was having his honesty as a trader questioned. Allusions to Jews and "sharp practice" infuriated him. As he had done in Selma, when he encountered anti-Semitism he fought back. Thus we find him, in 1867, when his banking house was not quite three years old, writing an angry letter to a Mr. Julius Hart who had called some of the Seligman deals "questionable." "Mr. Ridgely, a customer of ours," wrote Joseph, who now almost always used the royal "we," "informs us that you have made a statement to him that we had 50,000 pounds protested Exchange [bills] returned to us. The above statement being entirely untrue may still have a tendency to injure us, and we therefore ask you to retract all and every assertion of that kind made, previous to our handing the case to our lawyers."

Joseph was increasingly touchy about anti-Semitism. One of the most important developments after the Civil War, as far as international bankers like the Seligmans were concerned, was the laying of the first transatlantic cable by Cyrus W. Field in 1866. The Seligmans' first message on the cable was a congratulatory one to Field; their second, following the first by a few minutes, was addressed to Isaac in London: "California gold arrived will add hundred bonds after that hold up exchange unsalable—Josef."* But cable service at first was erratic, and Joseph began to notice that his cables seemed not to arrive in London as fast as those of other bankers. Joseph sent off one of his prickliest letters—going, characteristically, to the top—to Cyrus W. Field. He enclosed a long list of late cables, and added: "We have reason to know that dispatches sent from London at the time ours were forwarded have been received by other bankers twelve to eighteen hours in advance of ours."

His letter touched off an investigation at the Anglo-American Telegraph Company. No religious prejudice was unearthed, but it did turn out that downtown cable clerks accepted bribes from certain bankers to put their own messages through first and to delay others. A number of guilty clerks were dismissed.

Joseph, when the occasion arose, also enjoyed being magnanimous. In 1869, writing to a certain Henry Cohn of San Francisco, Joseph said: "Your letter of the 14th to Mr. Jesse Seligman, asks us to release Mr. Sternberg from his guarantee to repay us the $15,000 cash advanced you two years ago, and to take Mr. Lerlebach for $13,000 instead, keeping besides Mr. Lerlebach's note, the 300 shares water stock, and you add that Brother Abe has encouraged you to address us and

---

* Can this "unsalable" exchange have had anything to do with the "protested" exchange Mr. Hart was talking about? Probably not, because Hart did retract all his unkind remarks, and apologized.

promised to speak a good word for you, which he actually has done, and which is natural. . . ." And Joseph could not resist assenting to Cohn's request without a small self-congratulatory pat on the back for himself and his family, for he added: "Whoever knew of a Seligman who was not charitable and kind and served his neighbors, especially those who have been unfortunate?" (One can almost see Joseph smiling his sleepy little smile over this last touch.)

But his charitableness had its limits, nor was it in any way restricted to fellow Jews, as is clear from this poised and polished letter, written a year later, to an "unfortunate neighbor," the firm of Guiterman Brothers in Amsterdam:

> During your difficulties we have abstained from addressing you on the subject of the cash loaned you, which silence on our part you no doubt appreciated? But after this long delay we deem it not indelicate to remind you that we are still in the land of the living, and that periodical remittances even in small amounts would now be very acceptable, and we are sure on reflection you will agree.

Under Presidents Lincoln and Johnson, the Seligmans had enjoyed excellent relations with three successive Secretaries of the Treasury—Salmon Chase, William Fessenden, and Hugh McCulloch. When their old friend from Watertown days, Ulysses S. Grant, took Presidential office in 1869, they had every reason to look forward to the same preferential treatment. In the beginning the auspices certainly looked good. Grant appointed as his Secretary of State Elihu B. Washburne, who as a Congressman from Illinois had been one of the Seligmans' private clients. Joseph had once purchased, in Frankfurt, 200,000 U.S. bonds for Washburne,* saying at the time, "There is no necessity for you to send any Bonds as margin, as we require none from you, dear Washburne." (Dear Washburne was one of those Congressmen particularly influential in the allocation of land for railroads, in which, as the Seligmans were getting their feet wet, they were increasingly dabbling.) As soon as Washburne was appointed, the Seligmans wrote him, gently reminding him of their past good deeds, and offering their "full services" to the new administration.

But Washburne's appointment, it turned out, was only a courtesy one. He held the post for only twelve days, and was then made Minister to France. Grant replaced him with Hamilton Fish, who was less a friend. As the son of a Revolutionary officer whose father had been a friend of George Washington's and whose mother was a descendant of Peter Stuyvesant—who had once thrown every Jew in New York in jail—Fish

---

* On a Congressman's salary?

was very much "old New York," a social snob, and later one of the cornerstones of Mrs. Astor's Four Hundred. Then Grant did a startling thing. He contacted Joseph privately, and said he would like to make him Secretary of the Treasury.

The offer stunned Joseph. For three days he was unable to think of a reply. He was of course flattered, and had no doubt that he could do the job. With him in Washington, his brothers would no longer have to work at making Washington friends. But there was a shy side to Joseph's nature. He felt uneasy in the limelight, and he practiced a religion—or, as he himself always put it, "belonged to a race"—which for centuries had been disenfranchised, barred by law from politics and government office. He could not envision himself in this post. It seemed out of character to him. He was an American millionaire of fifty, but he was still a poor immigrant Jewish boy. In the end, the idea simply frightened him, and arguing the "press of business" in New York, he turned it down.

For every practical reason, he should have accepted. Grant appointed George Sewall Boutwell of Massachusetts instead, and Boutwell became a long Seligman headache.

At first, Joseph and Boutwell got along well. They worked together on a plan, carried over from the previous administration, to continue refunding the public debt, stabilizing currency, and building American credit abroad. Both men agreed on two main areas—that specie payments could not be resumed until confidence had been restored and that the high rate of interest—6 percent—then being paid on government bonds was a poor reflection on the state of American credit. With billions of dollars' worth of bonds at stake, the mood and temperature of the bond-buying market had to be gauged with extreme caution. A fraction of an interest percentage point either way could mean the success or failure of the issue in the marketplace. After a great deal of deliberation on the question, Joseph and Secretary Boutwell agreed that the interest rate on the new bonds should be 5 percent. Or so Joseph thought.

When Boutwell submitted his bond-issuing plan to Congress, his outline coincided with Joseph's in every major detail but one—the interest rate. The new bonds, Boutwell declared, would be offered at 4.5 percent. Joseph was flabbergasted. He hurried to Boutwell to protest that this was slashing the rate far too much and far too soon. The Seligmans, he insisted, could not sell bonds in Europe—or anywhere else—that promised such a low yield. But Boutwell was adamant. "I have decided," he said coldly, "that four and a half is proper." Joseph fumed.

"My father," Edwin Seligman wrote of Joseph many years later, "was the most tolerant of men. But he was also very intolerant of anything not quite up to standard, sometimes being a little unfair to stupid people." Fair or not, Joseph told Boutwell he was stupid.

To support his thesis, Joseph cabled his brother Henry in Frankfurt, asking him to canvass leading German bankers to see how they felt about the Boutwell plan. In Paris he asked William to sound out the formidable "Haute Banque" group—Hottinguer, Mallet, Marcuard, and De Neuflize. The brothers' wires came back; the European bankers felt as Joseph did: Boutwell's "cheap" bonds would not sell in Europe; 5 percent was the lowest sensible figure.

But Boutwell, who seems at this point to have fallen in love with the figure of 4.5 percent, refused to budge. Joseph, with the consensus of European bankers in his fist, marched to individual members of Congress to try to persuade them against what he called "Boutwell's folly." This did little to endear him to Boutwell, who complained loudly of Joseph's "unwarranted interference" with the Congress, and the coolness that had developed between the two men ripened into open hostility.

In the acts of July 14, 1870, and January 20, 1871, Congress authorized issues of bonds totaling $1.5 billion at rates which were, in a sense, a compromise. But it was a compromise which favored the Boutwell stand. A relatively small amount—$200 million worth— would pay 5 percent. The rest would all pay a lower rate, some as low as 3.5 percent. Joseph sulked in his Wall Street tent.

Still, in return for their help in devising the plan, at least part of which was being used, the Seligmans were certain that they would be offered a share in underwriting and selling the $200 million worth of 5 percenters. Other New York firms thought so too, for they began approaching the Seligmans for a share of the Seligmans' share. But the Seligmans were in for a hundred-million-dollar disappointment.

In March, 1871, William Seligman in Paris wrote a bitter letter to Elihu Washburne, who, since he was no longer in the Cabinet, could not have been expected to do much about the situation, saying:

> Last evening I was shocked and stunned by a telegram . . . saying Mr. Boutwell has appointed as agents in Europe for the conversion of U.S. Bonds [William lists several firms, the Seligmans glaringly absent from the roster]. . . . Thus we, contrary to our confident belief, are under the circumstances existing, slighted by our Government. We do not know what has caused us this neglect and injustice, whether it is personal aversion against us on the part of Mr. Boutwell or lack of

confidence, or whether it is the work of intrigue and selfishness on the
part of our competitors.

A moment's reflection should have cleared up William's mystification
for him. His brother Joseph had simply been the victim of overconfi-
dence. In his insistence that interest rates not be lowered too much and
too soon, he himself had moved too quickly and highhandedly. He had
overstepped himself, had stepped on toes in the process, and now was
being punished for it.

But the Seligmans were, to some extent at least, able to have the last
word. Boutwell capitulated somewhat, and agreed to "offer the loan to
everybody." (This did not please the Seligmans much; they did not like
to think of themselves as part of "everybody.") The brothers then took
a clutch of bonds to sell, though Joseph commented tartly, "The whole
business is doomed to failure unless more intelligence is infused into
it."

He was more or less right about that. The bonds sold so poorly that
Boutwell agreed to let Jay Cooke & Company form a banking syndicate
to try to dispose of the unsold balance. Two selling groups were set up,
one in London and one in New York, and the Seligman branches in the
two cities took part in both. This time the bonds sold very well indeed,
so well that President Grant was able to announce that the issue had
"established American credit abroad." And, grudgingly, the Seligmans
were able to accept a share of the responsibility for that development.

Socially, however, the Grant era was a merry time for Joseph Selig-
man. At Grant's inauguration, Joseph had stood near the President on
the platform when Grant took his oath of office. That evening, in full fig,
Joseph showed up at the Inaugural Ball and waltzed with Julia Grant.
(His modest little Babet, self-conscious about her poor command of
English, always eschewed such functions.)

There were lunches and dinners at the White House, where hilarity
ran high. After one of these Joseph wrote home to Babet that he had
been seated next to "the most beautiful lady that I've ever seen, yourself
excepted. It was a Mrs. Palmer from Chicago" (the famous Mrs. Potter
Palmer, whose sister later married Grant's son). At the table Mrs. Grant
asked Joseph whether he had ever seen anything more beautiful. Joseph
replied gallantly that he had not, but that he had a wife whom he found
even more beautiful and whom he loved even more. This, Joseph told
Babet, "made the President laugh heartily." There was more laughter
over such matters as black bread and pretzels. Julia Grant said she had
never seen *black* bread. Joseph replied that black bread was a staple of
German diet, but that there was something the Germans liked even
more—pretzels, which made Germans thirsty for lager beer, which made

them hungry for more pretzels. The table rocked with laughter. The President said that he had heard of a young banker in New York named Jacob Schiff, "a real comer." Joseph said, "But he is not as smart as me." At this, Mrs. Potter Palmer laughed so hard she choked on her cutlet and had to be pounded on the back by the President.

14

"THE D——D RAILROADS!"

In the years following the Civil War, the mergers, bankruptcies, organizations, and reorganizations of American railroads were creating an enormous field for stock and bond speculation. Railroads were being built competitively and haphazardly, which made them all the more interesting to speculators. By the late 1860's railroad stocks and bonds were not only the great "wonder" securities of the age; with the exception of government issues, they had become the chief interest of Wall Street and comprised 85 percent of all shares traded. There was great enthusiasm for railroad shares in Europe, and the ability to sell railroads in the Frankfurt, London, Paris, and Amsterdam markets was making many a banker wealthy.

By 1869 Joseph and his brothers had a working capital of over six million dollars, and their firm became the first of the German Jewish banking community to enter the railroad-securities field. They entered it, however, with reservations which, in retrospect, were more sound than not, and with Joseph's innate dread of land speculation, which, of course, was what railroad speculation was all about. A year before his banking firm was founded Joseph had turned down his brother James's suggestion that they invest in railroads, saying, "I consider this a speculation entirely out of our line. . . . Certainly none of us *know* enough of Erie, Central, etc. to keep them for an investment. We ought not to buy them at all. . . . We can make enough money in a legitimate way without gambling or hazard."* And yet, as railroads began to dominate the financial scene, Joseph quickly fell victim to railroad fever, an ailment that replaced gold fever. Railroad fever, in fact, visited Joseph Seligman with an almost fatal attack.

Not quite two years after his antirailroad advice to James, Joseph, already deeply involved in the "Erie, Central, etc.," wrote excitedly to Isaac in London: "We have just now seen Mr. Drew and he requested you to sell his 5000 shares of Erie in London. . . . Mr. Drew is a large operator and if satisfied will give us frequent orders in future."

Drew—the notorious "Uncle Daniel" Drew, an ex-cattle drover—was indeed a large operator, and was able to force the price of Erie stock up and down at will. Why did Drew want his shares sold in London and not New York? So New York wouldn't find out about it for a while. Allied with Drew in his operations were two other terrors of the age—"Jubilee Jim" Fisk, a former circus roustabout, and an ex-farm hand who became the leader of the threesome named Jay Gould. Joseph Seligman felt somewhat out of his league with these powerful roughnecks (which, perhaps, was why they employed him), but he did his best to keep up with them. At Drew's bidding, Joseph wrote to an important customer in Cincinnati, urging him to buy Erie because "it is now 59, but we have reason to believe that old Drew is at work and we should not be surprised to see it up to 65 or 66 before two weeks." The stock did reach that figure, then toppled again. In the great Erie "war" of 1868—when Drew, Fisk, and Gould sold millions of dollars' worth of Erie stock to Cornelius Vanderbilt, and then drove the stock down, leaving Vanderbilt two million dollars poorer—the Erie Railroad became known as "The Scarlet Woman of Wall Street." When Gould went to jail for this particular manipulation, the Seligmans, who had been acting as his brokers, loyally guaranteed his $20,000 bail bond and, with this action, more or less permanently committed themselves to Gould.

Just what brought the Seligmans and the Jay Gould group together to begin with is uncertain, but it was an alliance that has provided lasting controversy. Perhaps Gould—who himself admitted candidly that he was "the most hated man in America"—sought out the Seligman firm because he hoped their name would lend prestige, as a kind of ballast, to

---

* Curiously, when Joseph spoke of land-buying deals, he often contrasted them with "legitimate" business.

his own high-flying operations. (This, at least, is what the Seligmans have always said.) Or perhaps the Seligmans sought out Gould. Or, possibly, Gould simply had to settle for the young Seligman firm when older, more conservative gentile banking houses refused to act as his brokers. (One of these many years later told Frank A. Vanderlip, president of the National City Bank, "I made money because I stuck to one rule: I never dealt in Jay Gould bonds.")

Socially, Gould was ostracized from every group in New York. Even at the height of his success, when he controlled the Erie and had made millions in the stock market, he was never invited to Mrs. Astor's balls and, when he tried to join, was blackballed—almost unanimously—by the New York Yacht Club. He was an unappetizing little creature— sallow, frail, shy, and ill. He spent twenty years dying of tuberculosis, often in terrible pain and bleeding from the lungs, and, unable to sleep at night, he paced the sidewalk in front of his Fifth Avenue house under the eye of a bodyguard. By joining forces with Gould, the Seligmans did nothing to enhance their position with gentile society, nor did Gould profit socially from his association with the Seligmans. If anything, the relationship fanned the billowing anti-Semitism of the postwar period, and is perhaps responsible for the fact that many people today believe that Gould himself was Jewish. At the height of his unpopularity, Henry Adams referred to him as "the complex Jew," and many of his con- temporaries in Wall Street regarded him, as Dixon Wecter has said, "as a Shylock in habits and probably heredity." This notion was supported by the discovery that Gould was descended from one Nathan Gold, who had settled in Fairfield, Connecticut, in 1646, and that the "u" had been added to the family name as late as 1806. Still, as Wecter points out, "it is quite possible that Israel has been blamed unfairly" for Jay Gould. And the best reason for believing this is that Gould was a man who simply did not care what anybody thought of him. If he had been Jewish, he would not have troubled to deny it.

This was a period which has been labeled "one of the most sordid of United States political and economic history," what with the carpet- baggers in the South and, in the North, a high tolerance for "bribery, political gangsterism, and wild speculation."* Gould and Drew and Jim Fisk were, from that standpoint, very much in tune with their times. Gould admitted that he used bribery and blackmail to buy up Erie Railroad stock options from towns along his routes, and that he used Fisk's force of "plug-uglies" to take over by force and violence when other methods failed. Gould, furthermore, was by his own admission a raider and a ruiner. He had no interest in managing or improving railroads. He merely liked to drive a railroad's stock up, with rumors

* F. Redlich, *A History of Banking, Men and Ideas.*

and with trading, and then sell it and let it collapse of its own inflated weight.

The Seligman firm, in Joseph's words, did "an enormous amount of business" in the Gould manipulations of the Erie stock, selling short for their own account whenever Gould or Fisk or Drew sold short—as they did consistently—letting the triumvirate's operations provide the pattern for the Seligmans' own. In almost no time, the Seligmans had let the name of their old friend President Grant be linked with one of the most spectacular and scandalous financial coups of the decade—Jay Gould's attempt to corner the gold market.

The scheme boggled the minds of some of the brightest financiers of the day, and perhaps, in fairness to Joseph and his brothers, they never quite grasped what Gould was up to. Certainly President Grant was slow to realize what was afoot, as Gould had expected he would be.

In essence, it was a two-part plan designed to fill Gould's pockets by selling inflated gold shares and by collecting higher freight rates on his Erie Railroad.* Gould planned to start buying up gold and then, as the price climbed, to go to Grant—with the aid of the Seligmans and their entree to the White House—and persuade him that there was a shortage of gold. "What shall we do?" Grant was intended to ask, whereupon part two of the scheme was to go into effect. In order to build up the American gold supply again, it would be suggested that Grant step up United States grain sales to Europe, which would be paid for in gold. (This would be good for the American farmer, Gould pointed out charitably, though farmers were a class of Americans in which he had never shown much interest previously. It would also be good for his Erie Railroad, which was the major grain shipper from the Midwest to Eastern ports.)

Gould's stratagem was to raise the price of gold from $100 to about $145 and then unload it, meanwhile having got new freight contracts—at a higher rate—for shipping grain on the Erie. Gold began to climb as the Gould-Drew-Fisk group began buying, while the Seligmans, acting as the trio's brokers, also bought for their own account. Grant seemed to be falling into line perfectly, and gold did indeed reach $145. Then, apparently, avarice—one of Mr. Gould's most consistent emotions— took over, and Gould decided to let gold get a little higher—to $150— before selling. At this point Grant belatedly realized what was going on, and ordered his Secretary of the Treasury to release enough of the government's own stock of gold reserves to bring the price down again. On what became known as Black Friday, gold prices crashed.

But, it turned out, Gould had sold out at the top of the market

---

* Gould's scheme was not unlike the gold-inflating plot devised by the late Ian Fleming in his James Bond novel, *Goldfinger.*

anyway, and so had the Seligmans. It was almost, or so it seemed at the time, as though Gould and the Seligmans had been given some advance warning of the Treasury's forthcoming action. Had Grant tipped his old friends off? It was never proved, but this was widely assumed to be the case.

One thing was certain: though Jay Gould emerged from the scuffle not quite so rich as Fort Knox, he was some ten to twenty million dollars richer than he had been, and the Seligmans, though no figure for their profits exists, cannot have done badly even if they made no more than a straight commission. When Gould's role in the "gold conspiracy" was discovered, he was attacked by an angry mob and barely escaped being lynched. As an almost anticlimactic aftermath, it turned out that Gould had double-crossed his old partner, Jim Fisk, by not letting him know that it was time to sell.

In 1872 Gould was ousted from the presidency of the Erie, and there was a long overdue investigation of the road's management. Joseph Seligman was the first witness called. He pointed out that his firm had been merely brokers for, not manipulators of, the Erie. The line between a manipulator and a manipulator's agent is somewhat thin, but in those more tolerant days this explanation apparently satisfied the investigating committee. Gould himself went on to blow stardust in the committee members' eyes by telling a pathetic tale of how, as a poor farm boy, he "drove the cows to pasture and stung my bare feet on the thistles," and how, at the age of seventeen, he came to New York hoping to sell a mousetrap he had invented. "It was in a pretty mahogany case," he said, "which I carried under my arm. I went into a Sixth Avenue car, I think, and every now and then I ran out on the platform to see the buildings, leaving the case containing the mousetrap on the seat." He came back to find the mousetrap gone, and there, sure enough, was a sinister retreating figure hurrying down the aisle of the streetcar. Gould collared the man, who turned out to be a notorious criminal. For having helped apprehend the rogue, Gould said, he had surely done his duty to society. The mousetrap story also satisfied the investigating committee, and both Gould and the Seligmans emerged from the investigation unscathed. Or nearly so. The unholy light from the "Scarlet Woman of Wall Street" now bathed the Seligman brothers.

In the first months following the investigation, Joseph resolved to "stay out of the d——d railroads altogether." But the temptation was too great. Soon he had stepped up his railroad activities again, and was into them even more heavily than before. In 1869 America got its first transcontinental railroad when California's Governor Leland Stanford went to Promontory, Utah, to drive the famous "golden spike" into the link joining the Central Pacific and the Union Pacific. The portly

Governor aimed a silver mallet at the golden spike, swung, and missed. The miss was symbolic of the chaotic state of railroads, but no one perceived the symbolism. From that point onward, the growth of railroads was so rapid and disorganized that today there is virtually no American hamlet so small that it does not have its miles of rusted track approaching it, and a dilapidated station at its heart.

One transcontinental railroad might have seemed enough, but the first merely spurred dozens of rivals. One of these was called the South Pacific Railroad Company of Missouri, a line to run between St. Louis and the Kansas border. (Early railroads were named in the same helter-skelter fashion as they grew; what the South Pacific had to do with Missouri is unclear, except that the aim of the road was westward.) Joseph Seligman undertook to sell the South Pacific's first bond issue.

His system, a favored one of the period, was to loan a line money in return for bonds which were secured by the huge government land grants being given to railroads. It was a system which worked well when the bonds were marketable. In the case of the South Pacific the bonds sold poorly, and Joseph was briefly discouraged, suspecting that the country was becoming railroad-poor, "in view of the fact that nearly 200 railroads are being constructed within the borders of the United States." Nevertheless, Joseph agreed to take on a second bond issue for the South Pacific with the proviso that someone from his firm be put on the railroad's board. Thus Joseph himself became a director of the South Pacific.

Meanwhile, he was also helping to finance the Atlantic & Pacific Railroad, a much more ambitious project which planned to lay tracks all the way from Springfield, Missouri, to the California coast (going nowhere near the Atlantic, however). There were a few problems. To begin with, though the Atlantic & Pacific had been granted 42 million acres of land for its proposed 2,000 miles of track, only 283 miles of track had actually been laid. It was essential to the economics of railroads that the lines have, at their terminal points, cities, or at least markets, to provide the completed lines with revenue from freight. A project such as the Atlantic & Pacific had to make its way through a great deal of industrially barren Western land, and across the industrially dead Rocky Mountains, before it got to the commercially profitable Pacific Coast. There were, furthermore, only a few level or practicable crossings over the mountains and, at the time, only two possible crossing points on the Colorado River. In the case of the Atlantic & Pacific, it turned out that other lines had already preempted these points. The Atlantic & Pacific was, when Joseph took an interest in it, in effect a railroad to nowhere.

Joseph was demonstrating a curious weakness that would continue to plague him in all his railroad dealings: he had a poor sense of geography. He never seemed to know quite where he was. (This was literally true; his wife used to complain that whenever he came out of a theater or restaurant, he invariably started walking the wrong way.) He seems only dimly to have grasped the facts of such topographical features as the Rockies and the Colorado. Also, an even more serious defect, he had very little interest in the management, operation, or even in the reason for railroads. He didn't care how a line was run, or why, or even where, as long as it had iron wheels. He was only interested in its financial side. And so, when he financed railroads, he was really financing a business he did not understand.

Still, he went into the Atlantic & Pacific for several millions of dollars and took on its bonds to sell, which did even more poorly than the South Pacific's. As he had done with the SP, he joined the board of directors of the Atlantic & Pacific. A glance at the map, meanwhile, would have revealed to Joseph that, in addition to the two lines' individual problems, for a considerable distance across the state of Missouri they ran parallel to each other and only a few miles apart. Joseph's two struggling lines were competitors.

Joseph had also become interested in the Union Pacific Railway Company, Southern Branch. This line, which presently changed its name to the jawbreaking "Missouri, Kansas & Texas Railway Company"—called the K & T, or the "Katy"—was to be built on a north-south line from Fort Riley, Kansas, to New Orleans. Once more, a glance at the map would have revealed that the tracks of the Katy, moving southward, would at some point intersect—and collide—with the tracks of the Atlantic & Pacific, moving westward. And it was not so simple as building a bridge, or constructing a tunnel, at the meeting point, since both lines appeared to have identical title to the disputed land. In other words, whichever line got there first could effectively stop the other. On the board of the Katy, and laboring to sell her bonds, were such Wall Street figures as Levi P. Morton (of Morton, Bliss & Company), George C. Clark (of Clark, Dodge), August Belmont (of August Belmont)—and Joseph Seligman.

In 1870, while the South Pacific and the Atlantic & Pacific raced westward side by side, and the Katy raced southward to beat the Atlantic & Pacific, someone asked Seligman, "Which line are you for, Joe?" "I'm for railroads!" Joseph replied, no doubt with a trace of hysteria in his voice.

He also had other railroad commitments. He was involved with the Missouri Pacific Railroad, one of whose projects was to build a small branch line in St. Louis County from Kirkwood to Carondelet, Missouri. In the area, President Grant had a ramshackle and unproductive farm, and Joseph wrote the line's president, Andrew Pierce, saying: "When the Mo. Pacific R.R. builds the Carondelet Branch, I would advise by all means to take the route through General Grant's farm." "Why?" Pierce wanted to know. "Because I told Grant that's the way it would go," Joseph replied. Since Joseph was financing it, that was the way it went. Railroad fever seems to have come close to affecting Joseph's reason. While directing railroads through his friends' farms, he was able to complain, in the next breath, that railroad routes were being laid out "against all dictates of logic and sense."

Joseph's other railroads were nearing the point of battle, and in 1871 actual warfare broke out. Construction crews of the Katy and the Atlantic & Pacific met at the town site of Vinita (now in the state of Oklahoma), and went at each other with clubs, picks, crowbars, and heavy wooden railroad ties. It was a bloody encounter, and quite a number of men on both sides were killed before the Katy was declared the victor and Joseph decided that some of his railroad directorships "seem to represent a conflict of interests." To solve this, he resigned from the board of the Katy, remaining on the board of the other two conflicting lines. But he held on to his Katy stock anyway, just in case.

A year later Joseph found himself in a despondent mood about railroads and wrote to his brother William in Paris: "Now as to our various investments in R.R. bonds which have at present no market value I fully agree with you that we have too many for comfort." The letter continued on a note of high resolve: "I have concluded not to go another Dollar on any R.R. or State or City bond . . . and nothing will induce me hereafter [to put] another Dollar in any new enterprise until I have the moral assurance that the bond is as good as sold in Europe." And yet, halfway through this same letter, Joseph began to waver and to defend his activities in railroads, reminding William, "We have made a fortune these past 6 years & made it principally out of new R. Roads."

But Joseph began privately advising his clients to stay out of railroads. "We wish to give you our experience," he wrote to one of them. "New roads want no end of money . . . when you are in once for $25,000 they will draw you in for $100,000 and, subsequently, for half a million . . . it will take you many years to get your money back— and possibly never. This is our friendly caution."

It was good advice, but Joseph, addicted to the iron horse, was incapable of following it. In the years to come, his investments escalated from three railroads to over a hundred. At times he himself seemed confused by his activities. At one point he helped Jay Gould buy a controlling interest in the Missouri Pacific. A year later Joseph bought back a lot of the bonds he had sold to Gould. When Joseph helped Commodore Vanderbilt dispose, quietly in London—in the same kind of over-the-transom deal Joseph had performed for Drew—of some New York Central bonds, J. P. Morgan, Vanderbilt's banker, repaid Joseph by helping him sell 2 million dollars' worth of Gould's Missouri Pacific bonds—though Gould and Vanderbilt (and Morgan too) were bitter enemies. The Missouri Pacific bonds sold, as usual, poorly, and Joseph wrote William in a familiar vein: "I am heartily sick of waging a seemingly endless battle over Western railroads." Soon, however, he was back in again, selling Gould and Collis P. Huntington of San Francisco a controlling interest in the San Francisco line, which was supposed to provide the "missing link" over the Sierras from the Gould-dominated (at the time) Union Pacific into San Francisco. The Seligmans had no sooner sold the line to Gould than they bought it back again—and tried to sell it again, and finally did, to the Santa Fe on a share-for-share basis.

While Joseph was cautioning his clients to stay out of railroads, he was flirting with "a short but very promising little road" called the Memphis, Carthage & Northwestern. Soon after he had sunk $250,000 in it the M C & W found itself unable to pay for an engine. In an emergency move to help out, Joseph personally purchased a locomotive—which he named "The Seligman"—and rented the engine back to the line for a modest seventy dollars a week. (It was an idea borrowed from Vanderbilt, whose engine was called "The Commodore.") "The Seligman" chugged around for a while, but was unable to pull the line out of the red. Within three years it collapsed into bankruptcy and the engine was sold at auction for two dollars.

In 1873 Joseph wrote: "I am disgusted with all railroads, and shall *never again* be tempted to undertake the sale of a d——d railroad bond. I am daily engaged in two or three d——d railroad meetings and, therefore, cannot attend to office business as much as I want to." A month later he was writing dreamily of something called the "Great National, Atlantic and Pacific Railroad . . . a line never obstructed by snows, and of comparatively easy grades." A year later he was writing to William: "It would have been better if we had never touched [railroad] bonds at all . . . it was impossible for us to compete with the Barings and J. S. Morgan [father of J.P. and head of Morgan's London office] and others in the very best roads of the United States . . . we did not then understand the difference between finished first-class roads and unfinished second-class roads."

There was more than the difference between finished and unfinished roads that Joseph Seligman did not understand. But the above letter pinpoints one area of the Seligmans' railroad difficulties: J. P. Morgan and his bank and friends. In allying themselves with Gould, the Seligmans had made a powerful enemy of Morgan. To be sure, Morgan, in return for a favor (but never otherwise), would sometimes help them out. But the Seligmans' opportunities to perform favors for Morgan were rather few. Aligned with Morgan was August Belmont, a man never particularly eager to see the Seligmans succeed. Morgan, Belmont, and the Rothschilds formed an axis of financial power that Joseph Seligman was finding it increasingly difficult to beat.

15

"MY BANK"

Since Joseph Seligman was the leading Jewish financier in New York, the majority of his clients were also Jewish. This meant, of course, that when Joseph Seligman got nipped in one of his less successful ventures, many other New York Jews were also nipped. At the Harmonie Club, the select German Jewish counterpart of men's clubs of the era, members took to singing, *"On Seligman hab ich mein gelt verloren,"* when Joseph entered the room after one of his railroad misadventures. Joseph grew to care less for the Harmonie, and began to spend more time at the Union League Club, whose membership he sometimes seemed to prefer.

Around 1873 a curious change began to take place in Joseph Seligman. He was fifty-four and an established millionaire, but his outlook and attitude began to shift. Possibly it was a result of Grant's Treasury offer a few years earlier, or of lunches at the White House, where people like Mrs. Potter Palmer found him amusing. It was not that he began to long for a place in New York society, exactly, but he was becoming more Americanized, more gentilized, losing some of his feeling of Jewishness. None of the Seligmans kept kosher households at this point. Joseph continued to be a member in good standing of Temple

Emanu-El, but more often than not "the press of business" kept him away from Sabbath services. He had also met a young man named Felix Adler, a German rabbi's son who advanced ideas of a society based on ethics rather than religious piety, which Joseph found interesting.

This changed frame of mind began to have a strong effect on Joseph's approach to business. For years, the names dominating the note-issuing commercial banks—Willing, Morris, Hamilton (whose spiritual descendants still control commercial banking today)—were gentile. Commercial banking seemed the gentile banker's private niche, just as Jewish bankers such as Joseph had found a niche of their own as note-trading merchant bankers. There had been little crossing over from these two banking areas until Joseph, in the 1870's, decided that the Seligmans should re-establish their San Francisco business, and that this should be their first commercial bank. Joseph, aware that this would be a departure from what was considered "traditional" Jewish banking practice, chose a name with English overtones—the Anglo-California National Bank, Ltd.—and, to reinforce the bank's Englishness, turned over its organization to his brother Isaac in London.

It is certainly a testament to Isaac's financial ingenuity that he was able to plan nearly every detail of the bank in California (where Isaac had never been) by remote control six thousand miles away. In the process he became quite possessive about the project and began to refer to it as "my bank." (When Abraham Seligman, who considered himself a West Coast expert, traveled to London to discuss launching the new bank, Isaac was quite nettled at his brother's "interference," and wrote home to say that Abraham had come to London "probably because he has nothing better to do.")

In London, Isaac made a public offering of Anglo-California stock, and raised the impressive sum of £400,000—or about two million dollars in U.S. currency in those days. Isaac fussed endlessly over the tiniest matters and wrote to Joseph in a lecturing tone: "I need not call to your attention the great moral responsibility you now have. With God's help our reputation will be enhanced by the Success of your management of the Bank." He added sternly: "Should you mismanage affairs, you may rely upon it that our good name will suffer immensely, and nothing would be so deplorable as to suffer in reputation." Clearly, in the back of Isaac's mind through all this was his fear that Jews might be accused of overstepping themselves.

Isaac went on to instruct Joseph to send him *"weekly* summaries" of transactions and "intelligible reports," and urged him to be "exceedingly careful not to incur any bad debts, not to lock up your money in any unnegotiable security, and not . . . to lend money to prominent politicians with the prospect of having to wait years before getting it back"—

all of which sounded like Joseph's advice to his brothers several years before.

In the spring of 1873, the bank was getting ready to open its doors and Isaac wrote a series of insistent letters to say, "You will find some A-1 man to become head manager." Joseph replied that he had found two A-1 men—his oldest son, David, just twenty-two, and his brother-in-law (who was also his first cousin), Ignatz Steinhardt. Isaac was unhappy with these appointments. David, Isaac said, was "too green" to run a bank, "though at least he is American-born." Ignatz, said Isaac, spoke English poorly and "must be kept in a back room." He added that he hoped the boys would hire "a good corresponding clerk who can write a faultless business letter, for I should be ashamed to let the Directors read such rigamarole as dear David writes, and such ungrammatical English as Ignatz sends at present."

Just before the opening, Joseph made a surprise trip to San Francisco to check on things—a move Isaac had "scarcely anticipated," and which he considered scarcely necessary. But Joseph's inspection tour convinced Joseph that Isaac was right: David was not experienced enough to handle the assignment, and the whole family was astonished to see Joseph withdraw his own son and replace him with a man nobody had ever heard of, Richard G. Sneath, the first gentile and first nonfamily member to be given a place of importance in a Seligman enterprise.

Isaac was startled, but he understood. "There is not the slightest objection to the appointment," he wrote, "only the Board had better wait until form letters of resignation from David arrive, and some statement is received from you as to the gentleman intended to replace him. . . . You must bear in mind that things here are done systematically, and not reckless and slipshop [sic]."

During the early months of the bank, the New York stock market was unsteady. By September, prices began to drop and a number of firms failed. Joseph wrote to Isaac telling of "numerous failures, and the end is not yet. Jay Cooke & Co. suspended yesterday noon. . . . Let us thank God that we have made no losses." Banks were in desperate need of cash, and Joseph tried to persuade President Grant to deposit government funds in private banks, even though, as Joseph admitted, such a move would be "clearly illegal." By September 23 Joseph was writing Isaac: "Things look decidedly blue this evening, most of the banks decline to pay out Greenbacks or currency today, and the Chicago banks are reported suspended." The Great Panic of 1873 was under way.

Joseph now received word from Ignatz Steinhardt in San Francisco that he and Mr. Sneath were squabbling. The point of the dispute was which man was to receive top billing; Ignatz did not see why Sneath's name had been placed above his own on the bank's letterhead. A weary Joseph wrote to Ignatz: "Your letter, coming as it does in the midst of an unprecedented panic gives me such a pain . . . you must try to get along."

Ignatz wanted his name not only in the top spot on the stationery but also, of all things, in larger letters. Sneath's arguments for having top position were in themselves unsettling. It would "look better," Sneath insisted, in the San Francisco banking community if a "Christian name" headed the bank's list of managers. Joseph had foreseen such an argument, and had hoped to avoid it. To Isaac Joseph wrote: "Our friend Sneath imagines there is prejudice in the American mind against foreigners and Israelites (which we are sure there *ought* not to be and *is not* among intelligent Americans)." He added: "Last summer we discovered that he [Sneath] had an exalted opinion of himself. Steinhardt has also the same trait of character."

Joseph couldn't decide which man was right, or—perhaps—which to blame more. He could not bring himself to dismiss his wife's brother. In Sneath's case, there was a year's contract with the bank which had to be honored. Joseph wrote strongly worded letters to both men, whereupon Sneath, pronouncing himself outnumbered by Seligmans and their in-laws, huffily resigned. Joseph, aghast, wrote to Sneath saying:

> Your letter . . . has shocked and grieved me greatly . . . after your promise to give the bank a trial for twelve months, you suddenly ask the acceptance of your resignation, ostensibly for the reason that you disapprove of a co-manager. . . . You are now pleased to say that the Bank would have more friends among the Americans but for their foolish *prejudices* against the *religion of the bank.* . . . Don't you think, Mr. Sneath, that you err in this respect and do injustice to the mercantile community of San Francisco?

It was no use. Sneath refused to withdraw his resignation.

In Paris, William Seligman now chose this worst of all possible moments to announce that he wished to quit his brothers' firm too, and for suspiciously vague reasons. Angrily, Joseph turned William's problems over to Isaac, saying:

> Now I shall not have time to write Bro. Wm. It is criminal of him to bother us now when all our intellect and energy are required in a crisis of unprecedented dimensions. I shall invite that selfish Bro. Wm. to carry out his threat. Please inform him that he is mistaken when he expects that we will buy him out. We shall do no such thing. We shall want him to come here in Jan'y and take his ⅛th share of assets consisting of railroad bonds and shares, mining shares, property, bad and good debts, and attend personally to collecting them and, my word for it, he

will find himself in better health than by eating heavy dinners, drinking heavy wines, writing heavy letters to us, and doing nothing else.

From Paris, William airily explained that one reason why he wanted his brothers to buy him out was that he wished to buy his wife a diamond necklace. William seemed unaware of the panic, and had the impudence to say that he was "disappointed" with the size of his "one-eighth share of assets" at the close of 1873, the panic year. (In those days, all Seligman businesses were run as one and the profits divided among the brothers equally.) Joseph wrote to Isaac:

> Now Brother William has no practical sense and if he would only act as he preaches, things would go better. I am informed that while greatly discouraged at our statements he persists in giving grand balls and dinner parties which are in bad taste and do him (nor us) no good. We don't do it, and while the expenses of our three families with so many grown children are necessarily quite large (my own not larger than those of James and Jesse) we are trying to reduce them and certainly don't throw away money in parties, balls, and dinners, which lead to no benefit.

In the end it usually fell to Joseph to untangle family matters when they became too intricately knotted, when the "our dear Babette" syndrome made its familiar presence felt. Joseph sent Abraham, his best-natured brother, to San Francisco, and also hired Frederick F. Low, a former Governor of California, to comanage the bank with Abraham and Ignatz. Joseph had always wanted a gentile name on the bank's roster, and, interestingly enough, Low's name was now given top spot on the letterhead. Abraham didn't mind. Why didn't Ignatz? A sum— £3,000—was credited to Ignatz's personal account to get him to accept second billing. Joseph directed that this should be subtracted from his own share of the profits (but his brothers insisted that the £3,000 be deducted from all of them equally). Regine Seligman got her diamond necklace. Though a family rule forbade private speculation, an exception was made in William's case. He was allowed to speculate in a certain stock; it went up, and there was enough from the profit for the jewels—and for more parties. Richard G. Sneath vanished from financial history. The Panic of 1873 subsided, and the economy started up again.

But the trouble the Seligmans had opening their first commercial bank was prophetic. In the long run, the Anglo-California Bank was not so much a financial loss as a time-consuming nuisance. In a few years they relinquished control of the bank, though they held on to some of its stock. It exists today as the Crocker-Anglo Bank.

Joseph Seligman went on becoming more Americanized, more gentilized. His letters home to his wife during his 1873 inspection tour to San Francisco revealed a wholly new—for him—appreciation of the value of land. Along with the beauties of California scenery, he pondered the joys of real estate:

My Beloved Babet:

Last evening we went out to the country to see our friend Sneath, about 25 miles from here. How I wish you might have been with us! He owns 110 acres, for which, four years ago, when the land was still a desert, he paid 11,000 dollars. Just picture to yourself groves of the finest oaks and other trees, some of which branch out 100 feet. Then imagine as many kinds of roses, pinks, violets and numberless other flowers . . . all sorts of German berries and plums, oranges, figs, pears, various kinds of nuts and olives, in short everything the heart could desire! . . . A veritable paradise!!! Moreover, there are the horses and cows, four of which latter were valued at 800 dollars apiece and yielded 16 quarts daily.

If God grants us health you must surely spend a winter here. . . .

> Farewell, Beloved,
> Your Joseph

He had actually studied the figures of that least Jewish of businesses, farming. A few days later, he grew more enthusiastic, with more statistics:

My Beloved Babet:

Day before yesterday Abe and I went by train to San José and Santa Clara. Impossible to describe to you what a paradise is that tract of land sixty miles long and six miles wide where the farmer can glean two harvests of wheat, oats, corn in one summer and twelve crops of grass and hay, and all that without a drop of rain between April and October. Who does not see it cannot imagine it. I saw there a century plant which ten weeks ago was two feet high and now measures thirty-three and a half feet and is still growing taller.* There are farmers who sell in one year $100,000.00 worth of grain, and a gentleman whom we met told us that he makes 30,000 gallons of wine each year. . . .

Of course when Joseph got home he was met by the panic, and Babet never got her winter in California.

One of the gloomiest days of the panic coincided with Joseph's and Babet's twenty-fifth wedding anniversary. They had always lived in rented houses, and were at that time living at 26 West Thirty-fourth Street, where their landlord was John Jacob Astor. Almost opposite, and next door to the Astors, a forty-five-foot wide mansion was for sale.

---

* Some local booster must have been trying to impress Joseph with this tall tale. Century plants cannot grow at the rate of half a foot a day, even in San José.

Joseph (whose personal finances were unaffected by the panic) bought it for $60,000 and presented it to Babet as an anniversary gift. But, unlike her husband's, little Babet's heart still lay in the Old World. She was too much in the habit of hiding from the tax collector to live in a mansion. She was dismayed by the gift, and refused to move, so that Joseph sadly sold the house a few months later, at postpanic prices, for $62,000. (A number of years later, the building brought $750,000; Ohrbach's now stands on the site.)

It is hard to see how Joseph found time for philanthropy during these busy years, but he did. In his growing thirst to be considered an American more than a Jew, he had backed one particularly touching cause. The irascible and sharp-tongued Mary Todd Lincoln had not endeared herself to Washington during her years in the White House and, after the President's assassination, officialdom in the capital preferred to ignore her. Lincoln had left an estate of over $80,000, which should have been enough to keep his widow in comfort, if not in style, and yet, in 1868, she considered herself in such financial straits that she advertised in the New York *World* for aid. She followed this with an unsuccessful attempt to sell her personal effects, including her clothes, at auction, which further shocked and disgusted the public. One of the few people to come to Mrs. Lincoln's assistance was Joseph Seligman.

When she and her young son Tad moved to Europe, Joseph paid for the cost of the voyage. When she settled in Frankfurt, Joseph directed his brother Henry to look after her, and for several years Joseph and his brothers sent money to her. In 1869 a pension bill to care for the widows of Presidents was introduced in, and rejected by, Congress, whereupon Joseph Seligman wrote to Grant:

> The enclosed letter of Mrs. Lincoln was transmitted to me by my brother residing in Frankfurt, with the request to intercede with Your Excellency in her behalf. My brother states that Mrs. Lincoln's means are apparently exhausted and that she lives quite secluded. If your Excellency can consistently recommend to Congress to alleviate the pressing wants of the widow of the great and good Lincoln, I have no doubt that the bill now pending would pass to the satisfaction of the party and all good citizens.

From Frankfurt, in English grown rusty from his years in Germany, Henry Seligman wrote an even more moving letter to Senator Carl Schurz:

> My object in taking the liberty of writing you today is to plead on behalf of the widow of our late good and lamented President Lincoln. She is here living in a most retired and economical way, and has to the best of my information not enough to live comfortable. . . . I know it

is not a popular matter to vote away money or grant pensions except to Parties deserving them and I can assure there is no more worthier object that our Government can bestow than by giving to the wife of that great and good man who died in the service of his country sufficient means to live at least respectable. Why, had you dear Sir seen her as I have done last New Year living in a small street in the third floor in dirty rooms with hardly any furniture, all alone grieved and nearly heart broken, you would have said with me Can it be possible that the wife of our great man lives in such a way, and is our Nation not indebted to him, who gave up his life for the sake of freedom, that our great and rich Country cannot show at least its gratitude to his sacred Name by some small testimonial in giving to his family a comfortable Home. She . . . lives very retired and plain, sees hardly any one, and the shock of that terrible night's affair, which robbed us of one of the greatest and best of men has terribly affected her health and mind. . . . I have written also to the Oregon Senators . . . also Senator Corbil from California. . . . My brother Joseph can inform you that we all urge the matter only on account of our devotion to the Name of Lincoln whom we all loved and respected so much, and we should not like to see his family in want for anything— With my kindest regards to your honored self wishing you continued health and prosperity, I remain yours most respectfully

Henry Seligman

The letters had their effect; a pension bill was passed in 1870. Characteristically, Mrs. Lincoln, who later became insane, never thanked the Seligmans. But from their letters it is clear that they never expected her to be grateful; they were expressing nothing more than their "devotion to the Name of Lincoln."

America, "the land of infinite promise," had become a sacred object in Joseph Seligman's mind. It was one of the few things about which he would permit himself to be sentimental. In 1874 his third eldest daughter, Sophie, had consented to marry Moritz Walter, the son of another prominent German Jewish family (I. D. Walter & Company were woolen merchants). While plans for Sophie's engagement party were under way, a young justice of the Alabama Supreme Court arrived in New York from Montgomery to try to obtain a loan from New York bankers for his state. He contacted the pro-South Lehmans, who, in addition to their cotton brokerage business, had taken on the job of fiscal agents to Alabama shortly after the close of the Civil War. But the Lehmans were unable to help, and the judge was about to return home empty-handed when a friend suggested the Seligmans. With their reputation as ardent supporters of the Union cause, they seemed an unlikely source, but the judge was willing to try.

Joseph Seligman received him, listened to his plea, then said with his customary formality, "Will you do me and my family the honor of dining with us this evening? We are announcing the engagement of our daughter. Perhaps at the party we'll be able to give you a more definite answer about the loan."

It was a large party, with dozens of Seligmans, Walters, relatives, and friends. There were cheers, toasts, and speeches. Then Joseph, the leader of the family, stood up to speak—of Sophie's heritage, wandering back to the Baiersdorf he had known as a boy, his first trip to America with one hundred dollars sewed in the seat of his pants, his Mauch Chunk days, his peddling adventures in the South. While the bemused judge listened, Joseph began a long story about a young Jewish peddler in Selma who, as a result of an unjust accusation and religious bias, was about to be sentenced to prison until the young son of an Alabama judge stood up in his defense. "That friendless peddler," said Joseph, "was myself, and the judge's son is the Alabama Supreme Court justice who honors our table tonight." Turning to the Southerner, he said, "Sir, if you will call at my office in the morning, my brothers and I will be happy to advance your state one million dollars—at 6 percent interest."

"It was exactly the sort of grand gesture," commented one of his sons, "that my father liked to make."

But it was more than that. Family, friends, marriage, business— Joseph saw these as ingredients in a mixture of thickening consistency. Engagements, marriages, and the births of children all served to enrich the concoction; on these occasions money transactions nearly always took place, only to bind the elements closer together—the more the money, the tighter the bond.

The Southerner had felt a little odd and out of place at the party "among the Jewish *haute bourgeoisie*," as he wrote later. To Joseph, it was part of his new picture of himself. He had already served on boards (of the "Katy," for instance) with men like George C. Clark and August Belmont. His firm had begun to cosponsor multimillion-dollar issues with J. P. Morgan, who was becoming a major financial figure. With Felix Adler he had discussed founding the Ethical Culture Society, which Joseph did not think of as a "conversion" from, but perhaps an American substitute for, Old World Judaism. Having lunch at the White House or a gentile to dinner; commercial banking; Mrs. Potter Palmer's laughter; California's wheatfields, sixteen-quart-a-day cows, and fast-growing century plants; his wish to own his own house; caring for Mrs. Lincoln; even his hectic activities with "the d——d railroads" that were growing across the American landscape even faster than the fastest-growing century plant—in Joseph's mind they all added up to a perfectly assimilated Jew in America.

16

THE
ASSIMILATIONISTS

At the time of the Panic of 1873, *Harper's Weekly* published a three-panel cartoon depicting the three kinds of men who were, supposedly, involved in the debacle. In the first panel, above the caption "Lost," sat the disconsolate small-businessman, head in hand, brooding over his empty desk. In the second was "The Paying Teller," perspiring, in shirt sleeves, frantically paying out handfuls of greenbacks in the public run on commercial banks. In the third, above the word "Gained," was the private banker, sitting, with his hands on his knees, on his fat bags of gold. Though the name on the latter's window was the fictitious "Catch 'Im & Pluck 'Im, Bankers," the cartoonist's intent was immediately apparent, for the banker's gloating, bearded face was heavily Semitic.

If any of the German Jewish bankers noticed this slur at the time, as they must have, none of them commented on it.

Formal anti-Semitism is based on certain specific assumptions: that Jews are recognizable from all other people as a "nation," and should not be treated as fellow citizens; and that Jews are, from birth, unpatriotic to their adopted country. It argues an "international plot" of Jews to take over the world by such quaint measures as "the use of liquor to befuddle the brains of Christian leaders." (In 1903 these accusations were supported by the publication of a thoroughly spurious "document," *The Protocols of the Learned Elders of Zion.*) But anti-Semitism is not always formal, nor does it always display such definite symptoms. Often it is a vaguely defined "aversion," based on distrust or—when aimed at wealthy Jews—jealousy. Even New England, where Jews were widely admired, produced some anti-Semites for some thoroughly peculiar reasons. John Jay Chapman, for instance, was for many years what one might call a rabid *pro*-Semite. He claimed that the Jews represented a concentration of every human virtue, and insisted that they were smarter, braver, stronger, kinder, more pious and more moral than any other people. He considered them one of the world's great wonders, and compared them to the Parthenon and the Pyramids. Then Mr. Chapman took a trip to Atlantic City, where he witnessed Jewish families sunning themselves on the beach. He was so embittered at the discovery that Jews were no different from anybody else that he turned against them, and denounced them as stupid, uncritical, and "inferior."

In the years following the Civil War, as men like Joseph Seligman grew prosperous and performed feats that were reported in the newspapers, there was bound to be, among men less successful, a certain envy. And among the more powerful there were fear and a growing determination to keep men like Joseph Seligman "in their place." Joseph was now cooperating with John Pierpont Morgan, that curious and crotchety son of an expatriate New Englander who had turned to private banking, and who had returned to New York at a propitious moment, just before the outbreak of the war. If the Seligmans had been hurt by their association with Jay Gould and the "gold conspiracy" of a few years earlier, they were not helped by their new relationship with Morgan. Morgan was more feared than adored in Wall Street, and his own record for honest dealings was not entirely clean. Moreover, though Morgan was not an anti-Semite, he was a thorough snob. He treated the German-accented Joseph Seligman sniffily and condescendingly, and always insisted that Joseph come to *his* office to discuss business; he would not go to Joseph's. Joseph, meanwhile, disliked Morgan and was moved to comment, "Morgan—J. P. of Drexel, Morgan—is a rough, uncouth fellow, continually quarreling with Drexel in the office."

The term "social climber" had come into existence as New York society congratulated itself with the notion that "everybody and his cousin" who were outside its confines wanted desperately to get in. There were "nice people," and there were "common people," and as a rule of thumb all people with accents were common. German Jews who aspired to social acceptance, or even equality, encountered a heightening wall of exclusion. Furthermore, it was not a wall being built entirely by gentiles.

The Sephardic merchant families, "remarkable for their haughtiness, high sense of honor and their stately manners," according to a contemporary chronicler, occupied a quiet but secure place in society, Ward McAllister notwithstanding. A number of men of old New York gentile society, including a Hamilton and a DeLancey, had married Sephardic Jewesses. There were Sephardim in all the best clubs. The Union Club, New York's most exclusive, contained several Hendrickses, Lazaruses, and Nathans, along with Mr. McAllister. (In 1863 a group of dissident members resigned when the Union Club refused to expel Judah P. Benjamin, not for being a Jew but for being a Southerner and one of the financial wizards of the Confederacy; this group then organized the Union League Club and, in a flourish of Northern patriotism, immediately took in the North's financial wizard, Joseph Seligman.) Moses Lazarus, father of Emma, had been a founding member of the Knickerbocker Club, New York's second-most exclusive. The Sephardim made the most of their entrenched position, and, if German Jews found the gentiles in New York society indifferent, they found the Sephardic Jews almost unapproachable.

The German Jews, by the 1870's, were called "Forty-Eighters," after the pivotal year of their migration from Germany. A careful distinction was drawn between Jews of the "Nathan type," and those of the "Seligman type," between "the better class of Jews" and "vulgar Jews," between "Sephardic" and "German," and, finally, between "refined Hebrew ladies and gentlemen" and "Jews." The more the Germans insisted that they were "Hebrews," not "Jews," the more the Sephardim tried to disassociate themselves from the accented newcomers by stressing their ancient Spanish heritage.* In 1872 a New York society journal featured the news of a "fashionable Hebrew wedding," pointing out that the bride and groom were both members of "old American Sephardic families." It began to be clear that, no matter how much they might wish to be, immigrant Germans were not really quite "American." In exactly the same fashion, and for the same reasons, native New York Catholic families looked down on the newer-arrived Catholics from Germany and the "shanty Irish," who had come to escape the potato famine.

In the gaslit New York of 1876, the hand torch of the Statue of Liberty, the gift from France, sprouted surrealistically from a street

---

* To further confuse the situation, a number of Jewish families who had come to America before the Germans and who were not historically Sephardim began calling themselves "Sephardic" to escape the "Jew" label.

corner at Fifth Avenue and Twenty-sixth Street—part of a campaign to raise money to get the rest of the statue assembled on an island in the harbor, where it would welcome immigrants to the New World. (France had contributed $450,000 toward the erection of the statue, but expected the United States to contribute an additional $350,000 for the construction of a pedestal. For several years, while Americans bickered over who should pay this bill, the rest of Bertholdi's 225-ton lady reposed in a warehouse.) Emma Lazarus had written her lines, "Give me your tired, your poor . . ." to be inscribed upon the base of the controversial gift. Miss Lazarus' lines had a majestic ring. But—or so it seemed at the time—they also conveyed a somewhat condescending tone. Seligmans, Lehmans, and Goldmans may have arrived tired and poor, but did not enjoy being called "the wretched refuse" of some teeming European shore. Many German Jews in the 1870's, perhaps overquick to sense a slight where none was intended, interpreted Miss Lazarus' words as a snide comment on their own humble immigrant beginnings. Subscribing funds for the statue's erection on Bedloe's Island became largely a Sephardic project, eschewed by Germans. Such forces served to draw the Germans even closer to one another, into their own "Hebrew Select," with their own exclusive standards.

There was another force building against them. After the Panic of 1873 bankers as a class found themselves under a cloud. To be a "merchant banker" or a "financier" was becoming a less than praiseworthy occupation. "Wall Street," from the street of enterprise, was becoming a national symbol of avarice and evil—"the wickedest street in the world." Men like Joseph Seligman were in a line of work that was becoming less and less "respectable."

There was of course one German Jewish banker in the Union Club. His name was August Belmont. (There were more if one counted his sons, Perry, Oliver H. P., and August, Jr.) By the 1870's, however, another of his strange character changes had taken place. Though he still headed August Belmont & Company, bankers, he had begun to prefer to be known as a "diplomat." (In 1853 he had been made United States chargé d'affaires at The Hague, and from 1855 to 1858 he was the resident American minister there.) He had taken up the sport of kings, and the Belmont colors—and regal colors they were: scarlet and maroon—were established. The Belmont coachmen's livery consisted of maroon coats with scarlet piping and silver buttons embossed with "the Belmont crest" (which many said he himself had designed after studying those of European royal families), and black satin knee breeches with silver buckles. All his carriages were painted maroon with a scarlet stripe on the wheels. A lady correspondent of the day described the appearance of August Belmont in his coach-and-four as "overpoweringly commanding. One thought of . . . a King." Belmont's "image" was complete, but his ways remained difficult, contradictory.

Edith Wharton, in *The Age of Innocence,* presented a thinly disguised portrait of August Belmont in the fictional character of Julius Beaufort—a man whom, one of Mrs. Wharton's characters comments, "certain nuances" escaped. Said Mrs. Wharton:

> The question was, who *was* Beaufort? He passed for an Englishman, was agreeable, handsome, ill-tempered, hospitable and witty. He had come to America with letters of recommendation from old Mrs. Manson Mingott's English son-in-law, the banker, and had speedily made himself an important position in the world of affairs; but his habits were dissipated, his tongue was bitter, his antecedents were mysterious.

Beaufort's wife, who "grew younger and blonder and more beautiful each year," always appeared at the opera on the night of her annual ball "to show her superiority to all household cares." So did Mrs. August Belmont. On the social battleground of Newport, Caroline Belmont had also made several blood enemies, and there was a list of people in the Rhode Island colony to whom the Belmonts never spoke. Of Beaufort/ Belmont, one of Mrs. Wharton's characters airily explains, "We all have our pet common people." But, Mrs. Wharton adds, "The Beauforts were not exactly common; some people said they were even worse."

By the mid-1870's the "mystery" of August Belmont's past—his Jewish heritage—was probably the worst-kept secret in New York. But since it was considered an improper dinner-table topic, everyone in society pretended that there was, indeed, a mystery. They cleared their throats meaningfully when Belmont's past was mentioned, and let it go at that.

The thing about August Belmont that impressed the other German Jewish bankers was, of course, that astonishing religion change, that dazzling mixed marriage, that leap out of the ghetto into the perfumed upper air of New York society. The others were eager to be accepted by their new city too, but were unprepared for any move as drastic as his. Privately, they were shocked by the spectacle of Belmont; it seemed to them dishonest. It was one thing to wish to assimilate, but quite another to deny a whole tradition; one thing to embrace a new culture, but another to betray an old. Yet they regarded Belmont with mixed feelings—part admiration for his daring, part distrust of his motives.

Belmont's manner toward his former coreligionists was, in the meantime, disarming. "Belmont was a bit *too* jovial today," Joseph Seligman wrote in 1873. When the two met at their railroad board meetings, August Belmont always greeted Joseph with a "Hullo, Seligman!" in his gritty voice. Joseph, out of deference, always called Belmont "Mr.

Belmont," but one day in 1874, feeling bold, Joseph cried out, "Hullo, Belmont!" Belmont's face froze. He chose an interesting way to punish Joseph for his overfamiliarity. For the next few months, he elaborately misspelled Joseph's name on correspondence as "Selligman," "Seligmann," or "Suligman."

Then there was the matter of J. P. Morgan. While Morgan was willing to participate with the Seligmans on certain bond issues, he sometimes seemed a bit more willing to do business with Belmont. Actually, Morgan, who understood the Belmont-Seligman rivalry perfectly, was beginning to use both men to suit his own needs, playing one against the other whenever the opportunity arose. But Joseph was convinced that Morgan's freeze-and-thaw attitude toward him was simply because he was Jewish and Belmont wasn't.

August Belmont defined a dilemma for New York's other German Jewish banking families: how much Jewishness to abandon, how much gentile Americanization to absorb.

Over the years the Sephardim in America had gradually modified their religious services to conform more closely to the prevailing Protestant ways. Early in the 1800's Synagogue Shearith Israel had introduced English into the service. The cantors, or *hazonim,* began to assume the dignity, and the dress, of Protestant clergymen and were called "Reverend." The public auctioning of honors, which began to seem undignified, was discontinued. Other modifications evolved slowly. But the German Jews, though there had been steps toward Reform in a few big-city congregations in Germany and in England, felt they must Americanize their New York synagogue in a bold and abrupt sweep.

Partly, they wanted to catch up with the Sephardim in the assimilation-social-acceptance process. They were also concerned for their children. As early as 1854 the *Israelite* had gloomily predicted: "We will have no Jews left in this country in less than half a century" if synagogues did not rapidly adjust to the new age in America.

Temple Emanu-El became the symbol of the Germans' efforts "to become one with progress." When its new Fifth Avenue edifice was opened in 1870, with men like Joseph and Jesse Seligman on the building committee, it was hailed by the *New York Times* as one of the leading congregations in the world, "the first to stand forward before the world and proclaim the dominion of reason over blind and bigoted faith." Reason was the key, and the new temple seemed somehow a beacon for a new era when all men, regardless of race or creed, would join in a "universal communion" of reason. The Judaism that the temple proclaimed was "the Judaism of the heart, the Judaism which proclaims the spirit of religion as being of more importance than the letter." In 1873 Temple Emanu-El called Gustav Gottheil to its pulpit from

Manchester, England, to preach this enlightened Judaism "in impeccable English accents, comprehensible to all New Yorkers."

The attempt to bridge opposing worlds is apparent in the physical structure of Temple Emanu-El itself. Inside, with its pews and pulpit and handsome chandeliers—where hatted women worship alongside the men (unhatted), and not in a separate curtained gallery—it looks very like a church. But outside, as a kind of gentle gesture to the past, its Moorish façade calls to mind a synagogue.

Yet noble sentiments are often easier to express in rhetoric and architecture than they are in life. In some ways the temple seemed to emphasize the fact that Jews continued to live in two communities, the Jewish and the gentile, and the temple's congregation, by attempting to be a little of each, began to seem a little less than either. This duality of feeling only seemed to isolate the Reform Jew further. Emotionally and theologically, the results of this adjustment were complicated. When Reform Rabbi Sarner had been examined by an army board of chaplains during the Civil War, the notation placed after his name at the conclusion of the interview was "Lutheran."

While the congregation of Temple Emanu-El seemed uncertain as to just how "Jewish" and how "American" it wished to be, it seemed quite certain that it wanted to retain a third culture: the German. New York's German Jews began, in the 1870's, to say to each other, "We are really more German than Jewish," and were convinced that nineteenth-century Germany embodied the finest flowering of the arts, sciences, and technology. German continued to be the language the families spoke in their homes. The music children practiced in family music rooms was German music. When a Seligman, Loeb, or Lehman traveled to Europe, he sailed on the Hamburg-America Line; it was the best. When he needed a rest, he took the waters at a German spa—Baden, Carlsbad, or Marienbad. At their dinners they served German wines. When illness struck, the ailing were hurried to Germany, where the best doctors were.

The elite German Jewish club was the Harmonie, founded in 1852 and one of the oldest social clubs in New York. For forty-one years it was the *Harmonie Gesellschaft,* German was its official language, and the Kaiser's portrait hung in the hall. In some ways, however, the Harmonie was as progressive as Temple Emanu-El, where its membership worshiped. It was the first New York men's club to admit ladies at the dinner hour, and it was famous for its food. (Particularly celebrated was the club's herring with sour cream, which it put up in jars and the ladies carried home.)

Prosperous German Jewish men continued to return to Germany on their *Brautshaus.* One summer in Germany, Joseph Seligman encountered his friend Wolf Goodhart of New York, who had come over on just such a mission as Joseph had carried out two dozen years earlier. Joseph had recommended a particular young lady to Goodhart, but said Joseph in a letter home:

> He says he has a mind of his own and will not marry unless he gets a lady of the first water—handsome, highly educated, sprightly. In fact he wants something quite *recherché*, a *ne plus ultra*. I think he may, on his way back, drop in at St. James's Palace and look around there! His brother, Sander, in Lichtenfels who is more of a matter-of-fact man, tells him he is a d＿＿＿d fool if he does not try to get one with money. (Sander has one in view with *Sechs Tausend Gulden*.)

In their New York houses Loebs, Goldmans, and Lehmans employed French chefs, Irish maids, English butlers, but German governesses. When children reached college age, they were dispatched to universities at Berlin, Heidelberg, and Leipzig.

As for elementary schools, the German Jews had, from 1871 on, one of their very own on West Fifty-ninth Street—the Sachs Collegiate Institute, run by Dr. Julius Sachs. Herr Doktor Sachs was a stern, Old World schoolmaster whose uniformed boys, in smart black suits and starched stand-up collars, were seldom spared the rod. He emphasized the classics, languages (including German), and Teutonic discipline. He himself spoke nine languages fluently, including Sanskrit. At the height of his career, Dr. Sachs was turning out Lehmans, Cullmans, Zinssers, Meyers, Goldmans, and Loebs who were ready for Harvard at the age of fifteen. Julius Sachs also established a coordinated school for girls in New York, though it was less successful. It was considered less important to instill the German heritage in girls, and daughters were sent to Brearley or to finishing schools abroad. After a day at Dr. Sachs's schools, children came home for further instruction under German tutors.

Something of an exception in their approach to education—as indeed they often were to other things—were the Seligmans, led by Joseph, whose longing for Americanization was overpowering. Several of his brothers had early Americanized their first names. Henry was originally Hermann, William was Wolf, James was Jacob, Jesse was Isaias, and Leopold was Lippmann. As parents, they began naming their children after the great heroes of their adopted land. Joseph's sons included George Washington Seligman, Edwin Robert Anderson Seligman (after Robert Anderson, the defender of Fort Sumter), Isaac Newton Seligman, and Alfred Lincoln Seligman—a quaint compromise. Joseph planned to call the boy Abraham Lincoln Seligman, but decided the name Abraham was too Judaic to perpetuate in America. At the same time, Joseph and his brothers followed the Jewish tradition of naming their oldest sons David, after their grandfather, and the oldest daughters

Frances, after Fanny. William Seligman's David was David Washington. James modified David to DeWitt, thereby naming his first son after the first David Seligman as well as DeWitt Clinton. James also had a Washington and a Jefferson.

To educate his five boys, Joseph hit upon a dazzlingly American idea. He hired the creator of the great American boy hero, Horatio Alger, to live in his house and tutor his sons. James's five boys were invited to sit in on the Alger classes, where it was hoped they would all acquire the red-blooded standards of "Tattered Tom," "Ragged Dick," and Alger's other newsboy-to-riches heroes.

The experiment was not entirely a success. Alger may have been able to invent boy heroes, but he was far from one himself. He was a timid, sweet-tempered little man who, in his nonteaching hours, practiced his ballet steps. He was easily cowed, and his customary cry of alarm was "Oh, Lordy-me!" Ten lively Seligman boys were clearly too much for him, and he was forever having to rush to Babet or James's wife, Rosa, for assistance. Once, when he cried out for help, the boys jumped on him, tied him up, and locked him in a trunk in the attic. They refused to let him out until he promised not to tell their mothers.

The schoolroom was on the top floor of the Seligmans' brownstone, and, as Alger ascended the stairs the boys stood on an upper landing with lighted candles, aiming drops of hot wax at the top of his small bald head. But Alger, who had a classic inferiority complex, was endlessly forgiving. After lessons, such as they were, he liked to play billiards with the boys. He was extremely nearsighted, and when it was his turn at the cue, the boys substituted red apples for the red balls. Alger never caught on, and, as each new apple was demolished with his cue, would cry, "Oh, Lordy-me, I've broken another ball! I don't know my own *strength!*"

But Alger had his compensations. J. & W. Seligman & Company opened an account in his name, took his literary royalties and invested them for him, and made him a wealthy man. He remained a friend of the Seligmans and, long after the boys were grown, was a regular guest at Sunday dinner, where the practical jokes continued.

There was one favorite. Joseph's married daughter, Helene, and her husband lived with her parents. After dinner one of her brothers would steer Mr. Alger into the library and into a sofa next to Helene. There he would artfully drape one of Mr. Alger's tiny arms around Helene's rather ample waist while another brother ran from the room shouting, "Mr. Alger is trying to seduce Helene!" Helene's husband would then rush into the room brandishing a bread knife, crying, *"Seducer!"* The first three times this happened, Horatio Alger fell to the floor in a dead faint. Perhaps he did teach the boys to be Americans after all.

A few other German Jewish families altered their names slightly to make them sound a bit more American. Stralem, for instance, was originally Stralheim. Neustadt became Newton. Ickelheimer, which was certainly a mouthful, was telescoped to Isles. But the Seligmans rather frowned on this. It smacked of Belmont-ism.

Except for William. In the 1870's William Seligman, the most snobbish, probably, of the Seligman brothers, journeyed to New York from Paris for a conference with Joseph. William said, "Joe, now that we're getting to be men of substance, I suggest that we change our name."

Joseph looked at him for a moment with hooded, sleepy eyes, smiling his famous semismile. Then he nodded soberly. "I agree that you should change your name, William," he replied. "I suggest you change it to Schlemiel."

"THE HAUGHTY
AND PURSE-PROUD
ROTHSCHILDS"

There was one area in which August Belmont excelled. Its name was Rothschild. Belmont was not a spectacular, brilliant, or even "interesting" financier. He made few, if any, great financial coups. But men like Morgan liked to work with the European Rothschilds, and August Belmont, as their agent, was always there, helpful, collecting his percentage on the money that passed back and forth. When smaller bankers turned to him, he was never more than barely cooperative. When Goldman, Sachs, for instance, first dreamed of establishing an international operation, they approached a London firm called Kleinwort Sons & Company, to see if an English connection could be arranged. Since the Kleinworts did not "know" Sachs or Goldman, they discreetly inquired of the Rothschilds for a report on the New York firm's standing. The Rothschilds didn't know either, and passed the query along to Belmont. Belmont took his time about replying, but eventually sent back a note, via the Rothschilds, saying that Goldman, Sachs & Company was "one firm about which nobody can say anything against."

From a distance of years, this lofty comment sounds like damning with faint praise. But, apparently, coming from Belmont, it was enough to reassure the Kleinworts. The connection was established, and Goldman, Sachs & Company were almost deliriously grateful to Belmont "for so generously indorsing us"—an indication of the awe in which Belmont was held on Wall Street.*

When Joseph Seligman was readily acknowledged as the leading Jewish banker in New York, equaling, if not exceeding, Belmont's influence, Joseph made several suggestions to Belmont that "you introduce us" to the Rothschilds, suggestions which Belmont ignored. William Seligman tried to meet the Rothschilds in Paris, and Joseph, on his European journeys, tried in London. But the Rothschilds maintained their customary aloofness. Cultivating a Rothschild in Europe seemed every bit as difficult as cultivating a Sephardic Jew in New York.

In 1874 Joseph made a bid to Grant's new Secretary of the Treasury, Benjamin Bristow, to handle the sale of $25 million worth of U.S. bonds. This plum seemed about to fall into Joseph's lap when Bristow began to hedge. Bristow wanted, he said, "a stronger combination of bankers" behind the loan—a syndicate, in other words. He suggested "some strong European house," and though he did not say so in so many words, his implication was clear—he wanted the Rothschilds. Politely Joseph questioned "the propriety of giving the Rothschilds a participation," since they had given the Union such scant support during the Civil War. But the war had faded in everybody's memory, and Bristow stood firm.

Privately, Joseph was more specific about his misgivings. Writing to his brothers, he said: "Now the President and Mr. Bristow appear both anxious that we and the Rothschild group should work together, as they say no one could beat that great combination . . . [but] I fear that the haughty and proud Rothschilds would not let us come in as their peers, and I should not consent to join on any other terms."

Joseph's fears were well founded. The Rothschilds were the greatest private bank in the world and were unaccustomed to enter any deal they could not dominate. Joseph would have to come off his high horse a bit. Bristow contacted the Rothschilds, who replied from their citadel that they would handle the bond issue only if they were given a five-eighths

---

* The Kleinworts of London were held in almost equal awe. Walter Sachs recalls how, as a boy of fifteen, he was groomed for weeks by his parents on how to behave at a Kleinwort dinner in Denmark Hill, and remembers the "terrible humiliation" at a gaffe he made there. On the evening of the dinner, he was so nervous that, when the Kleinworts' front door opened, he bowed and then shook hands with the chief butler.

share of it. The Seligmans, "or any other reliable house," could have the "remainder."

Joseph tried to bargain. This, he replied, was acceptable provided the Seligman name was included in all newspaper advertisements for the bonds in New York and "either in Paris or Frankfurt." It was an important point. The position of a firm's name on the "tombstone," as a financial-page advertisement is called, is an indication of status.

Oh, no, replied the Rothschilds. They had said nothing about advertising, but now that Seligman had brought it up, they would have to make it clear that the Seligman name was not to appear in the advertising at *all*. A little nervously, Joseph wrote to Isaac in London: "If by next week the Rothschilds have not acceded to such terms as you and Paris can honourably accept, I will make it hot for Rothschild, as I cannot conceive that Bristow will ignore us and give the loan to Rothschild, even if they outbid us, as we can be of use to the Administration, and Rothschild cannot."

But Joseph was not able to make it quite hot enough. The Rothschilds grandly replied to Bristow that they "might consider" placing the Seligman name in the ads provided the Seligmans accepted an even smaller share of the issue than three-eighths. Two-eighths, for instance, might do. Joseph weighed the situation. From the standpoint of prestige, his name linked with the Rothschilds would be of great value. But he still felt it prudent to haggle. Perhaps, he suggested, they could settle somewhere between two-eighths and three-eighths—two-and-a-half-eighths, say, or six-sixteenths, or 31.25 percent. The Rothschilds appeared to grow bored with the argument, and replied that Joseph could, if he wished, have 28 percent of the issue and his name in the ads—below the name Rothschild, of course.

A weary Joseph wrote to Isaac: "We have at last advanced so far as to be able to join in a bid with Rothschild, which is, after all, a feather in our cap, and although our participation of 28% is small, I am contented." From wanting to go in as a Rothschild "peer," he had backed down to the point of accepting a little more than a one-quarter peerdom.

It took spunky Isaac in London to make the first face-to-face contact of a Seligman with a Rothschild. Isaac had had no qualms about confronting President Lincoln at a White House reception about Seligman coats, suits and uniforms. Now that the terms of the Rothschild-Seligman deal were set, Isaac marched off to Baron Lionel Rothschild's mansion in Piccadilly. This crusty Baron, when elected to the House of Commons, had for eight years refused to swear his oath of admission unless the Old Testament was substituted for the Holy Bible, and the words "upon the true faith of a Christian" were omitted. When he finally won, he sat in Parliament for fifteen years without saying a word. At the Baron's house, Isaac was passed through footmen and butlers to the Baron's drawing room where the Baron sat. It was a Saturday, and the Baron rose stiffly from his chair and said, "I am a better Jew than you. You go to business on Saturdays. I do not. My office is closed." It was a dismissal, and it was a snub, but Isaac looked quickly around the room and saw that the Baron's table was strewn with financial-looking documents. Said Isaac, "Baron, I think you do more business in this room on Saturdays than I do during the whole week in my office." The Baron looked briefly flustered. Then his lips curved upward. That evening Isaac wrote home to Joseph: "Old Rothschild can be a jolly nice chap when he wishes."

Now that Isaac had broken the Rothschild ice, Joseph wrote a three-page letter in elegant, almost obsequious praise of the Rothschilds, adding the instruction to Isaac, "Let the Baron read it." The letter said: "Please say to the Baron that we feel highly honored in participating with his great house in negotiating the 5% U.S. Bonds; that we never concealed the fact from the President and the Secretary that the House of Rothschild (properly successful in all they undertake) would be certain to make a good market for the U.S. 5%'s. . . . We were quite satisfied in leaving the sole management in London to the Messrs. Rothschild." Joseph continued his buttering up of the Rothschilds, name-dropping important American Seligman connections for several more lines, and concluded with a discreet sales pitch for future Rothschild business, saying he was sure that "the Baron will agree with us that our cooperation and joint management in New York will be of considerable advantage to the syndicate." Through the whole letter ran this between-the-lines theme: How much nicer it will be, dear Baron, working with us in New York than with August Belmont, who is such a poor Jew.

But Joseph's true feelings were best expressed in a note to Isaac in which he said snippily: "I am aware of the difficulty in dealing with so purse-proud and haughty a people as the Rothschilds, and were it not for the fact that it is an honor for us to be published in connection with them I would not have anything to do with the loan." And yet Joseph added: "Having broken the ice, I wish you to cultivate this connection."

There were other compensations. Joseph was able to write, with understandable pleasure: "Morgan—J. P. of Drexel, Morgan—is very bitter in his jealous expression about our getting the loan."

Then, in the autumn of 1874, Baron Rothschild summoned Isaac Seligman to his office to give him a piece of news. Some $55 million worth of United States bonds were to be offered for sale, and, the Baron suggested, the issue might be backed by a combination of three houses —the House of Rothschild, the House of Morgan, and the House of

Seligman. For the first time, August Belmont would act as agent for both the Rothschilds and J. & W. Seligman & Company. Needless to say, Isaac accepted. The Seligmans were now participating in the most powerful financial combination in the history of banking.

At last the Seligmans were able to consider themselves the Rothschilds' peers. The Seligman-Belmont-Morgan-Rothschild alliance, furthermore, was so successful that by the end of the decade there were complaints on Wall Street that "London- and Germany-based bankers" had a monopoly on the sale of United States bonds in Europe—which they virtually did. The Seligmans were now being called "the American Rothschilds," and Joseph, beginning to believe his own splendid myth, went so far as to suggest that his brother Isaac should be knighted.*

In Paris party-loving, party-giving William Seligman, now weighing over 250 pounds, was a social success, and was meeting, as he wrote home to Joseph, "all the nobs." Though Joseph had once disapproved of William's frivolous pursuits, he now applauded them. His earlier threats of defection were forgiven, and Joseph wrote to William assuring him of the importance of the contacts he was making, urging him to meet more nobs. Joseph wrote to Richard C. McCormick, U.S. Commissioner General, to ask: "In filling the offices for Commissioners in Paris, please do not omit to appoint Mr. William Seligman, of course as Honorary Commissioner, without pay, as brother William is at the head of a large American banking house in Paris and entertains all nice Americans." Joseph began instructing his other brothers to cultivate a Rothschildian kind of elegance and grandeur.

It worked with some better than others. At a large reception in Frankfurt, Henry Seligman found himself standing on the opposite side of the room from Baron Wilhelm von Rothschild of the Frankfurt branch. A friend whispered to Henry, "That's Baron von Rothschild. Would you like to meet him?" "Certainly," said Henry. "Bring him over." The friend hurried across the room to the Baron and said, "Mr. Henry Seligman is here and would like to meet you." "And I should very much like to meet *him*," replied the Baron. "Bring him over." Neither would cross the room. They never met.

In London Isaac understood the simple rule of Rothschild protocol. It was he who must always go to the Rothschild offices in New Court. The Baron would never deign to visit him, and Isaac would not have had the impertinence to ask him to.

But in New York the Seligman-Rothschild alliance did little to further the Seligmans' progress toward assimilation. As the decade drew to a close, there were more dark mutterings of an "international conspiracy"

* Isaac never was, but his son became Sir Charles Seligman several years later.

of Jewish bankers to take over the world's money. These were still rumbling undercurrents, but it would take no more than a single curious and sad episode, an episode that might have been no more than a tempest in a teapot, to make these feelings erupt into the public consciousness.

THE
SELIGMAN-HILTON
AFFAIR

Mr. Alexander T. Stewart was no stranger to Joseph Seligman. Stewart operated A. T. Stewart & Company, in Ninth Street, the largest retail store in New York. With its wholesale operation in Chicago, Stewart's was the biggest store in the country.

When the New York Railway Company was organized in 1871, with its plans for building the city's first elevated railroad, Joseph and Stewart were on the board of directors, along with Levi P. Morton, James Lanier, Charles L. Tiffany, August Belmont, and John Jacob Astor. The president of the line was a New York politician, Judge Henry Hilton. Judge Hilton's chief distinction was that he happened to be a friend and political crony of Mr. Stewart's, and a member of the Tweed Ring.

Despite their directorial connection, relations between Joseph and

Mr. Stewart were not cozy. Stewart was also a friend of President Grant's, and when Grant had offered the Treasury post to Joseph Seligman, and had been turned down, he had offered it to Stewart, who said yes. Stewart's friendship with Judge Hilton and the Tweed Ring, however, had made him a number of powerful political enemies, and his appointment was not confirmed by the Senate. This was a bitter disappointment to Stewart, who had wanted a Cabinet post as the capstone of his career. The Scotsman bristled whenever he thought of Joseph Seligman, who had refused the appointment without even bothering to see whether the Senate would approve him or not. Joseph had also been asked to run on the Republican ticket for Mayor of New York, but had replied, "The bank needs me, and my brothers beg me to leave politics and public office to others." It was no secret that Alexander Stewart wanted to be Mayor. When he heard of Joseph's refusal, Stewart said, "Who does Seligman think he is? He seems to think politics is only for tradespeople."

The uneasy situation was not helped when Joseph was appointed to the "Committee of Seventy"—a group of prominent New Yorkers whose purpose was to eradicate the Tweed Ring, and one of whose chief targets was Stewart's friend, Judge Hilton. Up to this point, A. T. Stewart & Company had been purchasing its bills of exchange from J. & W. Seligman & Company. When Joseph's membership on the committee was announced, this relationship suddenly terminated.

In 1876 Alexander Stewart died, leaving a fortune which turned out to be the largest ever recorded in America. Part of his estate was a two-million-dollar investment in the Grand Union Hotel in Saratoga. Stewart's executor was Judge Hilton.

Nobody in New York had paid much attention to Henry Hilton until he became the manager of Stewart's millions. Now he revealed to a society journalist that he was one of "a handful" of New York's most important men. Perhaps, but when Grant left the White House and Joseph and Jesse held a formal dinner at Delmonico's for the former President and "forty or fifty guests," Judge Hilton was not among those invited. Meanwhile, Joseph was going on to even greater triumphs. Wall Street jockeyed feverishly for position with the new President, Rutherford B. Hayes, and Hayes's Secretary of the Treasury Sherman. Early in 1877 Sherman summoned a representative group of New York bankers, including Joseph Seligman and August Belmont, to Washington, and sent each into a separate room "to work out a plan for refunding the balance of the Government war debt." Each man submitted his recommendations, and a week later Sherman sent for Joseph and told him that his plan was "by all odds the clearest and most practical," and would be adopted. (The plan called for building up a gold reserve of approximately 40 percent of the outstanding greenbacks through the sale of bonds for coin—something Joseph was good at.) *

After working at untangling the nation's finances through most of the spring, Joseph decided to take a vacation at Saratoga, and to stay at the Grand Union Hotel, which Judge Hilton now managed, where Joseph and his family had often stayed in the past.

Saratoga was then the queen of American resorts, outshining even Newport. Here, each summer, the cream of Eastern society arrived ritually to take the waters of its famous spa, to promenade in parasoled elegance down its wide main avenue, through the spacious public rooms of its large hotels, to perch with top hat and cane on the famous verandas, and to change clothes. A trip to "season" at Saratoga was not to be undertaken lightly, and the capacious Saratoga trunk was invented to accommodate the wardrobes these holidays required. John "Bet-a-Million" Gates once bet a famous dude of the period, Evander Berry Wall, that he could not change his clothes as many as fifty times between breakfast and dinner at Saratoga, and won. Mr. Wall made it through only forty complete changes of costume.

No one traveled to Saratoga without at least one valet, one personal maid, and a laundress, and to arrive with one's own chef was not uncommon. By far the grandest hotel in Saratoga was the Grand Union. In its day it was the world's largest hostelry, covering seven acres of ground with 834 rooms, 1,891 windows, 12 miles of red carpeting and a solid square mile of marble tiling. The edifice and its furnishings were said to weigh seventeen million tons, though how this figure was arrived at is unclear.

Still, there is evidence that by 1877 the Grand Union had begun to lose business, and Stewart—and his successor, Judge Hilton—decided that this was because the hotel's Christian guests did not wish to share the hotel with Jews. Joseph Seligman was therefore advised that the hotel had adopted a new policy and did not accept "Israelites."

In view of the tremendous fuss this decision kicked up, one question has become curiously obscured which, today, seems pivotal. That is, did Joseph and his family actually *go* to Saratoga that summer or were they advised of the hotel's new policy by mail? Accounts vary. One has it that Joseph "applied for accommodations," and was rebuffed. Another says that he was told, upon arrival, that he could stay at the hotel this time, but would not be welcomed back "in future." The majority of reports insists that a Seligman party did, physically, appear at the hotel and was turned away by a clerk at the desk, whereupon Joseph and party stalked out of the lobby and returned to New York.

* The plan worked so well that within two years the dollar was quoted at par for the first time since 1861.

If Joseph did go to Saratoga, he must have gone by train. When he traveled by train, he was usually supplied with a private car by one of his railroads, and he must have departed for Saratoga with the usual complement of trunks and retinue of servants. Did Joseph undertake this ponderous journey to a famous and popular hotel without a reservation? Or did he in fact go to Saratoga knowing quite well what awaited him at the Grand Union, and was the purpose of his trip to make a test case of the hotel's anti-Semitic policy? His subsequent behavior suggests this, and if that was his intention, he may have acted unwisely.

Joseph reportedly "treated the whole matter of his repulse lightly," but Joseph was a fighter and was not in a lighthearted frame of mind when he wrote a scathing letter to Judge Hilton which he then released to the newspapers. The letter was a bitter personal attack on Hilton, and it made front-page copy, with headlines running:

A SENSATION AT SARATOGA. NEW RULES FOR THE GRAND UNION. NO JEWS TO BE ADMITTED. MR. SELIGMAN, THE BANKER, AND HIS FAMILY SENT AWAY. HIS LETTER TO MR. HILTON. GATHERING OF MR. SELIGMAN'S FRIENDS. AN INDIGNATION MEETING TO BE HELD.

There followed threats of lawsuits under civil rights laws, charges, countercharges, talk of boycotts and recriminations, ugly name-calling. Judge Hilton did not soothe injured feelings by releasing a letter of his own in which he said: "I know what has been done and am fully prepared to abide by it," and, "As the law yet permits a man to use his property as he pleases and I propose exercising that blessed privilege, notwithstanding Moses and all his descendants may object." Fanning the already raging fire, he added: "Personally, I have no particular feeling on the subject, except probably that I don't like this class as a general thing and don't care whether they like me or not. If they do not wish to trade with our house, I will be perfectly satisfied, nay gratified, as I believe we lose much more than we gain by their custom."

The summer of 1877 was a lean one for news and, in the days that followed, the press—in San Francisco, Boston, Chicago, Cleveland, Baltimore, and in tiny towns across the country—leaped on the Hilton-Seligman story, featured it and editorialized about it, printing letters pro and con. In the middle of a performance of a New York play, a gentleman from the audience ran up on the stage and started to make an anti-Seligman speech while ladies in the boxes pelted him with their handbags. Both Joseph and Hilton received scurrilous and threatening letters. When Hilton ran a letter in the *New York Times,* dropping the unpleasant hint that the Seligmans were little respected by their fellow bankers in Wall Street, officials of Drexel, Morgan & Company, Morton

Bliss & Company, the First National Bank, and even August Belmont & Company, stepped forward in a paid announcement to say: "Judge Hilton is under a misapprehension as to the relations of the Messrs. Seligman and their associates, which always have been, and are, of the most satisfactory character."

Judge Hilton then added confusion to the chaos by announcing that if Joseph had "taken the trouble" to apply to him, Hilton, "personally," the hotel would have taken him in.

The furor grew more vicious, more barbed, with insinuations that the incident had actually nothing to do with anti-Semitism but was merely a business feud—that Joseph was miffed at having lost the Stewart account, and that Hilton was trying to ruin the Seligmans because of Joseph's role in the anti-Tweed group. It did begin to seem like a money battle when, led by a group of Joseph's friends, a massive boycott was undertaken against A. T. Stewart's store, which Hilton also managed.

Suddenly frightened, Judge Hilton pledged $1,000 to Jewish charities. A Seligman might have his price, but it was more than $1,000. *Puck,* the comic weekly, ran a two-page cartoon in its Christmas issue of that year, mocking Hilton and, in an accompanying editorial, praised Jews for refusing to be bribed:

> Alas! Poor Hilton.
>
> It is to be regretted that Mr. Hilton is as unsuccessful as a drygoods man and a hotel-keeper as he notoriously was as a jurist. But the fact remains. He took it upon himself to insult a portion of our people, whose noses had more of a curvilinear form of beauty than his own pug, and he rode his high-hobby horse of purse-proud self-sufficiency until he woke up one day to find that the drygoods business was waning. . . . Then Mr. Hilton arouses himself. He turns his great mind from thoughts of the wandering bones of Stewart; he brings the power of his gigantic brain to bear upon the great question, "How shall I revive trade?" He has remembered that he has insulted the Jews. Aha! we'll conciliate them. So out of the coffers that A. T. Stewart filled he gropes among the millions and orders the trustees of a few Hebrew charities to bend the pregnant hinges of their knees at his door and receive a few hundred dollars.
>
> But in this country the Jew is not ostracized. He stands equal before the law and before society with all his fellow-citizens, of whatever creed or nationality. And the Jew has stood up like a Man and refused to con-done the gross and uncalled for insults of this haphazard millionaire, merely because he flings the offer of a thousand dollars in their faces. All honor to the Jews for their manly stand in this instance.

At the height of the rancor, Henry Ward Beecher, the most noted clergyman of the day, made the Saratoga incident the subject of one of his most celebrated sermons. Titled "Gentile and Jew," Dr. Beecher declared from the pulpit:

> I have had the pleasure of the acquaintance of the gentleman whose name has been the occasion of so much excitement—Mr. Seligman. I have summered with his family for many years . . . and I have learned to love and respect them. . . . When I heard of the unnecessary offense that has been cast upon Mr. Seligman, I felt that no other person could have been singled out that would have brought home to me the injustice more sensibly than he.

But had Joseph been "singled out," or had he singled himself out? What had he wanted? Had he, knowing of the hotel's policy, appeared in Saratoga prepared to be excluded and hoping to create a *cause célèbre* in which he would emerge a hero, a champion of reason, in both the Jewish and the gentile communities? Or had he, knowing that the Grand Union barred Jews generally, simply not believed that it would bar him, a man of his position and distinction? Men like Beecher and the editors of *Puck* might hail him as a hero, but the Jewish community of New York was not sure that it had really required a champion of reason for resort hotels. As his old friend Wolf Goodhart said to him privately, "For God's sake, Joe, didn't you *know* that some hotels don't want Jews? The Grand Union isn't the only one!"

Months passed, and the affair continued to dominate the news as other clergymen, following Beecher's example, had their say and as all figures of importance in New York felt called upon to take a stand. As plans for the "mass protest meeting" in Union Square against Judge Hilton progressed, and as ill feeling continued to mount, with friends turned against each other over the matter, amid ugly cries of "Jew-hater!" and "Jew-lover!" and with anti-Semitic graffiti scrawled on walls, Joseph Seligman, now nearly sixty, grew increasingly aghast at the hornet's nest of hatred he had stirred up. Privately, he began to beg that the matter be forgotten. At last he approached William Cullen Bryant, who, saying that the incident had already been commented upon "from the mouths of everybody in public places," sensibly urged that the protest meeting be canceled. It was.

But the boycott on A. T. Stewart's store continued, and had a good deal to do with the store's eventual failure and sale to John Wanamaker.

Joseph tried to forget it. In the months that followed, he refused to speak of it.

The Seligman-Hilton affair was the first publicized case of anti-Semitism in America. But rather than extinguish anti-Semitic feeling, it kindled it. By pointing it up, Joseph had made it specific. He had solved no problem. He had merely defined one. Now the battle lines were

drawn. The Grand Union's policy gave other hotels and clubs a prece-
dent, and anti-Semitism in Adirondack resorts quickly became quite
blatant, with hotels boldly advertising, "Hebrews need not apply," and
"Hebrews will knock vainly for admission." At Lake Placid, Melville
L. K. Dewey built the largest club in the area, the Lake Placid Club,
whose members, Dewey said, would be "the country's best," specifically:

> No one will be received as member or guest against whom there is
> physical, moral, social, or race objection, or who would be unwelcome
> to even a small minority. This excludes absolutely all consumptives, or
> rather invalids, whose presence might injure health or modify others'
> freedom or enjoyment. [Dewey himself had come to the mountains for
> his hay fever, and his wife suffered from "rose cold," but apparently
> their sneezing was acceptable.] This invariable rule is rigidly enforced;
> it is found impracticable to make exceptions to Jews or others excluded,
> even when of unusual personal qualifications.*

Other Adirondack resorts, to complete the vicious circle, became exclusively Jewish.

At the height of the Seligman-Hilton affair, the New York Bar
Association blackballed a Jew. A year later, the Greek-letter fraternities
at City College barred Jewish members—a slight that Bernard Baruch
never forgave.

The affair would not end, and the ugly wound it had opened would
not heal. Soon Mr. Austin Corbin, president of the Long Island Railroad
and of something called the Manhattan Beach Company, which was
attempting to develop Coney Island into a fashionable summer resort
along the lines of Newport, followed Judge Hilton's lead—and borrowed
some of Hilton's language—with the announcement:

> We do not like the Jews as a class. There are some well behaved
> people among them, but as a rule they make themselves offensive to
> the kind of people who principally patronize our road and hotel, and
> I am satisfied we should be better off without than with their custom.

Following generations would have to live with the tensions which the
affair created. It was to have a profound psychological effect on German
Jewish life in New York, making it more defensive and insular, more
proud and aloof and self-contained, more cautious. These were tensions
Joseph's children and grandchildren would face. Jews had been snubbed
by hotels and clubs before. They had chafed at this treatment but, by

---

* In 1965 R. Peter Straus, a strategist in Senator Robert F. Kennedy's 1964
campaign, publicly criticized the Senator's brother-in-law, Stephen E. Smith, for
staying at the Lake Placid Club, "which is known to discriminate against Jewish
people."

overlooking it, had tried to rise above it. Now, however, it was out in the open and a fact of life: certain areas of America were closed to Jews.

The affair killed old Joe Seligman.

In the months that followed, it even seemed to affect his business judgment. His brother Abraham was his West Coast expert, but Abraham's advice was not always to be trusted. (It was Abraham who had got Joseph involved with Mr. S. H. Bohm and the Montana mining fiasco.) In 1878 Abraham urged Joseph to look into the doings of a German immigrant named Adolph Sutro in San Francisco, who had come up with a plan to build a half-mile tunnel beneath the Comstock Lode. Such a tunnel, said Abraham, "at once insures drainage, ventilation, and facilitates the work of getting the gold- and silver-bearing quartz above ground." All Sutro needed was half a million dollars to dig his hole, which he said would yield as much as six million a year in revenue.

Joseph was indignantly against it, and wrote to Abraham that the Sutro tunnel was "a visionary scheme doomed to failure," and that "it would injure J. & W. Seligman & Co. as bankers in foreign exchange to be known as investing money in speculations of this kind." But, because the tunnel plan involved putting railroad tracks through it, Joseph began quickly to warm up to the idea. Soon his firm had purchased 95,000 shares in the Sutro tunnel at approximately a dollar a share, and Joseph congratulated Abraham for his foresight. "I will do Brother Abm the justice that he was the only one who stuck through thick & thin to his scheme," Joseph wrote proudly. But by the time the tunnel was finished in 1879 it was too late to be of any aid to the diminishing Comstock Lode. Sutro himself, more farsighted than anybody, sold out his interest in the tunnel at a handsome profit. But the Seligmans hung on, and the stock became worthless.

That winter, looking ill and tired and old, Joseph traveled to Florida, with Babet and their son, George Washington, for a month of rest and sunshine. From there the Seligmans went to New Orleans, where Joseph's oldest daughter Frances and her husband, Theodore Hellman, were living.

March 31 was a hot and humid Sunday, and there was the usual large and heavy family midday meal. Afterward, Joseph said that he would like to take a nap and went upstairs.

A little later there was a cry from the floor above. The family hurried to Joseph's side, and Frances Hellman, writing to her brother Edwin who was then a student at Heidelberg, said:

> Our Papa said to me that he had such a strange sensation, just as if
> he were going to be paralyzed. Of course we laughed at this & told him

it was only the effect of the heat and his too heavy slumber. When the
doctor arrived, dear Papa brightened visibly . . . and when dinner time
came he insisted upon dear Mama going down stairs, saying he had a
good appetite also. We sent his dinner up, he ate it with relish, and all
of a sudden called to Mary [the Hellmans' maid] who was standing by
his side for brandy. She handed him the glass, he tried to take it with
his left hand, but it sank lifeless to his side—his left side had instanta-
neously become paralyzed. Mary put the brandy to his lips, he drank,
and then laid his head back in the chair, closed his eyes quietly, and
sank into the deep sleep from which he never woke. Just as his consciousness left him, he raised Mary's hand and gently stroked and patted
it several times, evidently thinking that dear Mama stood beside him.
So you see even his very last thought was a happy one.

During the final years of his life, Joseph had described himself as "a
freethinker." Nowadays he would doubtless be called an atheist. Under
the influence of Felix Adler, Joseph had helped found, and become
president of, the Ethical Culture Society. Joseph had directed that his
funeral services be conducted by the Society. But, since the Seligman-
Hilton affair had labeled Joseph "America's leading Jew," it was
unthinkable to Dr. Gustav Gottheil, chief rabbi of Temple Emanu-El,
that the temple should not conduct the rite. Dr. Gottheil was backed by
Joseph's brother James, who disapproved of Adler and who was president of the temple's board of trustees. The temple and the Society
argued over which should properly hold the services, while Joseph
became, even in death, the center of another religious controversy.

Finally Frances Hellman wrote, again to her brother Edwin in
Germany:

> After much (and what I consider simply *disgraceful*) resistance on
> the part of some of our relatives whom I don't need to mention, it has
> been decided that Felix Adler *only* will conduct the funeral services at
> the house—Gottheil and Dr. Lilienthal are to speak at the grave. I con-
> sider it wrong, and not in conformity with our dear father's life that
> Gottheil should speak at *all*. But it seems that it could not be prevented.

Frances then added proudly:

> Oh, my dear Edwin, if you could but read the papers, see the many
> letters received from Christian gentlemen, all but with one import, all
> bearing upon the goodness, the honesty, the nobleness, the talents and
> charity of our dear father, it would be to you as it is to us, a great
> consolation, the grandest legacy he could have left to his children.

There were other legacies, some large and some small. Among the
items in the papers was the note that the village of Roller's Ridge,
Missouri, through which one of Joseph's railroads passed, had voted to

change its name and would thereafter be known as Seligman, Missouri, in tribute to the great man's life.

The newspapers also speculated on the size of Joseph's financial legacy, which was assumed to be "in excess of fifty millions." When his estate was tallied, however, it amounted to slightly more than a million dollars. Out of this, a bequest of $25,000 was divided among sixty different charities, Jewish and non-Jewish, but he had given away far more than that figure in his lifetime. If he had lived longer, he would probably have died wealthier; all his brothers died richer than he.

There was no letter of condolence from Judge Henry Hilton.

And Joe Seligman was gone. To those closest to him, it seemed that something more important than his life had ended. To other German Jewish bankers, who had been waiting in the wings, it seemed as though something were beginning.

PART IV

THE AGE OF SCHIFF

19

"A COMPLEX
ORIENTAL NATURE"

By the 1870's nearly all the pivotal "Old Guard" names of German Jewish finance—with the exception of the Guggenheims—had migrated to New York City. Familiar on the streets of downtown Manhattan were the two Lehman brothers, prospering as cotton brokers. Marcus Goldman, with bits of commercial paper filling out the lining of his tall silk hat, was still a one-man operation. Two Strauses, Lazarus and son Isidor, who, like the Seligmans and Lehmans, had been peddlers and small shopowners in the prewar South, had moved to New York from Georgia and had opened the glassware and crockery department at R. H. Macy & Company. Solomon Loeb, at his wife's insistence, had come to New York from Cincinnati and, though not on a par with the Seligmans' operations, his Kuhn, Loeb & Company was becoming an important investment banking house.

In Philadelphia the Guggenheims were not doing at all badly. Meyer Guggenheim had sold his stove-polish and lye company for $150,000 and was branching out in other directions—importing herbs and spices,

Swiss laces and embroidery. He had also done some speculating in the stock market. He invested $84,000 in the Hannibal & St. Joseph Railroad, which, he had heard, Jay Gould had his eye on. Guggenheim bought in at $42 a share, and soon had the pleasure of watching his stock soar to over $200 and then selling his holdings for half a million. His wife was beginning to long for the headier atmosphere of New York, too.

In New York, after their mornings of shopping and errands, while their husbands marched the downtown streets, the ladies gathered in their uptown drawing rooms for their afternoons, in their little circle of friends, their little crowd. The ladies all owned silver tea services, and the tea service was the heart of the brownstone. In their best dresses and hats, with their reticules tucked in the cushions of the seats beside them, they discussed the feminine topics of the day—children, clothes, servants, health (with a heavy emphasis on obstetrics), and marriage—in formal German. (It was beginning to be considered bad form to use Yiddish.) Several women had marriageable daughters. There were a number of still unwed Seligman daughters, and there was Mrs. Solomon Loeb's Therese—a stepdaughter, yes, but as much a daughter as any of her others—who had developed into a beauty. There were eligible Seligman sons and Lehman boys. The ladies enjoyed planning matches for their daughters, asking each other, *"Waere sie nicht passend für . . . ?"* ("Wouldn't she be suitable for . . . ?") and considering the possible results.

There were also several young men who had recently arrived in New York from Germany. There was one particular bright and handsome boy who, barely out of his teens, had opened his own brokerage house. His name was Jacob Schiff.

Of course there were two schools of thought, among the ladies, as to whether it was wiser for a daughter to marry a German-born or an American-born boy. The German-born might at any moment decide to return to Germany, bearing off the daughter with him, forever. It was risky.

The ladies were not the only ones who were interested in young Jacob Schiff. American industry and government still relied heavily on European financing. New York bankers worked hard to cultivate European contacts, and looked over young banking talent from Europe with particular care. Here, very definitely, was talent of an unusual sort. At the same time, any young man with talent enough to enter the banking business was also expected to be able to enter the family.

Jacob Schiff has been described by one contemporary as "a patient, skillful man, a suave diplomat with a complex Oriental nature." Complex, yes, but out of the complexity of his character an extraordinary single-mindedness emerges as his most marked trait. From the very beginning, he seems to have known exactly what he wanted.

The Schiffs of Frankfurt-am-Main often compared themselves to the Rothschilds of the same city. (Jacob Schiff was of a younger generation of immigrants than the Seligmans, a generation that was coming not from poor country families but from wealthy city ones as well.) In the eighteenth century the Schiffs and Rothschilds shared a double house in the Frankfurt *Judengasse* where the identifying house signs, *"Zum Schiff"* and *"Zum Roten Schild,"* hung alongside each other until one of the Schiffs, already prosperous enough to move to London, sold the balance of the house to the first rich Rothschild, Meyer Amschel. If pressed, Schiffs usually admitted that, though not so collectively wealthy as the Rothschilds, theirs was the more august family. The Rothschilds were known only as big money-makers. The Schiff family tree contained not only successful bankers but distinguished scholars and members of the rabbinate. There was, for instance, the seventeenth-century Meir ben Jacob Schiff, composer of notable commentaries on the Talmud, and David Tevele Schiff, who in the late eighteenth century became chief rabbi of the Great Synogogue of England. The Schiffs can also demonstrate that they are a much *older* family than the upstart Rothschilds. The Schiff pedigree, carefully worked out in the *Jewish Encyclopedia,* shows the longest continuous record of any Jewish family in existence, with Schiffs in Frankfurt going back to the fourteenth century.

Jacob Schiff actually traced his ancestry even farther back than that—to the tenth century B.C., no less, and to none other than Henriette Seligman's ancestor, King Solomon and, thence, to David and Bathsheba, where he chose to stop tracing. Jacob Schiff took his descent from the King of Israel seriously, and a comparison of the careers of the two men, nearly three thousand years apart, is helpful. Like Jacob Schiff, Solomon was skilled in foreign commerce, importing, on a lavish scale, "gold, silver, ivory, apes and peacocks." Solomon, too, sought to make his position more secure by allying himself with his larger, more powerful neighbors and, to cement his relationship with Egypt, married the Pharaoh's daughter.

From the moment he made his appearance in the world, Jacob Schiff was a figure to be reckoned with. He was a restless, unpredictable child—sullen at times, then suddenly sunny, given to quick and violent bursts of anger that would just as quickly pass. He had something known as "the Schiff temper." As he grew older he grew more rebellious and temperamental. He was short in stature—even as a mature man he stood only five two in his stocking feet ("If," as an older member of the family says, "you can ever picture Mr. Schiff out of his shoes and spats")—and the shortness may have accounted for his

somewhat Napoleonic manner. But he was physically well knit and well
coordinated, careful about his waistline and a believer in fitness. Even at
ten, he was always exercising, walking, cycling. Older, bigger boys
thought twice before tangling with young Jacob—as they were to continue to do through his lifetime. He had clear skin, a wide forehead, and
large blue eyes that he inherited from his mother, who indulged him and
spoiled him. His relationship with his father was less secure.

Moses Schiff was a successful stockbroker on the Frankfurt Stock
Exchange. There were five Schiff children—a brother, Philip, and a
sister, Adelheid, older than Jacob, and two younger brothers. In 1863,
at the age of sixteen, Jacob went to work for his father. A year later,
Moses Schiff wrote to an American cousin in St. Louis:

> At present, all goes well with us. My eldest son, Philip, is of great
> assistance to me in my business. My daughter is engaged to be married
> to a very brilliant man, Alfred Geiger, the nephew of the philosopher
> [Abraham Geiger was then head of the Frankfurt synagogue], very
> clever and very orthodox. My second son, now 17—Jacob—is quite a
> problem because he already feels that Frankfurt is too small for his
> ambition. I would like to hear from you whether, if I gave my permis-
> sion, perhaps your brother-in-law would take him back with him, and
> he could continue to live the life of an orthodox Jew, which is of great
> importance to me.

In due time, the St. Louis cousin replied, saying that Moses was
certainly very lucky to have a son like Philip. He was sorry that Moses'
other son, Jacob, was a problem. He certainly knew what problems boys
like that could be. If Frankfurt was too small for Jacob's ambition, St.
Louis would be even smaller.

But Jacob Schiff had plans of his own. At the age of eighteen he left
Frankfurt, ostensibly for a few months' visit to England. In England he
spent several days writing a series of letters to his mother. He gave these
to a friend with instructions that they be posted, at regularly stated
intervals, until he could write to her from New York, where he was
headed all along, to say that he had safely crossed the Atlantic.

Every detail of his journey had been carefully worked out in advance.
He had $500 in savings, and he was met in New York, as arranged, by a
fellow Frankfurter named William Bonn, who was with the Frankfurt
house of Speyer & Company. Bonn took young Schiff back with him to
his boardinghouse and, to Jacob's "delight" (as he wrote home), invited
him to move in with him. The Bonns, he reminded his mother, were "of
the higher levels of the social layer cake" in Frankfurt. The two men sat
up all night making schedules and plans.

Bonn supplied Jacob with Wall Street introductions, and presently, in

1867, Jacob Schiff was ready to form his own brokerage firm with Henry Budge and Leo Lehmann (no kin to the single-"n" Lehmans), both ex-Frankfurt boys like himself.

When the partnership papers were drawn and ready for signature, it was a brief embarrassment to the new firm to discover that the youngest partner, Jacob Schiff, was not yet of legal age to sign.

20

"YOUR LOVING KUHN, LOEB & COMPANY"

In a photograph taken years later, after the great J. P. Morgan had admitted him as his only equal, Jacob Schiff stands squarely, solidly, addressing the world; his frock coat is smoothly buttoned across his comfortable middle; not a trace of humor lights his calm, impassive face. From his almost total lack of expression, one's eyes are drawn, instead, to the plump competence of his small hands. Yet in another portrait, a painting done at nearly the same time, we see a different Jacob Schiff. He is seated in a club chair, unbuttoned, relaxed, one hand draped carelessly across the arm of the chair, the other cradling his chin. His lips form the barest trace of a sardonic smile, and his blue eyes shine with a kind of wry amusement. He seems to be waiting for some pleasant event, which he has already predicted, to happen. Here is a man of wit, urbanity, and wisdom.

Somewhere between these two aspects of him lay the mysterious clue to his character, for Jacob Schiff could be exquisitely poised and logical and patient, and he could also be irrational and arbitrary and petty and demanding.

He liked large things—large cities, large houses, and large sums of money, such as those represented on two canceled checks which he eventually framed and hung on the wall of his office: one for $49,098,000 and another for $62,075,000, both written over his signature within a six months' period for loans he had floated for the Pennsylvania Railroad. He also liked to wield large authority. The very name Schiff rings with command. Historians have often speculated about the influence of names on personalities. Adolf Hitler might never have attained such heights of power and brutality if he had retained the name Schicklgruber. Could August Belmont have achieved the grandeur and social position he wanted as August Schönberg? The name Schiff has another connotation—the ship that would one day sail forth as one of the flagships of American finance. Could Schiff have reached his goals if he had worn the name of one of his ancestors, Zunz?

One thing was certain from the start: he could never be a good employee. He could not even be a good partner. He had to dominate. His partnership with Budge and Lehmann did not work out well, and Schiff began looking elsewhere. He was offered the managership of the Deutsche Bank in Hamburg and, in one of his rare steps backward, accepted the post and returned to Germany. But he was still restless, dissatisfied. Commercial banking bored him. Its business—taking deposit accounts, making cautious loans—was too cut and dried.

There was another problem. By 1870 the first openly anti-Semitic parties had been formed in Germany, and politicians were vying for the votes of anti-Semites. As the power of these corrosive elements grew, even Bismarck, who had ignored them in the beginning, then scorned them, now had to cater to them in order to have their votes and remain in power. This development gave anti-Semitism its first patina of respectability, and made the future for young Jews in Germany seem more uncertain. The most promising development during his Hamburg sojourn was Jacob Schiff's meeting the Warburg family, very much of the Jewish "social layer cake" in that city. Two of the sons of Moritz and Charlotte Warburg—Paul and Felix, who later became so important in Schiff's life—always remembered the elaborate toy fort the young banker presented to the Warburg children on one of his visits.

In Germany, one of the men Jacob Schiff met was Abraham Kuhn, the homesick founding partner of Kuhn, Loeb, who had returned to Frankfurt. Impressed with the energetic young man, Kuhn suggested he write to Solomon Loeb in New York and offer his services. In addition to supplying his name to the firm's letterhead, it was perhaps Abraham Kuhn's most significant achievement. Schiff did as Kuhn advised. Loeb accepted. When Schiff got to New York in 1873, he was twenty-six, Solomon Loeb was forty-four, and Kuhn, Loeb & Company was a babe of six.

In one of his earliest letters to his mother during his first stay in New York, Schiff had spoken of "the enormous opportunities in railroading and all that" in the new country. Now, in New York again, he began to concentrate on railroads in earnest. Here was the first indication that he would become a very different sort of financier from Joseph Seligman. Schiff had been watching the Seligmans' railroad activities carefully, and he was soon certain that he knew what it was the Seligmans were doing wrong. Joe Seligman had had no interest whatever in how railroads were run or why, and looked at them only as a means for taking profits. Schiff decided to make himself an expert on railroad management, on the reasons for railroads' existence, the needs they filled, their potentialities, and the role they could eventually play in relation to other industries and the American economy. With the somewhat edgy blessings of his senior partner, Mr. Loeb, Jacob began using the considerable resources of Kuhn, Loeb & Company to buy into—and befriend—railroads.

Soon Schiff, too, was on the board of directors of the Erie, which had caused the Seligmans so much woe. A railroad directorship, the details of which had been not much more than a nuisance to Joe Seligman, fascinated Schiff. He could now study a line from the inside as well as from without. Before long, his mind had achieved such a grasp of American railroading that a friend was able to say of him, "He carries every railroad in the country, every bit of rolling stock, every foot of track, and every man connected with each line—from the president down to the last brakeman—inside his head."

The kind of services Schiff began to perform for railroads were later described by one of his junior partners, Otto Kahn. "A railroad, or some particular officer of a railroad," Kahn said, "would come to us and would say, 'We have such and such a problem to solve. We would like to get your advice as to the best kind of security to issue for that purpose— a security which gives to the railroad the most powerful instrument, not only for immediate but also for long-term purposes, and gives the public the greatest possible protection without tying up the railroad unduly and beyond what is safe for it.' So, he says, 'Will you tell us what is the best kind of instrument to use for that purpose? Should it be a mortgage bond, a debenture, a convertible bond, preferred stock, an equity? We would like you to look into it and tell us. Here are a few facts and figures. Go through them.' "

Schiff and Kuhn, Loeb, Kahn admitted, "have sometimes been stuck by not knowing what kind of securities would be most advantageous from all standpoints to issue. We would know that in a short while from now other large security issues are likely to come upon the market. We would know what is the general disposition of the security market— favorable or unfavorable. Is there an investment demand, or isn't there an investment demand? And that situation varies. Sometimes we can sell nothing but equities. Sometimes equities are thrown into the discard and people want safety. Again, that is our job to know." Finally, Kahn repeated the motto that had been drummed into him by his mentor, Jacob Schiff: "Our only attractiveness is our good name and our reputation for sound advice and integrity. If that is gone our business is gone, however attractive our show window might be."

Jacob Schiff's approach to railroad financing was, in other words, very like that of J. P. Morgan. Schiff set himself up from the beginning as a friend of railroad management, as a champion of those whose money was actually invested in the stocks and bonds of the carriers. He stood opposed to the speculators and entrepreneurs and promoters, and to the deliberate wreckers of railroads such as the Seligmans' old client, Jay Gould. Schiff, furthermore, who was ten years younger than Morgan, was also able to get a significant head start on Morgan when it came to railroads. Morgan's first railroad achievement of any size was his ability, in 1879, to dispose of 250,000 shares of William H. Vanderbilt's New York Central, quietly, in London, so that the stock's price would not plummet on the New York market. For this sale, which totaled $36.5 million, Morgan received a fee of $3 million along with an elaborate tea service from a grateful Mr. Vanderbilt. But Jacob Schiff, two years before this, in 1877, had achieved a notable, if somewhat less profitable, feat of his own for the Chicago & Northwestern Railroad. His fee: $500,000.

Schiff was a young man in a position to move with the tide. For the next thirty years railroads would completely dominate the American financial scene, and Schiff from the beginning was determined that Kuhn, Loeb & Company should dominate the field of railroad financing. Morgan, lulled, no doubt, by his three-million fee from Vanderbilt, and by his belief that he had been "chosen by circumstance and inheritance as the heir of North America," joined the Union League and the New York Yacht Club. He bought a town house—the square brown mansion that still stands at 219 Madison Avenue—and a two-thousand-acre estate on the Hudson, called "Cragston." The sleek black hull of his *Corsair I* slid from its ways and into yachting history.

Jacob Schiff, meanwhile, was collecting railroad clients. Within a few years, these included the Pennsylvania; the Chicago, Milwaukee & St.

Paul; the Baltimore & Ohio; the Chesapeake & Ohio; the Denver & Rio Grande; the Great Northern; the Gulf, Mobile & Northern; the Illinois Central; the Kansas City Southern; the Norfolk & Western; the Missouri Pacific; the Southern Pacific; the Texas & Pacific; and the Union Pacific. He may have "sometimes been stuck," but apparently was not stuck often. Schiff, according to his biographer, Cyrus Adler, "rarely made a mistake in business judgment." As his handling of railroad finances grew more agile and adroit, so did Kuhn, Loeb's profits increase. Solomon Loeb, who at first had distrusted railroads—they seemed too risky— looked at the firm's balance sheet and was pleased. Schiff was never a man who willingly released figures, but Otto Kahn once said that for floating and selling a modest little ten-million-dollar railroad bond issue Kuhn, Loeb was compensated with "around or about a million dollars."

And there were other compensations, several of which Schiff considered more important than silver tea services. One was the permission he received from Solomon Loeb to "deal direct" with European bankers on money matters that concerned railroads. Schiff pointed out that he was "more up-to-date" on foreign banking methods than Loeb, and, besides, the older man should be relieved of some of his "heavy responsibilities." Loeb seems to have agreed to this without considering the consequences—which were, of course, that European bankers were suddenly corresponding with Jacob H. Schiff, the junior partner, instead of with the older members of the firm.

Another was the railroad education he was receiving from a doughty little Minnesotan—who everybody said was half Indian—named James Jerome Hill. Hill was being called Vanderbilt's chief rival for the title of America's most powerful railroad owner. Hill, like Vanderbilt, was a banking client of J. P. Morgan. "But I," Jacob Schiff said significantly, "am his *friend*."

Solomon and Betty Loeb had a large, comfortable town house at 37 East Thirty-eighth Street between Madison and Park, one of the prettiest residential streets in Murray Hill. The Victorian era is not celebrated for beauty of interior decor, and the Loeb house was no exception to other rich men's houses of the period. It was filled with large, ugly, and expensive objects; one had to thread one's way across the rooms through statuary, potted palms, pedestal tables with marble tops, and ottomans. The windows and doorways were heavy with hangings of pigeon's-blood velvet, and there were quantities of plush and long gold fringe everywhere. Solomon Loeb had collected a few good period paintings, mostly of the Barbizon School and works by Bouguereau and Meissonier, but his walls were also hung with huge, stilted family portraits, plus a number of Solomon's own pencil sketches which he copied laboriously

from prints as a form of weekend recreation. Also prominently displayed was a tinted photograph of baby James Loeb, naked on a red
velvet cushion. (Even when he became a young man and protested,
Betty Loeb would not take it down.) The house smelled cozily of wax
and varnish, of Solomon's cigars and Betty's dinners.

Betty Loeb had little interest in clothes, favoring sprawly prints and
large collars which did little to flatter her expanding figure. She loved to
serve good food and she loved to eat, and her Sunday dinners had
become famous in the little crowd—nearly as much an institution as the
Seligmans' Saturdays. Her food was famous for its quality and its
quantity. Guests, leaving her groaning boards, often had to lie down for
several hours. She always explained that she served "a little extra" on
Sunday so there would be enough left over for her to serve at her ladies
luncheon on Monday, but there was usually a great deal left over after
the Monday lunches, too.

Betty Loeb was as overpowering a mother as she was a hostess.
Therese, who knew that Betty was not her real mother, always treated
her as though she were. Among Therese's possessions was a small and
faded tintype of Fanny Kuhn Loeb, the only record of her mother's
existence in the Loeb house. It stood on a candlestand beside Therese's
bed, and whenever her young friends asked her who the woman in the
picture was, she shyly replied, "A relative." (Her half-sisters and
-brothers were grown before they learned that their father had had
another wife.)

Betty presented Solomon with four more children of her own—
Morris, Guta, James, and Nina—and she tended to all five with an
almost consuming passion. Betty was so fierce about educating them
that every minute of their waking lives was organized into lessons. There
were music lessons, dancing lessons, riding lessons, tennis lessons, singing lessons, sewing lessons, German, French, Italian, Hebrew, and
Spanish lessons. The children were so hovered over by tutors, governesses, nurses, and household servants that they could do almost
nothing for themselves. Morris, who had always been dressed by nurses,
was twelve years old before he learned that there was a difference
between his left shoe and his right. Therese, at eighteen, could do
exquisite needlepoint, but was unable to button her own dress.

Betty organized the four younger children into a piano and string
quartet—Guta at the piano, Morris at the viola, James at the cello, and
Nina at the violin—and there were Sunday morning concerts in the
Loebs' Pompeiian music room. If Betty liked what the children played,
she would say, with deep satisfaction, *"Das war Musik!"* If displeased
with a performance, she would mutter, *"Hmph! Musik?"* and there
would be extra hours of practice in the afternoon. To stimulate her

children's talents, she populated her Sunday dinner tables with visiting conductors, singers, composers, dancers, and musicians. She even hired musical servants. Apologizing for a particularly inept young butler, she said, "He's very musical. I promised to give him violin lessons in the front basement."

Her youngest daughter, Nina, had once told Betty that she wanted to be a ballet dancer. The ballet lessons were intensified accordingly. But Nina fell from a goat-drawn cart one summer at the family's country place on the Hudson, seriously crippling one leg. For several years the little girl wore a heavy weight on her injured leg which was intended to stretch it to the length of the other, but which did no good. Betty took her daughter to bone specialists all over the United States and Europe— and to a few quacks as well—trying to find someone who would help Nina walk normally again. One of the many doctors had said to Betty, "Don't worry. Your daughter will dance when she's eighteen." On the morning of her eighteenth birthday, Betty said to Nina, "You're eighteen. Now you must dance." And Nina rose from her wheelchair and, in terrible pain, with tears streaming down her face, danced, to please her mother.

Business consumed Solomon Loeb's life to the extent that the children consumed Betty's. Business absorbed him so much that, writing to one of his sons at school, he absent-mindedly signed the letter, "Your loving Kuhn, Loeb & Company."

When Kuhn, Loeb first opened its Nassau Street doors, the president of the National Bank of Commerce had come to Solomon and told him that he was sure the new firm would be a success. Solomon asked him why, and the president replied, "Because you know how to say no." This blossomed into a business rule of Solomon's: "Always say no, first. You can always change your mind and say yes. But once you have said yes you are committed." He used to tell his sons, "I have become a millionaire by saying no." But he found it hard to say no to Betty. Whenever she wanted something, she approached him briskly and said, "Now, Solomon, first of all say no. Then let me tell you what I have in mind."

One of the things she had in mind in 1873, when Jacob Schiff joined the firm, was the immediate future of Therese, who had just turned twenty. Jacob found himself a frequent guest at Betty's Sunday dinners and, more frequently than he may have realized, under the scrutinous gaze of the lady of the house. Jacob and Betty Loeb hit it off well; they discussed music, art, politics, but most particularly Jacob Schiff's future plans. Jacob's brief return to Germany worried Betty. Did that indicate a rootlessness on his part, an unwillingness to settle down? Betty had said her final farewells to the old country. She was committed to

America now, and had no intention of seeing any of her children carried off to any other part of the world. But Jacob assured her that he would never move back to Germany. He did as she suggested, took out his American citizenship papers, and this convinced her.

In Jacob Schiff, Betty began to sense a kindred spirit, a will as strong as her own, and an ambition as huge as hers. Now that he was a citizen, Betty seated Jacob next to Therese, with the other young people "below the salt." From her end of the polished table, above the salt, Betty watched as Jacob and Therese conversed. Therese was cameo-faced, blue-eyed, small, and dainty, and she blushed prettily when Jacob spoke to her. Whenever Betty saw Jacob speak to the lady on his left, Betty would exercise the hostess' prerogative and "turn the conversation," so that Jacob was confronted with Therese again.

By some mysterious process, the more the two young people saw of each other, the greater were the responsibilities given to Jacob Schiff at the Kuhn, Loeb office. When Solomon Loeb came home at night and mentioned a problem at the office, Betty would inquire, "What does Mr. Schiff think? Have you asked Mr. Schiff? Why don't you let Mr. Schiff handle that?" To Therese, Betty said, "Mr. Schiff is very handsome, isn't he? And your father says he is a brilliant businessman. The girl who marries him will be very lucky."

In 1874 Jacob Schiff wrote to his mother in Frankfurt, saying: "I know you haven't any clear conception of what an American girl is like. You may think she is rather uncultured and even a feminist—but don't imagine that of the girl I've selected. She might have been brought up in the best of German families."

Clara Schiff replied, urging her son to be gentle with this girl, cautioning him to curb his famous temper because "A word spoken hastily in anger would leave lifelong scars."

A few months later, Jacob wrote:

Beloved Mother,

I feel impelled to write to you by this mail, so that if I have calculated well, this letter will reach you on my wedding day.

My feelings for you and my thoughts, now that I approach this important time of my life, I cannot express in words. You have not only borne me, you have also guided me, so that, after some youthful indiscretions, I can now say to myself that I have become a good and moral man, and I may take the wife that I have chosen for life to the altar.

You, my dear Mother, I have to thank for all this guidance, for every good advice, every moral stems from you, and you gave me these precepts in such a way that they made a lasting impression on me.

And now on my festive day, you cannot be with me but I will be thinking of you. I know that in spirit you will be with us and bless us. More I cannot say to you today. Therese and I will always be your devoted children, and, God willing, I will be very happy with my girl.

Millions of kisses to you and my sister and brothers.

Your Jacob

As usual, he had not only "calculated well"; he had calculated perfectly. Jacob Schiff and Therese Loeb were married in New York on May 6, 1875, and Jacob's letter to his mother arrived in Frankfurt in that morning's mail. The young couple moved into a large brownstone at Fifty-third Street and Park Avenue, their wedding present from Solomon and Betty Loeb.

A loving Kuhn, Loeb & Company gave Jacob another present—a full partnership in the firm. He was on his way to becoming the most renowned of all the Schiffs, to eclipsing all the others except, perhaps, his ancestor King Solomon. And, already, in the Kuhn, Loeb offices, when a decision was to be made, men had begun to whisper—out of Solomon Loeb's earshot, "Why don't we see what Mr. Schiff says?"

Solomon Loeb had made a business asset out of saying no. His son-in-law, to any money-making proposition, usually had the opposite reply.

21

THE EMERGING
GIANTS

Jacob's Seligman-watching was teaching him several things. Joseph Seligman, by nature and by instinct, had been a moneylender who operated best out of his hip pocket. When it came to selling stocks and bonds at their best possible markets, he was brilliant. He was a manipulator. But Joseph Seligman had had a blind spot. He understood figures, but not the physical products or properties the figures represented. When it came to railroads, Joseph did not even use them much, and there is evidence that he considered them an essentially unsafe means of transportation. When he and his brothers helped finance New York's first elevated railway, Joseph ruled that no two Seligmans could ride the "el" at the same time lest, in case of accident, the bank suffered a wholesale loss of partners. He had made short trips in his private car between New York and Saratoga but, with the exception of his one trip to California, made few rail journeys of any length. He had, at one point, invited a group of fifteen tycoons for a two weeks' trip in private cars to promote shares in one of his lines, but the junket was a fiasco and most of the guests left the train before the trip was over. (One story has it that the men had expected Joseph to provide them with "female companionship" during the journey, and were furious to find that the entertainment planned for the whole two weeks was nothing but "cards, chess, and crokinole.")

The rationale of railroads, which Joseph never seemed to grasp, was that railroads opened up lands which could be sold to settlers who, in turn, would provide a traffic of goods and people which would make the railroads pay. In one of his more dismal railroad ventures, however, Joseph demonstrated that he had only a rudimentary knowledge of the kind of land which settlers liked to settle. This was his famous "Aztec Land" deal where, having failed to interest investors in a large stretch of Arizona—part of his Atlantic & Pacific Railroad holdings—Joseph suggested forming the Aztec Land and Cattle Company to use the land for cattle-raising. The only trouble was that the land, a vast stretch of unirrigated desert, was no more habitable for cattle than it was for people.

Jacob Schiff, on the other hand, saw that it was not enough to be merely a financier when dealing with railroads. One had to be an organizer as well. Before backing a railroad, he insisted on going over every mile of track. He interviewed shippers and line officials, poked about in warehouses, peered into cabs of locomotives, and talked to engineers, brakemen, and conductors. He inspected freight cars and signal mechanisms, and whenever he found anything out of order he made a note of it. Schiff's memoranda to the management of his lines pointed out such details as a mile of weed-grown track that left "a poor impression" on travelers; a passenger car whose windows needed washing; a tipsy conductor; a station that needed a fresh coat of paint; a "bumpy stretch" of track. No wonder he never backed a railroad—as Joseph Seligman had—that had no place to go, or no means of crossing the Colorado River.

The Morgan group had, for good reason, been leery of dealing with the Seligmans when it came to railroads. Morgan admired Jacob Schiff's approach. Morgan, too, was an organizer who dealt not only with the financial but also with the *physical* properties of industries, and who saw to it—by direct management and through the men he put on their boards—that they were *run,* once he had an interest in them, exactly as he wanted them to be. Soon after Joseph Seligman's death, Jacob Schiff was the only German Jewish banker whom Morgan—at least occasionally, and always begrudgingly—treated as a peer.

Schiff had studied the Union Pacific Railroad and its problems for four years before embarking on a project which everyone else in Wall Street considered hopeless. The Union Pacific, having joined the Central

Pacific with Leland Stanford's golden spike, had been having trouble ever since. An early engraving shows the crew of the little line shooting their way across the plain against a herd of belligerent buffaloes. Soon the Union Pacific's human adversaries were even more ferocious, and the *coup de grâce* was delivered by the Seligmans' old client, Jay Gould. By the time Schiff became interested in the line, Gould had bled it dry and abandoned it, and the company had collapsed into bankruptcy. Among the larger of the Union Pacific's debts were $45 million owed to the United States Government, plus 6 percent interest on government bond loans which it had used as collateral to raise another million from the public. Unpaid interest had accumulated for thirty years. The line's mileage had been reduced from 8,167 to 4,469, and its subsidiary companies were in a desperate tangle of debts. There was nothing left to show for the line but what Morgan, who had repeatedly refused to help bail it out, referred to as "two streaks of rust across the plains."

It was a bad moment for railroads. Two other lines, the Santa Fe and the Northern Pacific, had collapsed within a year of each other. J. P. Morgan, meanwhile, had become the one-man ruler of American finance. All other bankers, in endeavors of any size, had to defer to him. But Morgan was actually relieved when Jacob Schiff came to see him and asked, deferentially, whether Morgan would have "any objection" if Kuhn, Loeb "had a try" at reorganizing the Union Pacific. Morgan replied cheerfully, "Go ahead!" He said that he was "through with the Union Pacific," and added, "I don't even want a financial participation." This, as it turned out, was the greatest tactical error of Morgan's career.

For several months Schiff and Kuhn, Loeb busied themselves with the task of buying up Union Pacific bonds. But Schiff began to encounter a curious and invisible wall of opposition to his plans. There were strange and unexplained delays in Congress. For no reason Schiff could fathom, a portion of the press suddenly became hostile to him. European bondholders, on various mysterious pretexts, held off from signing definite agreements. As Schiff considered the situation, he decided that there was only one financial power in America strong enough to provide this subtle kind of antagonism. He returned to Mr. Morgan's office and, with a little smile, asked whether Morgan had changed his mind. Morgan said, "I give you my word. I am not responsible. But I will find out who is." A few days later, Morgan sent for Schiff and reported, "It is that little two-bit broker, Harriman, who is interfering. Watch out for him. He's a sharper."

"Ned" Harriman was more than that. He was one of the most disagreeable men of his period, and one of the most disliked. He was small and skinny and stooped, with watery eyes behind thick-lensed glasses. He had a prison pallor, a frightful cough, foul breath, and a nose that dripped. He was perennially ailing of one disease or another, and he spoke in a voice so low that it was rarely audible. When it could be heard, it had nothing pleasant to say. Harriman was incapable of tact. He never smiled. James Stillman of the National City Bank had called him "not a safe man to do business with." Yet Harriman's relatively small railroad line, the Illinois Central, was one of the best-run and most profitable in the country.

Up to that point, E. H. Harriman had been regarded primarily as a nuisance on Wall Street. He owned a small second mortgage on a few Erie Railroad bonds, and had once had the audacity to telephone the Erie's executive offices demanding that the Chicago express make a special stop at Goshen, New York, so that he could attend the races there. The request was curtly refused. Harriman, however, who knew that the express would be flagged at Goshen if passengers were boarding there for Buffalo or points west, telephoned a minion and had him buy a ticket from Goshen to Chicago. Harriman boarded the crack train at Jersey City, and when the train ground to a halt at Goshen, trainmen were surprised to find no Goshen-to-Chicago passenger but, instead, a debarking Ned Harriman. For exploits like these, he was distrusted and resented.

When Jacob Schiff first went to see Harriman, his approach was tactful. "We're having trouble reorganizing the Union Pacific, Mr. Harriman," Schiff said. "We seem to be meeting opposition. We wonder —is this opposition coming from you?"

"I'm your man," said Harriman.

"Why?" asked Schiff.

"Because I plan to reorganize the Union Pacific myself," said Harriman. "I want it for my Illinois Central."

"How do you plan to get it?" Schiff asked.

Harriman replied, "With my Illinois Central, I can borrow money more cheaply than you can."

The temerity of the strange little man impressed Schiff, who then said, "Perhaps we can work together."

"Perhaps," Harriman is said to have replied. "If I can be chairman of the executive committee."

Schiff flatly refused and departed. The opposition to his plans grew even stronger. Soon he appeared before Harriman again. "Suppose," Jacob Schiff said, "we put you on the executive committee of the line. Then, if it turns out you're the strongest man, you'll be the chairman in the end."

"Fine," said Harriman. "I'm with you. And of course I will be the strongest man."

Schiff's joining forces with Harriman was the beginning of a collaboration that would last for more than twenty years, during which the two men were in almost daily contact, which would lead to the amassing of the greatest single railroad fortune in the world—and which would lead the great J. P. Morgan, who referred to Harriman with such epithets as "punk" and "pad-shover," and who often called Jacob Schiff "that foreigner," to acknowledge both men as "my dear friends."

Harriman's Illinois Central did indeed provide a quick source of credit, but for a project as big as reviving the Union Pacific, Schiff saw immediately that foreign capital would be needed. He turned to a man who had been one of his boyhood friends in Germany, and who was now a London financier very nearly on a par with the Rothschilds, Sir Ernest Cassel.

Cassel was an unlikely sort of man for Schiff to have as a friend. He had become an elegant and an epicure, though his background was similar to Schiff's. Cassel was also, like August Belmont, a complete apostate of his faith. Schiff could be quite tiresome on the subject of religious observances. Schiff despised Belmont, whom he once called "an oyster, without a shell." Yet the very Belmont-like Sir Ernest became Schiff's chief financial contact in London and, as the years went by, his personal arbiter of taste in clothes, painting, furniture, and even table linen and silverware. Apparently the two never discussed religion.

If Joseph Seligman had virtually invented international banking in America, it was Jacob Schiff who took the invention, refined it, and made it an art, and his alliance with Sir Ernest Cassel is another example of Jacob's more up-to-date, streamlined approach. Joseph Seligman had devised a Rothschildesque, one-for-all, all-for-one, family-business setup, with a brother stationed in each important European capital. It had worked well enough for the Seligmans, particularly in the days before the radiotelegraph and the Atlantic cable, when blood ties across the sea with men you could trust were essential. By Jacob Schiff's time, however, this had become an old-fashioned, countrified system. In this faster, more competitive age, it was too rigid, too inflexible.

By moving as a unit, the Seligman family complex moved slowly and awkwardly. It was forever having to stop what it was doing to assist some brother who had made an expensive error, or to buy out a brother-in-law, or to help William in Paris buy his wife a diamond necklace. After Joseph's death, the Seligmans belatedly realized this. In 1897 the remaining brothers drafted a "Family Liquidation Agreement," not an agreement to liquidate the family but a plan to separate the New York, Paris, London, and Frankfurt firms from one another, and to divide their assets among the managing partners. The amount involved was $7,831,175.64, and it was portioned out in varying amounts with the largest share—$1,375,444.47—going to Isaac in London. But apparently nostalgia for the old, more familiar way of doing business quickly set in. The brothers had no sooner separated their assets than they began buying back in on one another—William, Leopold, Henry, and Isaac each buying a 10.4 percent interest in the New York house (for $800,000 each), and the New York house purchasing an interest in all three European houses. The Seligmans continued in their tight-knit way, causing Jacob Schiff to smile and say that, "The Seligmans have never really left their little family-village business in Bavaria."

Schiff distrusted such "standing alliances." He liked to be able to select alliances to suit the occasion. Jacob had brothers, too. (His brother Herman had gone to London and into banking, while the youngest Schiff boy, Ludwig, had remained in Frankfurt as a stockbroker.) But Jacob preferred informal contacts with correspondents and business friends, and this system enabled him to move unencumbered through the complicated reaches of international finance. "He was a man," said one associate, "who moved fast because he always traveled light."

He always carried his valuables with him, however. For instance, Sir Ernest had access to the highest levels of British financial and political power. He often lunched with the Chancellor of the Exchequer, and he even had the ear of the Throne. Now that Cassel shared Schiff's and Harriman's interest in the Union Pacific reorganization, bankers' ears pricked up on both sides of the Atlantic. Within three days of the news of Cassel's participation, Schiff and Harriman had received $40 million worth of pledges, and suddenly the project which had seemed "ridiculous" to Wall Street seemed distinctly less so.

Though Schiff knew a great deal about railroads, he discovered that Harriman was a railroading genius. After getting him his financing, he gave Harriman his head. The Schiff-Harriman group bought the Union Pacific on November 2, 1897, and Harriman was elected to the line's board of directors in December.

He then began a long struggle with his other board members for permission to spend $25 million for rolling stock, track, and improvements. It was an unheard-of sum at the time, and, once more, Wall Street soured on Harriman and called him a fool. But Schiff and Cassel backed him, and at last he prevailed. While a doubting Wall Street watched, the fortunes of the Union Pacific began to change. Schiff soon granted Harriman the chairmanship he wanted, but, as a good banker should, Schiff retained a position close behind the driver's seat. Presently the line had risen out of debt, and was even showing a profit.

But throughout the whole Union Pacific reorganization there was one question that puzzled certain observers. As Harriman, the ex-office boy and son of a poor Episcopal clergyman, was becoming one of the dominant figures in American railroads, his only rival of any importance in the field was the little Minnesotan, James J. Hill. While Harriman had been building up the Union Pacific, Hill, backed by Morgan, had been busily buying up the competing Northern Pacific. How long, people wondered, could both Hill and Harriman remain friends of Jacob Schiff?

22

MR. SCHIFF

VS.

MR. LOEB

If Jacob Schiff liked loose and informal business relationships which could be severed quickly and picked up again as he saw fit, he was correspondingly rigid and unyielding in his home. As Cyrus Adler, in his biography of Schiff, wrote, "He was accessible to all people on all subjects, though not easily persuaded when his mind was fixed."*

As a husband and father, he often seemed heartless. Those nearest to him, including his wife, had trouble feeling close to him. Therese Loeb Schiff was accustomed to discipline (from Betty) and to daintiness (her father's toy child, she could not even arrange a bowl of flowers without a

---

* This is as close as Dr. Adler lets himself come to an adverse comment on Schiff's character. Otherwise, his book is all praise, and one can see why. Schiff paid him to write it, and, when Schiff died, one of the items in his estate was six dollars in royalties on the book.

servant's help). But she had also been brought up to believe that her father was the final authority on any question that dealt with money. It was a little while before she fully understood the battle that was taking place in the office downtown. When her husband came home at night, he sometimes told her of developments, involving long lists of railroads whose names she never could keep straight, and plans. And sometimes she would interrupt him to ask, in her soft voice, "Well, what does my father think of it?" The question always seemed to make him angry, and so she learned to stop asking, and to listen to his evening discourse in respectful, if bewildered, silence.

There was almost nothing that Solomon Loeb and Jacob Schiff agreed upon. They did not agree on religion. Solomon was a professed agnostic, and there had been no religious observances at all in the Loeb house on Thirty-eighth Street. All this began to change when Jacob entered the family. He was the most "orthodox" of all the young German Jews of his generation, but with this he mixed a ritualistic liberalism which he had concocted for himself. He disapproved of the Loebs' amorphous attitudes. He lectured his father-in-law on his shortcomings as a Jew, and, though Solomon grumbled, Betty Loeb urged her husband to unbend a little for the sake of peace in the family. The nonreligious Loeb household became outwardly very pious.

Nor did Schiff and Loeb see eye to eye on spas, a serious matter for gentlemen of the era, and the arguments about which cure performed the greater service to the liver occasionally became heated. Mr. Loeb preferred the waters at Carlsbad. Schiff preferred Marienbad or Gastein—both, in those days, considered "grander" than Carlsbad. Whenever he mentioned Marienbad or Gastein, he enjoyed turning to his father-in-law to say, "I suppose you'll be at Carlsbad again—with the bourgeoisie." Both Solomon and Betty Loeb fretted privately over what seemed to them their son-in-law's—and now their daughter's—expanding taste for grandeur. (Once, after one of the young Schiffs' trips to Europe, which had included a sojourn at Marienbad, Betty Loeb asked Therese if she had bought anything in Paris. Therese replied, *"Nur ein einfaches schwarzes samt Kleid"*—"Only a simple black velvet dress"—and Betty Loeb was aghast at the thought that her daughter had become so elegant as to use the adjective "simple" in connection with a fabric as rich as velvet.)

But it was in the Kuhn, Loeb offices that the two men's differences were most pronounced. It was a battle of banking philosophies, and of generations. Solomon was cautious. Jacob was bold. Solomon was older and contented with his firm's success. Jacob was young and wanted to bend the firm to his will. Jacob made it a point to get to the office earlier than his father-in-law. There he started each day writing dozens of memoranda in small, meticulous longhand—plans, proposals, suggestions, ideas—and when Solomon Loeb arrived, he found his desk strewn with these notes. Some of Jacob's notions were too intricate for Solomon to grasp, and he would have Jacob sent in, and the two would try to discuss Jacob's ideas—Solomon reminding Jacob of the philosophy ("Always say no . . .") that had made him successful. When they emerged from their meetings, Jacob Schiff looked angry and Solomon Loeb looked tired.

Like so many self-made men, Solomon Loeb had prided himself on knowing, at any given time, just what was going on in every corner of his company. After all, he and his first partners had been retailers. As bankers, they had preferred to finance manufacturers and merchants whose operations they understood. Now the firm's railroad operations had extended Solomon's empire beyond his reach. As he studied the firm's figures he found it increasingly necessary to call for Jacob to explain. And Solomon had begun to worry about his health. After a day at the office, he would lie on a velvet sofa with his head in Betty's ample lap while she bathed his forehead with a handkerchief dipped in cologne. One morning Solomon called for Jacob. The clerk, as usual, hurried to Jacob's office to say, "Mr. Loeb would like to see you." But this time, without looking up, Jacob Schiff said, "Tell Mr. Loeb he may see me in my office."

The year was 1881. The Age of Seligman was over. While uptown Jewish society in New York might continue to argue about Jews of "the Seligman type" as opposed to those of "the Nathan type," there was no doubt among financiers in Wall Street that there was a basic difference between the Seligman and the Schiff types. American finance had entered the great Age of Schiff. Today, as a result, when the Kuhn, Loeb partners gather for a formal photograph, they do not assemble in front of the portraits of Abraham Kuhn, who looks wistful, or Solomon Loeb, who looks dismayed, but in front of the huge, mantel-crowning portrait of Jacob H. Schiff, who looks regal.

Early in the 1880's, scarcely ten years after Jacob Schiff became a partner in his firm, Solomon Loeb began to do what many in his family still call "a noble thing." Like all noble things, it was not an easy thing. But it had the blessing of Betty, who had helped him guide the fortune of Kuhn, Loeb from the beginning. He began to draw a distinction between "projects" and "policy." He would remain interested, he said, in Kuhn, Loeb projects. But policy would become the bailiwick of his son-in-law, Jacob Schiff. In effect, Solomon Loeb had abdicated. Though he continued to come to the office each day, he took the position of a silent partner. Jacob was given what he had always wanted—the reins of a company, a bank of his own.

One of the first things he did was to move its offices to larger and grander quarters, across the street in the new Mutual Life Insurance Building at 30 Nassau Street.

23

PORTRAIT OF
A FATHER

Therese Loeb Schiff tried to adjust herself to her husband's new leadership of the Loeb family. She tried to adjust herself also to her husband's piety. In their house on Fifty-third Street, Jacob paced daily through the rooms, prayer book in hand, reciting his prayers. Once, during this ritual, Therese noticed that he had placed, against the open pages of the prayer book, the daily stock market report. She made the mistake of chiding him about this. He was not amused. Jacob Schiff was not easily amused at anything. Therese learned never to approach her husband in a spirit of levity. She began spending her afternoons with Betty Loeb in the house on Thirty-eighth Street. When Jacob appeared at the end of the day and asked her, "Well, what did you do today?" Therese would reply shyly, "I went home."

Jacob's and Therese's first child, a girl whom they named Frieda, was born prematurely, scarcely eight months after they were married. This was an embarrassment to Jacob, and he blamed Therese for the untimely birth. Shortly after, Jacob stopped by the Loebs' house for a duty visit with his in-laws. While there, a friend of the Loebs, attempting to make a joke—though he should have known better—said to Jacob, slyly, "I want to congratulate you on the appropriate name you've given your baby—*Früh-Da*" ("early arrival" in German). Furious, Jacob strode out of the house and back to his own, where he demanded that Therese change the baby's name to something else. Therese wept. She loved the name, had selected it herself, and the initial "F" was in memory of her real mother, Fanny Kuhn Loeb. Jacob finally let her have her way, but he never spoke to the Loebs' friend again.

Their second child, a boy born a year after Frieda, whom Jacob and Therese named Mortimer, was even more of a problem to Jacob, though none of the family was ever sure why. Nothing young Morti did seemed to please his father. Jacob Schiff was of the old school when it came to punishments, and Morti was spanked for the slightest infraction of a rule. Spanking-Morti sessions became so commonplace in the Schiff household that the family began delicately referring to them as "seances." The ladies in the drawing room always tried to talk up more brightly and animatedly whenever they heard Morti's muffled screams from the seance upstairs. Early in life, Morti developed the tactic of befriending the servants, who sneaked trays of food up the nursery to him, to replace the meals he had been ordered to bed without. The servants became Morti's way of finding "home."

Jacob Schiff disliked the house at 57 East Fifty-third Street which his father-in-law had given him as a wedding present. He may have been justified, because certain of the Loebs—though not Solomon—seemed to treat the house in an annoyingly proprietary way. In the sitting room, for instance, there hung a tall mirror between two long, damask-draped windows, and from the time that she was able to walk baby Frieda loved to pose and pirouette before her reflection in the glass. Solomon's son, Frieda's Uncle Morris, announced that such vanity was unbecoming in a woman, even though the woman was still a toddler, and one day Morris Loeb appeared in his brother-in-law's house and completely covered the mirror with sheets of newspaper.

Jacob sold the Fifty-third Street house and bought another, larger house on West Fifty-seventh Street, which the family lived in only briefly. A neighbor built a wing which cut off Jacob's light, and he sold the Fifty-seventh Street house to Abraham Wolff, a Kuhn, Loeb partner who evidently didn't mind the gloom. Jacob then advised Therese that he had bought a lot at the corner of Seventy-second Street and Riverside Drive, where he intended to build.

At the news of this plan, Therese sat down and cried. Tears were her only defense against her husband. Poor shy Therese had very few friends—all first-generation Americans, all German Jewish, all wives of men in the little "banking crowd." The women's outlook was European and middle-class, their manners stiff and studiedly correct; they conversed in German, calling each other *"Frau,"* and never used first names. They paid calls and had teas; each woman had her regular day at home. (Therese Schiff's had become Tuesday.) They discussed their steamer crossings and their servants, and whether their deliveries had been "hard" or "easy." It was provincial and inbred, but too formal and self-conscious to be really intimate, yet these were Therese's friends. They lived in the East Forties to the Seventies, between Park Avenue and Fifth, and saw each other daily on their ritual rounds of shopping, visiting, and card-leaving. To Therese, being sent west to the edge of the Hudson meant that she would never see her friends again. If they visited her, they would have to come by carriage, and Therese was sure that none of them would bother. Besides, how far away it was from "home"!

Jacob relented and sold the Riverside lot, which later became the site of the Schwab mansion. He had eyed Fifth Avenue before, unquestionably the best address in New York for men of stature. In 1880, while the rest of the crowd mourned the death of Joe Seligman, Jacob Schiff decided to make the great social leap, to 932 Fifth Avenue at Seventy-fourth Street.

A move the size of this one clearly indicated some sort of celebration, and Jacob went busily to work planning an elaborate housewarming party. It must be given, he said, "At once!"—as soon as 932 was finished. Jacob was Belmontian in his approach to entertaining. He planned the menu, picked the guests, chose the wines, selected the flowers, and diagrammed the dinner table for the placement of cards. Therese, quite unsure of herself socially, was happy to let him, and was even grateful when a gown from Worth's arrived that he had picked out for her to wear. All New York's German Jewish elite were invited with notes that Jacob dictated to Therese.

Then tragedy struck. On the day the Schiffs moved to their new house, little Morti—displeasing his father again—came down with whooping cough. A large and thoroughly undignified sign was nailed to the front door of 932 Fifth Avenue. It read: "CONTAGION. KEEP OUT." The party was canceled.

Frieda Schiff later wrote that 932 was "a house full of horrors," heavily damasked, heavily marbled, even more cluttered with late Victorian furniture and *objets d'art* than the Solomon Loebs', whose decor Jacob seemed quite consciously to be trying to outdo and bring to its knees. Sir Ernest Cassel had not yet become Jacob Schiff's decorating mentor. Jacob had started collecting paintings, but he was not yet an experienced collector. Frieda wrote: "Father used to cough or give signals at the wrong time" when he went to auctions, and ended up with a great many things he hadn't planned to buy. He was required to find house room, for instance, for two enormous Chinese vases he hadn't wanted; they went into the dining room. (In the dark bowels of these urns, little Frieda and Morti sometimes hid from their father.) There was also a bronze bas-relief of the Schiff children by Augustus Saint-Gaudens, memorable to Frieda and Morti chiefly because they had to pose for it through an entire Christmas holiday.

At 932 Fifth Avenue the Schiff family life congealed into an unvarying pattern. The day began with the master of the house being helped into his overcoat by Joseph, the Schiff major-domo. "Do I need an umbrella today, Joseph?" Mr. Schiff would inquire. If Joseph replied, "Yes, I think so, sir," Jacob would answer, "Then I shan't take one." It was a rule of Jacob's: Joseph was invariably wrong about the weather. (Joseph, meanwhile, dabbled in the stock market quite successfully, and used to point out that he never took Mr. Schiff's advice, either; he liked to remind the Schiff children that he was rich enough to employ his own butler—and might, if he wasn't treated properly.)

While the exchange with Joseph was going on, the children were ushered by nurses into the front hall to say good-bye to their father. Jacob then inspected them, paying particular attention to the cleanliness of noses and fingernails, and, if satisfied, presented his bearded cheek to be kissed. Nurses then pressed a clean white hanky into the hand of each child. From the front door, waving their handkerchiefs and crying, "Good-bye, Pa! Good-bye, Pa!" the children watched Jacob Schiff descend the brownstone steps. A believer in walking, Jacob often walked as far downtown as Fourteenth Street before taking a cab.

When his children were old enough for school, he insisted that they walk. He disapproved of Mayer Lehman, who drove his children to school in a carriage. Father and children departed the Schiff house together. From Seventy-fourth and Fifth they proceeded to Fifty-ninth and Sixth, where Morti was deposited at Dr. Sachs's. Then Frieda and her father continued on to Forty-fourth Street, where Brearley was. It was a mile-and-a-half walk for Frieda. After school the children were met by their French governess, who escorted them on the long walk home. The children were required to converse in French all the way. There followed lunch with the governess, and then "afternoon lessons," which were private. There was riding in the park on Mondays and Thursdays, piano Tuesdays and Fridays, Bible on Wednesdays. Every morning from 7:30 to 8:00, behind the closed shutters of the music room, the children practiced their piano. Because her father thought she was overweight, fencing lessons were prescribed for Frieda. But, because he thought the dashing Spanish fencing instructor had a "devilish gleam" in his eye, Mr. Schiff directed that the French governess sit in on the class. (It was the governess who noticed the gleam and suggested this arrangement, and the fencing master's eye may have been on her and not little Frieda; the governess and the Spaniard were often seen in animated conversation, and were once discovered stretched out on the downstairs bowling alley where they explained they had "tripped and fallen.")

Dinner at 932 was at 6:30 sharp. Anyone arriving at table later than that missed his meal. Jacob insisted that his bowling alley be used. After dinner he asked, "Now, who will bowl with me?" Both children hated bowling, and this question was invariably met with silence. Jacob would then rise and, with a tap on the shoulder, select his bowling companion, and the two would descend to the alley. (The companion, of course, had the job of setting up the pins.)

Fridays were family nights. The Seligmans were in possession of Saturdays, and Sundays belonged to the Loebs. Once, when invited to a Friday night function elsewhere, Jacob replied, "I have made it a rule to spend Friday evening exclusively with my family, and I can under no circumstances vary from this."

Jacob Schiff's personality seemed to add a new rigidity to New York's German Jewish social life. On Friday evenings the family gathered in the drawing room in a circle where the patriarch blessed them each. Then he read a short service in German, after which the group descended quietly to dinner. At table Jacob Schiff pronounced a grace which he liked to say he had composed himself, though actually it was a pastiche of Talmudic blessings:

> Our God and Father,
> Thou givest food to every living being.
> Thou has not only given us life,
> Thou also givest our daily bread to sustain it.
> Continue to bless us with Thy mercy
> So that we may be able to share our own plenty
> With those less fortunate than ourselves,
> Blessed be Thy name forevermore. Amen.

He always stressed "With those less fortunate than ourselves."

E. H. Harriman was an antisocial man who never accepted invitations to dine, but James J. Hill was just the opposite, and was a frequent dinner guest at 932 Fifth Avenue. Hill was never given the nod by polite society, but Jacob Schiff admired him for the way, after the Panic of 1873, he had pulled a railroad out of a $27-million hole. Hill liked to talk, and when he started he was hard to stop. Ten o'clock was Jacob Schiff's bedtime, and at ten Joseph would bring his master his orange juice on a silver tray and say discreetly, "Mr. Hill, your taxi is waiting." "Send it away!" Hill would say airily, and launch into another anecdote while Jacob Schiff sat looking pained and discomfited.

Hill's breezy manner displeased Jacob on other occasions. Hill habitually carried with him a small bag of uncut stones which he played with nervously as he talked, like a Middle Easterner's worry-beads. One evening Therese Schiff admired one of the stones which she thought particularly pretty, and Hill gave it to her. She approached her husband and, in her small, soft voice, said, "Look what Mr. Hill gave me." Jacob looked at it and said, "Only I give jewels to my wife. Give it back." She did as he told her.

Everybody did. "Though small in size," said one of the family, "his presence always seemed to fill the largest doorway when he appeared. You only had to look once into those blue eyes to know he was someone to be reckoned with."

Schiff would have very much appreciated having Hill as a banking client. But Hill remained steadfast in his loyalty to Morgan, even though Schiff enjoyed reminding Hill, over their cigars, "I am very nearly as big as he," and once said, "Morgan may not be as big as he thinks he is." Certainly Schiff's alliance with E. H. Harriman was making him rich. In just three years since the reorganization of the Union Pacific, the line had become one of the greatest successes of the age. It had paid back all its debts, with interest, had unencumbered assets of $210 million within its system, and no less than two *billion* dollars' worth of outside investments which Schiff had helped place. Morgan at this point clearly regretted having relinquished his interest in the tracks he had called "two streaks of rust."

Those tracks were permitting Jacob Schiff to be one of the first in the German Jewish crowd to maintain not one but two summer homes—at Sea Bright, on the Jersey shore, and in Bar Harbor, Maine. (For all his devoutly religious views, Jacob always liked to step boldly into gentile areas where other Jews chose not to tread.) There was an unvarying schedule for opening and closing these houses. June and July were spent at Sea Bright. Then, on the last Thursday of July, the family had an early supper and boarded their private car—usually one of E. H. Harriman's cars of the Union Pacific—parents, children, nurses, governess, maids, and at least sixty pieces of luggage, many of them trunks. The car was presided over by Madison, the Schiffs' chef, and a helper. Sometimes a second private car was needed. The family would travel overnight to Ellsworth, Maine, then disembark and board a boat to Bar Harbor. The horses, meanwhile, were traveling, along with grooms, tack, and equipment, by boat from New Jersey. Once in Bar Harbor, everyone rested, and no wonder.

They stayed in Bar Harbor exactly a month. Then, in September, the whole process reversed itself, and everyone went back to Sea Bright again for another month. In October it was back to the city for the winter. If this schedule sounds arduous, it is well to remember that this was before regular visits to Florida were added to the Schiffs' yearly itinerary. Alternate summers, of course, were spent in Europe. If the first generation of Seligmans had taught the crowd how to do it, Schiff as the leader of his generation was teaching them how to do it better.

Considering the hugeness of the scale on which Jacob Schiff lived, while financing E. H. Harriman's railroads was making him steadily richer, it was strange that during these years his penuriousness was becoming more pronounced. He was miserly about the use of the telephone in his house and kept a little notebook on the stand beside it where each person was required to enter calls. "Telephone calls cost money!" he kept reminding them, and at the end of each month he carefully compared the calls in the notebook with those on the bill.

He was financial adviser to, and on the board of, the Western Union Company, and this gave him a franking privilege allowing him to send wires free. Naturally he preferred sending telegrams to telephoning. Each evening, during their summer months at Sea Bright, the two children were expected to dress up—with white cotton gloves and sailor hats secured by elastics under the chin—to meet their august parent when he arrived on the ferry *Asbury Park.* If, however, Schiff changed his mind and decided to take the train, he would send a telegram. These wires always arrived long after the family had departed for the ferry dock, and Schiff would be left waiting, unmet, at the station—furious.

Frieda and Morti were given their first spending allowances as children during one of their biennial summers in Germany. They were allowed fifty pfennig a week. When they returned to New York that fall, their father explained that this was computed at twelve and a half cents in U.S. currency, and that the children would therefore have to keep track of which was the twelve-cent week and which was the thirteen-cent week. At the end of the month he went over their accounts looking for discrepancies. (By the time she was engaged to be married, Frieda's allowance had been gradually increased until she was receiving a dollar a week, out of which her father required that she set one-tenth aside for the Fresh Air Fund.)

Mr. Schiff was a great maker of conditions. It was his tactic in both business and human relations: he seldom offered anything outright. There was always some sort of proviso attached. Sometimes his conditions were too stiff to be acceptable. But at other times they revealed an odd sort of logic. There was, for instance, the strange case of young Morti Schiff's long struggle to receive the kind of education he wanted.

Morti was an excellent scholar. He was first in his class at Dr. Sachs's school nearly all the time, but this did not delight his father. What Jacob Schiff considered most important was that Morti receive a grade of "excellent" in that marking category called "deportment." Like any boy, Morti did not always deport himself to perfection, and, regardless of his other grades, whenever his little gray report book showed a lapse in this respect, Morti and his father had another "seance" in the bathroom at 932 Fifth. After the spanking, Jacob Schiff would declare, "My son doesn't have to lead in his studies. But that *my son* shouldn't know how to behave—that's unpardonable!"

Morti finished school with honors when he was barely sixteen, but his father maintained that he was "not ready" for college. There then began a curious correspondence with the Reverend Doctor Endicott Peabody, headmaster of Groton. He would very much like, Jacob Schiff wrote Peabody, to enroll his son at the school for one year—but on one condition. He pointed out that Morti had been brought up "a conscious Jew," and therefore would have to be excused from all religious and chapel activities. There followed what the family described as "an exchange of dignified and amiable letters," which ended up with "mutual agreement" that Groton was not the school for Morti.

Now, why Jacob Schiff would even for a moment have suspected that Groton *might* have been the school for Morti is, at first glance, unfathomable. The year was 1893, and Groton was only ten years old. It had been founded by Peabody on the theory that the traditions and tenets of the Episcopal Church, combined with those of the English public school, would be most likely to produce ideal "Christian gentlemen" in the United States. The words "Christian," "Protestant Episcopal," and "Church of England" reappeared dozens of times throughout the school's prospectus; its first board of trustees included two bishops of the state of Massachusetts and a distinguished assortment of other gentile Easterners, including J. Pierpont Morgan. Schiff must have known these things.

It had been sixteen years before, in the summer of 1877 (the very month, coincidentally, of Morti's birth), when the episode of Joseph Seligman at the Grand Union had created such a storm in the press and among the clergy. Did Schiff have a notion of making a test case of his own over prep school admission policies? Schiff definitely felt that he had inherited Joseph Seligman's mantle as New York's leading Jew. If a test case was to be made, who better than Schiff to make it?

At the height of the Seligman-Hilton affair, there were unpleasant hints that wishes for business revenge were as much behind the affair as anti-Semitism. In the Schiff-Peabody exchange Wall Street rivalries may also have been involved. Peabody had close connections on the Street;

he had worked in Wall Street himself for a while, and his father had been a partner in Morgan's London office. Morgan himself was a cornerstone of the school. Jacob Schiff may have thought that Kuhn, Loeb could gain if its gentile rival—Morgan—could be discredited and embarrassed over an issue such as Groton.

Perhaps, if Schiff did briefly consider creating a Seligman-like affair, he remembered that the Seligman affair had ended in a thoroughly undignified and unamiable way. Schiff cared a great deal about deportment. Or perhaps he was not quite ready to do battle with the great Morgan.

Morti had never wanted to go to Groton; all he wanted to do was to go to Harvard. And so, to Morti's distress, as soon as his father abandoned the Groton idea, he announced that he wanted Morti to go to Amherst.

Schiff's opposition to Harvard is even harder to fathom than his flirtation with Groton. Harvard had already become something of a tradition in the family (Solomon Loeb's boys had gone there). Charles W. Eliot, Harvard's president, was a close personal friend of Schiff's, who admired Eliot enormously, quoted him endlessly (the heavily accented Schiff was fond of saying, "As President Eliot said to me in that peculiar New England accent of his . . ."), and the two men were frequent summer hiking companions in the hills around Bar Harbor. Yet he was adamant. Harvard, he said, was "too large," and "too many wealthy boys" attended it, both of which assertions showed a strange lack of understanding of what Harvard really offered in those days. Desperately, Morti wrote to President Eliot and asked him to intercede with his father, and Eliot tactfully mentioned to Jacob that he hoped Morti would "give a thought to Harvard." Huffily, Jacob replied that it was out of the question.

Jacob said that Morti was showing signs of being "too extravagant," and that Harvard would make Morti *more* extravagant. But Morti protested against Amherst so strongly that his father relented—part way. He offered a condition. If Morti would spend a year at Amherst, and could prove while there that he was not being extravagant, he could transfer to Harvard the following year. Morti agreed, and set off for Amherst where he installed himself in a boardinghouse for $3.50 a week; even students on full scholarships had better accommodations than his. The boardinghouse was a fair distance from the campus, and Morti wrote to his father asking if he could buy a bicycle. Jacob said yes, and Morti bought himself a shiny two-wheeler.

When Morti came home in June, he reminded his father of his promise: next year could be spent at Harvard. But Jacob shook his head sadly, and said, "No, my son—you proved just what I feared. You were extravagant at Amherst." Almost in tears, Morti demanded to know *how* he had been extravagant. "You bought a new bicycle," Jacob said. "You could have bought a secondhand one."

"You didn't *say* it had to be secondhand!" said Morti.

"I thought you understood," said his father.

In the fall Morti went back to Amherst. He was taken into a Greek-letter fraternity where the boys were trying to raise money for a billiard table. Morti wrote his father, asking if he could make a contribution. Jacob Schiff wrote back in an unusually expansive mood, saying that he would be happy to pay for the entire table—and a billiard table of the very finest make—if, in return, the boys would agree never to play billiards for money. The boys would make no such agreement, they never got their table, and Morti's popularity in the fraternity was somewhat lessened. This sort of thing went on all the time.

When Morti came home for the Christmas holidays that year, he came down with scarlet fever and so had to miss most of the balance of his sophomore year at Amherst. Even so, in June he made one final request. Could he spend his *junior* year at Harvard? "It was then," wrote Morti's sister Frieda, "that my father decided that Morti was ready for business."

Schiff asked his friend Hill to send Morti out to Duluth to work on the road gang of the Great Nothern Railroad, to learn railroad "from the bottom"—a fitting occupation for a bright young scholar with tendencies toward extravagance. Morti did this for a while. When his father decided Morti had learned enough railroading, Morti was sent to Europe to learn banking from the same level. He began working as an apprentice in various banking houses Jacob Schiff selected—first for the firm of Samuel Montagu in London (where Sir Ernest Cassel kindly took Morti under his wing) and then to M. M. Warburg & Company in Hamburg—moving further and further away from Cambridge, Massachusetts. When Morti spent his twenty-first birthday in Hamburg with the Warburgs, he realized that he would never get to Harvard.

Periodically, Jacob Schiff traveled to Europe to check on Morti's progress. Once, at a London party, Jacob encountered his son, who was color-blind like his Grandfather Loeb, wearing a lavender-gray suit and a yellow-gray topcoat. In front of two hundred assembled guests, Jacob Schiff told Morti to march right home and change his clothes and not to come back until he was properly attired. Of course Morti did as he was told.

Through all this Morti Schiff seems to have maintained an almost superhuman cheerfulness. Why did he put up with so much? "Morti," said his sister Frieda, whose experiences with her father were sometimes even more bewildering, "was passionately devoted to our father."

24

THE MITTELWEG
WARBURGS

Frieda Schiff, like her brother Morti, wanted to please her father. It wasn't always easy, for one of Jacob Schiff's specialities was demonstrating the shortcomings of others.

One of his philanthropies was the Young Men's Hebrew Association (Schiff had presented the Y.M.H.A. with its first permanent home at 861 Lexington Avenue, complete with gymnasium, library, clubrooms and classrooms), and this had led to his interest in its feminine counterpart, the Y.W.H.A. When plans were being drawn up for a building, Jacob promised a gift of $25,000 on the condition—again—that $200,000 more be contributed by others by January of the following year. The job of raising this extra sum was given to Frieda as a project, her first fund-raising experience of any importance. She went at it with diligence, but by the first of December she had contacted everyone she knew and she was still $18,000 short of her goal.

She knew that her father was a man of his word, and she was, understandably, "in a terrible state." She could envision the entire Y.W.H.A. project collapsing because the condition could not be met. To make her state even more terrible, her father went out of his way to remind her of his condition in mid-December. "You know," he told her, "I have it in writing that I shall not give the $25,000 unless the fund is completed." After days on the telephone she began to have sleepless nights.

"On January first," she wrote, "I was on the verge of despair"—still $18,000 short. Then she received a letter from her father. It was not addressed to her as a daughter, or even as a woman. It was addressed simply to "Chairman of Y.W.H.A. Building Committee." Writing to her as if she were a stranger, Jacob Schiff advised the Chairman that he had "persuaded Mrs. Schiff to give $18,000 in memory of her brother." The check was enclosed.

"It was absolutely typical of him," Frieda wrote later, "a man of his word, but his heart got around his word, and made it all legal." He was actually ashamed of letting his heart show. Doing it his way, he had provided just a peek of the heart without, as the English say, "letting down the side," or, as the Germans say, becoming "unbuttoned."

Not all episodes had such happy endings for Frieda. In 1894 she was having a particularly trying year. Her father had insisted that she could not make her debut until she was eighteen, and, since her birthday was in February, this meant she would miss the entire winter debutante season. Her best friend, Addie Wolff (the daughter of Abraham Wolff, another Kuhn, Loeb partner), was having her party at Sherry's, but Jacob Schiff would not let Frieda go. He said, "If you are seen in one place, you'll have more invitations. We'll have the same scene each time, and I can't make exceptions. For your own good, I don't want you to come out." So Frieda stayed home.

He often forbade her to do things "for her own good," and he had become obsessive about what he called her "innocence." In his determination that even her mind should remain virginal, he carefully arranged her life so that she would meet neither men nor girls her own age. He kept her busy with volunteer work and fund-raising. Anders Zorn painted Frieda Schiff's portrait during that lonely winter of her eighteenth year, and her dewy innocence shines from the canvas. She was high-cheekboned, with a thin, patrician nose, clear-eyed, dark-haired, slim-waisted, dressed in pink. She had one advantage to outweigh some of the drawbacks that went with being Jacob Schiff's daughter: she was beautiful.

She was permitted to have an eighteenth-birthday party, memorable because a musical teen-ager named Walter Damrosch sang and acted

out a parody on Wagner's Rhine Maidens while standing in a tin tub full
of water. But otherwise the year had been unexceptional and unreward-
ing. She had had no experience with boys whatever, beyond stiff and
formal conversations with male partners at her father's stiff and formal
dinner parties, where the young people were always seated "below the
salt." Whenever a boy spoke to her she blushed fiercely.

That summer Jacob and Therese Schiff took Frieda and Morti on
another of their ritual grand tours of Europe. One of the stops was,
naturally, Frankfurt, where the Schiffs were invited to dinner at the
home of some people named Dreyfus, who were Loeb cousins. "Are
there any young men I would like in Frankfurt?" Frieda whispered
furtively to a friend.

"Oh, you must meet Felix Warburg," said the friend. "He's the
handsomest man in town."

A Warburg family genealogy, prepared in 1937 and updated in 1953,
fills a volume very nearly the weight of Webster's International Diction-
ary, and the Warburgs take their family with even heavier seriousness.
The Warburgs put the lie to the much-repeated claim that "all the best
Jews are from Frankfurt" (whence, of course, come Schiffs and Rothschilds). The Warburgs are from Hamburg. The family is said to have
originated centuries ago in Italy (many Warburgs have a Latin look),
where the name was del Banco, "the bankers," since Jews were not
permitted personal surnames. Recorded history first places them, however, in Warburgum (or Warburg), a small town in central Germany,
from where, over three hundred years ago, they migrated north to
Hamburg.

The Warburg claim to being one of the world's noblest Jewish
families (and the Warburgs are far too proud to actually *make* such a
claim; they let it be made for them) is based on many things. A great
many Warburgs are wealthy, and have been for several hundred years,
but the splendid ring of the Warburg name has more to it than money.
The family bank, M. M. Warburg & Company in Hamburg, was an
ancient affair, founded in 1798, which lasted well into the Hitler era,
when it was forcibly confiscated in 1938 by non-Jews. The Warburgs
have also been distinguished in fields other than banking; they are a
particularly *rounded* family. There have been Warburgs prominent in
the military, in manufacturing, medicine, politics, book publishing,
diplomacy, education, and the arts. There have been Warburg authors,
scientists, composers, critics, inventors, and professors.

There are Warburgs today in every corner of the world—from New
York to London to Shanghai to Tokyo to Melbourne. One family habit,
which helps keep the Warburgs straight in various parts of the globe, is

to give Warburg children first names appropriate to the countries where they were born. Thus Elena, Oliviero, Gioconda, Francesca, and Italo Warburg are all Rome Warburgs. Eva and Charlotte Warburg, who became Israeli Warburgs, have children named Dvorah, Gabriel, Benjamin, Tama, and Niva. Ingrid is a Stockholm Warburg. When Renata Warburg was married to Dr. Richard Samson, she tried hard to conform to his mystic Indian cult of *Mazdasnan* and lived for a while with the Maharaja of Indore. Their child, Matanya, is therefore a Zoroastrian Warburg, or at least a Warburg from his mother's maharaja period. She later divorced Samson, left India, married a man named Walter Strauss, moved to Glasgow, and named her next child Carol.

Felix Warburg, who, Frieda Schiff had been told, was the handsomest man in town, was the son of Moritz Warburg, and Moritz Warburg was the youngest of six children of Abraham and Sara Warburg. Abraham Warburg died when Moritz was very young, but Sara Warburg, one of several strong-willed Warburg women, remained very much alive. Moritz's older brother Siegmund became titular head of the bank after his father's death, but as long as Sara lived Siegmund and Moritz had to report to their mother each evening after the Stock Exchange had closed. They brought their account books with them, and Sara grilled them thoroughly on each detail of each transaction. The two men's wives waited patiently at home until Sara was satisfied that the boys had put in a profitable day at the bank and dismissed them with a little wave of her hand. If Sara was not satisfied, she would sit very still in her thronelike chair, gazing at her sons hard and long. Then she would say, "Now. Explain yourselves. Siegmund, speak first." On such nights, the lights in Sara's big house in Rottenbaum Chausee burned late.

Sara was widely respected by men because she "thought like a man," and she had many influential men friends, among them the poet Heinrich Heine,* who once dedicated a poem to her (and it was not a poem about banking, either), and Prince Otto von Bismarck. Like her spiritual sister, Henriette Hellman Seligman in the United States, Sara was not a woman to be put off by royalty. She and the Prince corresponded regularly, and each year it was her custom to send him a package of Passover cookies. But one year the imperial court chaplain preached some anti-Semitic statements which incensed Sara. Bismarck was not really responsible for them, but he did not reproach the chaplain, and Sara decided that her friendship with the Prince should be terminated. At Easter, when the Prince had not received his customary cookies, he sent an aide to see Sara and ask what had happened. Sara told the Prince's emissary loftily, "If he doesn't know, tell him to come and ask me himself. But he won't ask. He knows quite well why he

* Heine also turns up in the Schiff family tree; his stepgrandfather was a Schiff.

didn't get his cookies." He never did ask, and he never received any cookies from Sara again.

Sara's son Moritz married Charlotte Oppenheim, and they had seven children—Aby M., Max M., Paul M., Felix M., Olga M., Fritz M., and Louise M. Warburg. Felix Warburg used to sign his letters:

because he saw the Warburgs represented in the heavens, with each of the Warburg children a star in the Big Dipper. This Warburg family lived at Mittelweg 17 and were known as "the Mittelweg Warburgs" to distinguish them from Siegmund Warburg's family, who lived on Alsterufer and were called "the Alsterufer Warburgs." To confuse things somewhat, both Siegmund and Moritz had sons named Aby, after their joint grandfather. But, to unconfuse them somewhat, the Mittelweg Aby—and all the other Mittelweg Warburgs—had the middle initial "M," which was not for "Mittelweg," but for Moritz, their father. Still, all those M's helped keep the Mittelweg Warburgs straight. Meanwhile, the Alsterufer Warburgs gave their children the middle initial "S," for Siegmund. This tradition has been carried on in both branches of the family.

Felix's mother, Charlotte, was like her mother-in-law Sara, a strong-minded woman who openly dominated her timid little husband, who, by the time she met him, was already used to being cowed. Charlotte also took pride in herself as a matchmaker, and was forever inviting young couples to dinner, where her practice was to send them out for walks in the twilight afterward, and then lock the French windows behind them. She would not let any of her "matches" back inside the house until, as she put it, "it" had happened.

Felix's father, Moritz, was the official leader of the sixteen thousand Jews in Hamburg. He thoroughly disapproved of the migratory wave of young Jews out of Germany in the 1850's, '60's, and '70's. For one thing, M. M. Warburg & Company was prospering, and he saw no need for any of his sons to "seek their fortune" in any such distant place as the United States. Also, as one of the family wrote of him, Moritz was a man "not distinguished by great physical courage." The thought of himself or any member of his family crossing the Atlantic terrified him. *"Das Wasser hat keine Balken,"* he used to say—"Water isn't very solid"—and once, when his mother ordered him to England on business, he begged her not to make him go. But Sara insisted, and Moritz crossed the Channel on his knees, praying all the way. When required to serve in the Hamburg City Militia, Moritz enlisted as a trumpeter. His wife, either proudly or mischievously, used to show the certificate he got for this service to everyone who came to the house. Moritz was also vain, and covered his baldness with wigs of varying lengths.

The Warburg children were, on the other hand, a bold, bright, and lively lot. Felix and his brothers were strikingly handsome youngsters, dark-haired with snapping black eyes. There is some argument today about "the Warburg mouth," which is said not to have been "good" where the boys were concerned. But the boys, as soon as they were able, wore the heavy mustaches that were the style of the period, so their mouths didn't matter. Felix, like his name, had a happy face, and his mustache curled upward. His brother Paul had a sad face, and his mustache turned down. Paul was a scholar. Felix was a blade. He loved beautiful things—beautiful women, music, books, paintings, horses, sailboats, clothes, and (in time) motorcars. He was also something of a rebel. He openly scorned the conventional Jewish orthodoxy of his home, which he used to say was "maintained more from tradition than from conviction." He was embarrassed by such rules as having to have a servant carry his textbooks to school for Saturday sessions, and having to adhere to the dietary laws whenever he went to a restaurant or traveled. He itched to go places and become his own man.

His oldest brother, Aby, was a rebel too. He had married a girl named Mary Hertz, described in the family as "an unusual girl"—unusual in that she was not Jewish. It was the first Warburg mixed marriage, and it stirred up such a storm that the couple were asked, "out of respect to the Jewish community of Hamburg," to leave the city to wed.

At sixteen Felix was taken out of school and sent south to Frankfurt to work for his mother's family, the Oppenheims, who had a precious-stone business there. His brother Max was already in Frankfurt, studying business, and the boys' mother wrote to Max telling him to take good care of Felix, and see that he took "language and violin lessons, select nice friends for him, prevent him from being too extravagant, and see to it that he takes one bath weekly." But Felix could take care of himself. He was already a *bon vivant,* and he cut quite a swathe in Frankfurt. In his snappy dogcart he drove his young friends and his Italian teacher (he had selected a very pretty young woman to teach him that language) on gay excursions to the Waeldchen, Frankfurt's prettiest park. In Frankfurt he met Clara Schumann, the widow of Robert

Schumann the composer, and Mme. Schumann developed quite a case on Felix Warburg. This raised an eyebrow or two. He was just eighteen; she was nearly seventy.

Felix Warburg very nearly didn't go to the Dreyfuses' party. The Dreyfuses, he said, gave "the dullest parties in Frankfurt," and he was not a man who liked dull parties. But his parents, who were visiting in Frankfurt, insisted because their old friend Jacob Schiff would be there, and they reminded Felix that Schiff had given the Warburg boys a toy fort during the period he had worked for the Deutsche Bank.

So, reluctantly, Felix went, and met Frieda Schiff, who was wearing the pale pink gown Zorn had painted her in. "I don't *think* I flirted," she said many years later, "because I had been brought up so strictly, and had gone out so little, that I was not too certain of myself."

That night Felix went home, long after midnight, knocked on his parents' door, and said, "I have met the girl I'm going to marry."

Matchmaker Charlotte was disgruntled because this was a match she had not arranged. Moritz Warburg was even more distressed when he heard that it was an American girl. Sitting up in his bed in his nightshirt and cap, he cried, "She will have to live in Germany, you know!"

25

MARRIAGE,
SCHIFF STYLE

The morning after Felix's announcement, Moritz Warburg paid a call on the Schiffs. The meeting did not go well. Mr. Warburg stalked out of the Schiffs' suite wearing a face of stone, and Jacob Schiff calmly announced that the family was moving on to Paris.

In Paris the Schiffs went to the races at Longchamp, and who should suddenly show up there but Felix Warburg, who had followed them from Frankfurt. He presented himself to the Schiff party, and stayed very close to Frieda while her father became increasingly agitated. At the end of the afternoon he told Frieda flatly that she was not permitted to see Felix again. "I took her to Europe to get her out of the way of temptation," he roared, "and now this happens!"

In addition to his wish to preserve Frieda's "innocence," there were several things that Jacob disliked about Felix Warburg. For one, Felix wasn't a banker. Though New York firms practiced nepotism extensively, there was a rule at the Warburg bank to prevent, or at least control, it: no more than two sons of a senior partner could enter the firm. Since Felix's older brothers, Max and Paul, were already in the bank, Felix could never work for M. M. Warburg & Company. If Frieda wished to marry a Warburg, Jacob said, why didn't she marry Paul or Max? But in any case Jacob would never permit her to marry a man who would make her live in Germany. Behind these illogical arguments there hung the fact that Schiff distrusted Felix's manner. Felix was witty and lively, and Schiff was uncomfortable when faced with anything as intangible as bounce. He did not like jokes; *bon vivants* alarmed him. Felix's nickname was "Fizzie," after the Vichy Celestin "fizzie water" he loved to drink, but "fizzy" also described his personality. There was a slight cleft in Felix's chin which Schiff saw as a sign of weakness of character. The real truth, however, was that he didn't want his daughter to marry anyone.

When the Schiffs arrived at Gastein, Felix Warburg turned up again. While Jacob was taking the waters one afternoon, Frieda and Felix met secretly in the park. They walked for a while, and then he stopped her under a plane tree and said, "Isn't it a beautiful day?" "Yes," said Frieda. "This is a beautiful place," he said. "Yes," she agreed. "Would you ever like to live in Germany?" he asked her. Frieda was terrified. She ran home to her mother and gasped, "I think he proposed!"

Immediately, a council of war was called and an elaborate set of plans was developed. It was decided that the Schiff and Warburg families should have a summit conference on the matter, and on neutral territory. Ostend on the Belgian coast was selected. First, a formal dinner was given by the Warburgs at their favorite kosher restaurant. That went reasonably well (Schiff was a great believer in the power of formal dinners to solve most problems). Next, Mr. Schiff gave a luncheon for the Warburgs at his hotel. The headwaiter suggested fresh Channel lobsters, which were nonkosher. Schiff ordered filet of sole. But somehow a mistake was made and the lobsters were served anyway, and Mr. Schiff flew into one of his towering rages. The lunch was a disaster.

A tactic was at last agreed upon, however, which, though not very entertaining for the two young people, assured them of remaining in some sort of communication. Frieda and her family would return to New York, and there, her father explained, Felix would write a weekly letter to Schiff, who would respond with a weekly letter to Felix. Frieda was to institute a similar schedule of letters between herself and Felix's mother. Frieda and Felix were under no circumstances to write each other. This program was to continue until such time as Felix was able to come to New York. The two young people parted without so much as a farewell kiss.

In New York, the letter-writing began. Sometimes her father showed Frieda his letters to Felix before posting them. Written in German, they used the formal *"sie,"* a form reserved for use when speaking to one or more persons with whom one is not on familiar terms. But once Frieda noticed that her father had at last written to Felix using *"du,"* the familiar form. She was overjoyed and hugged and thanked her father for unbending this much. Without a word, Jacob Schiff took out his gold penknife, scratched out every *"du,"* and substituted *"sie"* throughout. It was a letter, furthermore, inviting Felix to join Kuhn, Loeb & Company in New York.

Felix Warburg did not particularly want to work for Jacob Schiff. He was never to become a great financier (though he did possess other talents which, in time, became very useful to Schiff). But he did love Frieda, and Schiff had set an unalterable condition: Felix could not have Frieda unless he took, in the bargain, Kuhn, Loeb. As Felix was preparing to leave Germany for New York, his father called him aside and said, "My son, I have just one request to make of you." Felix was certain that his father was about to make him promise to bring his young wife back to Germany or, at the very least, to ask him to keep the dietary laws. But his father said, "Do not take the iced drinks that spoil Americans' digestions and force them to go to Carlsbad for a cure." Felix arrived in New York in 1895, and immediately went to work.

Schiff's attitude toward his future son-in-law did not soften much during the "courtship" period that followed. He arranged things so that the young couple saw almost nothing of each other. When they did meet, they were heavily chaperoned. His concern for Frieda's innocence continued, and he enjoined both her mother and her grandmother from mentioning "ugly" truths.

Therese Schiff obeyed her husband, but Grandmother Betty Loeb had her own ideas. She had become interested in nursing and obstetrics, and was getting a reputation as an "advanced" woman. Betty even read the novels of Zola openly! On her book shelves behind locked glass doors were books dealing with the physical side of marriage, and she was determined to have a talk with Frieda. But Jacob got wind of this, and refused to let Frieda see her grandmother unless there was a third person present. Betty Loeb did manage to get Frieda alone one afternoon and to say to her, "It's normal for a girl to be upset and nervous at a time like this. Being engaged is unnatural. A girl should either be not engaged at all or married." It was some help, but not much.

The dashing young man about to carry off their loviest young princess was referred to by German Jewish society as "The Black Prince." As the day of the ceremony approached, tensions in the Schiff household mounted. It was to be an at-home wedding at 932 Fifth, and, adding to the other complications, was the caterer's news that no more than 125 guests could be fitted into the house, and, a week before the wedding, 145 had accepted. Jacob Schiff struck a seerlike pose and announced, "Twenty will not come." Later, Frieda Schiff Warburg wrote: "As always his forecast was right. Two days before the ceremony, Mrs. James Seligman died, and her entire family, numbering exactly twenty, couldn't come."*

Frieda Schiff's and Felix Warburg's marriage was called "dynastic," and it did seem to represent a consolidation of Kuhn, Loeb power. There they all were—old Solomon Loeb, who had founded the firm but had withdrawn altogether a few years earlier in favor of his son-in-law, the father of the bride. There was Solomon's old partner, Abraham Wolff, whose daughter Addie was a bridesmaid and who—in another Kuhn, Loeb wedding—would very soon marry another partner, Otto Kahn. There was Solomon's son Morris, not a banker but married that same year to Abe Kuhn's daughter, Eda, another bridesmaid. The bride's aunt, Nina Loeb, was maid of honor, and Paul Warburg had come from Germany to be his brother's best man. These two met for the first time at the wedding and fell in love, which would give Solomon another son-in-law in the firm, which would make Nina her niece's sister-in-law and make Paul Warburg his brother's uncle.

Since the Schiffs belonged to two congregations, Temple Emanu-El and Beth-El, two rabbis performed the ceremony—Dr. Gustav Gottheil and Dr. Kaufmann Kohler. It was a glittering occasion, but the business overtones of the union almost overshadowed the happiness of the newlyweds. While the women speculated about the suitability of Felix as a husband, the men considered his promise as a partner. But the most historically significant fact was that Frieda Schiff had achieved her first victory over her father, and had managed to marry the man she loved.

From the house the couple went to the Plaza, where Felix, in his nervousness, forgot to register his bride. From there, they went on a short trip to Washington, where Frieda, in *her* nervousness, realized that she was without a personal maid for the first time in her life. Faced with the problem of packing suitcases and not knowing how to begin, she burst into tears and Felix had to help her, wrestling manfully with unfamiliar crinolines. They returned to New York long enough to board the S.S. *Kaiser Wilhelm II* for a cruise to Italy, but this time Jacob Schiff assigned one of his wife's personal maids, Hermine, to accompany Frieda. Hermine proved to be quite a trial. Felix Warburg used to say, "I spent my honeymoon with a German governess." Hermine would not let Frieda wear any of her trousseau on the boat so that the dresses

---

* Frieda's nervous state may have played tricks on her memory, because Rosa Content Seligman did not die until twelve years later. But some member of the crowd with twenty relatives apparently did die that week.

would be fresh for Italy, where the senior Warburgs were to meet them, and she scolded Frieda whenever she got a spot on any of her other dresses. Also, possibly acting on instructions from Jacob Schiff, she was reluctant to let the newlyweds spend any private moments together. She was forever fussing around the stateroom and seemed miffed that she had not been given an adjoining cabin. Still, Frieda and Felix managed to find some time together. Frieda Warburg became pregnant with her first child on her honeymoon, just as her mother had done.

Frieda was delighted with this news, and said to her mother that she believed in young marriages, and "If this one's a boy, I'm going to take up the rug in his room, take out his bed, and make him sleep on a cot as soon as he's old enough to marry," to force him out of the nest. Therese Schiff looked disapproving, and announced that, on the contrary, she was turning an upper floor of 932 Fifth into a bachelor's apartment for Morti, "So my son may stay with me as long as he wishes."

During Frieda's wedding trip, her father wrote:

Dear children,
    You shall not come home without receiving at least one letter from me, but as I telegraphed you frequently [using his Western Union franking privilege, of course] I suppose you are in any event satisfied. . . .

"Satisfied." On this stiff note he seems to realize how unfeeling he sounds, and suddenly the tone of the letter changes, loosens, expands, letting a bit more of his heart show as he swiftly continues:

    . . . I need not tell you how happy dear Mama and I are in your own young happiness, which, God grant it, may last for many years without a cloud obscuring it, and if trials come, without which hardly any human life exists, your deep love for each other will give you strength to bear whatever God destines for you.

When the young Warburgs returned to New York, they moved to a hotel while their first house was being finished for them. But Jacob, upset at the news of his daughter's condition, at the loss of her precious innocence, would not come to the hotel to see them, or even telephone, refusing to ask for Frieda by her new name.

Frieda and Felix did go to the Schiffs' house for dinner. At one point during that dinner, Frieda turned to her father and asked him a question. It was a simple question—she could never remember, afterward, just what it was because her father suddenly lost his composure completely and cried out, *"Why do you ask me? You have your husband to turn to now!"*

26

"THE BATTLE OF THE GIANTS"

Jacob Schiff was never quite sure whether he approved of young Otto Kahn. For one thing, Kahn, though he had not gone as far as August Belmont and changed his name, was something of a religious turncoat. (Otto Kahn has been called "the flyleaf between the Old and New Testament.") Also, Kahn, like his friend and contemporary, Felix Warburg, had a taste for high life and, of all things, Bohemia. Kahn liked to surround himself with painters and poets and playwrights and, as a boy growing up in Mannheim, he had dreamed of being a poet himself. (His mother, however, who steadfastly maintained that he had no talent, finally convinced him to burn all his manuscripts, including two five-act plays in blank verse, so the Otto Kahn works were lost to the world.) Kahn spoke with a clipped English accent, ordered his suits from Savile Row, quoted Ibsen and Walter Pater and Carlyle, and sang in the office—all of which Schiff found disconcerting. But Schiff had to admit that Kahn was a promising financier.

From Mannheim, Kahn had gone to London in 1888, where he

became a British subject and worked for the English office of the Deutsche Bank. Within a year he had become the bank's vice manager, and was hobnobbing with such intellectual and theatrical figures of the day as Richard Le Gallienne, H. G. Wells, Beerbohm Tree, Maxine Elliott, Henry Irving and Harley Granville-Barker. He went to parties with the Prince of Wales, whom he had been told he resembled. He also knew the London Warburgs and, for a while, shared a bachelors' flat with Paul Warburg during the latter's stay in England on family business. At the invitation of Speyer & Company,* Kahn had come to New York in 1893. He was then twenty-seven. There he met Abe Wolff's daughter Addie, and in 1896, a few months after Frieda Schiff's marriage to Felix Warburg, he entered Kuhn, Loeb & Company in what was becoming a time-honored way, by marrying a partner's daughter.

Kahn's initial contribution was an unusual one. People, seeing pale, wheezing E. H. Harriman coming down the street toward them, darted into doorways to avoid him. Yet Otto Kahn saw something in this strange little man that was deeper than his unappetizing appearance. Kahn, in fact, found himself getting along with Harriman even better than Schiff did. It was surprising, really, because Kahn's nature was smiling and expansive, Harriman's dour and withdrawn. But because Kahn seemed to understand him and respect him, and was willing to converse with him, Harriman liked and respected Otto Kahn. Jacob Schiff was happy to watch this unusual friendship ripen. He himself had always regarded Harriman more as a business associate than as a friend, and since the Union Pacific reorganization this relationship had been secure.

Of Harriman, Kahn wrote candidly:

> His was the genius of the conqueror, his dominion was based on rugged strength, iron will, irresistible determination, indomitable courage and, upon those qualities of character which command men's trust and confidence. He was constitutionally unable either to cajole or dissemble. He was stiff-necked to a fault. It would have saved him much opposition, many enemies, many misunderstandings, if he had possessed the gift of suavity. . . . I ventured to plead with him that the results he sought could just as surely be obtained by less combative, more gentle methods, while at the same time avoiding bad blood and ill feeling. Invariably his answer was: "You may be right that these things could be so accomplished, but not by me. I can work only in my own way. I cannot make myself different, nor act in a way foreign to me. They will have to take me as I am or drop me. This is not arrogance on my part. I simply cannot achieve anything if I try to compromise with my nature and to follow the notions of others."

* Which had given Jacob Schiff his first contact in New York.

Gradually, Otto Kahn became the bank's chief liaison with Harriman, while, in the meantime, Jacob Schiff cultivated the garrulous, easygoing company of James J. Hill. With this arrangement—having the two most powerful railroad men of the age as virtually daily visitors to the Kuhn, Loeb offices—it must have seemed to Schiff in 1900 as though, except for a few details such as J. P. Morgan, he had American railroads in his pocket.

To unify his Union Pacific system, Ned Harriman had, with the help of Kuhn, Loeb, purchased two smaller lines, the Oregon Short Line and the Oregon Railroad & Navigation Company. This accomplished, he decided that he also wanted a line called the Chicago-Burlington & Quincy, a rich line which fanned through some of the richest country in the West. Its fingers stretched to Mississippi River ports, to mining towns in Colorado and the Black Hills, and to farm lands in Illinois, Iowa, and Nebraska. Harriman wanted the Burlington, as he explained, partly because it was a competitor for business in Union Pacific territory, but also because he feared that at any moment the Burlington might extend its main line from Denver to the Pacific Coast. This would make the Burlington a Union Pacific competitor on a transcontinental as well as a local level.

However, when Harriman began quietly to dicker for the Burlington, he found his way blocked by "subtle but powerful forces." Someone else was interested in the Burlington, and had already been quietly buying up its stock. Harriman mentioned his fears to Otto Kahn, and the two men approached Kuhn, Loeb's senior partner, Jacob Schiff. Schiff listened in silence, and then said, "I will ask Hill about it." That evening, at his house, Schiff asked Hill point-blank, "Are you buying Burlington?" Hill laughed and replied, "Absolutely not." Schiff then returned to Harriman and assured him that Hill had no interest in the line.

Hill, however, had not been telling the truth. He had, early in 1901, decided that he wanted a feeder line for his Great Northern and Northern Pacific. His banker, Morgan, had recommended that Hill buy the St. Paul Railway, but Hill was convinced that the Burlington was the better line. Morgan gave in and, long before Harriman had let his hungry gaze fall upon the line, Hill-Morgan interests had begun buying up the Burlington on behalf of the Great Northern and Northern Pacific. As the two railroading giants, one with a monopoly on the Southwest and the other controlling the Northwest, squared off to do battle, two facts were pertinent. Morgan, who represented Hill, had a personal, almost psychopathic hatred of Harriman and fumed at the mention of his name. Schiff, on the other hand, who represented Harriman, was Hill's friend. If anyone was to mediate, or referee the fight, it would have to be Schiff.

Schiff paid another of his polite visits on Morgan and asked him the same question he had asked Hill. Morgan, who could be ruthless but was seldom devious, admitted that he and Hill were in fact buying the Burlington. Schiff then began to argue for a "community of interests." It was to become one of Jacob Schiff's key phrases, but at the time it belonged to Morgan, who had defined it, saying, "The community of interests is the principle that a certain number of men who own property can do what they like with it." Schiff was using the community-of-interests argument deliberately, aware of the appeal of the concept to Morgan, to try to persuade Morgan to let Harriman have an interest in the Burlington purchase, and a share in the management. Morgan refused. A grim-faced Jacob Schiff now sent for James J. Hill.

On a balmy April evening in 1901, Jim Hill arrived from Washington. He was in a buoyant mood. That afternoon he had finished negotiations for the purchase of the Chicago-Burlington & Quincy, and the contract was to be signed the following morning. His railroads, the Northern Pacific and the Great Northern, would then own more than 96 percent of the Burlington stock, for which he and Morgan had paid as much as $200 a share, far above the market value. The young man who met Hill at the ferry dock was nervous. It was Morti Schiff. "Father is waiting for you at Mr. Baker's house," said Morti. "Did you get his message?"

"Yes," said Hill. "Is Harriman there also?"

"I believe so."

"Good!" said Hill breezily.

The two set off. The meeting, arranged by Schiff, was a last-ditch effort to ward off a battle, and was to be held on neutral territory at the home of Hill's friend, George F. Baker, the so-called "Sphinx of Wall Street," president of the First National Bank, the city's largest.

With Hill's arrival, the atmosphere of the gathering in Baker's library grew tense. Schiff's customary regal poise was overlaid with frost, and, after greeting Hill curtly, Schiff said a few brief words about their long friendship and then asked Hill abruptly, "Why did you lie to me a month ago and say you had no intention of buying the Burlington?"

Hill's candor was as remarkable as his good spirits. "I *had* to," he replied. "After all, I knew you were interested in the Union Pacific."

Schiff gave him a contemptuous look, and then asked once more that Harriman be given at least a small share in the Burlington purchase.

"Oh, I don't think so," said Hill cheerfully. "You see, I want it all."

Harriman, who at that point had been pacing the floor "in suppressed excitement," sprang at Hill and said, "Very well! This is a hostile act and you must take the consequences!"

Hill merely waved his hand and walked out of the room.

On April 20 the announcement of Hill's purchase was made. Morgan, his duties as Hill's banker over, set off for Europe to take the waters at Aix-en-Provence and to visit his beautiful French mistress. Hill, in even better spirits than he had been in at Mr. Baker's house, boarded his private train for a long holiday in the American Northwest. Nobody had reckoned with the rage of Ned Harriman, who had once boasted to Otto Kahn, "Let me be but one of fifteen men around a table, and I will have my way."

To get his place at the Burlington's table, Harriman's scheme was simple—and outrageous. If Hill's Northern Pacific now owned the Burlington, Harriman would buy up the Northern Pacific. If, in other words, he could not buy Hill's railroad, he would buy up Hill. The boldness of the scheme boggled the imagination. And it quickened the pulses of a a number of Wall Street figures, among them James Stillman of the National City Bank, and one of Stillman's most important customers, Rockefeller and Standard Oil. Wall Street might have laughed at Harriman once, but—with the help of Schiff—he was the man who had helped turn the defunct Union Pacific into one of the country's most profitable lines. Harriman had been given complete control of the Union Pacific's finances, and now, to implement his great plan, he demanded permission of the Union Pacific's board to issue $60 million worth of new bonds.

Whether or not to participate in Harriman's plan was the most agonizing decision of Jacob Schiff's career. What was at stake was merely everything, so far as he was concerned. One did not lose a battle with a man like Morgan and survive. All night long, he paced the floor of his Fifth Avenue house, weighing the possibilities, while Therese begged him to come to bed. The sun was up before he decided. He would go along with Harriman.

It would take $60 million and more to do what Harriman had in mind. After all, the goal this time was not just to buy up a defunct railroad at twenty or thirty cents on the dollar. To succeed, Harriman and Schiff would have to go into the stock market and to private investors all over the country and, as quickly and secretly as possible, to buy up, from the strongest railroad–Wall Street combination in the world, the controlling interest in a $115 million corporation.

Schiff had warned Harriman that the price of Northern Pacific stock would begin to rise as soon as Kuhn, Loeb's brokers went into the market and started buying it. To account for the rise, Schiff suggested an explanation of childlike simplicity. He would start a rumor on the Street that Northern Pacific was rising because of Hill's purchase of the Burlington. The Northern Pacific was nicknamed the "Nipper," and Kuhn, Loeb men began saying, "Nipper's going up, now that Hill's got a new line." Ironically, the explanation satisfied partners at the House of

Morgan as well as Hill's men on the Street, who cheerfully began selling large blocks of stock to the enemy. Playing right into Harriman's hands, the House of Morgan disposed of $14 million worth of Northern Pacific by the first of May—all of which found its way into the hands of Schiff and Harriman.

One begins to sense the size of Edward Harriman's ego here. Harriman wanted to corner the Northern Pacific not for money, nor even for power. He wanted nothing but revenge on Hill and Morgan—to get even with them for excluding him from the Burlington's board. Privately, Jacob Schiff began warning him that he might be going too far. But Harriman at this point was intractable.

Jim Hill was superstitious and a believer in omens, and he was in Seattle on the last day of April when "a dark-complected angel" appeared to him in a dream as he lay in his canopied Louis Seize bed in his private car. The vision told him that all was not well in New York, and he immediately ordered his train turned around and headed East at top speed. He arrived in New York on Friday, May 3, breaking a transcontinental record. He went immediately to Kuhn, Loeb, walked into Jacob Schiff's office, and demanded to know why Northern Pacific had risen so rapidly. With a smile, Jacob Schiff informed him that Kuhn, Loeb was buying Northern Pacific "on orders from the Union Pacific"— or Harriman.

Angrily, Hill said, "All right. Do your damnedest. But you can't get control. Morgan and my friends alone hold $40 million worth of Northern Pacific, and as far as I know none of them has sold a share."

"That may well be," said Schiff carefully, knowing that Hill's statement would have been true a week earlier, but was no longer. "But we've got a lot of it, Jim. After all, you secretly bought the Burlington and wouldn't give us a share. Now we're going to see if we can get a share by buying a controlling interest in the Northern Pacific."

Hill pressed Schiff to find out how much stock he had, but Schiff would only repeat, "A lot of it, Jim. A lot." Nervously, Hill took out his little bag of uncut stones and began to worry them between his fingers.

At that point, Schiff made a final peace offer. He and Harriman would stop buying, he said, and would gradually return the Northern Pacific stock to the market, if Hill would give Harriman a place on the Burlington's board. It was all Harriman had wanted to begin with. Hill seemed to waver, and Schiff said quickly, "Come to dinner at my house tonight. We'll talk it over."

The stock market closed that afternoon at a new high, led by the Northern Pacific Railroad. The stock had also leaped ahead on the London Exchange. Outside speculators were moving in, and brokers were selling short. The mood of the street was feverish.

One must admire the poise and Himalayan coolness of Jacob Schiff at this moment. It was a Friday evening at the Schiffs. Fortunes hung in the balance, to say nothing of Jacob Schiff's own future as a businessman, yet no detail was altered from the family ritual. In the upstairs sitting room the Sabbath candles were lighted, and the children gathered in a circle to be blessed. Then their father read his Friday evening service, and the family descended to the dining room to meet their dinner guest. Jacob Schiff said grace as always, and the children recalled later that when he came to the words, "For those less fortunate than we," his blue eyes traveled briefly and humorously to rest on Mr. Hill. Dinner continued in its customary stately way.

After dinner, in the library over their cigars and brandy, the two men got down to business. Jacob Schiff explained that his group now controlled 370,000 shares of Northern Pacific common stock, and about 420,000 shares of preferred—or $79 million worth on a basis of par valuation. Hill, nodding jerkily, immediately said that Harriman could go on the Burlington board. There was no question of it. "You have won," Hill said. "I salute you." The two men talked on for hours, and it was well after midnight when Hill rose to go. He clasped Jacob Schiff's hand and said once more, "Harriman shall go on the Burlington board tomorrow. You have my word for it." As the two said good night, Hill is said to have brushed aside a tear.

If so, it was a crocodile tear. Once more, Hill was showing himself to be a man who could not be trusted. Before appearing at the Schiff house for dinner, Hill had gone to the Morgan office, conferred with the partners, and had sent a cable to Morgan himself asking permission to buy 150,000 more shares of Northern Pacific to strengthen his position. Morgan had wired back approval. Hill had never intended to admit Harriman to the Burlington board. He had just begun to fight.

Harriman, meanwhile, was nervous. The shares he and Schiff had acquired, both common and preferred, did, taken together, constitute a clear majority of the two classes of stock. Taken separately, however, Harriman lacked—by some forty thousand shares—a majority of the common stock. On Saturday morning, therefore, he telephoned a Kuhn, Loeb broker named Heinsheimer and ordered forty thousand more shares of Northern Pacific "at the market."* But Schiff, having taken Hill at his word, had left instructions at the office to buy no more Northern Pacific. In a dilemma, Heinsheimer tried to find Schiff—it was a five-million-dollar order—and learned that he was at the synagogue. Heinsheimer rushed uptown to Temple Emanu-El and looked for Schiff among the worshipers. Finding him, and making his way into a seat beside him, Heinsheimer whispered, "Harriman wants forty thousand more NP." Without lifting his eyes from his prayer book, Schiff replied, "Do not buy it. I'll take the responsibility."

* In those days the New York Stock Exchange was open on Saturdays.

Perhaps it was because of the unusual surroundings in which Schiff issued his instructions that an oversight of considerable proportions took place. For some reason, Harriman was never advised of Schiff's advice to Heinsheimer, and Harriman spent the weekend confident that he owned a majority of both the preferred and the common stock. On Monday morning, Jim Keene, a famous stock manipulator of the era, hired by Hill and Morgan, moved into the stock market with his team of brokers and began buying up the 150,000 shares Hill had ordered—$15 million worth. The price of Northern Pacific began to climb. By noon, it had reached 110 . . . then 117 . . . then 127. By Tuesday it had jumped to 149¾, and it was then that Harriman learned, to his dismay, that his order had not been executed. At the stock's inflated price, he could no longer afford to buy.

Brokers still speculate why Schiff stopped Harriman's order. (In his characteristic way, Schiff himself never offered an explanation.) The most common reason given is that the pious Jacob would not handle the transaction because it was ordered on a Saturday, which is ridiculous. Others have said that Schiff prudently foresaw the panic that was coming, and decided to let Hill and Morgan charge on alone, wreck the economy, and take full blame for it. This is possible, but unlikely. The plain fact was that Schiff had believed Hill, and could not imagine that Hill would betray him a second time. Still—though, as it turned out, it would have made no difference—somebody should have told Harriman. On Wednesday morning the Northern Pacific hit 180, and Wall Street went wild. The stock was behaving similarly in London, and British bankers were cabling furiously for more shares. When the stock reached 200, many speculators sold, anticipating a break and hoping to buy in again at lower prices. They did not realize, however, that neither Hill nor Harriman intended to sell and take profits. Harriman had locked up his shares, and Hill, having got as many more shares as possible, was also sitting tight. Speculators had taken over.

By mid-week European bankers had become alarmed and reversed their previously liberal policies on American loans. The Bank of England warned the London joint-stock banks against New York. While American credit teetered, the two antagonists stood firm, refusing to move. At the height of things, sickly Ned Harriman was suddenly stricken with appendicitis and was rushed to a hospital. Coming out of the anesthetic, he demanded a telephone and attendants were astonished to hear him put in a call to James J. Hill. "Hill?" he said when he reached his party. "This is Harriman. I just wanted to tell you that the operation is over and I'm still alive." He then collapsed on his hospital bed.

By Thursday Jacob Schiff was speaking of a "deplorable situation" that had developed. The Northern Pacific had hit 1000, and it was suddenly clear to Wall Street that the stock had been cornered. Millions of dollars' worth of shares had been sold which did not exist, and millions of dollars would be needed to settle the debts. It was, in the words of one financial historian, "finance run mad." Suddenly, the Northern Pacific broke violently, and the market followed, with some of the soundest stocks declining by 50 percent or more. Cornered brokers scurried frantically—and futilely—to cover themselves, but Wall Street had become literally insolvent. Others placed pistols to their temples. It was the most ferocious financial panic in history.

Later, the Northern Pacific corner and the panic that followed became known as "the Battle of the Giants," and the four main partici- pants—Hill and Morgan, Harriman and Schiff—were depicted as raven- ous gorgons, fattening themselves on the American public. Hill and Harriman and their respective bankers were portrayed as having deliber- ately and singlehandedly set out to smash the economy. Harriman, whose unpleasant nature and aspect had already made him thoroughly hated, gained no new popularity, and Jacob Schiff now shared Harri- man's notoriety. Morgan, meanwhile, did not become more publicly beloved when he returned from Europe and, asked by a reporter whether he didn't owe the American public an explanation, made his famous and contemptuous reply, "I owe the public nothing."*

Who really was to blame? Hill, likening the panic quaintly to "an Indian ghost dance—they whirl about until they are almost crazy," blamed the public. "Perhaps they imagine that they have a motive," he said, "in that they see two sets of powerful interests which may be said to be clashing. Then these outsiders, without rhyme or reason, rush in on one side or the other. They could not tell you why they made their choice, but in they go, and the result is such as has been seen here for the past few days." Harriman tried to divorce himself from any respon- sibility whatever, pointing out that he had stopped buying Northern Pacific stock before it started on its upward spurt (though, of course, he had at first wanted to buy), and that during the whole so-called "battle" he had withdrawn from the battlefield. Morgan blamed Harriman, and Schiff blamed Hill. There is evidence, though, that all four principals in the affair were secretly ashamed of the havoc they had caused.

And who had really won? At best, the Battle of the Giants must be considered a draw. Hill and Morgan came out with a majority of the Northern Pacific's common stock. But Harriman and Schiff had a majority of the preferred and a majority of all the shares outstanding. One thing was certain. Morgan had finally met his match in Jacob Schiff.

---

* It was an era when it was fashionable for the rich and mighty to disparage the public. In 1883 William H. Vanderbilt had uttered his famous "The public be damned!"

Never again would one man control the finances of the country. From that point on, there would be another to consider.

A few days after that terrible Black Thursday, Jim Hill appeared at the Kuhn, Loeb offices and asked to see his old friend Schiff. Felix Warburg came out to meet Hill and explained that his father-in-law was temporarily indisposed. "How is he?" Hill wanted to know. "Not very happy," said Felix politely. "Is he still mad at me?" asked Hill. "Yes," said Felix, "I would say so." Hill, with another little wave of his hand, said, "Oh, Schiff takes these things too seriously."

A week to the day after the collapse of the market, Jacob Schiff, gently glorying in his new position as Morgan's equal, wrote Morgan a long and masterly letter, full of delicate irony, in which, almost apologetically, he called Hill a double-crossing liar. He had, Schiff wrote, perhaps misconstrued Hill's words and intent; for this he would beg to be forgiven. The letter concluded on this note of almost fawning suavity:

> I trust you will accept my assurance that nothing was further on the part of Union Pacific interests than to do aught meant to be antagonistic to you or your firm, and that, as far as my partners and I are concerned, we have at all times wished, as we continue to do, to be permitted to aid in maintaining your personal prestige, so well deserved. You will find Union Pacific interests, and certainly my firm and myself, entirely ready to do anything in reason that you may ask or suggest, so that permanent conditions shall be created which shall be just to all interests and not bear within them the seed of future strife, discord, and possible disaster.
>
> Trusting, then, dear Mr. Morgan, that you will understand the spirit in which this letter is written, and hoping that the rest of your stay abroad may be pleasant and not interrupted by any unsatisfactory events, I am, with assurances of esteem,
>
> > Yours most faithfully,
> > Jacob H. Schiff

Schiff was never a man to make an enemy when he could keep a friend, especially a friend who could be useful to him. And so it is not surprising to see him, a few weeks later, writing a similarly conciliatory letter to "My dear Hill," saying:

> It made me unhappier than I can tell you to find myself, for the first time in fifteen years, in a position where you and I could not go together arm in arm. . . . I believe that your own interests and those we represent can be knitted together so tightly and profitably that before long we shall all feel that what had to be gone through during the past few weeks was not for naught.

He was quite right, and Morgan agreed. Soon after the panic, Morgan formed the Northern Securities Holding Company to protect Hill's interests, and, in a gesture that Morgan must have made with great difficulty, he asked Harriman to sit on the board and have a vote in the new company. It was Harriman's first admission into the councils of J. P. Morgan, and, for a while at least, everyone was happy. Harriman and Hill, it turned out, never did have anything against each other personally. They greeted each other cheerfully with "Hullo, Ned!" and "Hullo, Jim!" Jim Hill showed how much he continued to admire Schiff by sending Schiff not one, but two portraits of himself, whereupon Jacob wrote back: "There are few men with whom I have come into contact during my business career for whom I feel as great and real attachment as I do for you."

Schiff always seemed to have the last word. Long after the battling giants had shaken hands and made up, Schiff wrote to his friend Sir Ernest Cassel saying how "very much attached" he had become to "dear Morgan," and how "very obliging and considerate towards me" Morgan had been, "especially since the Northern Pacific Affair. He understood very well that it was his interests that had brought us into conflict." Schiff, who had proved himself a powerful fighter, was also an effective peacemaker.

During the Northern Pacific Affair Otto Kahn's name had been mentioned merely as one of Schiff's "lieutenants." But while he may not have played a major role in the episode, he had been watching very carefully from the sidelines. Kahn always insisted that Jacob Schiff taught him everything he knew, and Kahn must have learned his lessons well. A few years after the panic, Kahn, in a brisk battle at Duveen's, was able to capture a Franz Hals painting from the next-highest bidder for $500,000. The man he had outbid was J. P. Morgan.

"The Battle of the Giants" was watched by Kuhn, Loeb's founder, old Solomon Loeb, from a distance and with stunned amazement. He had never trusted railroads, and the scope of what his son-in-law was doing was beyond him. It had been two years since he had been inside the Kuhn, Loeb offices. He had developed a sad cast to his blue eyes, and had become increasingly preoccupied with his health. Whenever a disease was mentioned in his presence, he would nod and say miserably, "*Ja*, I have also had that one." (Once, after the family doctor had treated Betty for a complaint, the doctor went downstairs to inform Solomon of his wife's condition. As he was about to utter his familiar statement, the doctor raised his hand and said, "Mr. Loeb, I assure you that this is something you have *not* had.") Solomon loved to have Betty fuss over him, and was jealous of every moment she failed to spend with him. She played the piano for him in the afternoons, but he was even jealous of her absorption in the music and would interrupt the playing to say, "Betty, I don't know why, but I have the strangest pain here." And she would break off playing to tend to him.

At their camp in the Adirondacks, his sensitive skin suffered from prickly heat, and she would lay him down and, at the age of seventy, powder him like a baby. She also consoled him with enormous meals; they became two plump little old people who worried over each other endlessly. Betty had developed diabetes in her fifties, and was told that she must not fast on Yom Kippur. Still, she thought she *ought* to, and so developed a tactic which, she felt, satisfied three things: doctor's orders, her son-in-law Jacob's orthodox views, and her appetite. On Yom Kippur she would not go to the dining table but had a series of little meals brought to her on the porch of the house—this way feeling that she was not fasting and not really eating either.

One summer Solomon saw Betty reach for another serving of Nesselrode pie which her diabetic diet forbade her to have, and cried, "Betty, don't!" But the indomitable Betty, whose will was a match for her husband's any day, said, "I don't care if it costs me ten years of my life. I'll take a second helping of this excellent dessert." With a little smile, she did and within a few hours she was dead. After her death Solomon was a husk of a man. He died a little more than a year later, in 1903.

27

"DER REICHE LEWISOHN"

Adolph Lewisohn's father had a curious theory. He told his son that the Passover matzoths, or *Aphikoman,* had, when properly blessed, a special virtue: if a bit of this unleavened bread was tossed into the sea, it would calm the water. Adolph's father said he knew that this was true because he had tried it once, and it had worked. When Adolph was eighteen in 1867, crossing the Atlantic to America, he had carried one of these blessed matzoths with him. The ship hit a storm, and young Adolph struggled to the rail and cast his *Aphikoman* on the water. Nothing happened. It was one of his last attempts to conform to his father's orthodoxy. It was symbolic of his break with the past.

Adolph had been born in Hamburg, the youngest of seven children of Sam and Julie Lewisohn. He was a plump, silent, introverted child, devoted to his mother. One afternoon when he was six years old he was sitting with her when she suddenly said that she felt a little dizzy. Within a few minutes she was dead. Soon afterward his father remarried and started a second family. There were soon four more sons. Adolph, the outcast, had in the meantime been ordered by his father to visit the synagogue every day for a full year to say his *Kiddush,* the orphan's prayer.

The senior Lewisohn operated a business that had been in the family since 1740, dealing in wool, bristles, horsehair, ostrich and other ornamental feathers, and, eventually, in metals. Sam Lewisohn was proud of his reputation as a businessman and of the fact that he was known locally as *"der Reiche Lewisohn"*—the *rich* Lewisohn. He was also proud of the Lewisohn pedigree, which he traced back to 1609 when the Lewisohns came to Germany from Holland. Sam's mother had been Fanny Haarbleicher, the daughter, Sam pointed out, "of a very good English Jewish family." And *her* mother's father was Solomon Goldschmidt, a London financier.

Sam was a strong-willed little man. In 1848 he became concerned about a Parisian milliner who appeared to have defaulted on payment for a shipment of feathers. Sam set out for Paris to collect the bill in person. News traveled slowly in those days, and he had not heard about the Revolution that had broken out in France (which was one reason why Paris ladies were not buying ostrich-plumed hats that year). As he reached the frontier, he was warned repeatedly to stay out of France. But he continued on, in the face of hordes of escaping refugees, into Paris, right up to the barricades. When challenged, he cried out, *"Je suis un Républicain d'Hamburg!"* Since Hamburg was recognized as a free city, he was permitted through the battle lines and went on to the milliner's shop, where he demanded and got payment of his bill.

He was a martinet when it came to disciplining his children, and Adolph had a dreadful respect for his father that was a long way from love. The German backhanded slap was his father's favorite form of punishment, and young Adolph received many of these. When he was seven, still during the year of mourning his father had imposed upon him, his older sister was married in a gay ceremony. At the wedding a traditional collection was taken for the poor, and young Adolph made a comment about collections that was, for his age, unusually perceptive (and, for a future philanthropist, interesting). He said he had heard that in Christian churches and cathedrals there were two kinds of alms boxes. Those of solid wood earned pennies, but those with glass sides— where donations were visible—always yielded larger coins and bills. He was slapped for bringing up "churches and cathedrals" at a Jewish wedding.

Once he ate lamb chops and cream puffs at the same meal, which was against the orthodox dietary law, and was slapped for that. He took lonely walks in the fields outside Hamburg. He picked wildflowers which he pressed between books, and built a little glass herbarium, planted with mosses and herbs, and placed it in his bedroom window overlooking the canal. One day it was gone. His father had decided it was "not manly."

He tried to please his father by taking an interest in the business. During the Sabbath—from sunset Friday to sunset Saturday—the Lewisohn offices were closed, but after sunset Saturday business commenced again in an informal sort of way, upstairs in the parlor. Here Adolph's father and uncles and clerks gathered to discuss the week's transactions, and to receive an occasional visiting salesman. On one of these evenings a salesman from Russia arrived selling bristles. Russian bristles were an important item for export, and Adolph's uncle, after examining samples in various colors, placed an order for bristles in white, yellow, gray, and black. Adolph, who had been quietly listening, said suddenly, "In New York they won't want black bristles." He was thereupon dealt another slap by his father. Later his father said, "You were right about the black bristles, but that makes no difference. You have no right to speak out against your uncles and elders."

Adolph was nearsighted, and heavy-lensed spectacles were prescribed. The glasses, at least, protected him from the slaps, and he seemed to withdraw behind them into a private world of worry and hope. At the age of ten he had heard terrible news. His dead mother whom he had loved so much had suffered from "melancholia." Now one of his older sisters showed the same disturbing symptoms, and had to be carefully watched. Adolph himself began to nourish a secret fantasy—a dream of escape, and travel, and of riches with which to buy treasures that even *"der Reiche Lewisohn"* could never afford, riches that could buy not only freedom from the black cobbled streets of Hamburg but something that Adolph began to see as a kind of grandeur and stature. The squinting, overweight boy became, in his own mind, a secret potentate.

Aside from the Scriptures, there was little to read in the Lewisohn house. But there were newspapers of sorts. There were two Hamburg dailies—*Der Freischutz* and *Nachrichten*—but these were not sold outright; they were loaned or rented. The papers were delivered, read for an hour or so, then picked up again and carried on to another family. Naturally, when each paper arrived at its appointed hour, the senior member of the family—Adolph's father in his case—got to read it first. By the time it got to Adolph it was usually time for it to be collected again.

An exception to this publishing practice was *Die Fremdenliste,* "the list of strangers." This stayed in the house because it was not so much a newspaper as an advertising handout paid for by various Hamburg hotels, listing the commercial and other travelers who arrived from out of town. At first glance, *Die Fremdenliste* may not seem much more exciting than reading a telephone book, but for Adolph Lewisohn poring over the list of strangers had a special fascination. The strangers had strange names, and they came from exotic ports, and he could let his imagination go and create exciting histories and daring exploits for them all. The strangers became his intimates as he fleshed them out and let them populate his waking and sleeping thoughts. Many were titled personages, and *Die Fremdenliste* carefully listed each arrival according to his status, wealth, and importance. Royalty came first—the visiting kings, princes, and dukes. Then came courtiers and those with powerful royal connections. Then came religious titles, then generals and counts and barons. After these came the *rentiers,* the landed gentry who lived on their incomes. And last of all, at the bottom of the list, were placed the *"Kaufmanner,"* or merchants. Adolph, the merchant's son, set his sights on the princely category.

At times *Die Fremdenliste* published bits of general news. Here, for instance, Adolph learned of the rich gold fields that had been discovered in California. He also read how fellow Germans and fellow Jews like the Seligmans were becoming titans of American finance. And the Seligmans had originally been simple countryfolk, not even successful merchants!

At the age of fifteen Adolph went to work for his father. He was sent on a two weeks' business trip to Frankfurt and Zurich, his first taste of travel outside Hamburg and, as it turned out, his first real taste of the kind of grandeur he had dreamed about. Returning from Frankfurt he made an illicit side trip to Wiesbaden, one of the grand spas of the day, and one starry night he stood outside the window of the great gambling casino and watched women in furs and jewels and men in monocles and cutaways move slowly through the gilded and mirrored rooms under heavy chandeliers where, as he said later, "to me everything looked beautiful!" A few months later his father sent him on another business mission to Schleswig-Holstein, and from Schleswig he was required to visit a small island off the coast, a half-hour's boat trip away, his first sea voyage. He was seasick both over and back, and when he returned to Germany, he said, "I was seasick, but I shouldn't have been because I'm going to America." His father laughed at him.

Adolph's father had sent an agent to New York to be the firm's sales representative, but it turned out that the man was not as trustworthy as the senior Lewisohn had supposed. Two of Adolph's older brothers, Julius and Leonard, were sent over to replace him and soon wrote home to Germany asking for another brother.

Adolph's father knew that Adolph had "liberal tendencies," and Sam had the usual parental fear that, once in America, Adolph would abandon orthodoxy. But at last Sam consented. Adolph was to sail on the Hamburg-America packet ship *Hammonia,* and all the way down the

Elbe on the tender his father lectured him on the importance of keeping the dietary laws, asking him to swear never to give up the tenets of his faith, and Adolph "tried to promise." As young Adolph started up the gangplank, his father became terribly agitated and cried out, "It's natural that you should be upset too, my son!" But Adolph wasn't a bit upset. And when his father gripped his hand and said, "If you'll promise not to cry, I won't cry either," Adolph Lewisohn stood for several minutes, trying to cry to please his father, but, as he wrote later, "I could not dissemble. To me, there was nothing to cry about." It was the happiest moment of his life.

When he got to New York—it was 1867, just two years after his contemporary, Jacob Schiff, had made his first trip to America—Adolph wrote home to his father:

> The city leaves nothing to be desired. . . . Everything is as grandiose and animated as possible. Life here not only corresponds to my expectations but even exceeds them. We have very nice rooms, which, of course, cost also a nice sum of money ($55.00 a week with board, on Broadway). The business hours are from eight o'clock in the morning until half-past six in the evening without interruption, but then you have the evening for yourself. . . . I like this very much, as in Hamburg I mingled with strangers. I am getting along quite nicely with my English.

He also assured his father that, "of course," the firm did not do business on the Sabbath. It was an assurance he would be required to repeat up to the time of his father's death, even though, in fact, the opposite was true.

"What I did resent," he wrote in an unpublished memoir dictated when he was an old man, "was that my father was so bent on the strict orthodox forms that he insisted on our devoting ourselves entirely to that way of life, letting everything else go that might interfere with it." In New York the Lewisohn boys bought some lard for export to Hamburg. When old Sam Lewisohn heard of this transaction, he cabled the boys with orders to dispose of the lard immediately; he would not accept it, and he refused to deal in it. He could, and did, deal in pigs' bristles because bristles were inedible. But lard was edible and violated kosher restrictions. Sabbath strictures stated that the orthodox Jew could carry nothing on his person except his clothing, unless it was carried within an enclosed courtyard. Sam Lewisohn had no courtyard, and, as Sam pointed out, since the city gates were not closed on Saturday, the entire city could not be considered a courtyard, either. This meant that nothing could be carried, not even a handkerchief. If one of his children needed a handkerchief on the Sabbath, Sam said the handkerchief must be knotted about his arm—worn, in other words, as part of his clothing.

Sam Lewisohn would not even allow the key to his house to be carried on the Sabbath. Since some coming and going was necessary, and since Sam did not like to ring his own doorbell, the key to the house was ritually placed on a little ledge outside the door, next to the lock, on Friday, so it could be used on Saturday without carrying it. Adolph could never understand why his father bothered to lock the door in the first place.

No fire could be lit in the house between sundown Friday and sundown Saturday. In the pregas days some of Sam's Jewish neighbors in Hamburg brought hot dishes to a community stove on Friday, where they would be kept warm for Saturday. But since this involved carry-ing—from public stove to the house—on the Sabbath, Sam would not permit it, and the Lewisohns ate only cold dishes on Saturday, even in the coldest winter, in a cold house. "Every Saturday and every holiday morning," wrote Adolph, "saw us all at the synagogue. I suppose Jesus Christ did the same, because the New Testament tells us that he drove the money-changers from the Temple and that at times he preached in the synagogue." He added, somewhat slyly: "As a pious Jew, he must have attended the synagogue, although I suppose that toward the end of his life the authorities would not let him preach. Perhaps if he were to appear today and preach as radically as he did then, he would not be allowed in the more conservative Christian churches."

From his study of his *Fremdenliste,* Adolph had observed how German society of his day had become rigidly stratified. Unless en-nobled by a "von," no businessman, merchant, or professional man was *hoffähig,* or received at court. It was a stony rule that the nobility and the common people never mixed, nor spoke to, nor even acknowledged each other—nor was it as simple as that. The nobility was stratified within itself, as was the nonnobility. Each German belonged to his *Kreis,* his little group, and any intercourse between these groups was not only not done; it was considered dangerous. Mingling of the classes invited disorder, a state the German feared the most. The wife of a doctor did not speak to the wife of an architect; the architect's wife did not speak to the merchant's. This continued down the many rungs of the social ladder until the wives of tailors refused to speak to wives of shoemakers. The Jew, of course, occupied his own isolated position, and Adolph, who wanted friends almost as much as he wanted to be rich, came to America believing that a preoccupation with Jewish ritual and "feelings of Jewishness" only intensified the Jew's isolation from the world around him, and made him seem—and feel—more alien and aloof.

In New York, once, arguing with a friend who said, "Jewishness is drawn in with our mother's milk," Adolph replied with a smile, "Well, that doesn't apply to me. I had a Christian wet nurse. Perhaps that explains why I get along with the Christians better than you do, and why I have so many Christian friends."

"I could never see," he said on another occasion, "why it should be considered *bad* to be a Jew. Some Jews are noisy and offensive. So are some gentiles. Noisy, offensive gentiles should be avoided. So should noisy and offensive Jews."

When he encountered anti-Semitism, he liked to analyze it in a businesslike way. As a fifteen-year-old in Hamburg, he had seen a performance of *The Merchant of Venice,* and had been startled by, and "did not approve" of, the portrayal of Shylock in the play. He proceeded to make a careful dissection of Shylock's character and behavior. "I could not understand why Shylock should be regarded as a mean character," he wrote. "Shylock had not asked for credit from anybody or committed any wrong or crime. He was simply living his own life with his family." Then, said Adolph,

> Along came some Christian gentlemen who wanted a loan, and they applied to Shylock who must have been pretty good at thrift as he had plenty of ready money. One of these gentlemen proposed to borrow a large sum and Shylock drew a queer contract, but Antonio did not have to sign if he did not want to agree to it. Of course, Shylock could not have been entirely sane or he would not have exacted the cutting off of a pound of flesh. That certainly was not good business, as he would not have benefitted by it.

Later on in the play, Lewisohn pointed out,

> Shylock was offered three or five times the amount of the loan and could have made a small fortune out of his contract. If he had done this, there might have been some reason for making him out a bad character. But Shylock's sense of honor was stronger than his desire to gain. They had treated him cruelly, taking his daughter and through her had stolen his property. Considering what it meant to be a Jew at that time, to have his daughter marry outside his faith, Shylock's feeling of outrage and revenge was not unnatural.

Then Lewisohn added: "I think that history tells us that the Jews did not always act as impractically as Shylock did in the play."

Adolph drew a business moral from Shylock's story: never to make a "queer contract," and never to extract an excessive profit from a trade. In 1873 he was still an employee of his father and his older brothers, but he occasionally had a chance to buy and sell on his own. In the summer of that year he was sent back to Europe on a feathers-and-bristle-buying assignment. He had wanted to sail on the fancy new Hamburg-America liner *Schiller,* one of the most luxurious of its day.

Reluctantly, however, he decided that "it looked better for business" if he took an older, less showy ship, and so he chose the *Hammonia* again. It was a lucky decision. The *Schiller* went down in mid-Atlantic with no surviving passengers. Another passenger aboard the *Hammonia* who had changed his booking from the *Schiller* was Senator Carl Schurz. Adolph used the booking coincidence as an excuse to introduce himself to Schurz (a former major general in the Union Army, later to become Secretary of the Interior under Hayes), and made a friend.

Adolph disembarked at Plymouth, went up to London to visit the bristle market, and made plans to continue on to Hamburg. But he was still an inexperienced traveler. After buying his rail and steamer tickets and paying his hotel bill, he found that he had no money left to pay for meals on his journey. On the train to Dover he struck up a conversation with "a Christian gentleman" who mentioned that he had meant to buy some chamois gloves while in London. Adolph replied that, as it so happened, he had bought several pairs, which he would be happy to sell. He sold them, and at a little profit "which seemed fair, since I was by then the exporter of the gloves from London, and the gentleman would have had to pay considerably more in Paris," and the money was enough to feed him until he got to Hamburg. Like Shylock's, Adolph's "sense of honor was stronger than his desire to gain."

Adolph Lewisohn was then twenty-four, and he had not seen his father in six years. When he arrived in Hamburg, it was a Saturday, and when he entered his house, his father, in his long Sabbath robes, rose to meet him and cuffed him soundly on the ear. Adolph had been carrying his valises.

"Sometimes, in those days," he wrote, "my dreams seemed a long way from coming true."

28

THE POOR
MAN'S METAL

Copper, "the ugly duckling of metals," had long been considered the poor man's metal, despised for its very abundance. Because there was so much copper in the world, it was one of the world's least expensive and most neglected metals, used as the basis for the cheapest coins and utensils. There was copper all over the Western Hemisphere, from Alaska to Tierra del Fuego, and the thrifty Mormons ignored one of the largest copper lodes of all, just outside Salt Lake City; no one bothered to put money into the relatively expensive recovery process to turn crude into finished ore. The dawning age of electricity, however, was beginning to change all this.

Adolph Lewisohn first became interested in copper in the 1870's when, with a visiting cousin from Germany, he made a bristle-selling trip to Boston. While there he watched a demonstration by a young man named Thomas A. Edison. Edison claimed he could record human voices on little metal spools. Adolph spoke into Mr. Edison's contraption and, to his amazement, heard his voice played back. Edison then told Adolph that the day was not far off when voices would be transmitted across continents by wire—copper wire. Talk such as this began to make copper shares fluctuate wildly on the market.

At that point most American copper was mined in the Lake Superior region of Michigan, and in 1877 the American market found itself glutted with copper and a great deal of the metal was sold for export to Europe at a low price. Then, in 1878, there was a sudden copper shortage and the price of copper rose sharply, so high that American manufacturers were having to import cheaper copper from European mines. This unusual situation gave Adolph and his brothers an unusual idea.

All copper imported to the United States from Europe was subject to five cents per pound duty. But there was a loophole in the customs regulations, and American-mined copper—such as the hundreds of tons of the stuff that had been sold cheaply to Europe the year before—could be reimported without the payment of any duty at all. There were a few technicalities. In order to be reimported duty-free, American copper was to be shipped back to this country in the same casks in which it had been shipped out, as proof of its American origin. Also, the European seller of this copper was to provide a certificate saying that the re-imported metal had, indeed, originated in America. In a fast-moving market, after a shipment had changed hands several times, certification was not easy to get.

The copper Adolph and his brothers ordered carried no such certification. Also, it was no longer in its original casks; it had been uncrated and repacked. But, even with the cost of shipping, it was cheaper per ton than copper available in the United States. The ingots, to be sure, were stamped with the names of the Michigan mines, and perhaps—the brothers hoped—this fact would be sufficient to satisfy customs. Rather like American tourists who have overspent their quota and pray that customs won't poke too deeply in their luggage, the Lewisohn boys waited for their copper to arrive praying that customs would not hew too closely to the regulations. It was a gamble, and it worked. The shipment passed customs untaxed, and the boys sold the copper quickly.

A year later, with their growing reputation as copper factors, the boys were offered a chance to buy their first mine in Butte, Montana. The price was low, and Adolph set out for Montana to look over the situation. There was plenty of copper in the hills around Butte, but much of the ore was of low grade and, furthermore, there was no way to get copper out of the area except by mule team, which was prohibitively expensive. Still, Butte was a wide-open town—Montana had not yet become a state—and was full of eager speculators. Adolph bought up a claim called the Colusa mine, and formed a company in Butte called the Montana Copper Company.

Now the Lewisohns were owners of a mine which produced a product they could not ship. They went to work. The first person they approached was Henry Villard, president of the Northern Pacific Railroad, whom they asked to build a line from Helena into Butte. Villard agreed, but there was a sizable string attached. If the Lewisohns wanted a line built into Butte, they would have to guarantee large freight shipments of ore out—guarantees the brothers were not at all sure they would be able to keep. Next, they approached Jacob Schiff's sometime friend, James J. Hill, head of the Great Northern, and asked him to build the Great Northern into Butte by way of Great Falls. Great Falls was important because there was water power there, which the Lewisohns figured they could use to set up a smelting and reduction works. Hill also agreed, but only after extracting additional guarantees. The Lewisohns now had $75,000 tied up in one mine which was yielding them no income. The brothers were, Adolph confessed, "very nervous."

Their ability to persuade railroads to reroute their lines was only the beginning of a larger problem—how to meet those guarantees, which actually presented a double challenge: first, to find sufficient ore to make up the guaranteed tonnages and then, if possible, to ship even more. In their contracts with the two railroads, the Lewisohns had clauses to the effect that the more ore they shipped, the lower the freight rate would be. (Since then, shipping laws have been passed that give small manufacturers an even chance, but in those days the biggest shippers got the best breaks.)

While the railroad tracks were being laid, Adolph came up with one of his best ideas. He looked at all the low-grade ore dumped from the Colusa in giant slag heaps. Considered unsalable, it was being discarded as waste. But, Adolph calculated, if all those tons of waste were shipped by freight—somewhere, anywhere—they would give him his guaranteed tonnage and mean that his high-grade ore could be shipped much more cheaply. The notion reminded him of something he had done as a boy. When he made his first selling trip for his father, to Frankfurt, he had been embarrassed, checking into hotels, by the tiny store of personal effects he was carrying with him. He had bought a large suitcase and filled it with rocks.

Adolph's rock idea, applied to mining, was simple enough, but nobody had thought of it before. Mining engineers had studied the problem, but it took a boy from Hamburg, whose only experience with digging had been in his window-ledge herbarium, to come up with a solution.

His idea of shipping supposedly worthless low-grade ore turned out to have even more value than its worth as a decoy, since there *was* a market for low-grade copper ore in England. Here again, the cost of shipping had always been considered too high. Still thinking of his valise full of rocks, Adolph expanded upon the idea. Suppose, when the railroad was built, the low-grade ore were to be shipped to a West Coast port—San Francisco, Portland, or Seattle. Suppose, from there, it could be loaded on a ship for little or no cost—as ballast. Suppose, from there, it traveled around Cape Horn to New York and suppose, at last, from there it could be loaded on another ship—as ballast again—for England. When the Northern Pacific tracks reached Butte, this was exactly what the Lewisohn brothers did.

The boys were on their way.

29

FURTHER
ADVENTURES
UNDERGROUND

To a large number of the crowd, they were simply—and rather sniffily—known as "The Googs." "Are they asking the Googs?" people would ask if someone was having a party. The Seligmans acted as though they were coming down in the world when James's daughter, Florette, married a Goog. (After all, another of James's daughters had married a *Nathan.*) The Guggenheims, in fact, never seemed quite to "fit in" with the crowd, no matter what they did. They always seemed just a bit outside of things. There are several possible reasons for this. For one thing, the Guggenheims were Swiss, not German. For another, they were quite opposed, in their financial philosophy, to men like the Seligmans (though they were closer in their thinking to Jacob Schiff). But the best reason for their special position, perhaps, is that the Guggenheims as a family group managed to make more money—in barely twenty years' time—than any other individual in the United States, if not the world, with the possible exception of John D. Rockefeller. (It is very likely that the Guggenheims made more money than Rockefeller. But when one deals with hundred-million-dollar fortunes, accurate figures become very hard to get.)

Meyer Guggenheim was well past fifty before such spectacular prospects began to present themselves to him, though the family's lace and embroidery business in Philadelphia had not done at all badly. By the 1880's he and his sons ran several small companies, including their own lace-making factories in Switzerland and their own importing and distributing company. Meyer was rich. But he had still not reached his goal, "One million dollars for each boy"—and there were seven of these—when a friend named Charles H. Graham came to talk to him about mining shares. The curious thing about that visit is that, for all its profound effect on the Guggenheim lives and fortunes, no one today is sure what transpired.* Graham, a Quaker, operated a grocery store in Philadelphia and had been speculating in Western mining lands. Perhaps he went to see Meyer to sell him some mining shares. More likely, Graham owed Meyer some money and persuaded Meyer to accept mining shares in lieu of cash. In any case, in return for a consideration of either $5,000 or $25,000 (there are two conflicting reports), Meyer, who had never been west of Pittsburgh, became a one-third owner of two lead-and-silver mines called the "A.Y." and the "Minnie" outside Leadville, Colorado.

Since he was always more interested in finance than in management, Joseph Seligman had been content to leave his mining interests in the hands of custodians who, as in the case of Mr. Bohm, often turned out to be untrustworthy. Perhaps Meyer Guggenheim had learned what not to do from Joseph. In any case, he immediately set off for Leadville to inspect his new holdings. He cannot have expected to find much because he brought with him, as insurance, a large stock of Guggenheim laces and embroidery. When a Leadville merchant bought some of his goods, Meyer muttered, "That's about all I'll get out of Leadville." And, sure enough, both the A.Y. and the Minnie, though they descended from a mountainside ten thousand feet above sea level, were flooded with seepage from the Arkansas River which raced nearby. (Meyer determined this by dropping a stone down the shaft of each mine and waiting for the splash, an experiment so simple that it would not have occurred to a Seligman.) To find out what was in them, they would have to be pumped out or, as Meyer put it, "unwatered." He installed pumping equipment.

---

* Even Meyer himself, who died in 1905, was always hazy on the details of Mr. Graham's call.

During the next few months, more and more of Meyer's money was required to keep the pumps going, and by August, back in Philadelphia for a fresh supply of laces and embroidery to help support the pumps, he had very nearly abandoned hope when he had a telegram from Leadville. It read: "You have a rich strike." The A.Y. mine, unwatered at last, was yielding fifteen ounces of silver—or nearly twenty dollars' worth—per ton, along with considerable copper ore. The amount of silver in the mine was encouraging—as much as $180,000 worth of pure silver from a single stope. At the same time, the preponderance of copper was disappointing.

Immediately, Meyer called all his seven sons to Leadville, including Benjamin, who was still an undergraduate at Columbia, and William, who was barely in his teens; the two were told to finish their studies locally and to learn some practical metallurgy on the spot. Meyer and the older boys would perform purchasing and marketing tasks and, above all, devote themselves to finding a method of smelting copper ore that was not exorbitantly costly.

This did not take long, thanks to a circumstance even luckier than Mr. Graham's visit. Of several existing processes, one that had been developed but had still not been tried was the brain child of R. J. Gatling, the inventor of the rapid-fire machine gun. The financing of the Gatling process of ore recovery had been turned down by J. P. Morgan, but there was one young, little-known, lone-wolf speculator who believed in it. His name was Bernard Baruch. On Baruch's advice, Meyer gambled on the Gatling process, which almost immediately lowered the price of refining copper to a practical seven or eight dollars a ton.

One of the great "troubles" with the Guggenheims, socially, in the New York crowd they soon entered was that nearly all nineteenth-century fortunes up to that point had been built systematically, and possessed a kind of inevitable logic. But Meyer Guggenheim's money had been made in such an erratic way—from stove polish to lye to spices to Irish linen and Swiss embroidery, leaping from one business about which he knew little to another about which he knew even less, and landing, at last, with a rich strike in silver and copper from a waterlogged mine shaft. There were rumors that Meyer was a little unbalanced, and had succeeded not by his brains but by fool luck. But the consistent element in Meyer Guggenheim's career was that he was always essentially a middleman, refining and marketing a product made by someone else.

Just as he had succeeded in improving an existing brand of stove polish, he had now succeeded in improving the smelting of copper. As he went about liquidating his lace business, he continued in this pattern. He decided to concentrate not on the production-ownership end of the copper business but, as he saw it, on the part of the business where the money really lay—in smelting and refining.

Meyer's theory was very like one held by another underground expert of the day, John Davison Rockefeller. Rockefeller never deigned to own an oil well, considering drilling companies far too risky and preferring to leave them to lesser speculators. He liked to own refineries. The well owners then had to bring their oil to him, which he bought at the lowest price (which got lower the more the producers produced, and which hit bottom when overproduction set in). Similarly, whenever Meyer bought copper lands, he bought them primarily for the purpose of setting up smelters; he then either kept his mining ownerships as subsidiaries or sold them to buy more smelters.

By 1882 Meyer's holdings were large enough, according to one biographer, to "enlist and hold the attention of his sons," who had been working for him all along. Meyer formed M. Guggenheim's Sons for this purchase, in which each of his seven boys was an equal partner. Meyer began lending his sons money to go out and buy and build smelters. In 1888 the boys bought their first smelter in Pueblo, Colorado, for $500,000, and soon they had another in Mexico. The profits they divided were enough to hold anybody's attention. In 1890 the Minnie mine alone was worth $14,556,000. A year later the Guggenheims had made so much money that they decided to form a trust of their own, consolidating about a dozen of their refining operations under the name Colorado Smelting & Refining Company.

The first issue of stock in this new company was to have been underwritten by J. & W. Seligman & Company. But at the last minute Isaac Seligman (whose family had not yet become connected to the Guggenheims by marriage) backed out. He did not think the issue would sell.

It did, however. In 1895 the Guggenheims bought a huge refinery in Perth Amboy, New Jersey, and four years later a separate Guggenheim Exploration Company was formed, called Guggenex, which very quickly led the brothers into copper and silver mines in Nevada, Utah, and New Mexico, gold mines in Alaska, tin mines in Bolivia, diamond mines in Africa, more copper mines in Mexico, copper and nitrates in Chile, and even a rubber plantation in the Belgian Congo.

By 1900 the Guggenheims had made so much money that the two youngest brothers, Benjamin and William, decided to give the family enterprises less attention. Having been assured that, for sentimental reasons, they would continue to partake of the profits, both boys retired, leaving digging, smelting, and exploration to Isaac, Daniel, Murry, Solomon, and Simon. Meyer, meanwhile, according to William Guggenheim, "kept books of small neat figures," enjoying the fact that each new entry "improved his financial status."

He had laid the foundation for what is now the United States copper industry. Such giants as Kennecott, Braden, and Anaconda Copper all had their genesis in Meyer Guggenheim's operations, and if Mr. Graham had not stopped by Meyer's store, none of it might have happened.

As news of the Lewisohns' and Guggenheims' mining successes reached the Seligmans in New York, their old enthusiasms for adventures underground were rekindled. Not that they had ever really died down. Dreams of hitting a bonanza had kept them sending good money after bad in any number of mining ventures. They had bought mines, despite their lack of knowledge of the productive end of mining. They had financed operations they had never seen. At the height of the Panic of 1873, the most severe the country had ever known, the Seligmans cheerfully invested in a totally worthless gold mine, the Oneida, and went on holding a number of other valueless mining shares. But mining shares were becoming nearly as glamorous as railroads, and the Seligmans were unable to believe that they would not soon find a winner. In the 1870's Joseph had written to his brothers: "I want no more mines at any price! Even for nothing! As the assessments* are always the worst!" But of course he had gone right on buying mines. In fact, one of the greatest credits to the Seligman firm is that it was able to remain solid and afloat, without visible financial injury, despite its many mining losses.

After Joseph Seligman's death Jesse became head of the New York firm and, perhaps because Joseph had had bad luck in Montana, Jesse determined that he would have better. There was not much logic behind this decision, but there had been little of that commodity evident in any of the brothers' mining operations. Jesse's Montana enterprise was called the Gregory Consolidated Mining Company, and was located southwest of Helena. "It sounds very promising," he wrote to his brothers—without bothering to visit Helena; the mine's impressive name satisfied him. He purchased a sizable share of the Gregory, and then dispatched an expert to look at the mine—his young son Albert, who had actually studied mining engineering. "We shall not trust strangers this time," he wrote confidently, congratulating himself that he was being smarter than Joseph, who had trusted the thieving Bohm.

Young Albert found conditions in the Montana mining regions somewhat different from those on campus. He also found the Gregory to be a mine that was operating at a heavy loss, and soon after he arrived it was

---

* Sellers of mining securities often "assessed" buyers of the stock to put up additional sums of money if the cost of whatever development the stock was to pay for exceeded the original estimates. If the stockholder did not come forth with these assessments, he lost his participation.

unable to meet its payroll. Albert wanted to close the mine immediately, but Jesse wanted to hold on. While father and son argued by telegraph, the miners went unpaid. Finally, when salaries had not been paid for a full two months, the miners captured Albert and held him hostage. In New York there were dark rumors that the Gregory's general manager, in collusion with Albert, had staged the kidnaping as a means to keep the men working. But as soon as Jesse Seligman paid the miners' wages, Albert was released and the mine was closed. It was never worked again.

Though Jesse continued to dabble in mines, they became a taboo subject at the Seligman dinner table when Jesse's wife Henriette discovered that Jesse's balance sheet showed holdings in six different mining companies—with a total value of six dollars.

30

TWILIGHT OF
A BANKER

Jesse Seligman was twenty years older than Jacob Schiff, he headed the more venerable banking house, and in the 1880's the title, inherited from his brother Joseph, "New York's leading Jewish banker," undoubtedly still belonged to Jesse. He was one of the toughest, hardest-to-ruffle Seligmans, and one of the brightest. He was stockily built, with an earnest, square-jawed, homely-handsome face that seemed incapable of imposture. The *Daily Graphic* described Jesse as "cool, circumspect and conservative. . . . He carefully weighs all his opinions before expressing them, and his word, once given, is as good as his bond." The *Graphic* also called the head of the Seligman firm "simple almost to austerity."

Jesse was actually a more popular man in New York than his brother Joe had been. Joe's life had been pretty much all business, but Jesse had found time for considerable philanthropies. He had been one of the founders of the Hebrew Orphan Asylum, the Montefiore Home, the United Hebrew Charities, and served as a patron of the Metropolitan

Museum of Art and of the American Museum of Natural History. He did a great deal to enhance the "social distinction" of the Seligman family, an eminence which families such as the Guggenheims were finding it so difficult to achieve. And so it is a particular pity that this esteemed man should have embarked, soon after his brother's death, upon a project which, though it left the Seligmans a great deal richer, left their business reputation considerably damaged.

In 1869, after ten years' building, the Suez Canal linking the Mediterranean to the Red Sea was opened, and the great "impossible" dream of Ferdinand de Lesseps had become a reality. In the years that followed, De Lesseps turned to other notions for joining places together. A great railroad from Europe to the Pacific coast of China was one. Another was to flood the Sahara Desert from the Atlantic, and turn northwestern Africa into an inland sea. At last he turned his attention to an idea that had been considered by many governments and explorers before—a canal between the Pacific and the Caribbean at Panama.

Whether, if Joseph Seligman had been living, he would have tried to bridle his brother's enthusiasm for the De Lesseps project is a good question. Joseph always approached all new projects with some caution. But he also had a way of flinging caution to the winds and leaping boldly into schemes—railroads, tunnels—which he had originally distrusted, so perhaps he would have done just what Jesse did. Jesse, however, admitted that the Panama Canal appealed to him for sentimental reasons. He liked the idea of carving a trench through the mountains he had crossed on muleback thirty years before with his sick brother and their supply of dry goods, heading for the gold-rich land of California. Sentiment, of course, is not always a reliable business guide.

Jesse had little trouble getting the French Panama Canal Company to let J. & W. Seligman & Company handle its stock issue. In fact, the French company seemed so eager to employ the Seligmans that a curious arrangement was made. The sum of $300,000 was paid to the Seligmans outright as a kind of extra fee, "for the privilege of using the Seligman name as patrons of the undertaking," or so it was airily explained at the time. No one had realized that the Seligman name alone had such value—$37,500 a letter.

A stock-selling syndicate was formed, headed in America by the Seligmans, along with Drexel, Morgan & Company and Winslow, Lanier & Company. (It always delighted Jesse when he got top billing over Morgan.) In France the committee in charge of selling canal subscriptions was headed by Seligman Frères and the Banque de Paris. The initial estimate for building the canal—considered ample—was $114 million, and the total stock issue contemplated was 600 million francs' worth.

The proposed canal would be operated by the French Government, and from the moment the De Lesseps project was announced there was a great deal of adverse criticism of it in the American press. No one wanted a European power in control of the passage. Furthermore, the United States had been negotiating on and off for many years, with Britain and various Central American countries, to build a canal across the isthmus. The route favored had always been through Nicaragua, where a series of natural lakes and rivers provided a partial waterway, and which many early gold prospectors had used successfully to get to California. American engineers considered the Nicaragua route superior, and, in fact, an American company had been about to start digging when the Panic of 1873, and the depression following it, brought the project to a halt. Now here was presumptuous France stepping in to steal the glory from America.

When it was announced that American bankers, led by the Seligmans and including Morgan, intended to back the French canal, the editorials grew angrier and more biting. Speakers rose in the House and Senate to denounce the project and the men behind it, and editors screamed of Jesse Seligman's intention of "selling America to France." Once more there were vicious hints of "an international Jewish conspiracy," and one reporter, trying to make Morgan's participation fit this notion, went so far as to say that Morgan, unable to beat them, had "decided to join the Jews."

But in a coolheaded interview for the New York *Herald,* Jesse Seligman said, "It is a private undertaking altogether, and we have every confidence that an enterprise of this kind will pay. Naturally, the United States will receive the largest share of the benefit from it. All the machinery to be used in the work of the construction will be bought here. When the scheme is fully understood and appreciated, there will be many eager to subscribe to it, but as it is, all the necessary capital is already assured."

It certainly was. With the French hero De Lesseps behind it, Panama Canal shares had no difficulty selling in France. And, though American public opinion continued to run heavily against the canal, the public also seemed to think that with men like Seligman and Morgan behind it there was money in it. So shares sold rapidly in New York as well. The initial stock issue was oversubscribed, and digging was immediately begun.

De Lesseps had determined on a sea-level canal, without locks, and for seven years he and his engineers labored against mountains and valleys and watersheds and the scourge of Panama fever and, most of all, against the extravagance and dishonesty involved in the pricing and purchasing of supplies and equipment. Suppliers and the canal's purchasing agents were in perpetual collusion, and tons of material were shipped to Panama that the company never needed and never used. The American press and public continued to grumble, and in 1884 the Frelinghuysen-Zavala Treaty was negotiated with Nicaragua for the construction of a rival, and roughly parallel, canal. For a while it seemed as though there would be two canals.

This treaty was not ratified by the U.S. Senate, but immediately a group of private citizens in New York organized the Nicaragua Canal Association and obtained concessions to build from both Nicaragua and Costa Rica. Soon this project was being known as the "American," and therefore "legitimate," canal, whereas the Panama was the French, or enemy, canal. More than ever, men like the Seligmans and Morgan seemed to be at war with their own country. The more talk there was of Nicaragua, the harder Jesse Seligman worked to sell Panama.

By the time the Nicaragua group had started digging (and some distance was actually excavated before the project collapsed), De Lesseps and his friends were in serious difficulties. De Lesseps decided that he would have to build locks, and at this he struggled on for another two years. At last, after nine years' work, $400 million had been spent—almost four times the original estimate—and the canal was not quite one-third completed. The Panama Canal Company went under and De Lesseps was sent home to France, disgraced, to face a Parliamentary investigation. In Washington a Congressional committee was set up to find out why tens of thousands of American shareholders had lost money on the canal venture, while men like the Seligmans and Morgan, in commissions for selling the shares, had made so much.

J. Hood Wright, a Drexel, Morgan partner, was summoned to Washington, where he was interrogated by Senator Patterson, the chairman of the investigating committee. Mr. Wright artfully managed to disclaim any responsibility for the disaster. Drexel, Morgan's role, he piously explained, was merely to "help" the Seligmans. He testified that his firm had nothing to do with the Canal Company's purchases, expenditures, or other banking business, but he did admit that his firm had helped the Seligmans purchase the American-built Panama Railroad for the French company.

Senator Patterson wanted to determine how much pressure the banking firms had exerted to swell public confidence in, and promote, the now bankrupt company. He asked Wright, "Was not the moral and business influence of these three great banking houses given to the enterprise?"

Wright replied hedgily, "In what respect?"

"As far as affecting public opinion in the United States was concerned."

"I presume so," said Mr. Wright.

"Was that not sufficient, in a large degree, to mold public opinion in favor of the Panama Canal Company?" asked the Senator.

"That," replied Wright with extreme caution, "I am not prepared to answer."

Of course an honest answer would certainly have been "Yes." It soon turned out that the Seligman-Morgan-Lanier alliance had gone to considerable lengths to appoint men to the American canal committee whose names would add luster and prestige to the project. The investigation unearthed the fact that Jesse Seligman had offered his old friend ex-President Grant the chairmanship of the canal committee at a salary of $24,000 a year—which Grant could certainly have used at that point. But Grant declined the offer, and Jesse had then approached President Hayes's Secretary of the Navy, Richard W. Thompson, who had resigned his Cabinet post to take the job. Obviously, placing a former Navy Secretary in the Canal Company was just the sort of thing Senator Patterson was talking about. Thompson's duties for the company were partly those of a lobbyist—a man who could influence the opinion of Congress (and help persuade it to block the progress of the Nicaragua Canal Company)—and also to strengthen the "image" of the company with the American press, and to inspire the confidence of American stock purchasers.*

The investigation also disclosed that the Seligmans had more reasons than sheer altruism for working so hard for the Canal Company. They themselves had certain juicy contracts for the procurement of machinery and equipment, and, finally, that $300,000 fee for the privilege of using the Seligman name had had certain strings attached. It had been paid "for services rendered" in influencing American public opinion in favor of the canal. The Seligmans were considered to have done their job so well that an additional $100,000 had been paid.

When Jesse Seligman was called before the investigating committee, he proved a more straightforward witness. The entire Panama Canal undertaking, he admitted, had been badly planned and riddled with "corruption, fraud, and thievery."

Senator Thompson was curious about some of the appointments that had been made to the canal committee, and asked Jesse, "Why was Mr. Thompson selected as chairman? He was not a great financier, was he?"

---

* It was the dawn of national advertising, and the value of having a "big name" endorse a product had been early discovered. An ad of the period depicts none other than President and Mrs. Rutherford B. Hayes touting the virtues of an appliance called a "Cold Handle Sad Iron." Lucy Hayes is saying to the President, "We cannot leave until we visit the Enterprise Mfg. Co. and order some of Mrs. Potts' Cold Handle Sad Irons like this." The President replies, "But my dear they are for sale by all Hardware Stores in this country."

Jesse replied, "No, but he was a great statesman and lawyer."

"But you offered the place to General Grant. Now he was a great soldier, a popular idol, but he was not a great lawyer, or financier, or great statesman, was he?"

With a smile, according to the *Congressional Record,* Jesse began, "Well—"

Senator Geary interjected, "There may be some difference of opinion on that point."

Sitting forward in his chair, Jesse Seligman said calmly, "General Grant was a bosom friend of mine, and I always look out for my friends."

Jesse then admitted that he knew American sentiment had been against the Panama Canal at the outset, and he added with candor, "A committee of representative men here, identified with the Canal Company, would have the effect of creating a more favorable sentiment among the American people."

A surprising and not unrelated fact also emerged from the investigation. Secretary Thompson may have accepted the appointment because he, like Jesse, felt obligated to look out for his friends. A few days after Joseph's death, he had written to Jesse:

> In my official capacity as Secretary of the Navy, I have had especial opportunities to understand and appreciate his [Joseph's] character. My first intercourse with your house was had through him, in the summer of 1877, soon after the Department was placed under my charge. At that time, its financial condition was seriously embarrassed, being indebted to your house several hundred thousand dollars, which was steadily increasing on account of drafts drawn by Naval pay officers in all parts of the world, and which were accepted and paid by you in London. It was impossible to discharge the whole of this debt, or even any large proportion of it, without adding to the existing embarrassment and causing serious injury to the Service. When he came to understand this condition of affairs, he at once proposed to carry the debt to the beginning of the next fiscal year and to allow drafts to be continued until then without regard to the amount. The proposition was liberal and in the highest degree patriotic; and having been thankfully accepted by me the Department was enabled to bridge over all its pecuniary trouble. But for this, the injury to its credit and to the Service generally might have been irreparable.

And so, unusual though it seems, the immigrant Seligman brothers, who had crossed the Atlantic in steerage only a few years before, were, for a while, personally meeting the payroll of the United States Navy. This fact Jesse was eager to get into the record.

The investigating committee eventually decided that the banking firms had been guilty of no wrongdoing, had sold the Panama Canal issues in good faith, and that a certain amount of public relations mixed with banking was excusable. But the whole Panama Canal scandal troubled Jesse, now in his sixties, who felt he had let his dead brother down. For it had been Joseph who had always insisted on "our reputation for the strictest integrity."

What had happened to the Seligmans' reputation was no worse than what was happening to the financial community generally. Wall Street itself had serious public-relations problems. Americans no longer spoke with admiration and respect of "the men who guide our Nation's financial future." Instead, the "broker tribe" had become a small and greedy band of self-interested villains, and Wall Street had become the wickedest street in the world

Congress, at this point, decided to step in and make the canal a United States project once and for all, and once again the favored route was through Nicaragua. (Partly, this was because American engineers wanted to disassociate themselves from the French fiasco at Panama.) The Seligmans might have quietly withdrawn, with their considerable profits, from the whole canal arena. But they were too psychologically and emotionally involved to do so. And there was more to it than sentiment now. They had a certain interest in any assets (there was a railroad, for instance, and a few partially finished terminals) of the old company which could be salvaged and sold to the new U.S. company. So naturally the brothers were committed to a Panama route. They therefore embarked upon a long campaign to reverse American public opinion and discredit Nicaragua.*

While debates about canal routes were continuing in Washington, the Seligmans approached a friend of theirs, Senator Mark Hanna. A committee called the Inter-Oceanic Commission had been appointed to study possible canal routes, and the Seligmans asked Hanna to ask the Congress to make no recommendation until the commission's report was in. Hanna agreed, and Congress, at his request, agreed to wait. Then, to the Seligmans' disappointment, the commission delivered its report— overwhelmingly favoring Nicaragua.

Now, in a costly desperation move, the Seligmans in New York and Paris approached a man named Philippe Buneau-Varilla. Buneau-Varilla has been called "the man who invented Panama," and yet, in a sense, it was the Seligmans who invented, or helped invent, M. Buneau-Varilla. He was a suave, mustachioed little man who had first caught the

---

* Which modern engineering studies have determined would actually have been a better route.

attention of the Seligmans through his activities in the Dreyfus case.* To the Seligmans, M. Buneau-Varilla seemed uniquely talented when it came to shocking the public into a change of heart. By the most delightful coincidence, it turned out that Buneau-Varilla had been devoted to the idea of a canal through Panama since the age of ten, ever since hearing of De Lesseps' feat at Suez. Without hesitation, he agreed to take the job.

He arrived in the United States and immediately launched into a heavy schedule of speechmaking. Nevertheless, a few months after Buneau-Varilla's arrival, Congress voted unanimously in favor of the Nicaragua route. Now, backed by the Seligmans, Buneau-Varilla moved into high gear in a last-ditch attempt to swing the Senate. Buneau-Varilla fought so hard and made so many heated speeches that the French Foreign Minister in Washington wired Buneau-Varilla's brother in Paris, saying that Philippe's activities were embarrassing to France, and suggesting that Philippe had lost his mind. The brother hurried to America, only to discover that Philippe was out to win and would not be stopped.

An Old Testament Deity stepped in to help the Seligmans and their chief propagandist. A volcano on the island of Saint Vincent in the West Indies erupted, killing several thousand people. Two days before that, the supposedly dead volcano of Mount Pelée erupted on Martinique, and thirty thousand people died. Nicaragua had a volcanic history. Panama did not. Buneau-Varilla suddenly remembered something he had once seen. He rushed to a stamp store and there, sure enough, was a five-peso Nicaraguan stamp depicting the smoking mountain of Momotombo. Buneau-Varilla bought ninety volcano stamps, affixed each to a letterhead, and wrote below each: "An official witness of the volcanic activity of the isthmus of Nicaragua." He mailed one to each Senator three days before the balloting. He and the Seligmans waited. The Senate declared in favor of Panama with only eight dissenting votes. The Seligmans cheered.

Buneau-Varilla then bought enough volcano stamps for the House of Representatives, and soon the House too had reversed itself. But there were new troubles. The Isthmus of Panama was then a part of Colombia, and Colombia now changed her mind about granting a new right of

---

* He had been a classmate of Colonel Dreyfus at l'Ecole Polytechnique, and, at the time of Dreyfus' conviction, Buneau-Varilla and his brother had been publishers of *Le Matin* in Paris. It was the Buneau-Varilla brothers who, in 1896, had startled the world by publishing photographs of two letters—one the incriminating letter Dreyfus had allegedly written to the German attaché, and the other, in a totally different handwriting, a letter Dreyfus had actually written a few years earlier to Philippe Buneau-Varilla. This bit of journalism reopened the case, and led to the whole affair that followed.

way. Buneau-Varilla began applying pressure, and certain sums of money began finding their way into Colombian officials' hands. Colombia seemed about to change her mind, but then voted not to ratify the canal treaty. "There is nothing left," Buneau-Varilla explained to the Seligmans, "but to have Panama secede from Colombia. That will mean a revolution." James Seligman wanted to know, "How much would a revolution cost?"

That would, of course, depend. Buneau-Varilla rented a suite at the Waldorf-Astoria and invited a group of would-be secessionists to a meeting there. The cost of a revolution was the chief topic on the agenda. The Panamanians insisted that they needed at least six million dollars to pay for their guerrillas. Buneau-Varilla hurried to the Seligmans, who said that six million was a bit too high. Buneau-Varilla returned with the Seligmans' best offer—$100,000. It would have to be a cut-rate revolution, but the Panamanians accepted the terms.

Buneau-Varilla then went quickly back to the Seligman offices. At a desk in the partners' room he wrote a Panamanian Declaration of Independence and a constitution. He went to Macy's and bought silk for a Panama flag, which he had designed himself and, at James Seligman's summer house in Westchester, he spent a long evening stitching his new flag together. The following Monday he boarded a train for Washington and, as he said later, "I called on President Roosevelt and asked him point-blank if, when the revolt broke out, an American war ship would be sent to Panama to protect American lives and interests [including Seligman interests]. The President just looked at me; he said nothing. Of course, a President of the United States could not give such a commitment, especially to a foreigner and private citizen like me. But his look was enough for me."

And of course the warship *Nashville* did go to Panama to oversee the crisis. It stood offshore, and its presence was a considerable morale factor for the seceding Panamanians—and helped persuade the Colombians to put down their weapons. The day was won for Philippe Buneau-Varilla, and for the Seligmans. The hand-stitched flag fluttered aloft, saluting one of the greatest public-relations triumphs of the age.

The Seligmans, understandably, were eager to show their gratitude to their new friend. They made a series of discreet suggestions to certain of *their* friends in Washington, and presently the most implausible event in an altogether unlikely career had come to pass: Philippe Buneau-Varilla, a citizen of France, was appointed the first Ambassador of the Republic of Panama to the United States.

Old Jesse Seligman had, in the meantime, withdrawn almost completely from the Panama Canal and its problems. After the failure of the first canal company, and the ordeal of the Congressional investigation, he too had begun to fail. Now Jesse's pride was assaulted again—from a place that wounded him even more.

The situation in New York's private clubs had become, in the 1890's, as it continues to be today, a complicated one. The Knickerbocker had a Jew among its founding members—Moses Lazarus, the father of Emma. The Union Club, older and far grander, had several Sephardic Lazaruses, Nathans, and Hendrickses. It had also had August Belmont, and it now had his sons—August, Jr., Oliver, and Perry—and it had at least one acknowledged German Jew, the banker Adolph Ladenburg. Though James Speyer campaigned vigorously against organizations which discriminated against Jews, he himself was considered "the only Jew in the Racquet Club." For years, the most steadfastly anti-Jewish club in New York was the University, though the Yale seal, partly in Hebrew, on the club's McKim façade, often led people to suppose otherwise. The University Club had reciprocal privileges with the Bath Club in London, to which Isaac Seligman, and several of his sons, belonged. Yet when Isaac Seligman visited New York and attempted to stay at the University Club, he was advised against it. Other clubs operated on policies that were consistent only in their inconsistency.*

The Union League was Jesse Seligman's favorite club. He and his brothers Joseph and William had been virtually founding members. Joseph had been a vice president of the club at the time of his death, and now, in 1893, Jesse also was a vice president. Yet, though perhaps Jesse hadn't noticed it, or refused to believe it, the Union League Club had already begun to adopt a certain "policy." Jesse's son Theodore was a young lawyer, recently out of Harvard, and had come to New York to practice. It seemed natural, to both Jesse and his son, that Theodore should join the Union League, which the Seligmans fondly thought of as part of the family. Theodore's membership was sponsored by Mr. LeGrand Camon, a founding member, and he was seconded by General Horace Porter. Many other distinguished members, including Joseph Choate and Elihu Root, were stanchly behind him. Yet, when action was taken on his membership application, Theodore Seligman was rejected. With exemplary lack of tact, the membership committee explained to Jesse that it was "not a personal matter in any way, either as to father or son. The objection is purely racial."

Jesse immediately tendered his resignation. Equally quickly, and apparently at a loss as to why Jesse should be in the least bit upset about it, the club's members voted unanimously not to accept it. Jesse stalked out the front door.

Being a Seligman and unable to take an insult lying down, Jesse

---

* At Yale the leading senior society, Skull and Bones, for years never took in a Jew, though it did take in the Negro football player, Levi Jackson. *That* led to the observation, "If his name had been the other way around . . ."

released the story to the newspapers. There were the usual tongue-clicking and head-shaking and what-have-we-come-to editorials, but the fact was that it was a drearily familiar tale. The Mayor of New York, Thomas F. Gilroy, announced himself "shocked" over the club's treatment of Jesse and, the very next week, revealed that a way had been devised by which the entire City of New York could "pay tribute" to Jesse Seligman, and demonstrate the "great honor" in which he was held by his fellow citizens.

It was a strange tribute that Mayor Gilroy devised. The Spanish Duke of Veragua was due to arrive in the city on a more or less state visit, and was to be driven down Broadway to City Hall, where he would be presented to the Mayor. The Mayor announced that his tribute would be to borrow Jesse's coach—not Jesse himself, nor Henriette, nor young Theodore, whose reaction (unbridled embarrassment) to the hubbub the snub was causing was totally overlooked, but just the Seligman landau, horses, coachman, and footmen, to transport the Duke and Duchess. Whether this novel form of bestowing an honor comforted or merely amused Jesse is not known, but it thoroughly annoyed Henriette. The Mayor was commandeering her coach at an hour that coincided with her daily drive through the park.

The city flocked to cheer and ogle the royal couple, who, at the center of a long procession—including a full military regimental escort, marching bands, and mounted police—moved grandly downtown in the Seligmans' landau, with the Seligman footmen wearing rosettes of the Spanish colors.

Though he was still technically a member, Jesse never set foot inside the Union League Club again. His bitterness over the episode probably shortened his life, just as the affair with Judge Hilton shortened his brother's. Soon afterward Jesse's health began to fail. Tired and suffering from Bright's disease, he and his wife, their three sons and two of their daughters, boarded their private railroad car for California. (Travel, often elaborately undertaken, was considered good for the ailing in those days.) Ostensibly, the trip was for Jesse's health, but privately he had said that he never wanted to live in New York again. The family arrived at Coronado Beach in April, 1894. There, in the land he had come to as a gold-seeking pioneer half a century before, Jesse Seligman died.

Now New York undertook a prolonged display of guilt. Collis P. Huntington, a fellow railroad enthusiast and president of the Southern Pacific, ordered a special three-car funeral train to bear Jesse's body, and his widow and children, back to New York. Huntington commanded that the train be given precedence over all others, and as it made its long journey eastward its progress was followed in daily bulletins by all the New York papers.

A large delegation of mourners met the train at the station, and a throng of more than two thousand people appeared at Temple Emanu-El for the funeral, including a sixty-man delegation from the Union League Club who, led by the club's president, came on foot from the clubhouse to the temple. The mourners' names read like a Who's Who in banking, commerce and government of the era, and included Seth Low, Cornelius N. Bliss, Oscar S. Straus, Mayor Gilroy, Emanuel Lehman, John Wanamaker, Carl Schurz, Abraham Wolff, James Mc-Creery, John Crosby Brown, and Bishop Henry C. Potter. A hundred and fifty children "whose rosy cheeks and cheerful looks betokened the care that is taken of them" entered the temple from Jesse's Hebrew Orphan Asylum. Outside, on Fifth Avenue, the police struggled with mourners who could not get in and, in the only unseemly moment of the day, arrested two of them, Moritz Rodeburg and James Back, who were identified as Nos. 23 and 2018, respectively, in the rogues' gallery and who had been circulating among the wealthy throng as pickpockets. After the services, a slow procession carried the body to the Seligman mausoleum at Salem Fields, where Victor Herbert, "the violinist," played at the grave.

Newspaper eulogies for Jesse continued for days. Several editors drew morals from his career. For example, the Bath, Maine, *Times* commented with Yankee common sense: "The late Jesse Seligman . . . came to this country in 1840, and when he landed, inquired for a place where he could board for one dollar a week. He died worth $30,000,-000. Young man, if you follow his example, especially about the one dollar a week, you may be able to do the same thing."

In New York the *Morning Advertiser* made Jesse the occasion of tart political comment:

> The conditions under which he flourished would still exist but for some of the unreasonable exactions of Labor Organizations and but for the unwholesome doctrine that has been promulgated by political demagogues that labor has no fair chance and must look to legislation to do for the workingman what Mr. Seligman and thousands of others have done for themselves. These successful men, working with their hands and spending less than their small earnings, did not look for any easy road to success. Industry, thrift, and caution, turning a deaf ear to the allurements of fleeting pleasures and to the harangues of the demagogue, comprise all the secret of their success.

One point was missed. This was that Jesse's funeral bore overtones of a deeper, more poignant tragedy. A whole era was over. Joseph, Jesse, and Abraham Seligman were all dead, and so were two of their sisters, Babette and Sarah. The other five brothers were old men now, and losing their effectiveness. (James Seligman, seventy, whose peddling innovation, the horse and wagon, had done so much to improve the Seligmans' fortunes, now distrusted "that new gadget," the telephone, and required an underling to place and accept all his calls.) Fanny Seligman's dream for "the boys, the boys" was being intercepted by the logic of mortality.

The great era of J. & W. Seligman & Company, as a firm, was also over. It had really ended fourteen years before when Joseph died and was no longer there to tell his brothers what to do. Joseph and his brothers had many children, but who would carry on? The company was beginning its long decline, from a great international banking house with offices in New York, San Francisco, New Orleans, Paris, and London to what it is today—a small, prestigious investment house with but a single office in New York.

31

THE LADIES

In the glorious, innocent 1880's and 1890's Wall Street, when it wasn't undergoing panics, had been a jolly, happy-go-lucky place. As *Harper's Magazine* pointed out, "The nervous force necessarily expended in rapid reasoning and quick decision is often directed into other channels to relieve the overtasked brain."

The younger members of "the broker tribe," as they were called, relieved their overtasked brains with such affairs as an annual regatta in the harbor for their rowing association. Beer flowed plentifully, and the men showed up in jaunty straw boaters. (A star oarsman in these events was Isaac Newton Seligman, Joseph's son; Ike had rowed on the Columbia crew, and had helped his college defeat both Harvard and Yale on Saratoga Lake.) There were also baseball games against college teams, and "friendly struggles among themselves, in which the 'Good Boys' pitted against the 'Bad Boys.' " Lunchtime wrestling matches on Bowling Green were also popular.

The biggest party of all took place at Christmas, and all merry hell broke loose on the Street when members of the financial community "luxuriate in the blowing of tin horns and bugles, smashing of broker hats, pelting with blown bladders, wet towels, and surreptitious snowballs, and in the sly insertion of cooling crystals between the collars of unsuspecting brethren. Hot pennies are sometimes used."

But for the German Jewish bankers, the horseplay and the fraternity-lodge equality tended to halt at the close of the business day, and the men returned to their houses and womenfolk uptown, and to a social life that was increasingly family-centered and self-contained.

Each woman had her group of women friends whose husbands were also her husband's friends, and often these friendships led to tighter business connections, and, in the younger generation, when sons and daughters of friends married each other, friendships were cemented into kinships. The mothers of the crowd studied the marriage market for suitable partners, while fathers studied the upcoming crop of young men as possible business partners. Marcus and Bertha Goldman were particularly good friends of Joseph and Sophia Sachs, the poor tutor and the rich goldsmith's daughter who had run away to America in 1848. In the United States Joseph had worked as a schoolteacher—and, for a period, as a rabbi—in Baltimore and Boston before settling in New York. It was Joseph's oldest son, Julius, a scholar like his father, who had established the Sachs Collegiate Institute, and who taught most of the children of the crowd, and Julius married the Goldmans' daughter, Rosa—a match both Bertha Goldman and Sophia Sachs had promoted. Now, in the 1880's, another Goldman daughter, Louise, was marriageable, and Bertha and Sophia decided that she would be perfect for Sophia's second son, Sam. The young people agreed, and Marcus Goldman invited Sam to be his first partner in the commercial-paper business which, up to this point, he still carried on singlehandedly, with the help of his hat.*

To join his new father-in-law, Sam Sachs was required to liquidate a small dry-goods business which he had been operating, and, to facilitate this, Marcus loaned Sam $15,000. The loan was to be repaid in three promissory notes of $5,000 each, over a three-year period. By the time Sam's and Louise's third son was born, Sam had repaid Marcus two of the three notes, and Grandfather Marcus, in his old-fashioned German script, wrote formally to his son-in-law to say that, in recognition of Sam's "energy and ability" as a partner, and in honor of little Walter's arrival, he was forgiving Sam the final payment. Louise Goldman Sachs, a sentimental sort, always kept her father's letter, along with the canceled note, in the little strongbox where she kept, tied in faded bows, her little boys' silky blond ringlets and, dated and labeled, all their baby teeth.

"And thus," Walter Sachs was able to say years later, "it appeared

---

* By 1880 the Goldman topper transported as much as $30 million worth of paper a year.

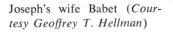

Joseph Seligman as a young
man (*Courtesy J. & W. Seligman & Co.*)

Joseph's wife Babet (*Courtesy Geoffrey T. Hellman*)

The house in Baiersdorf's "Jew Street" where all eight Seligman brothers
were born (*Courtesy J. & W. Seligman & Co.*)

A nineteenth-century peddler, prosperous enough to buy a horse and wagon of his own, offers his wares to rural housewives (*Bettmann Archive*)

"The Royal Feast of the Money Kings" as caricatured in the New York *World,* 1884. Jesse Seligman, former peddler, is third "king" from right (*Courtesy J. & W. Seligman & Co.*)

William Seligman (*Courtesy Geoffrey T. Hellman*)

Joseph Seligman in later years (*Courtesy Geoffrey T. Hellman*)

Jesse Seligman (*Courtesy Geoffrey T. Hellman*)

The locomotive "Seligman" which Joseph purchased, then rented back to the line for $70 a week (*Courtesy J. & W. Seligman & Co.*)

Jefferson Seligman, family eccentric, was interested in noise abatement, street-washing methods, was opposed to handshaking, preferred kissing (*N.Y.* Daily News *photo*)

CITY OF NEW YORK
OFFICE OF THE MAYOR

TO WHOM IT MAY CONCERN:

Mr. Jefferson Seligman is observing traffic conditions in the City of New York and any courtesies which may be extended to him will be appreciated.

John L. Hylan
M a y o r.

March 33, 1923.

(*Letter courtesy J. & W. Seligman & Co.*)

Isaac Newton Seligman and his daughter Margaret (*Courtesy Mrs. Joan L. Simon*)

Kuhn, Loeb founder, Solomon Loeb (*Courtesy Kuhn, Loeb & Co.*)

Offices of Lehman, Durr & Co. on Court Square, Montgomery, Alabama, shortly after the Civil War (*Courtesy Lehman Brothers*)

The Guggenheim boys: (*left to right*) Benjamin, Murry, Isaac, father Meyer, Daniel, Solomon, Simon, William (alias "Gatenby Williams") (*Culver*)

"Christmas Carnival in the New York Stock Exchange" as *Harper's Magazine* saw it in 1885 (*Courtesy J. & W. Seligman & Co.*)

August Belmont, né Schön-
berg, shortly after his marriage (*Museum of the City
of New York*)

The beautiful Caroline Slidell
Perry Belmont, around 1850
(*Museum of the City of New
York*)

August Belmont as an established social success (*Culver*)

Mrs. August Belmont in her carriage outside "Bythesea," her Newport home (*Culver*)

Jacob Schiff, a believer in physical exercise, often walked more than sixty city blocks before taking a cab to his downtown office (*Culver*)

The Schiff children, Morti and Frieda, posed for this bas-relief by Augustus Saint-Gaudens during their Christmas holiday, 1888 (*Metropolitan Museum of Art, Gift of Jacob H. Schiff, 1905*)

Frieda Schiff Warburg's upstairs sitting room at 1109 Fifth Avenue. Her portrait hangs above mantel (*Jewish Theological Seminary of America*)

Battle site: the Warburg house at 1109 Fifth Avenue (*Jewish Theological Seminary of America*)

Felix Warburg aboard his yacht *Carol* (*Courtesy Mrs. Walter N. Rothschild*)

Frieda Schiff Warburg (*Courtesy Mrs. Walter N. Rothschild*)

Entrance hall at 1109 Fifth Avenue, looking into Felix Warburg's study where he kept his print collection (*Jewish Theological Seminary of America*)

Under Jacob Schiff's portrait, the present generation carries on at Kuhn, Loeb. (*From left*) Gilbert W. Kahn, son of Otto Kahn, and Schiff's grandsons, John M. Schiff and Frederick M. Warburg (*Courtesy Kuhn, Loeb & Co.*)

Adolph Lewisohn in the garden of his Westchester estate with grand-daughters (*from left*) Marjorie, Elizabeth, and Joan (*Courtesy Mrs. Joan L. Simon*)

Adolph Lewisohn's top-floor art gallery at 881 Fifth Avenue. Paintings (*above, from left*) by Degas, Cézanne, Renoir, three Cézannes, Rousseau, Van Gogh (the celebrated "L'Arlésienne"), Renoir (?), Manet. (*Below, from left*) Picasso, Degas, Cézanne, Manet, Renoir, Degas, Monet. Sculptures by Renoir, Rodin, Bourdelle. Table cases held Shakespeare first folios and illuminated Bibles (*Photos courtesy Mrs. Joan L. Simon*)

Otto H. Kahn and his daughter on a visit to Berlin to study conditions in Germany (*Bettman Archive*)

Otto Kahn's Italian Renaissance palace at 1100 Fifth Avenue

Otto Kahn's house at 1100 Fifth Avenue. (*Above*) His private office with enclosed stairway at rear leading to his bedroom. From the small window at top he liked to have the last word before retiring. (*Below*) Mr. Kahn's library

In the autumn of 1915, a number of "Our Crowd" gathered at the Seligmans' Fish Rock Camp on Upper Saranac Lake, N.Y., to celebrate Aunt Guta Loeb Seligman's 50th birthday. Of the 31 people in this picture, 28 are either descendants or married to descendants of David Seligman or Solomon Loeb, and a 29th is a relative by legal adoption. *From left to right, top row:* Mrs. Isaac N. Seligman (the former Guta Loeb, a daughter of Solomon Loeb); her husband, Isaac N. Seligman (grandson of David Seligman); Mrs. Theodore Hellman (née Frances Seligman, a sister of Isaac N.); Mrs. Edwin R. A. Seligman (née Caroline Beer, married to a brother of Isaac N. and Frances); James Paul Warburg (son of Paul M. Warburg, nephew of Guta Loeb Seligman, and a grandson of Solomon Loeb); Paul M. Warburg (Guta's brother-in-law); Hugo Seligman (son of Leopold Seligman, first cousin of Isaac N. Seligman); George Beer (brother of Mrs. Edwin R. A. Seligman, married to Edith Hellman, a niece of Isaac N. Seligman); George Washington Seligman, a brother of Isaac N.; Mrs. George Washington Seligman (née Alice Benedict) with her dog; Dorothy Borg (whose mother was a Beer, a sister of George Beer and Mrs. Edwin R. A. Seligman); Eleanor Beer, adopted daughter of the George Beers. *Second row, from left:* Mrs. Hugo Seligman; Mrs. George S. Hellman (married to a grandson of Joseph Seligman); Mrs. Paul M. Warburg (née Nina Loeb, Guta Loeb's sister Mrs. Edgar A. Hellman (married to anoth grandson of Joseph Seligman); Mrs. Georg Beer (née Edith Hellman, a granddaughter Joseph Seligman) with her dog, Daisy; an u known guest, visiting from Germany. *Third ro from left:* Joseph L. Seligman, son of Guta a Isaac N. Seligman (a grandson of both Josep Seligman and Solomon Loeb); Joseph L. Seli man, Jr. on his mother's lap; Mrs. Joseph Seligman; Margaret V. Seligman, a daughter Guta and Isaac N. (later married to Sa Lewisohn); Eustace Seligman (son of t E. R. A. Seligmans) wearing what appears be a German Iron Cross in his lapel; Eustace sister Hazel Seligman; Bettina Warburg, daug ter of the Paul M. Warburgs; Rhoda Hellma a grandniece of Guta and Isaac N. *Bottom, fro left:* A Hellman cousin, Janice; her father, Edg A. Hellman; an unidentified man in a mas who many in the family think must have bee a relative—he seems to be making a Jewis peddler-parody gesture, and how would he ha had the effrontery to do this if he weren't r lated? On his knee is Margaret Hellman, Janice sister. *Lower right:* Professor Edwin R. A. Seli man, father of Eustace and Hazel, brother Isaac N. and George Washington Seligman an of Frances Hellman, brother-in-law and unc by marriage of George Beer (*Courtesy M H. E. Hellman*)

that on the very first day of my entrance into this world, I concluded my first business deal for Goldman, Sachs."

The Goldmans and the Sachses, however, were still relatively minor figures, socially, in the crowd. Two ladies had for years contended for social leadership—Mrs. Solomon Loeb and Mrs. Jesse Seligman. Betty Loeb was famous chiefly for her dinners, whereas Henriette Seligman was renowned for the large scale on which she lived and for her grand manner.

Henriette was a creature of habit. Her carriage always arrived at her door at precisely the same moment each day for her drive through Central Park, and neither the length nor the route of the excursion ever varied. She and Jesse entertained frequently, and, since Henriette believed that punctuality was not only a duty of royalty but a courtesy that royalty deserved, whenever her butler announced dinner, she arose and proceeded into the dining room, regardless of whether or not all her guests had arrived. When she traveled to Europe, as she did at intervals of clocklike regularity, she always engaged the same stateroom on the same steamship and, since her itinerary never varied, the same suites in the same hotels.

In Paris her hotel was, naturally, the Ritz, and once the old Kaiser Wilhelm was planning a state visit to Paris coincidental with Mrs. Seligman's. The Ritz, who knew Mrs. Seligman's preferences only too well, deemed it wise to go through the German ambassador to see if, just possibly, Mrs. Seligman would be willing to relinquish her suite for the Kaiser and accept another. Henriette replied that she was "not ready for a change of suite," and that, though she was very sorry, nothing could be done. The Kaiser slept elsewhere.

She had, on the other hand, a true sense of *noblesse oblige* when it came to the sleeping habits of the working classes. Early one morning in her New York house, Henriette was awakened by a noise belowstairs. Convinced of the presence of a burglar, she rose and, in wrapper and slippers, descended to the parlor floor to find the culprit. She found no one there, and so, though she was extremely nearsighted and had left her glasses upstairs and had only a candle to light her way, she continued to the basement. There, in the darkness ahead of her, she heard the sound of running footsteps as the frightened prowler hurried to an open window and made his way out. Henriette proceeded to the window and cried out imperiously, "Do not return!" to the retreating figure in the street. Then she closed and bolted the window and went upstairs to bed.

The next day she told her friends and family of this episode at her customary hour for telling things, teatime. Someone asked her why she hadn't waked her husband. "Mr. Seligman was recovering from an illness," she replied. "I couldn't think of disturbing him."

"But, Auntie," said a nephew, "why didn't you ring for one of the menservants?"

She gave the young man a disapproving look. "My servants," she said, "had done their day's work. It was my duty to put my home in order."

The Seligman house stood in Forty-sixth Street near Fifth Avenue, and the Jay Gould mansion was a block to the north. Between these two residences stood a hotel called the Windsor, which burned down with a great loss of life. During the fire Henriette, with her customary considerateness, opened the lower floors of her house for use as a temporary hospital for the wounded and dying, and her daughters and maids served sandwiches and coffee to the firemen. Mrs. Seligman herself could not come down; the fire occurred at that hour of the day which she customarily devoted to her embroidery. It was here, over her needlework in her upstairs sitting room, that she agreed to receive the Fire Commissioner of the City of New York, who said he had come to deliver a message of some urgency, even though it was not the proper hour for callers. The Commissioner was ushered in, and explained that the shell of the Windsor seemed about to collapse, and that very likely a large portion of it would fall on Mrs. Seligman's house.

"Then, Commissioner, I do feel that the lady of the house should be present when that happens," said Henriette, completing a stitch.

"Your roof has already caught fire three times," said the Commissioner and, clearly aware that he was in the presence of a Personage, added, "I have come here to have the honor of escorting you out."

"Thank you very much," said Henriette, "but my menservants—" there were four—"are taking care of the roof."

"Exactly. And I want them to continue doing just what they're doing—putting out the flames on the roof."

Henriette gave him another of her stern looks. "Mr. Commissioner," she said, "are you suggesting that *I* leave and my servants *stay?*"

"Of course."

"If a house is safe enough for the servants, it is safe enough for the mistress," said Mrs. Seligman, and went on with her embroidery.

At ten o'clock, her usual hour, she prepared to retire. As she rose to go to her bedroom, she said to one of her nephews, "If things become *too* dangerous, I count upon your waking me." In her bedroom she undressed and turned down her bed. This was her only concession to the situation, that she did not ring for one of her maids to turn down the coverlet for her.

A few feet away from her bedroom wall, a tower of flames rose into the night. Above her, through the night, her roof caught fire repeatedly. Just before midnight, the blazing husk of the Windsor tipped, swayed, and came thundering down, missing the Seligman house by inches and scattering fiery bricks on the roofs of the Seligmans' and the Goulds'. Mrs. Seligman slept on. The Goulds had evacuated their house hours before.

Babet Seligman, Joseph's widow, was a much more modest lady, who was always rather awed by the ways of her aristocratic sister-in-law. After her husband's death Babet went into heavy mourning, and, though she survived Joseph by nearly a quarter of a century, she never emerged from her widow's weeds and never again appeared at any large social gathering or public function. Her entertaining was limited to little family dinners. Edward, her coachman, also went into perpetual mourning for his master, in a black uniform with the monogram "J.S." stitched in black on the sleeve. Edward, in fact, became Babet Seligman's one male friend. On their rides through the park they chatted through the speaking tube.

Quite another story was James Seligman's wife, Rosa. Rosa was a Content, and James married her when she was just seventeen, a beauty with a highly bred, olive-skinned Modigliani face and huge dark flashing eyes. But she had a violent and unpredictable temper, and the Contents had made it quite clear that they thought Rosa was marrying beneath her station, and that they had consented to the union simply because James Seligman was rich.

By the 1880's James's and Rosa's had become a notably unhappy marriage. Rosa was an excellent dancer, but James was not. "Germans," she used to say contemptuously, "are always heavy on their feet." She took her Content heritage seriously, and enjoyed referring to the Seligmans as "the peddlers." It soon developed that she was an almost compulsive spender. James was miserly in his personal spending, but the family said that this was because it cost him so much to pay Rosa's bills. She demanded furs, dresses, jewels, and beautiful houses, and James got them for her. She insisted on numerous servants, and he hired them for her, even though she often pointed out that the servants had more distinguished pedigrees than the Seligmans. She had an English butler whose first name was the same as her husband's, and it amused her to say, in front of dinner guests, "James, will you please tell Jim that dinner is ready?"

She raised eight children, but would let none of them bring friends into the house, claiming that other people's children were inferior and probably germy. In her youth Rosa's behavior had been attributed to "temperament," and she was considered "high-strung." As she grew older, her conduct grew increasingly erratic, her outbursts and tantrums more frequent and alarming. Soon Seligman family letters began to refer darkly to "our family skeleton"—not a reference to Rosa, but to the fact that James had sought solace in a young mistress. Rosa began to spend most of her days in department stores, where she would astonish sales-girls by leaning across counter tops and whispering confidentially, "When do you think my husband last slept with me?"

Rosa Content Seligman may have been odd, but her children were even odder. One daughter, Florette, married Meyer Guggenheim's son, Benjamin (the "smelter" of the Seligmans' cablegram), and that union produced the art-collecting Peggy Guggenheim, who, in her autobiography, wrote that most of her Seligman aunts and uncles were "peculiar, if not mad." She also insists that James and Rosa had eleven children, though *The Seligman Family Register,* privately published in 1913, lists only eight. What became of the other three, if they ever existed, is a family mystery. The eight remaining were certainly colorful.

One aunt, wrote Peggy Guggenheim,

> was an incurable soprano. If you happened to meet her on the corner of Fifth Avenue while waiting for a bus, she would open her mouth wide and sing scales trying to make you do as much. She wore her hat hanging off the back of her head or tilted over one ear. A rose was always stuck in her hair. Long hatpins emerged dangerously, not from her hat, but from her hair. Her trailing dresses swept up the dust of the streets. She invariably wore a feather boa. She was an excellent cook and made beautiful tomato jelly. Whenever she wasn't at the piano, she could be found in the kitchen or reading the ticker-tape. She had a strange complex about germs and was forever wiping her furniture with Lysol. But she had such extraordinary charm that I really loved her. I cannot say her husband felt as much. After he had fought with her for over thirty years, he tried to kill her and one of her sons by hitting them with a golf club. Not succeeding, he rushed to the reservoir where he drowned himself with heavy weights tied to his feet.

Another of Rosa's daughters grew to be enormously fat. Despite this handicap she convinced herself that she had had a long and passionate love affair with a druggist. She even knew his name—Balch. The family tried to persuade her that the druggist Balch was imaginary, but to no avail. She was so overridden with guilt and remorse that she became "melancholic" and had to be placed in a home.

James's son Washington had curious dietary theories, and lived on charcoal and cracked ice and almost no food. His teeth were black from chewing charcoal, and the ice he sucked between the bites of charcoal made him a somewhat noisy dinner companion. Whiskey was also a part of his diet, and he always had a glassful before breakfast. He had his suits constructed with a special zinc-lined pocket to hold his ice cubes, and once, when his tailor mistook Washington's instructions, Washington cried out, "No! No! The *right* pocket is to hold the ice! the *left* pocket is for the charcoal"—to the bewilderment of other customers in the shop. At a very early age he had adopted the practice of threatening to commit suicide unless his father gave him what he wanted and, as a result, he was permitted to keep his very own mistress in his room—a room none of the rest of the family was permitted to visit. He was certainly a trial. Finally, however, he carried out one of his threats and shot himself in the temple.

Another brother had a neurosis the opposite of his mother's. He refused to spend any money at all. In order to eat, he showed up at his relatives' houses at mealtimes, usually saying he wasn't hungry and then devouring everything in sight. He repaid his hosts with after-dinner entertainment; it was always the same. He placed chairs in a long row, and then slid and wiggled along the seats on his stomach. His act was called "the snake."

Brother Eugene had been an infant prodigy, and was ready for college at the age of eleven. So as not to be conspicuous, he waited three years and graduated from Columbia at eighteen with the highest honors in his class. He became a practicing lawyer, and a bachelor, whose only pronounced peculiarity was his obsession about cleanliness. He bathed six or seven times each weekday, and much oftener on Sundays. De Witt Seligman also had a law degree, but he never practiced. His favorite pastime was writing plays, none of which was ever produced. Playwriting experts used to say that De Witt had talent—at least for getting his characters into suspenseful situations and predicaments. The only trouble was, he could never quite figure out solutions for the troubles his characters had got themselves into. Invariably his plays ended in a way that reflected their author's dilemma: a gigantic explosion took place, eliminating everybody.

Jefferson Seligman had ways more beguiling than any of his brothers and sisters. Jeff married a girl named Julia Wormser for whom he cared little. The couple soon separated, and Jeff took two small hotel rooms in the East Sixties where he began a life devoted to keeping young ladies clothed and warm. Peggy Guggenheim has said that her uncle's rooms were stocked with fur coats, and "Almost any girl could have one for the asking." Geoffrey T. Hellman, on the other hand, has written that Jeff kept closets full of dresses from Klein's which were equally available to all his friends. Probably he went through a fur-coat period, and then, for reasons of economy, followed this with a dresses-from-Klein's period. It is known that his sister Florette once visited him and seized a supply of dresses in her size, saying, "I don't see why I shouldn't have some, too!"

Jeff had some charming social theories. Once, in a newspaper interview, he came out strongly against the practice of shaking hands, saying that this custom sped the transmission of germs. Instead of handshaking, he recommended kissing. He also suggested that the New York Street Cleaning Department should not sprinkle streets their entire length, but leave little dry gaps every block or so, so that old ladies could cross without getting their feet wet.

Jeff Seligman had the health and welfare of the whole human race at heart. He had been made a partner in J. & W. Seligman & Company, but he was never really interested in banking, and there is no evidence that he did any work, executed a single order, or participated in a single decision. But instead, as Geoffrey Hellman has written, "Somewhere along the line he got off on a novel tack. He began to establish himself as the fruit-and-ginger Seligman." He had a theory that plenty of fruit and ginger was good for the body and good for the brains, and he arrived at the office each morning with his basket of fruit and his box of ginger. Starting in the partners' room, where the brains of the company were supposedly concentrated, he distributed his goods to his cousins and uncles. "On even the busiest days, the partners would accept the fruit and ginger Jeff offered," a former Seligman employee told Hellman. "He would then distribute the remainder to the lower echelons. One day, when I was talking to one of the partners in the partners' room, Jeff gave me a banana. I went back to my desk in another room, and a little while later Jeff showed up and started to hand me an orange. He peered at me, and withdrew the orange. 'You've already had your fruit,' he said."

J & W. Seligman eventually established a dining room on the top floor of their Wall Street building, and, having checked to make sure that the kitchen contained plenty of fresh fruit, Jeff was able to discontinue his fruit line, but he continued to serve ginger. Jeff Seligman was Peggy Guggenheim's favorite uncle. She called him "a gentleman of the old school."

Peggy's mother, Florette, was not without her little quirks. She had a strange nervous habit of repeating phrases three times. Once, when stopped by a policeman for driving the wrong way down a one-way street, Florette replied, with some logic, "But I was only going one way, one way, one way." Another family story insists that Florette once told a clerk in a department store, "I want a hat with a feather, a feather, a feather," and was sold a hat with three feathers.

Peggy Guggenheim has referred to her mother's and grandmother's circle of friends as "the most boring ladies of the haute Jewish bourgeoisie." But Peggy was a rebel, and the bore is in the eye of the beholder. Certainly these ladies did not bore each other. They gathered in their uptown drawing rooms over their silver tea services, on their regular afternoons, and discussed the topics of the day, one of which, by 1888, was "What shall we do about the Guggenheims?" The others were children, clothes, health. Mrs. Semon Bache advised that children under three years old should be fed fruit sparingly. Bananas were especially dangerous. "After a baby is one year old, he may be fed a teaspoonful of orange juice occasionally," she commented. "But only if he's in perfect health." Mrs. Lazarus Hallgarten was concerned about "promiscuous bathing," for not only were women appearing on the beaches in snug-fitting bathing skirts and blouses but, of all things, stockings that exposed the *toes*. Mrs. Mayer Lehman commented that "The laced shoe is rapidly gaining followers," and wondered how the others in the group felt about this development. Mrs. Solomon Loeb had heard of a new cure for whooping cough: "A handful of dried chestnut leaves boiled in a pint of water—a wineglassful once an hour." And so it went.

In the evenings the families entertained each other at dinners large and small. The women were particularly concerned about what was "fashionable," and why shouldn't they have been? Many of them had been born poor and in another country, and now they found themselves stepping out of a cocoon and into a new and lovely light. They felt like prima donnas, and, now that their husbands were becoming men of such influence and substance, they wanted to be guilty of no false steps in their new land. They wanted desperately to be a part of their period, and as much as said so. Beadwork was fashionable. One had to do it. It was the era of the "Turkish corner," and the ladies sewed scratchy little beaded covers for toss pillows. At one dinner party, while the ladies were discussing what was fashionable and what was not, Marcus Goldman rose a little stiffly from the table, folded his heavy damask napkin beside his plate, and said, "Money is *always* fashionable," and stalked out of the room.

32

SONS, DAUGHTERS, REBELS

The eight original Seligman brothers had sired, between them, thirty-six sons, and their sisters and brothers-in-law had been responsible for eight more. It was an impressive total. But out of it, as the nineteenth century drew to a close, it began to seem that there were painfully few boys who had any interest in, much less talent for, banking. Joseph's oldest son, David, accepted a partnership at J. & W. Seligman, but he showed up at the office only once every week or so, usually to check on the state of his own portfolio. Another son, Edwin R. A., taught political economy at Columbia, and another, Alfred Lincoln, was artistic. He and his wife Florine, who were childless, conducted salons.

Still others of the second generation had become gentlemen of leisure, or had succumbed to what the *Morning Advertiser* called "the allurements of fleeting pleasures." In fact, the only Seligman boy out of the forty-four who appeared to have marked financial ability was Joseph's second son, Isaac Newton, who, upon his Uncle Jesse's death, became head of the firm at the age of thirty-nine.

With the easygoing *nil admirari* attitude they often seemed to affect, the Seligmans never appeared to be unduly concerned about their lack of able and dutiful sons to carry on. Boys were permitted to drift along whatever paths they chose (Jeff, for example, with his nutritionist theories, had once wanted to be a doctor, and had studied medicine in Germany before settling on a Seligman partnership.) Other fathers of Joseph's and Jesse's generation, however, cared desperately about turning their sons into bankers like themselves, and when twigs did not bend naturally in that direction, force was sometimes used.

The Lehmans were lucky. All three of the original brothers had competent sons, and by the 1890's there were five Lehmans in the firm: in addition to Mayer and Emanuel, there were Mayer's son Sigmund, Emanuel's son Philip, and a nephew, Meyer H. Lehman, the son of Henry Lehman who had died in the South. The Lehman firm had been cautiously expanding—investing money in an early automobile company, a rubber manufacturer—but it was still a commodity house, trading in cotton, coffee, and petroleum, and was therefore ranked far below other New York banking houses in prestige and importance.

Solomon Loeb, on the other hand, had founded a banking house that now rivaled the Seligmans'. Forced into the background by his brash son-in-law, Jacob Schiff, Solomon's one hope had been that the Loeb name could be perpetuated in the firm through his two sons, Morris and James, who, by the time they reached their twenties, began to collapse under the weight of their parents' towering ambitions and to wilt from the intensity with which they had been trained as children.

Morris Loeb ran away from home, was found in Philadelphia and returned, and after that point he was carefully watched. He became a shy and nervous young man with quick, frightened gestures and a hunted look in his eyes. He had a terror of mirrors (it was he who had papered the mirror in the Schiffs' sitting room), and an even greater dread of becoming a banker. He began to have a fetish about money, and a fear of spending it. He quarreled frequently with his mother about the lavishness with which she set her dinner table, and he once offered her a prize if she could produce a Sunday dinner so simple that there would be no leftovers. (Needless to say, she never won the prize.) Morris scrimped and saved pennies and squirreled them away. (When the Loeb house was demolished many years later, some of Morris' deposits were discovered behind moldings and beneath floor boards; the wallpaper of one room was interlined with thousand-dollar bills.)

For all the quirks of his personality, Morris was a splendid student at Dr. Sachs's school, and though his father explained to Julius Sachs that "He is to be trained, of course, as a banker," Morris' best subject was science. He graduated at sixteen, went on to Harvard into the class of 1883, and, since he was the first of his father's children to go to college, Solomon Loeb said to him, "I have no idea how much an American education costs," and gave him a blank checkbook. Morris never wrote out a single check, though he got through Harvard with honors.

By the time Morris was graduated, his father had despaired of making him into a banker. Seeing that their son was, whether they liked it or not, a chemist, Solomon and Betty bent all their efforts toward making him the greatest chemist in the world. His parents proceeded to build him his own, fully equipped laboratory, right on the grounds and next door to their summer house at Elberon. Here Morris seemed happy with his burners and test tubes and lixivia, and his young cousins remember a gentle, absent-minded man who, when they tapped on the door of his lab, would sometimes let them in and entertain them by blowing glass in bright, strange shapes for them. Eventually, Morris got a job as Professor of Chemistry at N.Y.U.

Morris was married rather late, in 1895 at the age of thirty-two (but it was a Kuhn, Loeb marriage, which pleased his father), to the handsome and statuesque Eda Kuhn, a sort of cousin (Eda's aunt was Solomon Loeb's sister, and another aunt had been Solomon's first wife). If Morris and Eda had had children, the cousinships among the Loebs and Kuhns would have become even more tangled, but theirs was a barren, lonely, and difficult marriage. Sometimes Morris would approach his father and say that he had to get out, away from the world of silk-covered walls and gilt and mirrors; he wanted to run away again— somewhere, anywhere. "But your laboratory is here, Morris," his father gently reminded him. "Right here on the place. What else could you want?"

Morris began to have an obsession about the cleanliness of his food, and a fear of being poisoned. Driven, haunted, he subjected every morsel he was served to elaborate chemical tests. Ironically, at a chemical convention in Washington, far from his lab, he ate a bad oyster, developed typhoid fever, and died.

Having given up on Morris, Solomon had concentrated on James. Jim Loeb was, at first glance, totally different from Morris—handsome, strong, with a vivid personality full of life and humor. He was a scholar and an esthete and a talented musician, playing the cello as well as the piano and organ. After Dr. Sachs's and Harvard—again near the top of the class—he was offered a chance to study Egyptology in Paris and London, with a curatorship of the Boston Museum of Fine Arts and a teaching post at Harvard to follow. For months Jim Loeb begged his father to let him take this study offer, but Solomon was adamant. One of his seed line had to join the bank, and there was no alternative. Finally, Jim acquiesced and joined Kuhn, Loeb & Company. Jim's brother-in-law, Jacob Schiff, liked assistants and advisers, but not peers. It was not easy for Jim in a line of work he hated and yet from which so much was expected of him. He also soon realized that his young nephew, Morti Schiff, was the more dutiful son, and that Kuhn, Loeb, if Jacob Schiff had anything to say about it, would one day be turned over to Morti. But Jim tried to do as he was told and, in his after-work hours, played the cello, began a collection of early Greek figures, and fell in love.

The name of the girl whom Jim Loeb loved and wanted to marry is one of those which has been written out of family records, but it is known that she was beautiful, loved him very much, and was a gentile. She is said by some to have been the daughter of a prominent New York family who, in fact, were friends of the senior Loebs. But the religious barrier—to Solomon, even though he was a professed agnostic—was insurmountable, and the union was considered out of the question. There was pressure put on Jim Loeb to give up the girl, and it came from Solomon, Betty, from all the Kuhns and Wolffs, from the giant Kuhn, Loeb Company itself, and, most powerfully, from Jacob Schiff. Jim Loeb resisted for a while, and then, as the family has put it, "extreme pressures" were applied.

"Life in New York," wrote his niece Frieda Schiff tenderly, for she admired her handsome Uncle Jim very much, and they were close in age, "began to press on him, and he went abroad to consult a neurologist." The neurologist was Dr. Sigmund Freud, and for a while Jim Loeb lived in Freud's house. Then he settled in Germany. A generous sum of money was given him, and he built a large house on a deeply wooded estate at Murnau, near Munich, where he lived as a recluse, filling his hours by building his art collection, a vast collection of rare books, and by sponsoring the now famous Loeb Classified Library. Over the fireplace in his sitting room, Jim Loeb hung a portrait of his father to remind him of what he had left behind. Back home in New York, Jacob Schiff summoned his lawyers and had his will rewritten to stipulate that either of his unmarried children would be disinherited if he or she married a non-Jew.

To add to the sad story of the Loeb children, there was also Solomon Loeb's "beautiful, temperamental, musical" daughter, Guta, who, in 1883, had married Isaac Newton Seligman—"the first real American," as the Loebs proudly pointed out, in the conventional, German-speaking Loeb-Schiff household. Ike and Guta had one son, Joseph, but Guta's life was blighted by a series of nervous breakdowns. "Her mother overtrained her," one of the family said. "She had been so regimented and disciplined that she had no resources of her own." Most of poor Guta's married years were spent in sanitariums.

Emanie Sachs wrote a novel of German Jewish society in New York as it existed around the turn of the century. It was called "Red Damask," and depicted a closed and cloistered social order, strikingly consistent in its attitudes, a world governed by obedience and traditions where, if one had diligence and character, one "didn't need religion"; where behavior was a matter of "having high standards and living up to them"; where "Right was right, and wrong was wrong; in doubt, your conscience would tell you what to do." It was a world whose figures moved with the mechanical precision of Venetian clock figures, where life was scheduled for the proper thing at the proper moment, and where a woman "did not do bead-work when embroidery was fashionable."

In a world the novel's heroine sees as rigid and prisonlike, she longs for escape, to break out of the pattern, to "pioneer" in some new city where she is unknown and where her family name stands for nothing. At a crucial point in the story, the heroine cries:

> "Good heavens! What's life for? . . . Our crowd here. They cover their walls with the same silks. Why, there isn't a house we go to, including Sherry's, that hasn't a damask wall! They go to the same dentist and the same grocer and the same concerts. They think alike and act alike and they're scared to death not to talk alike. The men go to jobs their fathers or grandfathers created, and all they do is sit at desks and let the organizations work . . . they go in for art collections with an expert to help. They wouldn't risk a penny on their own tastes. They wouldn't risk anything."

The place this rebellious spirit wants to go is El Paso. But, in the end, she goes nowhere. The silken web is too strong. She is trapped like a figure in a crystal paperweight, "where even the snowstorms seem private," and where "engagements, scheduled weeks ahead, were changed only for serious illness, or death, or steamer sailings."

Though men like Solomon Loeb and Jacob Schiff had been rebels and runaways and gamblers (immigration itself had been a gamble), they found it difficult to understand such impulses in their children. They expected, instead, an attitude of *Pflicht und Arbeit.*

A child in this gilded ghetto was not supposed to have a life of his own.

33

ELBERON,
AND POINTS
NORTH AND SOUTH

The incredible "Gilded Age" of the 1880's and 1890's was also an age of list-making, and, as each new list appeared, a new delineation between first- and second-rate Americans was established. In 1887 the *Social Register* was copyrighted, and its first volume appeared for New York City the following spring. There were less than two thousand families in this "record of society, comprising an accurate and careful list of its members, with their addresses, many of the maiden names of the married women, the club addresses of the men, officers of the leading clubs and social organizations, opera box holders, and other useful social information." With the birth of the *Social Register*, New York society felt that it had at last organized itself into an aristocracy. In his *Saga of American Society*, Dixon Wecter wrote: "Here at last, unencumbered with advertisements of dressmakers and wine merchants, enhanced by large, clear type and a pleasant binding of orange and black—which if anything suggested the colors of America's most elegant university—was a convenient listing of one's friends and potential friends. It was an immediate triumph." The *Social Register,* of course, rather conspicuously included no Jewish names, but it was such a success that Ward McAllister suggested that "our good Jews might wish to put out a little book of their own, called something else, of course."

McAllister himself—who was called "Mr. Make-a-Lister"—was the author of an even more abbreviated list of names of New York's "best" —his Four Hundred for Mrs. William Waldorf Astor. Since Mrs. Astor's ballroom only held four hundred, McAllister started saying in 1888, soon after the *Social Register* appeared, that there were really only about that number in society, the *Register's* two thousand families notwithstanding. "If you go outside four hundred," McAllister said, "you strike people who are either not at ease in a ballroom or else make other people not at ease." Whether McAllister intended to include August Belmont, owner of one of New York's first ballrooms, among those comfortable in ballrooms has never been clear. Mrs. Belmont and Mrs. Astor had become social rivals, and McAllister was on Mrs. Astor's side. Though McAllister began talking "four hundred" in 1888, he did not publish his official list (which ran to slightly more than three hundred people) until 1892, two years after August Belmont had died and been buried with full Christian ceremony. McAllister's published list (printed in the *New York Times,* which is an indication of the attention paid to such matters in those days) included several widows, but it did not include Caroline Belmont. Both Belmonts, however, made the earliest editions of the *Social Register.*

"Our good Jews" did not put together a *Social Register* of their own, perhaps because those who composed Jewish society knew too well who belonged and who did not, and did not need to refer to a list. "In the years following the Seligman-Hilton affair," one member of the crowd said, "the German Jewish elite became . . . well, not *non*assimilationist, exactly, but less *actively* assimilationist." Referring to the Mrs. Astor group as "the butterflies," Jews watched the activities of the Four Hundred from a distance and with a certain cool disdain.

Though Jacob Schiff remained on Fifth Avenue, there began to be a general German Jewish migration to the West Side of Manhattan, and the blocks between Seventieth and Eightieth streets, Central Park West and Columbus Avenue, became the first recognizably German Jewish upper-class neighborhood. In this period there was talk of Central Park West becoming "the Jewish Fifth Avenue." The area south of Seventieth Street was still a shantytown, with herds of goats grazing among the rocks at the edge of the park, but north of Seventieth, in handsome four- and five-story brownstones, many of which stand today as rooming houses, several families of the crowd arranged themselves. Marcus Goldman and his son-in-law, Sam Sachs, purchased adjoining houses in West Seventieth Street. On West Seventy-first lived the Cullmans; on Seventy-second the Meyers. Harry Sachs, Sam's brother, bought a large house on West Seventy-fourth Street, and Marcus Goldman's son Henry bought an even larger one on West Seventy-sixth.

The second generation was continuing to be just as intramural when it came to marriage as the first. The last decades of the nineteenth century were a period of consolidation, of gathering in. Mayer Lehman's son Sigmund married his first cousin, Emanuel's daughter Harriet. Just as Joseph Seligman and his wife had been first cousins, now Joseph's sister's son, Eugene Stettheimer, married Joseph's brother Henry's daughter, Grace. William Seligman's daughter Leonore married Max Wassermann, and William's son David married Max's sister, Sophie, while Jesse Seligman's daughter, Emma, married another Wassermann brother, Edward. In 1878 young Adolph Lewisohn married into the crowd. His bride was Emma Cahn, who was related to the Cahns of J. S. Bache & Company, who were related by marriage to the Baches.

Along a wide stretch of New Jersey shore—in Elberon and such adjacent resort towns to the north and south as Long Branch, Deal Beach, Sea Bright, Allenhurst, and West End—a German Jewish summer colony was developing: "The Jewish Newport." Peggy Guggenheim described Elberon as "a sort of ghetto," and so it was—but then so was Newport. The space of Atlantic Ocean that separated the two places became, like the width of Central Park between Central Park West and Fifth Avenue, symbolic of the social separation of the two communities, each of which had begun to look inward, upon its own problems and satisfactions, rather than outward upon the world.

Life at Elberon was remarkable for its sense of isolation and tranquility, as well as for the amenities it contained the feelings of conviction and complacency that seemed to surround each day's scheduled activity. Of course there were some who found Elberon stifling in its addiction to Victorian conformity. Emanie Sachs described the residents of the colony as "padded with red damask, built of a pattern in a piece, dancing round and round in a golden trap, getting nowhere." But much the same could have been said of Elberon's gentile counterpart on the Rhode Island shore.

Peggy Guggenheim called Elberon "the ugliest place in the world. Not one tree or bush grew on this barren coast. The only flowers I remember were rambler roses, nasturtiums and hydrangeas, and since then I have not been able to endure them. My grandfather had a family mansion in West End . . . a hideous Victorian house." Nearby lived several of her Guggenheim uncles, one in "an exact copy of the Petit Trianon at

Versailles," and another in an "Italian villa with marble Pompeiian inner courts and beautiful grottoes and sunken gardens. Compared to these, my grandfather Seligman's house was a modest affair." The Guggenheims were still considered *nouveau riche.*

Sam Sachs also chose a European theme for his Elberon house—"a kind of an adaptation of an Italian palazzo" of white stucco, with a red-tiled roof and fountains and formal gardens "adapted from Versailles." Both Solomon Loeb and Jacob Schiff had houses on this shore, the latter's predictably grander than the former's. Jacob Schiff was the first man of the crowd to rent his own private stateroom for the season on the ferryboat, *Asbury Park,* on which he commuted from Manhattan. He used the stateroom as an office, and he spent the trip (it took just over an hour) sitting in a wicker chair writing tense little memoranda on scraps of paper.

Many Seligmans—Jesse and his son Henry, Joseph's sons Isaac and David, Joseph's daughter Frances Hellman, and James's son Jefferson (of the fruit and ginger)—had summer homes on the bluffs around Elberon, and theirs were more typical of the style and mood of the place: large Victorian houses, hectic with gingerbread, millwork, and decorative cupolas, surrounded on all sides by wide porches that were covered with high-backed rocking chairs that rocked all day long by themselves in the offshore breezes, where Seligmans and their friends gathered to sit in long rows, and rock, and look at the sea, and smoke their cigars, and talk business. The women, under parasols, took little walks between the nodding blue heads of hydrangeas, and some of them must have asked themselves why, when they had all this ease, anyone would have preferred the Grand Union Hotel at Saratoga?

The salt air made for hearty appetites, and twice a day the families gathered in walnut-paneled dining rooms for enormous dinners that began with tomatoes stuffed with caviar and anchovies, continued through delicious clear soups, to roasts "with the most beautiful spinach," to fruits and cheeses and red wine. After meals, while the gentlemen lingered over more cigars and business talk, the ladies retired to the drawing room to sit on plush-covered ottomans and discuss what they had just eaten. One encountered many of the same features in most of these rooms—the whatnot in the corner with its collection of Dresden figurines, the gold-fringed lamp supported by a ring-a-rosy of bronze cherubs, the marble-topped table crowded with photographs, the palm tree in the Sèvres pot, and the climax of every such drawing room, the family portraits gazing solemnly from the walls in heavy gilt frames suspended by velvet ropes: the children in their long ringlets, standing stiffly in black velvet dresses, their faces grave above white lace collars, posed with birds, Bibles, or hoops in their hands. The houses might have been "ugly," but they were ugly to a point of Victorian perfection.

From the drawing room, it would soon be time for the little walk among the hydrangeas again, that walk that was so good for the over-taxed liver, and which gave one an appetite for the next meal. At night one retired early—there were few late parties—between fine linen sheets in a bedroom that smelled of the best French soaps, lavender sachet, and sea air.

The seemliness of Elberon's summer panorama was hardly ever broken by an untoward event, or, indeed, by undue jollity—as once happened when a hotel in Allenhurst which did not accept Jews caught fire and burned to the ground. While it blazed, a number of well-connected German Jewish children stood nearby and cheered.

In Elberon the Seligmans always seemed to manage to have the most distinguished dinner and weekend guests, particularly favoring celeb-rities from the worlds of politics and government in Washington. At one of the Seligmans' Saturdays, it was never a surprise to find a former U.S. President, a Supreme Court Justice, several Senators and a Congressman or two. The Seligmans' old friend Grant had, at their suggestion, bought a summer home at Long Branch and was a frequent, if somewhat unreliable, guest.* President Garfield was another Seligman friend. When Garfield was shot less than three months after his inauguration, he was taken to a cottage in Elberon where Jesse Seligman—"with," as Postmaster General Thomas Lane later recalled, "that thoughtful con-sideration and tenderness which distinguished the man"—opened his house to the official family of the dying President. "The Seligmans," said another observer at the time, "displayed the closest American equivalent of the European concept of *noblesse oblige.*"

And certainly at some point during these great Elberon years New York's German Jewish financiers and their families had begun to think of themselves as an American aristocracy of a certain sort. With their moral tone and their emphasis on family, they had begun to regard themselves as perhaps just a little bit "better" than "the butterflies" of Newport.

* Poor old Grant, who had long since given up marching in temperance parades, had always wanted to be a capitalist. After leaving the White House, he set himself up, with the Seligmans' help, as an investment banker in partnership with a glib young fellow named Ferdinand Ward, whose seemingly Midas touch had earned him the label of "the young Napoleon of Wall Street." In 1884 Ward told Grant that the Marine National Bank, in which Grant & Ward had deposits, was in trouble and needed $300,000 for one day only. Again with the Seligmans' help, Grant managed to raise half this amount. Ward pocketed it and disappeared. Three days later, the Marine National closed as a result of overdrafts by Grant & Ward, and it soon turned out that Ward had embezzled more than $2 million from the firm and that its books showed $27 million in nonexistent assets. Once more, the Seligmans came to the aid of their old card-playing friend from Watertown days, and gave him funds enough to live comfortably until he had completed his memoirs and died. Grant's *Memoirs,* of course, finally made his estate rich, and helped pay for his famous and imposing tomb.

In 1892 the Seligmans had a visit from a true European aristocrat. He was Prince André Poniatowsky, a nephew of King Stanislaus of Poland. He called on the Seligmans in New York to open an account, and he noted that their offices were "very much like those of the bankers in the City of London, of great simplicity, located on the first floor of the Mills Building, in those days the largest building of that type in New York. It was of no special architectural style, but, as the British say 'substantial.'" Here, the Prince wrote, the Seligmans "received me immediately and with a courtesy that demonstrated to me on what complimentary terms their Paris house had written to them about me."

Jesse Seligman was in Europe that summer, and so Isaac Newton Seligman, Joseph's son, took over entertaining and smoothing the way for the Prince. After opening his account, the Prince asked Isaac whether there were any other businessmen in the United States who might be helpful to him, and Isaac

> responded with a rapidity of decision characteristic of businessmen the first of this type I met personally. With a few words he outlined to me what course of procedure to adopt and which people to see. While I was trying to express my appreciation to him, he held in one hand the telephone through which he arranged a meeting for the same day . . . while with the other hand he was ringing the bell for a stenographer, to whom he dictated a letter of introduction accrediting me in Chicago to Mr. Lyman Gage, President of the Bank that was their correspondent in that city.*

Saying, "Come have a bite," Isaac took the Prince to lunch on the top floor of the Mills Building, "where there was a sort of grillroom reserved for the tenants and the owner of the place," and introduced the Prince to the other Seligman partners. Here, the Prince suspected, the partners were in psychic financial communication with one another. By Isaac's manner toward him, the others were able to judge the exact size and importance of the Prince's account.

> To explain my unexpected presence to four Christians seated around a table, it would have been necessary to advise each of them successively that my letters of introduction had been signed by So-and-So, that I had important matters to cable to Paris, and heaven knows what else! Four Christians, I said, but I should have specified the denomination, since for four Protestants these hints would not have been enough.

But in the presence of the Jewish bankers the Prince found no such tiresome need to offer his credentials.

* Once more the Seligmans were displaying their uncanny way of getting to know the right people. Their friend Lyman Gage later became Secretary of the Treasury under President McKinley.

Words were superfluous; the attitude of the head of the firm amply sufficed. His partners now knew as much about me as he did. They had watched him from the moment we sat down, and from his expression had gauged the precise degree of consideration to which he judged me entitled. I suspect, in fact, that if it had been a question of a bank statement, each partner could have scribbled the exact amount on the tablecloth without appreciably deviating from his senior's estimate.

This ability to communicate without words the Prince ascribes to something with which "nature seems to have wished to compensate this astonishing race for the insecurity against which it has struggled for centuries by endowing it with an ability, which escapes us, to understand each other in silence."

The Prince was also relieved to find that the Seligman partners did not appear to be overawed by the fact that they were lunching with royalty. "I felt in them," he wrote, "a shade—oh, scarcely perceptible!—of that reserve which a name and title had already earned for me, and for many years would earn for me, in the presence of businessmen, who automatically thought of me as a personality." But this scarcely perceptible shade of deference was not enough to be off-putting.

Isaac invited his Highness to spend a weekend with the Seligmans at the Jersey Shore, and, at the outset at least, the Prince was not at all sure what he was getting into. On the ferryboat crossing, he wrote: "As soon as we left New York, the iced drinks circulated on the deck, and with more avidity than prudence I accepted the offer Seligman made me of sarsaparilla, a hygienic drink, something like a cross between beer and a mouthwash." But as soon as the boat had docked at Elberon the Prince began to see what New York's German Jewish society was all about. He realized that he had entered a special world not quite like anything he had ever seen before in America or on the Continent. It may not have been an aristocracy, precisely, that the Prince encountered in Elberon, but it was a world of grace and ease and bonhomie which captivated him completely and haunted him for years to come. Years later he reminisced that he met people that weekend "of whom no counterpart then existed in Europe, and probably no longer exists in America."

This is what the Prince's wondering eyes beheld:

Upon the arrival of the boat, a large number of carriages, mostly driven by wives or daughters, came to pick up the passengers, whose residences spread out for several miles along the coast, and also inland, as was the case with the Seligmans, whose house faced Rumson Road.

Isaac Seligman's wife was a daughter of Mr. Loeb, founder and partner of the house of Kuhn, Loeb, already well-known at this time but eventually to take on world importance. They had one child, then three or four years old, whom I unwittingly disappointed at breakfast when he saw that I was not wearing a crown.

The house was simplicity itself—comfortable, of course, but without any show. Of brick and wood painted white, brightened by green shutters, it must have had four or five bedrooms, a bathroom—possibly two, but I doubt it—a dining room, and a drawing room giving on a porch where one spent most of the time. . . .

The next day I was able to see that the neighboring houses, of much the same style and size, were occupied by more or less distant members of the family. To the left, next to Isaac Seligman's, an almost identical house was occupied by his sister Mrs. Hellman, with whom we dined that evening—a charming woman, whose husband was the brother of the head of the Seligman firm in Paris. . . . To the right lived an older sister of Mrs. Seligman, who had married Jacob Schiff . . . a little farther along, Mrs. Seligman's and Mrs. Schiff's mother, Mrs. Loeb, whose husband was in Europe that year, lived in a considerably larger house with the youngest of the three sisters, Nina, a charming girl and an excellent musician, who later married Paul Warburg. . . . Finally, still farther off, on the seashore, lived a brother, David Seligman, with his wife and daughters, of whom one, Mrs. van Heukelom, resides in Paris today, and the other, Mrs. Lewisohn, comes to Cannes every year.

In each of these households, the male servants were limited to a coachman, generally a Negro, who took care of the horses, and a gardener. Otherwise the servants were women—cooks and housemaids. If after more than forty years I can so distinctly recall the circumstances in which the numerous members of this family lived, it is because I was profoundly surprised at the time by the contrast that their private lives offered to those of most bankers and businessmen of Anglo-Saxon ancestry whom I met in America that year. In Wall Street, their financial power placed them all on an almost equal level with the big Anglo-Saxon bankers.

Now the Prince made a particularly significant point about the Jewish bankers:

> *Money in itself, however, had no significance for them outside of business.* Any observer, listening to their talk during leisure hours would have taken them for good *rentiers,* given to sport, literature, art, and especially to music, who contributed generously to charity and still more to the finances of their political party, and, above all, were devoted to family life with an intensity to be met with today only in the French provinces.

The Prince kept trying to put his finger on just what it was that was special and appealing about these German Jewish families, and concluded that they reminded him most of French provincials: "Moreover, apart from their taste for sport, the men's private lives resembled rather closely those of the heads of the old banking houses of Lyon." (The Prince's repeated emphasis on "sport" is a little puzzling. Some tennis was played at Elberon, and a bit of croquet, and there was a good deal of walking. But in 1892 there were as yet no real "sportsmen" in the crowd. The Prince was probably overinfluenced by oarsman Ike Seligman, who was an exception.)

The Prince found the atmosphere of the crowd foreign—small-town European—yet very American:

> In the preceding generation, the father and the uncle, the founders of the firm, had played a major role in politics . . . the men of this generation had inherited the business and worked to keep it going. . . . Born in the United States, they had breathed the invigorating air of that country at an early age, and their childhood, like their adolescence, was patterned after the current model of the "American College Man" . . . imbued with confidence in the future of his country as well as pride in the glory of its past. It was a rather limited past at the time, but because of that very fact so much closer, more vital, and more to be cherished. With the most sincere emotion, they spoke to me of the heroes of the War of Independence as well as those of the Civil War—the first epic antedating the selection of this new country by their parents—for, excellent citizens that they were, they had preserved an affinity for preceding events through legends with which their mothers had rocked them to sleep in their childhood, and which had later jelled at college with the study of Goethe, Schiller, and Heine.

Prince Poniatowsky never visited Newport, but it is hardly possible that he would have found it as beguiling a place as he found Elberon to be. Clearly the nobleman felt very much at home there. Yet this is the same stretch of Jersey shore that critic Edmund Wilson, who grew up near Deal, has called a resort "of the second-rate rich."

On Monday morning, still starry-eyed, the Prince returned to New York and, that evening, was taken to dinner at the Knickerbocker Club. Over dinner he happened to mention the delightful weekend he had spent with the Seligmans at Elberon. A ghastly hush fell on the table, and the Prince began to grasp the social facts of life that existed in New York. After dinner he was taken aside by one of the club's members who,

> with a little embarrasment, indicated his surprise at seeing me associate with Jewish families outside of business hours. Very much surprised myself, I listened to his description of the worldly conventions that kept Israelites away from the "inner circle," no matter

what their merits, their culture, or the outstanding roles they might
have played in the development of the country! There was on his part
neither passion nor animosity. He talked to me as though he were
making a statement of facts, just as he might have briefed me on the
fundamental differences between the Republican and Democratic
parties.

But the Prince was a prince, and was not to be put down by a stuffy
clubman. "I must undoubtedly have scandalized him," he writes,

when I told him that I had accepted an invitation to go back the following weekend, this time to Mrs. Hellman's home, and that I could
not and did not wish to change this plan—first, because I had met
some particularly interesting people there, and, more important, being
a foreigner in this country, I did not feel justified in changing rules
that I had followed up to now in this connection. Whether in France
or in England, I had always maintained the most cordial social relations with the Rothschilds and the families of certain Jewish bankers
with whom I had business associations, and I really had no reason to
behave differently in the present case.

In the face of this coolly royal response, the American clubman turned
and walked muttering away.

34

THE
GUGGENHEIM-
LEWISOHN BATTLE

After meeting Adolph Lewisohn, a New York businessman once commented, "I guess his brother Leonard must be the smart one." A few weeks later, he met Leonard Lewisohn. Following this meeting he said, "No, I guess Adolph is the smart one."

Neither of the Lewisohns was a Schiff-like financial genius. But they had gone about the business of getting rich with diligence, and had the assistance of a considerable amount of luck. By the 1890's the brothers were considered copper kings—one of their mines had paid $35 million in dividends alone—and the impression one gathers of them at this point is that they had ceased caring about making money. Adolph himself once said, "I made as much money as I wanted to make, and then I stopped."

Having stopped, he started to spend, and here again he was the opposite of tight-fisted Mr. Schiff. He bought the E. H. Harriman mansion at 881 Fifth Avenue, a huge place at Elberon, and a hilltop castle in Westchester County, and quickly began filling all these places with friends, flowers, coolers of champagne, pretty women, and collections of precious stones in lighted cases. Though short and round and myopic—he never quite *looked* the part—Adolph Lewisohn became the crowd's first certifiable playboy.

His approach to life was inevitably reflected in his approach to business. In 1898 Adolph and his brother decided to join forces with William Rockefeller and Henry H. Rogers, one of the guiding lights of Rockefeller's Standard Oil, to form, with some five million dollars' capital, the United Metals Selling Company. The Lewisohn contribution to this combine consisted of their Perth Amboy copper works and all the copper interests of Lewisohn Brothers. The Rockefeller-Rogers group contributed the Amalgamated Copper Company, which controlled Anaconda and other copper producers. Adolph Lewisohn was made president of this trust, and Rogers' son-in-law became treasurer. The merger was almost immediately successful, and soon 55 percent of all the copper produced in the United States was being sold by the United Metals Selling Company.

The success of the selling trust led Adolph to the next step—the formation of a smelting trust. Including again the Rockefeller-Rogers group, this was a far more ambitious project with a capitalization of over $100 million. It was called the American Smelting & Refining Company, and it represented a merger of twenty-three different smelting concerns. Clearly, this was a trust designed to dominate the American mining scene—to give Rockefeller interests virtual control of everything under American soil, with Adolph and Leonard Lewisohn riding along as very important hitchhikers. There was only one difficulty. The Guggenheim interests, when asked to join the American Smelting & Refining Company, politely declined. It was one of old Meyer's strictest rules: Guggenheim smelters must not be allowed out of the family. Perhaps Adolph Lewisohn felt, at this point, that he had already made as much money as he "needed," and was ready to stop. In any case, he seems not to have grasped the importance of the Guggenheims' refusal to become part of his merger, and to have been satisfied with their assurances that they would act "in harmony."

With the formation of their Guggenheim Exploration Company, the family had entered upon its most ambitious era. Its aim was to corner the best mines in North America in a great sweep from South to North, starting in Mexico and moving across the hemisphere through the United States, Canada, and Alaska. At the head of this vast plan was the most ambitious of Meyer's sons, Daniel, the second-eldest. In the partners' room at Guggenheim Brothers in New York, the various Guggenheim men are immortalized on canvas and, according to a persistent rumor, the square footage of each man's portrait bears a direct relationship to the size of his contribution to the family fortune. Certainly the portrait of "Mr. Dan," as he was called, is rather larger than the others. He was seven years younger than Adolph Lewisohn and in 1899 was still in his peppy mid-forties. He was a little man, like his father, but, according to Bernard Baruch, Daniel Guggenheim was "one of the three small men I've known—the others were Sam Gompers and Henry Davidson—who sat taller than most men stand. I see Dan . . . a little fellow sitting in a big chair and dominating the entire room from it." His most arresting features were his greenish-blue eyes, which (it seems to have been a prerequisite for turn-of-the-century tycoons) have always been described as "piercing." Daniel Guggenheim had also decided that he wished to dominate the American mining scene. His companies were earning a million dollars a year, but with the formation of the American Smelting & Refining Company he was on the defensive for the first time. He was less interested in "harmony" than in victory.

At this point, one begins to get the impression of Adolph Lewisohn fiddling while Rome burns. Busy with his parties, he seems to have assumed that the sheer size of his American Smelting & Refining Company, and of his associates, Rockefeller and Rogers, would win the day. Rogers, too, seems to have been under this misapprehension, while Rockefeller, as he often did, was leaving everything to Rogers. Daniel Guggenheim, meanwhile, made several bold moves. He gathered on his team a speculator named William C. Whitney, who had married the sister of Oliver H. Payne, a large Standard Oil stockholder. Whitney had speculative capital to spend. Next, Guggenheim had a stroke of luck. A strike crippled a number of the American Smelting & Refining Company's properties, making the trust temporarily vulnerable. Dan Guggenheim took advantage of this by heaping lead on the market and forcing the trust to sell below cost. Dan began buying up A S & R shares. In December, 1900, the trust made Dan Guggenheim another offer to buy him out, but this time the trust was leading from weakness. Guggenheim knew it, and made the most of it. He would sell, he announced—for $45.2 million. And for this price the trust would receive all the Guggenheim properties except the best ones—the Colorado and Mexican mines and the Exploration Company. With the remaining properties, came, as well, the Guggenheims. And so, all at once, the American Smelting & Refining Company *was* the Guggenheims. Daniel Guggenheim was president, and four other Guggenheims were on the board of directors. It all happened so fast that it seemed like sleight of hand.

Dazed, Rogers and the Lewisohns realized that the "impossible" had happened. Buying out the Guggenheims, they had, simultaneously, put the Guggenheims in control. The Seligmans were this time delighted; they led the syndicate that put the A S & R's first issue on the market— an offering at par of $40 million worth of preferred stock, which sold with great ease.

The Rogers-Lewisohn group now tried to retaliate. They hired David Lamar, one of several speculators who had earned the title, "The Wolf of Wall Street," and told him to drive the price of A S & R stock down until the company was ruined. But the Guggenheims had Whitney, who was no less powerful a speculator than Lamar, and who was enjoined to do the opposite. The battle between the two speculative wolves, as a result, ended close to a draw. The stock fell only a meager seven points, and the Guggenheims held fast. Next, Rogers and the Lewisohns took their case to the courts. The law certainly seemed to favor the Rogers group but, when the Guggenheims agreeably offered to compromise, the result of the compromise seemed to further favor the Guggenheims. When the smoke of the lawsuit disappeared, Daniel Guggenheim was Chairman of the board of the American Smelting & Refining Company, his brother Simon was treasurer, and three other brothers were still on the board.

Winning control of the A S & R was the greatest single moment in the career of the Guggenheims. It marked them as mining kings of the world, and, from then on, with the self-generative power that money often seems to have, the Guggenheim fortune mounted. Adolph Lewisohn, meanwhile, still had his A S & R shares. The fact that he had lost a battle didn't seem to matter. At some crucial point in it, he had simply lost interest. He was not that acquisitive. Besides, he was too busy spending and enjoying his own millions.

Financial historians have described the Guggenheim-Lewisohn struggle for control of the copper industry as "a battle of epic proportions." But, in terms of the amount of fun both families managed to have afterward with their respective fortunes, it seems to have been all a lark.

In New York the waltz and the two-step were gradually being edged off the dance floor by the ragtime tempo of such dances as the turkey trot, the grizzly bear, the bunny hug and the Latin maxixe. Soon, women's skirts would begin to climb to the accompaniment of whistles, while stuffed birds appeared on umbrella-sized hats. Even "men of distinction," it was said, were showing up in peg-top pants, two-button shoes and spats.

Some men of distinction, that is. The Guggenheims refused to be fashion leaders and remained conservative, one foot still in the nineteenth century. The last of Mrs. Astor's great balls were taking place—balls the crowd had no part of anyway. But the balls and Mrs. Astor's friends had served their function. If, while gentile society in New York appeared to be growing more factionalized and self-serving, Jewish society could reassure itself that it was becoming more solid and responsible. "Mrs. Astor's sort of society," wrote one of the crowd, "was quite a different sort of thing from ours. You might say hers was the opposite. Hers was based on publicity, showiness, cruelty, and striving. Ours was based on family, and a quiet enjoyment of the people we loved." This is a reasonable estimate of it. The exclusiveness was mutual and double-edged. If gentile society chose to be flashy, the Jewish crowd would be inconspicuous.

"Inconspicuous," in fact, had become a key concept in German Jewish life. It was to be inconspicuous that Meyer and Barbara Guggenheim, and so many others, had abandoned the orthodoxy of their parents and become Reformed (or less noticeably Jewish) Jews, and had joined the German Jewish Temple Emanu-El. To be inconspicuous, many Guggenheims had scattered themselves in large, but anonymous, brownstones on the less fashionable West Side. Inconspicuousness was synonymous with decorum. Whenever Meyer Guggenheim took his sleigh or carriage through the park, he drove alone, managing the reins himself, avoiding the showiness of a coachman and footmen. There was almost a rule of thumb: the richer one was, the more decorous and inconspicuous one endeavored to be.*

Of course it was a little hard to be inconspicuous with the kind of fortune the Guggenheims were amassing. There was also, in the case of the Guggenheims, that unlucky ability to create scandal. The year 1900 was the dawn, in America, of a new attitude toward love and sex. It was the era of the kept woman, and it was naturally assumed that every man of property had one. (Even those who didn't pretended that they did.) Newspapers devoted yards of chatty print to this or that gentleman of distinguished family who had been "glimpsed looking gay" with this or that "curvaceous miss" or "bit of fluff." Society, gentile and Jewish alike, buzzed with whispers of "love affairs" and "mistresses" and lovers. Even very young children seem to have been affected because little Peggy Guggenheim was only a child of seven when she said to her father, Benjamin, "Papa, you must have a mistress as you stay out so many nights"—and was banished from the dinner table.

Meyer Guggenheim's Barbara died in 1900, and, shortly afterward, who should come forward but a woman named Hanna McNamara, age

---

* And for some intensely practical reasons. The 1900 Cudahy kidnapping, with its then-record ransom demand of $25,000, had been a grim reminder of what could happen if one made too much point of being rich.

forty-five, to say that she had been Meyer's mistress for twenty-four years, charging breach of promise and asking $100,000 in damages. Meyer denied everything, including her assertion that she had been a domestic in the Guggenheim house. He went so far as to offer $10,000 reward to anyone who had ever seen him in the plaintiff's presence, and the suit was dropped. Still, the episode left the impression that old Meyer, in his seventies, was a rake, and Peggy Guggenheim has said in her autobiography, "When my grandmother died, my grandfather was looked after by his cook. She must have been his mistress." Peggy based this assertion on having once seen the cook "weep copious tears" when old Meyer Guggenheim was ill.

Peggy's father, meanwhile, *did* indeed have a series of mistresses (several of whom made embarrassing demands on his estate when he died). One of these, technically titled his "masseuse," lived in his New York house; Benjamin's lady friends were apparently tolerated by his wife Florette. Another was the Marquise de Cerutti, whom he kept in Paris and always referred to as "T.M." (for The Marquise). Once, taking their regular morning walk in the Bois de Boulogne, Ben and Florette Guggenheim encountered T.M. out walking also. She was wearing an elegant suit made entirely of baby lamb fur, and Florette scolded Ben for being so extravagant. "You are quite right, my dear," said Benjamin and, to do the proper thing, gave her the money to buy an identical lamb suit of her own. (A practical woman, Florette took the money and used it to add to her portfolio of stocks.) Though the rest of the crowd—particularly Florette's family, the Seligmans—was aghast at Ben Guggenheim's carryings on, he rather enjoyed his reputation as a philanderer. He once told a fourteen-year-old nephew, "Never make love to a woman before breakfast for two reasons. One, it's tiring. Two, you may meet someone else during the day that you like better."

For all this jaunty talk, Ben was not so tolerant of the activities of his brother William, the last of Meyer's sons, who has been described as "just one Guggenheim too many," and also as "the handsomest of the boys." Certainly one of Will's problems was his feeling that he was a leftover Guggenheim, and also his conviction that he did not *look* Jewish. He began to nourish a fantasy that he was not a Jew, and somewhere along the line invented another identity for himself, whom he named Gatenby Williams. It was hard to say whether Will Guggenheim admired Gatenby Williams more than Gatenby Williams admired Will Guggenheim; they were lifelong fans of each other. In fact, Gatenby wrote an appreciative book about Will, "in collaboration with Charles Monroe Heath," in which Gatenby said of Will that all the Guggenheim brothers "except Benjamin and himself were dark," and that anyone seeing Will's "light complexion and the cast of his features

. . . would not have surmised his Semitic ancestry." Will, says Gatenby, "was a nice-appearing young man. . . . Well proportioned . . . he carried himself erect and with dignity. His hands were expressive, the gestures indicating refinement. . . . He dressed neatly. . . . His eyes were a grayish-blue; his lips met in an even line, yet they seemed extraordinarily sensitive, belying the arduous activities and responsibilities that had long been his."

One of Will's activities and responsibilities that Gatenby Williams kindly does not mention was Will's marriage in 1900 to Mrs. Grace Brown Herbert, a divorcee from California. Will brought his bride proudly home to his father and brothers, who immediately recognized her as "the fancy woman of a prominent New Yorker." The Guggenheims presented Will with an ultimatum: get rid of Grace or be disinherited.

It cost the family $78,000 in cash and a trip to Illinois for Grace's divorce where, it was hoped, the scandal would not reach the New York newspapers (it did), and even that wasn't the end. Will married again, had a child, and Grace reappeared, suing to annul the divorce on the grounds of fraud, saying neither she nor Will had been residents of Illinois at the time. Had Grace won this action, she would have made Will not only a party to fraud but a bigamist, and would have illegitimatized his son. Fortunately, Grace's case was thrown out without further cost to the Guggenheims.

When Gatenby Williams' book, *William Guggenheim: The Story of an Adventurous Career,* was published, a few people noticed that the publisher, the Lone Voice Publishing Company, had the same address, 3 Riverside Drive, as Will Guggenheim. Pride of authorship prevailed when Will prepared his *Who's Who* biography, however, and Will's paragraph read: "Author: William Guggenheim (under pseudonymn Gatenby Williams)."

Some Guggenheims were less inconspicuous than others. Benjamin Guggenheim bought an elaborate house at Fifth Avenue and Seventy-second Street which featured a marble entrance hall with a fountain and, on a wall facing the double front door, a stuffed American bald eagle, its wings spread as if in full flight, secured to the marble wall with brass chains. The eagle was Mr. Guggenheim's own touch. He had shot it himself one August at his place in the Adirondacks. Whenever it was pointed out to him that it was against the law to shoot American bald eagles, and also to stuff them, he protested that *he* had never been told of such a law, and that when he had taken the bird to the taxidermist the man had said simply, "Whatever you say, Mr. Guggenheim!"

Upstairs was the "Louis Seize Parlor," decorated with tall mirrors, tapestried walls and tapestried furniture, along with a concert grand piano. But on the floor was a huge bearskin rug with its mouth open in a vicious snarl. Its teeth were forever falling out, and occasionally its tongue, which was disconcerting, but Mr. Guggenheim liked the bear also, and so it stayed amid the Louis XVI gilt chairs and tables. The central parlor, where Mrs. Guggenheim entertained her lady friends at tea, was decorated with an enormous floor-to-ceiling tapestry depicting the triumphant entry of Alexander the Great into Rome.

The Guggenheims never appeared able to do things with quite the *ease*—or at least the attempt at ease—that others in the crowd did. When they traveled, for instance, the Guggenheims never seemed to understand tipping. As they moved from one grand European spa to the next, vengeful porters and bellhops drew meaningful symbols in chalk on the Guggenheim trunks and suitcases, and the Guggenheims never realized why their luggage was always being dropped and crushed and lost.

Benjamin Guggenheim was the Guggenheim on the *Titanic* who refused a weeping steward's offer of a life vest and, instead, went to his cabin and dressed in his evening clothes in order to go down like a gentleman. He insisted, furthermore, that his young valet do the same and, as a woman was entering one of the lifeboats, Ben Guggenheim placed a note in her hand which read: "If anything should happen to me, tell my wife I've done my best in doing my duty."*

But had he done his best? A persistent piece of Guggenheim gossip has it that a surviving *Titanic* passenger was traveling as "Mrs. Benjamin Guggenheim," and she has been identified as "a young blond singer." The family has repeatedly pointed out that the *Titanic*'s passenger list contained no such name. Yet Peggy Guggenheim has spoken of the shock at going to the pier to meet the survivors on the *Carpathia,* still not knowing that her father was dead, and watching her father's mistress descend the gangplank.

Ben's brother Will (or "Gatenby Williams") did not fare much better where women and notoriety were concerned. After separating from his second wife, Will "reverted to his old love, the theatre, taking on a succession of showgirls as protégés." His protégés often held informal press conferences, and one of these young ladies, an actress playing in *Ballyhoo,* told reporters she had met Will because "I was reading a copy of the *Literary Digest* and that caught his eye." When Will died, his entire fortune was bequeathed to "Miss America" of 1929, "Miss Connecticut" of 1930, and two other showgirls of roughly the same vintage. The papers speculated avidly on how many millions the four

---

* A more touching example of courage in the crowd was provided by Mr. and Mrs. Isidor Straus, who each refused, on that terrible night, to enter a lifeboat without the other, and went down together.

girls would divide, but, alas, Will's second wife, whom he had neglected to divorce, had a claim on the estate. The estate itself, furthermore, had been considerably depleted by Will's spending. The four young ladies divided only $5,229.

But the most spectacular playboy of all the Guggenheims was Dan Guggenheim's son, Meyer Robert. M. Robert had a total of four wives and, at one point, upon marrying the second one, became a Roman Catholic. ("I'm delighted," said Dan Guggenheim at the time. "My son has always been a very bad Jew. I hope they'll make a better Catholic of him.") He did not, in any case, remain a Catholic long. M. Robert was briefly the American Ambassador to Portugal. When he was sent home, *persona non grata,* by the Portuguese Government, he laughed off the whole thing, saying that it was all because he had accidentally dropped a teaspoon down the front of a Portuguese lady's dress. Witnesses to the event, however, said that the dropped teaspoon would not have got Robert Guggenheim tossed out of Portugal if only he had not been so insistent on going after the silverware with his hands. His fourth wife was the well-known Washington hostess, Polly Guggenheim, now Mrs. John A. Logan, who took her husband's waywardness with tolerant good humor. After Robert Guggenheim's death, his name popped up in the papers again. The federal government wanted to collect some $169,548 in taxes, which, it claimed, should have been paid on gifts of cash, jewelry, and "a comparatively modest home in Georgetown" made to "an unidentified woman friend."

At that point, it was remembered that M. Robert Guggenheim had died one evening while getting into a taxi in front of a comparatively modest home in Georgetown, after dining with a friend there.

35

MONSIEUR
JOURNET'S
NIGHTGOWN

At least two important media for the communication of social news had come into being in New York by 1900, neither of which was entirely reliable. One was a weekly gossip sheet called *Town Topics*. The other was the telephone. *Town Topics* was devoted almost entirely to the shocking carryings on of Vanderbilts, Webbs, Whitneys, Goelets, Goulds, Morgans, Huntingtons, Schwabs, and Ryans. The publication dramatized the fact that to be "in society" had certain drawbacks, for *Town Topics* earned considerable revenue through simple extortion; if a Vanderbilt, Webb, Whitney, Goelet, Gould, Morgan, Huntington, Schwab, or Ryan did not want his latest indiscretion printed, he had to pay up. Because they were not considered society, the families of the crowd were mercifully spared (though Jimmie Speyer was once approached by a *Town Topics* "representative," and gallantly said, "I don't care what you write about me, as long as you don't say anything disagreeable about my wife." He was left alone).

Meanwhile, thanks to the telephone, gossip traveled faster and more efficiently than ever before. Most women of the era spent at least two-thirds of each morning on the telephone, and many felt unable to start their day until the telephoning was done. And all at once (or so it seemed), uptown circuits were busy from nine to noon with talk of mistresses, lovers, showgirls, and scandal. Frieda Schiff Warburg, her children remember, "used to look as if she had been drawn through a knothole" when she emerged from her morning telephoning. And well she might have.

Just how many of the romances and harrowing tales were real and how many were imagined is, obviously, open to great question. The word "mistress" had become so commonplace that any woman a man was seen speaking to at a Schiff Friday night could be labeled his mistress by Saturday morning. One day, Mrs. Alfred Liebmann, the wife of the brewer, was lunching with her friend Hulda Lashanska, the opera singer. Girlishly, Mlle. Lashanska told Mrs. Liebmann when they met that they might be joined by "a beau." Who should show up but the glamorous "Black Prince"—Felix Warburg! Scandal! News of that affair and "mistress" filled the telephone hours for days afterward. But, since it had been an in-the-crowd lunch, news of it never got outside. (And Lashanska, meanwhile, was a good friend of Frieda Warburg's also, which made it seem like a tempest in a teapot.)

Sometimes, as was the custom of the era, when divorce was "not done" except in a Guggenheim-like emergency, the mistress did indeed join the household and become, in Mary McCarthy's phrase, "a friend of the family." At other times this proved difficult, and there were permanently bruised feelings all around. There were husbands and wives who, though they traveled and entertained together, never spoke, and there were couples who, even though they went to the same dinner parties, were not on speaking terms with other couples over affairs of the heart.

There was one much-liked member of the crowd whose wife, it was suddenly announced, had taken a lover, himself a married man. The affair eventually terminated itself, and, some time later, the young wife died. Though this might have been considered the end of things, it wasn't, and a family conference was called to see what should be done about the dead wife's shocking treatment of her husband while living. Her desk was searched and, sure enough, certain letters turned up which "proved" her guilt. These were then bundled up and shipped—not to their sender but to his wife as "evidence" of his behavior. It was then deemed necessary to tell the dead wife's young children of their mother's transgressions. These exchanges of information were harsh, but also protective, for now where else could the talk fly? It had flown full circle, and all "within the family."

Not all affairs could be terminated with such surgical neatness, as was demonstrated by another unfortunate "family problem," involving, of all people, the Seligmans. By the turn of the century very little scandal had attached itself to that elegant and redoubtable family, though they had been around longer than anybody else. They had their "peculiar branch," but otherwise they seemed serenely above the tribulations certain others had to endure. In fact, it didn't seem fair, and the Seligmans were resented for this.

In 1900 the Seligman veneer began to crack. Alfred Lincoln Seligman, Joseph's fifth and last son, was—like a number of his brothers and cousins, like Solomon's two sons Jim and Morris Loeb, and like Ben and Will Guggenheim—not interested in business, and was more disposed to be a gentleman of leisure. Alfred was an easygoing, soft-spoken fellow with a dilettantish interest in the arts. He played the cello nicely, and was also an amateur sculptor. He was fond of children, though he and his wife had none, and gave a charming monument to New York, a bronze statue in Morningside Park, at 114th Street, which depicts a fawn cowering under a rock while a fierce bear crouches above. The inscription reads:

> To the children of New York City,
> Given by Alfred Lincoln Seligman,
> Vice-President of the National Highways Protection Society,
> and erected under their auspices, 1914

The fawn's position is symbolic of the position Alfred found himself in fourteen years earlier. He was married to the former Florine Arnold, and he and his wife liked to consider themselves "Bohemian." They loved to entertain artists, writers, composers, and musicians in their big apartment in the old Murray Hill Hotel. And, wrote the late George S. Hellman in an unpublished account of the Seligmans, "Alfred's kind heart beat with a childish faith in the goodness of human nature—a faith so childish, so unbelievably trustful, that it was to lead to the first profound tragedy of the Seligman family." (Mr. Hellman is a bit of a romantic when it comes to his Seligman relatives.)

The year 1901, as old New Yorkers will remember, was the year of the great fire in the Murray Hill Hotel. The building was rocked with a series of violent explosions, the wounded and dying lay in the corridors, and much of the hotel was destroyed. But, for some reason, the Forty-first Street side of the building was completely untouched by the fire, and Alfred's and Florine's apartment was in this northern side. Alfred was out of the building when the fire occurred, but a Seligman nephew happened to be in the neighborhood and, explaining that he had a relative who lived in the building, he was allowed through the fire lines to check on Florine. (Mr. Hellman does not say that he was this nephew but, from the evidence he presents, this seems likely.) "He found Florine," writes Mr. Hellman, "seated in her drawing-room. She was alone, looking lovelier than ever, with a tinge of excitement heightening the color of her peach-blossom cheeks." (She was, in other words, exercising perfect Seligman composure in the crisis, and the "tinge of excitement" can be excused by the fact that she was in a burning building, and the noise of the blasts, the screech of the sirens, and the screams of the dying must have been perturbing.) The gallant Mr. Hellman cannot resist adding at this point, "Fair-haired, blue-eyed, perfect nose and mouth, Florine Arnold was one of the most beautiful of New York women."

Graciously, beautiful Florine Arnold Seligman arose from her chair, thanked her young nephew for so considerately dropping by—"But as you can see, I'm perfectly well"—and then said, almost gaily, "I want to show you how terrific the explosions were!"

She then led him through her own bedroom, into an adjoining bedroom, and said, "Look what's happened to Monsieur Journet's nightgown!"

(A nightgown, Mr. Hellman explains, is what men of the period wore instead of pajamas.)

The nephew looked at the nightgown in question. Clearly male, it had been flung, by the force of the blast, from the surface of the bed where it had obviously been lying, and now hung from the ceiling over the bed, draped across a crystal chandelier. But the young nephew was less impressed by this phenomenon than by the news that Monsieur Journet occupied a bedroom in the Seligman apartment next door to Mrs. Seligman's, while Mr. Seligman's bedroom was across the hall beyond the sitting room.

Monsieur Journet was Marcel Journet, a handsome French opera singer, who was filling an engagement at the Metropolitan Opera House at the time.

"Perfectly astonishing," murmured the young nephew, recalling, as he said this, certain related facts. Alfred and Florine Seligman had recently returned from California, traveling with Journet, and they were now due to leave for Europe soon, again accompanied by M. Journet. Clearly, a "situation" had developed that required the most delicate handling by the family.

In the days that followed the fire, Florine continued to tell the story of the remarkable flying nightgown, taking visitors into Journet's bedroom to see where it had happened, oblivious, apparently, of the appearances of the thing. More and more eyebrows were raised. Finally, the story reached the ears of Alfred's older brother Isaac and their sister Frances, and it was decided that a confidential talk with Alfred was in order.

"Of course, Alfred," the older Seligmans said, "we are all very fond of Florine, and we *know* there's nothing wrong. But we think you have been somewhat . . . indiscreet."

Alfred's reaction was so shocked that the others were convinced he was sincere when he cried, "I don't know what you're talking about!"

Isaac was more specific. "Well, you've recently come back from California, where you were traveling with Journet. Now he has a room in your apartment. Next Saturday you are going to Europe together. People are beginning to talk."

"You aren't implying—" gasped Alfred.

"Of course not," said Isaac. "But there is talk, and you should take that into account. It's embarrassing for all of us."

"But, Ike," said Alfred, "you don't quite understand. I'm just as much devoted to Journet as Florine is."

"Certainly," said Isaac a little stiffly, "and I like him very much too. But people are gossiping more than you realize."

Isaac then went on to point out a solution. Alfred was to go home, without mentioning their conversation, and tell Florine that "the press of business" would mean that he could not take the Saturday boat to Europe. Journet would depart alone. The talk would stop. With obvious reluctance, Alfred agreed.

When he approached Florine with the proposed change in plans, Florine became agitated. She was counting on the trip. She was tired of New York and had to get to Europe. It was her favorite boat. She didn't believe the trumped-up story about the "press of business." Alfred had no "business." Isaac ran the investment house. The more she protested, the more excited she became.

Finally, Alfred said flatly, "Well, whether you like it or not, I've decided that we're not sailing Saturday."

"*We are!*" she screamed. "At least *I* am!" She burst into tears and cried, "You might as well know! *Journet is my lover!*"

Thunderstruck, Alfred Seligman walked out of the Murray Hill Hotel. He went to live with his mother, who then shared a house with his sister Frances, and for months was sunk in a terrible depression. He would sit for hours in his chair, refusing to speak or leave the house, staring into space, seeing no one. At times, tears would well in his eyes.

Meanwhile, the Seligman family took sides. Frances, though she loved Alfred, blamed her brother for his laxness and his blindness. Florine's aunt, who was married to one of James Seligman's sons, also insisted it was Alfred's fault. Edwin Seligman, to save the good name of the family, led a sturdy band of Seligmans who blamed Florine.

A deep breach between the James and Joseph branches of the family—which had begun over religion, and James's insistence that a rabbi speak at Joseph's grave, and which had continued over the "family skeleton" of James's mistress—widened and deepened as that most terrible of things was contemplated: a Seligman divorce. "One could see it happening to people like the Googs," wrote Henriette Hellman Seligman despairingly, "but not to *us!*"

As the Seligman lawyers began preparing their briefs, fate stepped in. Florine became ill and was rushed to a hospital, where she underwent an emergency operation and then developed blood poisoning. Dying, she summoned Alfred to her side. In tears, she told him that the affair with Journet had been nothing more than an "obsession." It was, she said, just like his cousin Angeline's dream of her love affair with the druggist Balch. She begged Alfred to forgive her, but there was really nothing to forgive. She swore that Alfred was the only man she ever loved, and that she had made a will leaving everything she owned to him (which was true, and Alfred, in turn, donated everything she left him to charity). She died in his arms.

Alfred went on with his life, painting, sculpting, playing his cello, working for causes devoted to children's welfare, and never married again. He was killed, a few years later, in an automobile accident.

Florine was buried in the Seligman mausoleum at Salem Fields. Though he had been specifically forbidden to enter, M. Journet used to manage to visit the mausoleum on each of his trips to America through the years until he died. He always left a small nosegay of flowers at the foot of the marble entablature that bore her name.

Florine's story had a pretty-picture, almost operetta ending. A year later when Henry Seligman's son, Jesse II, shot and killed his wife, who had been "unfaithful," and then killed himself, it was not so pretty.*

Even though it was a murder within the family and "within the crowd," the Seligmans seemed to be having trouble maintaining their "social distinction."

---

* His remains were not admitted to the Seligman mausoleum, but were, for some reason, to the one belonging to his murdered wife's family—where one would think they would be in even less friendly company.

36

THE
GREAT BATTLE OF
1109 FIFTH AVENUE

In 1904 Jacob Schiff was at the peak of his career. That summer he had met in London with Baron Korekiyo Takahashi, Financial Commissioner of the Japanese Government and president of the Yokohama Specie Bank. At the heart of their meeting was Japan's need to raise at least five million pounds sterling—in days when the British pound was worth some six U.S. dollars—to finance its war with Russia. Britain was Japan's political and commercial ally, but now London bankers were having difficulty supplying Japan with war financing, and in New York Japan's chances of winning the war were considered remote. For several days Schiff and Takahashi discussed Japan's problems. The meeting ended with Schiff's agreement to handle the loan. It was, as Frieda wrote, "not so much my father's interest in Japan, but rather his hatred of Imperial Russia and its anti-Semitic policies, that prompted him to take this great financial risk."

Schiff had been outraged by the Czarist pogroms, and had made a number of public statements in which he had called the Russian Government "the enemy of mankind," and in which he had urged an armed revolution against the Czar. Takahashi quotes Schiff as saying, "A system of government . . . capable of such cruelties and outrages at home as well as in foreign relations must be overhauled from the foundations up in the interests of the oppressed race, the Russian people, and the world at large . . . and taught an object lesson." Now Schiff set about singlehandedly to abet this overhauling process by helping Japan win her war.

In his new position of peerdom with his old adversary, J. P. Morgan, Schiff approached both Morgan and George F. Baker of the First National Bank, inviting them to join in the loan. When they agreed, there remained only the Rockefeller-Stillman interests, and the National City Bank, to be persuaded. With both Schiff and Morgan sponsoring the loan, the National City group quickly agreed to participate also. It was the first time in history that Japan had been able to obtain money outside of London, and it took three massive loans, engineered by Schiff, before Japan was declared the victor in 1905.

Now began a long series of honors bestowed upon Schiff. England had backed Japan too, and King Edward VII invited Schiff to luncheon at Buckingham Palace, where Schiff found the King "an amiable fellow." Next, the Japanese Emperor asked Schiff to come to Japan and receive one of the Empire's highest honors, the Second Order of the Sacred Treasure. Schiff was to be given a private audience with the Mikado himself, and lunch at the imperial palace, where, he was pleased to note, "It is the first time the Emperor has invited a foreign private citizen to a repast at the palace, heretofore only foreign princes having been thus honored." (The more successful he became, the more formal grew his literary style.)

As a great American railroad financier, he was able to move as grandly across continents as he moved across rooms. Leaving New York for San Francisco, on the first leg of the journey, the Schiff party ensconced itself in two private railway cars, plus a baggage and officers' car. With Mr. and Mrs. Schiff were Ernst Schiff, an unmarried nephew; Mr. and Mrs. Alfred Heidelbach (of the Heidelbach, Ickelheimer Heidelbachs); Mr. and Mrs. Sigmund Neustadt (of Hallgarten & Company); Mr. and Mrs. Henry Budge (Budge had been Mr. Schiff's partner in his first brokerage business); a personal maid for each lady; and Joseph, the Schiff butler. They were accompanied by ninety-odd pieces of luggage, many of them large trunks. They were apparently cramped because they hitched on a fourth private car, a dining car, in Chicago. As the Schiff train rolled from one railroad line to another, it was ceremoniously greeted by railroad presidents and vice presidents who were keeping track of the progress of the entourage.

Most of the passing landscape Mr. Schiff found uninteresting. But perhaps this was because it was considered proper private-car etiquette to travel with one's curtains closed. Pausing in Salt Lake City, Schiff wrote that it contained "little of particular note or attraction except the Tabernacle and the Temple, the latter not accessible to those not belonging to the Mormon Church." In San Francisco the Heidelbachs received news of an ailing relative and were forced, regretfully, to turn back for New York. The rest of the party boarded the S.S. *Manchuria*, where a large section of first class had been set aside for them.

In Honolulu Mr. Schiff had word that Queen Liliuokalani wished to receive him and his party. Schiff was not one to turn down an invitation from a queen, even though Liliuokalani at that point was only an ex-queen, but there was a small difficulty. The *Manchuria* was scheduled to spend only an hour or two in Hawaii before continuing on to the Orient; the Queen's invitation was for the following morning. Mr. Schiff took up this problem with the captain, who finally agreed to hold the ship in Hawaii an additional sixteen hours. (How the other passengers on the *Manchuria* felt about the delay is not recorded.)

Even so, it was going to be nip and tuck. The Queen's invitation was for 9:30 A.M. The Captain had explained that, because of the tides, he could not possibly hold the ship after 10 A.M. And Mr. Schiff, who was nowhere near so secure with steamship companies as he was with rail-roads, became quite nervous that the boat would sail without him. Jokingly, one of his party suggested that he kidnap a member of the *Manchuria*'s crew and hold him until the audience was over. Schiff thought this an excellent idea and, without more ado, commandeered the *Manchuria*'s captain to escort them to the Queen—"as hostage, in order to be certain not to be left behind," as he explains in his journal of the trip. Jacob Schiff was not one to fool around with cabin boys.

He found the Queen a "stately looking old brown lady, surrounded by some of her ladies-in-waiting who, we understand, are relatives." This must have seemed quite appropriate to Schiff, who was surrounded by his own relatives.* It was a little after ten when the party reboarded the ship, which, as Schiff points out, "could not very well have left without us."

That evening at the captain's table, where of course the Schiffs sat, Mr. Schiff said, "Captain, will the *Manchuria* be calling at any more ports where there will be kings or queens?"

"No!" the captain replied. "No! No!"

* In addition to his nephew, he had the Neustadts, who were parents-in-law of his son Morti.

The rest of the trip was unremarkable.

Schiff was a man of will and a man or tradition. Driving to lunch in the Japanese imperial palace, Schiff announced to the Imperial Chief of Protocol that he wished to propose a toast to the Emperor. In a dither, the Protocol Chief urged him not to, since a toast was a thing "not done" in the Japanese court; the Emperor might misunderstand. Nevertheless, when the guests were seated, Schiff rose and lifted his glass; "To the Emperor. First in war, first in peace, first in the hearts of his countrymen." To everyone's relief, when the Schiff statement had been translated, the Emperor looked pleased.

Not all Schiff's remarks in Japan led to peaceful solutions. At dinner one evening Mr. Schiff found himself seated next to Baron Takahashi's fifteen-year-old daughter, Wakiko, and, in the course of conversation said to her, through an interpreter, "You must come and visit us in New York some time." A Schiff statement clearly carried as much weight in Tokyo as it did on Wall Street, for the next morning the Baron bowed himself into the Schiffs' apartments and said that, though it was highly unusual for a young Japanese girl to leave her home and country at such a tender age, and to undertake such a long and arduous journey to a foreign land, he had, since Mr. Schiff had proved himself such a friend to Japan, agreed to let Wakiko return to New York with the Schiffs, but he truly felt—and he hoped Mr. Schiff would understand—that Wakiko should not visit the Schiffs for longer than three years.

"Mother," wrote Mr. Schiff in his diary, "believes it somewhat of a responsibility we are undertaking in assuming charge of the responsibility of the girl and her education but we have decided to assume the responsibility." There is a hint of Schiff hysteria here, for Mr. Schiff was usually too cautious a stylist to use the word "responsibility" three times in one sentence. And what actually happened was that "Mother"— Therese Schiff—hadn't protested any action of Jacob's so hotly since he threatened to move her to Riverside Drive. But Mr. Schiff was a man of his word. Wakiko joined the Schiff party, returned to America with them, lived her three years with them, and was educated here.*

Meanwhile, Frieda and Felix Warburg had had, in fairly rapid succession, five children—four of them lively boys—and were beginning to feel crowded in their Seventy-second Street house. They already had, to be sure, quite a comfortable summer place in White Plains. Called "Woodlands," it was an estate of a mere thirty acres to start, but Felix, who always liked to "square off" his property, enlarged it repeatedly

---

* Wakiko is an old woman now, living in Japan, but she still corresponds with the Schiff grandchildren she played with as a child, and not too many years ago her own grandchildren visited America, where they played with Schiff's great-grandchildren.

until it composed some six hundred acres. (Penurious Morris Loeb wanted to call it "Moneysunk.") It was built in the Tudor style around a large central tower, and it had an indoor swimming pool which was also a hothouse filled with orchids and tropical plants. It had—another idea of Felix's—the "Presidential benches," a series of wooden benches, each engraved with the name of a United States President, stretched along five miles of bridle paths. (The Franklin Pierce bench, at a far corner of the property, was forever being stolen by neighbors for firewood.) Felix loved vistas, and cut down great sweeps of the surrounding forest to create them. When Nina and Paul Warburg first saw Woodlands, Nina said that it was lovely, but she liked a water view—to remind her of Koesterberg on the Elbe, where a number of German Warburgs had summer places. Felix immediately ordered another vista cut down, this time all the way through to the golf pond of the Scarsdale Country Club. (Nina liked it so much that she and Paul came to live there, and built their own house on the estate, where Paul built her a beautiful rustic "outdoor study" with a pool of its own.) Felix was a man of sudden enthusiasms. Once Frieda said, "Wouldn't it be nice to rent two cows so we could have our own milk for the children." "Oh!" cried Felix, "I've always wanted a Guernsey herd." So they acquired one.* He also laid out a few golf holes on the polo field, which had more or less occurred while he was building his driveway.

Mr. Schiff, however, didn't like Woodlands. He was probably jealous because Frieda and Felix seemed to enjoy it so much. He became very difficult whenever the young couple tried to stay at Woodlands beyond the second week in June, when he expected them to join him on the Jersey shore. Whenever he came to White Plains, he made disparaging remarks about the place, and used to say, "I can't wait to have the children breathe the good sea air at Rumson Road." Also, to make Frieda even more nervous, whenever her father visited Woodlands, things had a way of going wrong—there would be a heat wave and the wells would run dry, or there would be a thunderstorm and the electricity would go off.

But Mr. Schiff's objections to Woodlands were as nothing compared to the fuss he kicked up over the Warburgs' new plan, which was to build themselves a new house in the city.

While his father-in-law was traveling in Japan, Felix bought a 100 x 100 piece of land at Fifth Avenue and Ninety-second Street, a particularly beautiful corner facing the Central Park Reservoir. Felix, with his

---

* And with it a herdsman as flamboyant as Felix, who immediately ordered stationery printed which said, at the top in large letters, "WOODLANDS FARM, WILLIAM B. JONES, SUPERINTENDENT," and, at the bottom, in very small letters, "Felix M. Warburg, owner."

usual exuberance, liked the Gothic style, and had always admired the old Fletcher house on Seventy-ninth Street and said, "If I ever build a house, I want the architect of that house to design it." The architect of the Fletcher house was C. P. H. Gilbert and, when he had his property, Felix hired him.

It was to be quite a house that Mr. Gilbert designed. The ground floor was to contain a large entrance hall with an adjoining "etching room," to house Felix's print collection, and the kitchen and pantries. On the second floor was a music room built around an Aeolian electric pipe organ for Felix to play; a Red Room to house the Italian paintings, Raphael's "Madonna and Child" among them; a huge conservatory with stained-glass windows; and the formal dining room. On the third floor Gilbert placed a joint sitting room for Frieda and Felix where they would both have desks on which to array family photographs and where they would place their Friday evening candles; a family breakfast room; Frieda's boudoir and bathroom; their joint bedroom; and Felix's dressing room and bath. The fourth was the children's floor with their rooms and schoolroom, and Felix had designed an elaborate electric toy railroad with tracks snaked in and out of the doors through all the rooms on this floor. The fifth floor was taken up with the squash court and guest rooms (and, later, Edward Warburg's art gallery). The sixth floor and the basement were servants' quarters. Felix had also purchased an adjacent lot where he had conceived the idea of building an apartment house, to be used by Warburg relatives, connected to the main house by an umbilical bridge. (This plan, however, never came to be.)

The minute Mr. Schiff heard of the Warburgs' plans to build 1109 Fifth Avenue he flew into one of his terrible rages. The trouble was, nobody seemed to know quite what his objections were. "Perhaps," Frieda said, "he was angry because we hadn't consulted him. Perhaps he felt we were doing it behind his back." At the time, he denied this. The closest he could come to putting his objections into words was to say, "It's conspicuous. It will add to the social anti-Semitism in New York if a young couple build such an ornate house right on Fifth Avenue." But this didn't make much sense. Schiff himself had an ornate house on Fifth Avenue too, just a few blocks to the south, and a new one to boot. He had acquired No. 965, and, when his son married Adele Neustadt, he had given 932 to Morti as a wedding present, who commented, "It's nice to own a house in which I got so many spankings." Pacesetter Schiff had, in fact, led the crowd's march to Fifth Avenue.

As the building of 1109 got under way, it became most difficult for Felix, who had to suffer his father-in-law all day long at the Kuhn, Loeb office. The house became a closed subject between the two men, and the atmosphere between them became icy. At one point, Felix confided to

Frieda, "I just don't think I can go on working with your father under circumstances like these," and Felix went so far as to go to Schiff and offer his resignation. Mr. Schiff stared at him stonily and said, "If you leave this company, I'll see to it that you never work anywhere in America again." It was a sizable threat, and Jacob was a man capable of carrying it out.

The situation was no easier for Frieda. Her father would not discuss the house with her. Though he walked past the site of the construction each Sunday morning with Samuel Sachs, on their way to Montefiore Hospital, where the two men ritually visited patients and checked on the upkeep of one of their favorite charities, when he came to the corner of Ninety-second Street he made a point of turning his head in the opposite direction. Finally, desperate, Frieda said, "Perhaps it's the fact that it's Gothic that upsets him so. Perhaps he'd like it better if we changed it to a Renaissance style." She went to Gilbert with this suggestion, but he pointed out that, since the exterior walls were already built, it was a little late for a change of theme.

The house was completed in the autumn of 1908, a year in the building. Fortunately, the Schiffs were in Europe when it was time for Frieda and Felix to move in, so they were spared having to invite Jacob to take part in this. They decided to move in on their son Frederick's birthday, October 14. But once in the house Frieda was faced with what might happen when her father returned to New York. She became convinced that he would never speak to her again. The night before he was due to arrive, she could not sleep for worry and, the next morning, was too ill and tired and frightened to go to the pier to meet her parents, as she had always done. Felix went alone.

That afternoon her father came by to see her. He was ushered into 1109 Fifth Avenue and up to her bedroom. He sat on the bed beside her for over an hour, telling her about the summer he had had in Europe, without once mentioning that he was in a new house.

But the next day a note was delivered to Frieda. It said: "Your mother and I wish you much happiness in your new home. Though it looked very complete to me, there must be something you still need, and we hope this check will help toward it." The note was not signed, but of course the check was. It was for $25,000.

Certain night watchmen in the Warburg mansion, which is now the Jewish Museum, insist that the house is haunted. A mischievous ghost patrols the galleries at night, rattling the display cases. If so, it is probably the restless shade of Jacob H. Schiff trying to find his daughter.

37

"WITTY AND INTERESTING PERSONALITIES"

In 1870 the number of Jews in New York City had been estimated as eighty thousand, or less than 9 percent of the city's population; as such, they were no more than the object of casual curiosity. By 1907 ninety thousand Jews were arriving in the city every year, most of them from Russia and Poland. (Because the Russians and the Poles seemed indistinguishable, they were all grouped as "Russians.") The Jewish population of the city stood at close to a million, or roughly 25 percent of the total. By 1915 there would be nearly a million and a half, or 28 percent. These statistics presented the Americanized German Jews in New York with the most pressing and painful problem they had ever faced, and a deep rift had developed between the Germans and the Russians, between uptown, where the Germans lived, and the Lower East Side.

In Czarist Russia of the 1870's and 1880's, life for the Jews had become intolerable. The vast ghetto known as the Pale of Settlement, which included the Ukraine, Byelorussia, Lithuania, and much of Poland, had become a morass of overpowering poverty, and the situation for Jews who lived outside the Pale was not much better. In the 1880's the tyranny over Jews became legalized under the May Laws, which prohibited Jews from owning or renting land outside towns and cities and discouraged them from living in villages. The increasing economic pressures triggered the "spontaneous" outbreaks of 1881, the massacre at Kishinev in 1903, and the massive and savage pogroms that followed. In 1891 thousands of Jews were expelled without warning from Moscow, St. Petersberg, and Kiev, and six years later, when the government seized and monopolized the liquor traffic, thousands of Jewish innkeepers and restaurateurs were thrown out of business.

One reason for the pogroms, of course, had been the desperate, and largely unsuccessful, attempts of Jewish workers to organize trade and labor unions. In 1897 the General League of Jewish Workers in Russia, Poland, and Lithuania—*Der Algemayner Idisher Arbeter Bund*—had been organized and, in the next three years, led several hundred strikes of cobblers, tailors, brushmakers, quilters, locksmiths, and weavers who had been working eighteen hours a day for a wage of two to three rubles a week. But many of these strikes were marked by violence, bloodshed, and arrests. In the first years of the twentieth century, thousands of persons were arrested for political reasons, most of them Jews. In 1904 of thirty thousand organized Jewish workers, nearly a sixth were thrown into prisons or exiled to Siberia. The Pale of Settlement had become a hotbed of revolutionary activity. Then the Revolution of 1905 seemed to erase all hope. The only answer was to escape to America, the land of the free.

In the years between 1870 and 1905, more than a third of the Jews of Eastern Europe left their homes. Over 90 percent of these came to the United States, and most of these settled in New York City.

In New York they found a small, established, Americanized colony of German Jewish families who were solid, well tailored, capitalistic in their outlook, and wealthy. They found, in fact, what the Germans themselves had found in the Sephardim fifty years before. The new arrivals from Eastern Europe were ragged, dirt-poor, culturally energetic, toughened by years of torment, idealistic, and socialistic. Aside from the single fact of their common religion, the Germans and the Russians could not have been less alike.

To the older-established Germans, who had acquired the patina of manners and respectability, this vast mass of gruff-voiced, "uncouth, unwashed" Russians who had the temerity to call themselves fellow Jews and therefore brothers was a distinct embarrassment. Newspaper stories of "horrible conditions in the Jewish quarter" on the Lower East Side—with reports of overcrowding in tenements, vermin, garbage, marital disorders, violence, starvation, and crime—were a grievous thorn in the German Jewish side. To be identified as a Jew, along with "those people," became increasingly irksome. "Those people" were loud, pushy, aggressive—"the dregs of Europe." They made a bad name for everybody. In this period Mrs. Solomon Loeb counseled her children and grandchildren, "When traveling on a train for short distances, never hurry for the exit when it reaches your stop. People will think you are a pushy Jew." Adolph Ladenburg cautioned his chauffeur—and it was intended as a rule of life for everyone in the family—"Never try to get through the traffic. Wait your proper turn before going. The stricter it's run, the better for everybody's good." And he repeated it for emphasis, *"Everybody*'s good." In blaming the Russians for the anti-Semitism that existed in New York, the Germans themselves began to display anti-Semitic attitudes.

German Jewish anti-Semitism had begun to take form when Rabbi Kaufmann Kohler of Temple Emanu-El, touting German superiority, stated that German roots meant "peace, liberty, progress, and civilization," and that German Jews were freed of "the shackles of medievalism," with their minds "impregnated with German sentiment . . . no longer Oriental." By a queer rationale, the Germans began to speak of the Russians as something akin to the Yellow Peril and Russian "Orientalism" became a repeated theme. The German Jewish press echoed this, speaking of the "un-American ways" of the "wild Asiatics," and referring to Russian Jews as "a piece of Oriental antiquity in the midst of an ever-Progressive Occidental Civilization." The *American Hebrew* asked: "Are we waiting for the natural process of assimilation between Orientalism and Americanism? This will perhaps never take place." The *Hebrew Standard* stated it even more strongly: "The thoroughly acclimated American Jew . . . has no religious, social or intellectual sympathies with them. He is closer to the Christian sentiment around him than to the Judaism of these miserable darkened Hebrews." Yes, the Russians *did* seem to have a different color skin. Because many Russian names ended in "ki," they were called "kikes"— a German Jewish contribution to the American vernacular. (Germans are also said to have invented the term "Bohunk," referring to Jews from Bohemia.)

Looking around them, the immigrant Russians saw German Jewish millionaires and quickly learned that these men had started as peddlers. If that was the avenue to success, they would take it. The future for peddlers in the 1880's and '90's wasn't what it had been in the '40's and '50's, but Russian Jews would have to learn this the hard way. The

Russian Jewish peddlers, with packs or behind pushcarts, took to the streets of Manhattan. In their dark baggy suits, hats, shoestring ties, and sausage curls, they chanted what became a familiar street refrain: "Suspendahs, collahbuttons, 'lastic, matches, hankeches—please, lady, buy!"

There was also the touchy matter of the Yiddish language which the Russians spoke. Yiddish newspapers had sprung up which the Germans denounced as "socialistic"—or worse. They called the Yiddish theater "barbarous." Yiddish itself they called a "piggish jargon," and insisted that it was "a language only understood by Polish and Russian Jews." But the truth was that Yiddish, which is Judeo-German, was perfectly intelligible to Germans who were *not* Jewish. Yet Yiddish, like the foot peddler's pack, was another symbol of a buried past. Yiddish stood for poverty, meanness, the ugliness of the *Judengasse*—for everything the German wanted to escape.

At the moment when language seemed at the heart of all the bitterness, two young German Jewish girls took a somewhat different stand. They were Alice and Irene Lewisohn, daughters of Leonard Lewisohn, who made a pact that they would never marry, but devote their lives instead to the welfare of immigrant Jews, and to the girls' greatest love, the theater.* The girls began giving funds to build the Neighborhood Playhouse as a headquarters for the performing arts in the heart of the Lower East Side ghetto. Their plan was to produce plays in both English and Yiddish, and yet, when their first play, *Jephthah's Daughter,* was offered in English, the Yiddish press accused the girls of catering to uptown groups and not supporting Yiddish theater, which the immigrants needed and missed so badly. While the girls continued to present most plays in English, subsequently several Yiddish-language plays were performed at the Neighborhood Playhouse. Uptown, of course, the sisters were treated as scandalous rebels, especially when it was learned that the *Folksbühne* group was performing at their Playhouse. (The *Folksbühne* was sponsored by the "Socialist" Workmen's Circle.) The Neighborhood Playhouse also gave the noted actor-director, Ben Ami, his first chance to present himself in the United States, even though he spoke no English.

To most well-to-do Germans, one of the most terrifying things about the Russians was their interest in forming trade unions. This threatened the Germans' pocketbook, always the most vulnerable part of the anatomy of any rich man. And so, to the uptown German, the Lower East Side Russian became the Enemy. The division between the two camps widened. It was worker versus boss, mass versus class, vulgar

* Alice later broke the pact, and married Herbert Crowley.

versus genteel, "foreigner" versus "American," Russian versus German, Jew versus Jew.

Still, though there was literally nothing about the Russians of which the Germans approved, one Russian could not be ignored. There were simply too many of them. Clearly, the Germans would have preferred it if the Russians had never come, but there they were. For a while, the United Hebrew Charities and the Baron de Hirsch Fund—a £493,000 trust established by the German capitalist for the specific purpose of helping Jewish immigrants settle in America—embarked on programs to inspire Eastern Europeans to settle elsewhere than New York. These organizations, trying to sound charitable, pointed out that the "country air" in New Jersey or the Catskills would surely benefit the immigrants. They met with little success. In 1888 two hundred Jews were shipped back to Europe in cattle boats. But what were two hundred out of hundreds of thousands? Uptowners, increasingly alarmed, attempted to have laws passed in Washington to restrain further immigration. But the tide could not be stopped.

The next logical step, as far as the Germans were concerned, was to try, if possible, to reshape these shabby immigrants along what the Germans considered "acceptable" German lines—to clean the immigrants up, dust them off, and get them to behave and look as much like Americans as possible. The East Side settlement houses, originally little more than delousing stations, were set up. The United Hebrew Charities began providing free lodging, meals, and medical care for immigrants, and sponsored entertainments and lectures—on manners, morals, marriage, and the dangers of socialism—designed to show the poor Russians the unwisdom of their former ways. When refugees overflowed Castle Garden and the rooming houses nearby, the New York Commissioner of Emigration opened the Ward's Island buildings, and Jacob Schiff contributed $10,000 for an auxiliary barracks.

Others contributed in their own way. A particularly busy lady of the period was Mrs. Minnie Louis, a voluble woman whose ample body was overstuffed with good intentions. Minnie was not exactly a member of the German "crowd" of the highest social standing, but she represented its point of view. And if, since the Sephardim had Emma Lazarus, the Germans wanted a poet of their very own, Minnie filled the role. In a poem, addressed to the immigrant Russians, she explained "What It Is to Be a Jew." She started by declaring what a Jew wasn't:

> To wear the yellow badge, the locks,
> The caftan-long, the low-bent head,
> To pocket unprovoked knocks
> And shamble on in servile dread—
> 'Tis not this to be a Jew.

But, she added:

> Among the ranks of men to stand
> Full noble with the noblest there;
> To aid the right in every land
> With mind, with might, with heart, with prayer—
> *This* is the eternal Jew!

Be a man, in other words, like Jacob Schiff or Solomon Loeb or the Lehmans, Warburgs, Seligmans, and Lewisohns. It was a large order. Jacob Schiff admired the poem. The Russians admired it less.

Minnie Louis, in her stone marten cape, became a familiar figure on the Lower East Side, where she passed out cookies and exhorted immigrants to stop speaking Yiddish and cut off their curls. But to the Russians Minnie became an object of suspicion. On the Lower East Side it was widely rumored that she was not a Jew at all but a Christian missionary.

It would take more than poetry and cookies to elevate the immigrant to what the Germans considered his proper station. And so, led by men like Jacob Schiff, the massive programs of philanthropy began. As the *American Hebrew* sorrowfully observed, "All of us should be sensible of what we owe not only to these . . . coreligionists, but to ourselves, who will be looked upon by our gentile neighbors as the natural sponsors for these, our brethren." The Germans took up this task with a heavy collective sigh, as if assuming the white man's burden. This was the atmosphere of philanthropy—money was given largely but grudgingly, not out of the great religious principle of *Zedakah,* or charity on its highest plane, given out of pure loving kindness, but out of a hard, bitter sense of resentment, embarrassment, and worry over what the neighbors would think. Many wealthy gentile families were enlisted to aid the Germans in their heavy chore of uplifting the Russians. In the 1890's Mrs. Russell Sage, Warner Van Norden, and Henry Phipps all contributed importantly to the United Hebrew Charities, and Mrs. Josephine Shaw Lowell established her East Side Relief Work Committee to "put our poor 'Hebrew Jews' at work and to clothe the poor Negroes of the Sea Islands."*

As the wheels of philanthropy began to turn, pulling its heavy load of impoverished humanity behind it, any spirit of benevolence that might have existed at the outset grew less. Philanthropy became something very close to patronage, with the Germans, the patron lords, doling out funds to the poor, the miserable, the dependent and the patronized, the new "huddled masses." From a tithing system of raising money, some-

---

* In this period, the Germans were forced to face another irritating fact: They were being increasingly equated with Negroes.

thing painfully like taxation developed, and wealthy Germans, having been brusquely informed of how much they were expected to contribute, emerged from meetings of the United Hebrew Charities with red and angry faces.

Not surprisingly, the Russians, on the receiving end of this charity, had no trouble sensing the spirit in which it was given. Uptown social workers and investigating teams invaded the Lower East Side, poking through blocks of railroad flats, clucking about filth and garbage, and asking impertinent personal questions—often to people who, in their own circle, were considered men of consequence. The Germans, however, were frequently surprised that the Russians, having accepted their largess, did not always respond with gratitude. As the *Yiddishe Gazette* reported in 1894:

> In the philanthropic institutions of our aristocratic German Jews you see beautiful offices, desks, all decorated, but strict and angry faces. Every poor man is questioned like a criminal, is looked down upon; every unfortunate suffers self-degradation and shivers like a leaf, just as if he were standing before a Russian official. When the same Russian Jew is in an institution of Russian Jews, no matter how poor and small the building, it will seem to him big and comfortable. He feels at home among his own brethren who speak his tongue, understand his thoughts and feel his heart.

Alas, it is possible that this reporter is speaking of just such German philanthropists as Jacob Schiff. Schiff, for all his giving, lacked the common touch. His buttoned, German sense of superiority was too great. When faced with a Russian, his blue eyes glazed. When the son of a German friend of Schiff's announced that he had fallen in love with, and wished to marry, a Russian girl, his father cried, "You must have got her pregnant!"

It was not surprising that, as Russian Jewish families grew prosperous, they established charities to care for their own. Needy Russians began turning their backs on German philanthropy in favor of Russian. Though the United Hebrew Charities opposed it, East Side doctors organized the Jewish Maternity Hospital in 1906, where Jewish mothers could be certain they were being served kosher food (which the Germans also frowned on), and where the relationship between doctor and patient was not one of benefactor to beggar, but of equality. Uptown, at Mount Sinai Hospital, though 90 percent of the patients were Eastern Europeans, there was a rule that no Eastern Europeans could be admitted to the staff.

Some Russian and Polish Jewish families did, as they began to make money, attempt to copy the German model and assumed German airs.

They became the "Kavalrier Datch," and boasted, *"Mayn waib is gevoren ah datchke un ich bin gevoren ah datch."* ("My wife has become a lady and I have become a gentleman.") But, for their attempts to bask in the glow of German respectability, they were also looked down upon. Many Russians Germanized their names; Selig became Sigmund, and so on. Others took German surnames, but this was often because, if one had a Russian name, it was impossible to obtain credit at an uptown German bank.* And no matter how successful a Russian became, or how hard he tried to Germanify himself, he found the sacred circle of uptown German Jewish society closed to him. Though the Germans gave away millions to the Russian immigrants, they never extended them invitations to their dinner parties, clubs, and dances.

When, on rare occasions, Russians found themselves inside a German's Fifth Avenue mansion, they reacted with awe. Felix Warburg, who was even more philanthropic than his father-in-law, Mr. Schiff, had a private little joke which used to amuse his family whenever a recipient of his charity came around. As a boy in Berlin, when the Kaiser's car sped by it played a little four-note melody on its horn. The joke in Germany used to be that the words to this tune were *"Mit unser Gelt"*— "With our money." Sometimes a Warburg pensioner would come to the Warburg house with a little gift for Felix. Accepting it, Felix would hum the little tune under his breath. It made his children giggle.

Once Felix invited two Russians to a Jewish charities meeting at his house. He had never met them before, but he knew how to spot them. They were the two who didn't come in dinner jackets. He overheard this pair standing in front of one of his Italian paintings and saying, "When Communism comes and there's a division of property, I hope I draw this house." Felix stepped over to the improperly attired men and said, suavely, "When Communism does come, and there is a redistribution of goods, I hope that if you do get my house, you will also invite me to be your guest, because I have always enjoyed it," and walked away.

But Adolph Lewisohn, who was always something of an individualist and who often did offbeat, rather surprising things, once decided that he would invite some Russian Jewish families to his Fifth Avenue house to dine. They came, and, to his astonishment and delight, he and the Russians hit it off very well. The crowd was shocked, and asked, "How can Adolph *do* that?" But Adolph defended his action, and insisted that his Russian friends were not boorish and uncouth at all but that, on the contrary, they were "witty and interesting personalities" and had con-

* As a result, in Jewish circles in New York today one can always speculate whether so-and-so, with his German name, is really a German or a secret Pole or Russian.

versed intelligently about music, literature, and art. "They had read more Shakespeare than I had," he said.

But, despite such gestures, the stern wall between German and Russian persisted. In the early 1900's a group of East Side Jews began to envision a United Hebrew Community, "to effect a union of Jewish societies and congregations in New York City." But it would take events of violence of a world-wide and unimagined sort to bring this about even partially.

38

THE EQUITABLE
LIFE AFFAIR

One of the most colorful and written-about young men in turn-of-the-century New York was James Hazen Hyde. He had been nicknamed "the hayseed" by his Harvard classmates, but now, five years out of college, he was considered a hayseed no longer.

Upon the death of his father, H. B. Hyde, the young man had found himself, at the age of twenty-three, the custodian of a billion dollars' worth of life insurance, and was in charge of the savings of 600,000 individuals who held policies in the senior Hyde's Equitable Life Assurance Society of the United States, "Protector of the Widow and Orphan," the largest insurance company in the country. The Equitable had over $400 million in its treasury. Young Hyde, whose father had built the company from scratch, owned 51 percent of it.

The minute the Equitable passed into James Hazen Hyde's hands, he became, in view of the vast ramifications of the Equitable, a director of forty-six other corporations, including the Metropolitan Opera, but whether he had the intellectual equipment to cope with these directorships was doubtful. He was far more interested in enjoying himself. He had a barber imported from Paris to cut his hair and trim his beard in the French style, and, in the restaurants where he liked to stop, he positioned various French chefs, who had nothing to do but await the moments when their employer might drop in and wish some specialty. Hyde loved costume balls, indeed parties of all varieties. He threw a *bal masqué* at Sherry's that cost him $200,000. He had a country château on Long Island, with a private "office" in the stables where he entertained "actresses" and other friends, and where "French costume dramas and other entertainments were performed." A reporter from the Paris *Figaro* described Hyde's country office as

> a room full of telephones and electric bells, furnished with fine carpets, old mahogany furniture, sporting photographs and prints, coaching trophies and hunting horns; next to his office is the kitchen, which permits him and his guests to come when the whim seizes them and have supper in the stables more freely and gaily than in the château; I remember a very festive supper that we had there with the thermometer outside fifteen above zero, where ladies donned old postilion hats or bull-fighter bonnets and blew hunting horns while everybody danced the cake walk.

Life in the city was every bit as vivid as it was in the country, and another reporter describes the dashing young exquisite on his way to his office at the Equitable, "driving jauntily downtown in his private hansom cab, a bunch of violets nodding at the side of the horse's head, another bunch nodding from the coachman's hat, and a third bunch breathing incense from the buttonhole of the young man himself." For all this—and probably *because* of all this—the financial community suspected that Hyde hadn't the slightest idea how to run an insurance company. They were quite right. Among the many financiers who wooed him after his father's death, offering to help him run his company and see to it that he "did the right things" with it, the first to gain Hyde's confidence was Ned Harriman. With Harriman, also eager to help, came Jacob Schiff and Kuhn, Loeb & Company. Schiff was placed on the board of the Equitable in 1900.

There were, however, others deeply involved in the affairs of the Equitable. They were the Alexanders, a family of such age and distinction that they snubbed Mrs. Astor, whom they considered "an amusing little upstart." So grand were the Alexanders that they preferred not to identify themselves with New York at all, and referred to themselves as "an old Princeton family." The Alexanders were not only large Equitable stockholders. James W. Alexander, head of the clan, had been made trustee, by the elder Hyde, of the younger Hyde's estate until he reached the age of thirty and, it was hoped, discretion. It was Mr. Alexander's opinion that James Hazen Hyde's affairs were in serious need of management—an opinion which, needless to say, young Hyde did not share. Ned Harriman announced that he was stoutly on Hyde's side, and he said that he "did not think that the Alexanders' method of management of the Equitable was the right one."

J. P. Morgan, meanwhile, had a large interest in another insurance company, the New York Life, and was following events at the Equitable closely. What Morgan had in mind was to buy up the Equitable and add it to the New York Life; he and his client, Jim Hill, thought that the Equitable's half-billion-dollar treasury could be put to excellent use financing railroad ventures, and this, of course, is exactly what Harriman and Schiff had in mind for *their* railroads. Soon after Schiff's appointment to the Equitable's board, the insurance company began investing in railroad issues recommended, not surprisingly, by Kuhn, Loeb.

And so the alignment for control of the Equitable—and Hyde—was the same as in the Northern Pacific battle, Morgan and Hill against Harriman and Schiff. The Equitable's fifty-two directors began taking sides.

Alarmed with the deteriorating situation, James Alexander, along with other officers in the company, drew up a protest in which they demanded that Hyde give up control of the Equitable and that the company be "mutualized"—that is, that the right to elect directors be taken from Hyde and given to the policyholders themselves. (But Alexander had great influence with Equitable policyholders and so really wanted nothing more than to be able to vote the Equitable's shares himself.)

With both the Harriman and the Morgan groups pressing Hyde to sell his Equitable interest to them, Hyde may have felt himself surrounded. Perhaps he simply didn't care. In any case, for reasons that have never been quite clear, he suddenly sold all his stock in the Equitable to a lone-wolf speculator named Thomas Fortune Ryan. Moreover, the price Ryan paid for controlling interest in the insurance empire was startlingly small—$2,500,000. And when it was announced that dividend income on this amount of stock was only $3,514 a year, things seemed decidedly fishy. "Why?" cried the New York *World* editorially. "What is the real motive?" For the moment, as the Schiff and Morgan groups silently withdrew, no one was quite willing to say.

In the storm of threats, inprecations, charges and accusations that followed, James Hazen Hyde departed for Paris. He never returned. In 1929 he appeared briefly in the news again when it was revealed that

Durand's restaurant in Paris offered, as a dessert, a peach flambéed in kirsch called "Poached Peach à la James Hazen Hyde."

By leaving when he did, Hyde conveniently avoided getting involved in what followed, which was a full-scale investigation by the Armstrong Committee of the New York State Legislature into the securities dealings of the big insurance companies, particularly the New York Life with Morgan on its board, and the Equitable with Jacob Schiff. Schiff, Morgan, Harriman, and Hill were all called before the committee and its investigative counsel, Charles Evans Hughes. Hughes turned up a number of interesting things. Morgan's New York Life, in order to hide the fact that it owned stocks—and so it could say in its annual report, "The Company does not invest in stocks of any kind"—had made a number of fictitious loans to its employees. A bond clerk, for instance, was on the books as having received a loan in the sum of $1,857,000, and a fifteen-year-old Negro messenger boy had, according to the company's accounts, been granted a generous loan of $1,150,000.

Hughes was particularly interested in Jacob Schiff's stock sales to the Equitable. The New York State insurance law provided that any director of an insurance company who profited by "selling or aiding in the sale of any stocks or securities to or by such corporation shall forfeit his position . . . and be disqualified from thereafter holding any such office in any insurance corporation." Had, Hughes asked, the firm of which Mr. Schiff was a partner, Kuhn, Loeb, sold any securities to the company of which he was a director, the Equitable? Yes, Schiff admitted, he had, but the stocks had been sound and the prices had been fair.* Many of them were for his favorite railroads. He added that, after all, his firm had sold "only" $49,704,408 worth of stock to the Equitable, and this paltry amount of business had been done over five years' time. He also pointed out that the $49,704,408 worth which Kuhn, Loeb had sold was "only" 16 percent of the total bought by the insurance company over the same five-year span, and finally—the most extraordinary percentage figure of all—that $49,704,408 worth of sales was "less than 3 percent" of Kuhn, Loeb's business. Schiff had never before revealed a figure that indicated Kuhn, Loeb's size. Now he had. In the five years from 1900 to 1905, the firm had sold $1.75 billion worth of securities. That meant $350 million a year. In those golden pre-income tax days, such Kuhn, Loeb partners as Schiff, Felix Warburg and Otto Kahn must have brought home very nice pay checks indeed.

The modest presentation of these heady figures must have satisfied the Hughes committee. At the close of the investigation it was reported that

---

* In similar cases it had been decided that, though such sales were a "technical offense," they were not "ethically offensive" if the conditions of soundness and fairness of price were met.

Jacob Schiff "was one of the few men prominently identified with the Equitable who came through unscathed in reputation." Nevertheless, the investigation led to far stiffer insurance regulations. And it offered, in passing, at least one explanation why the Equitable stock which Ryan had bought from Hyde for $2.5 million yielded such a niggardly dividend income as $3,514 a year. The company's charter, it seemed, stipulated that all profits except 7 percent of the $100,000 par value of stock should go to policyholders. The stock itself, however, could be used as a massive borrowing tool, to secure loans far in excess of its par valuation. As the investigating committee noted, "The stock must be regarded as affording enormous collateral advantages to those interested in financial operations." Thomas Fortune Ryan clearly felt that way about it. He went on to buy a huge house on Fifth Avenue, added a private chapel, and converted the house next door into an art gallery which he filled with tapestries, Limoges enamels, and busts, mostly of himself—three of them by Rodin.

Jacob Schiff, meanwhile, as soon as the investigation was over, quietly resigned from the Equitable board.

39

"I ENCLOSE MY
CHECK FOR
$2,000,000 . . ."

Glamour, on a magnificent, even international scale, was introduced to the New York crowd in the person of Otto Kahn. Like his friend and partner, Felix Warburg, Kahn was a blade—and more so. He was so sartorially splendid that, when appearing before the New York Board of Estimate to submit a fiscal plan for the city, the New York *World* devoted half a column to his remarks and three-quarters of a column to a description of his clothes—the pearl-gray cutaway, the cashmere trousers, the stickpin of an egg-size black pearl, even the tiny orchid in his buttonhole.

Through Otto Kahn the city's Jewish and gentile elite would embark on a new relationship, and, for this, Kahn had arrived at exactly the right moment. When Mrs. Astor had died in 1908, it was said that "With her passed not only a social dynasty but also the whole idea of hereditary or otherwise arbitrary social supremacy in America; with her, indeed, passed 'Society' in the old sense." For over thirty years, attendance at her ball had been the one and only test of social importance in New York. "If she invited you, you were in; if she did not, you were out," explained a contemporary. With the aid of Ward McAllister, she had defined society's limits, and at the height of her social powers, her box—No. 7—at the Metropolitan Opera House was "a social throne. It was always Mrs. Astor who gave the signal as to the proper time to leave. The time bore no relation to the stage to which the opera had advanced, but was selected because it happened to suit the matron; the time she chose was usually just after an intermission."*

American society had for a long time taken a rather proprietary interest in opera. The reason why was fairly simple. In the early days of American cities, when the rich entertained one another, they often found themselves all dressed up with no place to go. After an elaborate dinner party in New York, there was nothing to do but go home and go to bed. As Henry James wrote, "There was nothing, as in London or Paris, to go 'on' to; the going 'on' is, for the New York aspiration, always the stumbling-block. A great court-function would alone have met the strain . . . would alone properly have crowned the hour." In the absence of court functions, opera and the opera season filled this dreary gap. Later, James called opera "the only approach to the implication of the tiara known to American law" and "the great vessel of social salvation."

Opera was more fashionable than the theater for several reasons. The theater has always provided a more personal, speculative experience. One never knows what one will encounter at the new play. But the very formality and artificiality of grand opera makes it reliable; in turn-of-the-century New York, one could go to the opera certain that one would hear nothing untoward, "vulgar," or particularly surprising. In much of Europe opera had belonged to the common man, but by the early 1900's the situation abroad had begun to change also. The upper classes seized and took over opera. In Berlin the opera season had taken on the appearance of a "court function," and in England it was said of Edward VII that "he only talked freely when he went to the opera."

In America each city had its own set of rules involving the opera. In San Francisco, which had built its opera house and established its "season" while it was no more than a miner's town with unpaved streets, the fashionable night was Thursday, where one showed that one was able to entertain in style regardless of the convention of "maid's night off." In New York the smart night for opera-going was Monday, for the

* *Our Times, Pre-War America,* by Mark Sullivan (Scribner).

simple reason that Mrs. Astor and McAllister had chosen Monday as their night to go. Mrs. Astor, who established the chic practice of leaving early, also—à la August Belmont—made it fashionable to arrive late. The great horseshoe of gilded boxes surrounding Mrs. Astor's throne contained others of her "Four Hundred." Outside the narrow, locked, and curtained door of each box, the boxholder's name engraved on an oblong brass plate was a kind of proclamation that that person had reached the pinnacle of social success. Aspiring climbers fought in vain for opera boxes of their own, which sold for as much as $30,000 apiece, in the Diamond Horseshoe, and even younger members of old, box-holding families had to wait many years for gilt-and-velvet shrines of their own. The opera boxes had further rules. It was considered "vulgar," for instance, to visit other boxes until the second intermission. A pair of Lemaire opera glasses, encrusted with diamonds and sapphires and costing $75,000, was, on the other hand, not vulgar. It went without saying that no Jew could be a Metropolitan Opera box holder.

The opera ritual had become so stiff and studied by the early 1900's that the quality of the music performed and sung was of extremely small importance. Appearing at the opera had become of far greater concern than hearing it. One spent such a short time at the opera anyway—sort of a digestive interval between dinner and an Assembly ball—that one hardly bothered to listen. Nor, considering the rigid sameness of the programming—it was nearly all Italian—did one really *need* to listen. Harriet Beecher Stowe, attending the opera, was surprised to hear, during a soft passage in the music, a woman's voice saying, "I always cook mine in vinegar." So dilatory was society's interest in the actual music that the Metropolitan's impresario had said candidly, "I have never discovered a voice in my life. I don't go around discovering operas. I am not musician enough for that. Opera is nothing but cold business to me."

It was, of all things, the Equitable Life affair that first got Otto Kahn involved with the Metropolitan. When James Hazen Hyde went on the Met's board, and when Jacob Schiff became Hyde's banker, it was natural that Schiff should have been more concerned with Hyde's insurance assets than with his opera-house connections. Hyde, however —despite the anti-Semitic cast of the Met—did invite Schiff to sit with him on the Met's board. Schiff declined, suggesting that Hyde consider his young partner, Mr. Kahn.

Kahn, at first, was doubtful whether to accept Hyde's offer. As a banker, he was eager to keep a hand in whatever went on downtown. But he also loved music and the theater, played three instruments, and the romance of the opera appealed to him. He was also worried that an opera directorship might damage his position as a businessman. As Kahn said,

> At that time I was on the threshold of my business career. There were more people then than now looking askance at art.* They looked upon the joy of life and art as incongruous elements in the general harmony of the sphere of existence. I was warned by well-meaning friends that I had better not fool with operatic and theatrical matters; that I would lose standing among serious-minded people if I did so; that it was *infra dig* for a staid and reputable banker to have his name connected with an opera company; that my motives would be misunderstood and misinterpreted.

Faced with these temptations and warnings and misgivings, Otto Kahn consulted Ned Harriman, who gave him some astonishing advice.

"You just go ahead and do your art job, but don't *dabble* at it," Harriman told him. "Make it one of your serious occupations. As long as you do not let it interfere with your other work, with your business duties and ambitions and thoughts, it will do you no harm. On the contrary, it will exercise your imagination and diversify your activities. It ought to make a better businessman out of you."

Kahn became a member of the board of the Metropolitan Opera, and immediately began following Harriman's advice. In those days the structure of an opera company was quite different from what it is today. The Metropolitan Opera and Realty Company was a shareholding corporation which owned the opera house building; the corporation leased the building to an impresario whose responsibility it was to hire the company and put on opera. Otto Kahn initially purchased two hundred shares of stock in the corporation. Hyde had had three hundred shares of Metropolitan Opera stock, and when he departed for Paris, Otto Kahn had bought these. Henry Morgenthau, another director, soon retired, and Kahn bought his three hundred shares. Suddenly Kahn was the opera's leading stockholder. He began buying up opera stock wherever it was available, and presently he had 2,750 shares and virtually owned the Metropolitan Opera. As his mentor, Jacob Schiff, would have agreed, owning the company was the first prerequisite to making it one of his "serious occupations."

One of his first moves in 1903 was to hire a new impresario from Germany, Heinrich Conried, who, according to critics who instantly materialized, possessed no qualifications whatever. At the time, a writer for the New York *Herald* commented: "The only explanation of Kahn's motive in the Conried selection was that the latter's very ignorance

---

* On Wall Street, certainly. One of the Street's reasons for thinking young Hyde a featherweight was his "fancy, Frenchy" interest in opera.

of music might have given his sponsor a chance to superintend, direct, and manage." The same writer warned Mr. Kahn that Conried was "out for big game himself," and was "out to be the head of the opera not only in name but in fact also," and that Otto Kahn had used "Wall Street tactics" to get Conried appointed—rushing the new director in by getting busy board members to sign over their proxies to Kahn. (Kahn, who had already begun his lifetime practice of demanding that newspapers print retractions of stories he considered inexact, made no comment on this one, so we may assume it contains the truth.) No one noted that a great revolution in the Metropolitan Opera was under way, and Conried's first opening night, which marked the American debut of a young Italian tenor named Enrico Caruso in *Rigoletto*, was received with the same bored languor as usual by the Diamond Horseshoe, and got mixed notices in the press.

It was not until December of Conried's first season that the New York newspapers and the opera-going public realized that an important change had taken place at the stately Met. This was Conried's brilliant staging of the first American performance of Wagner's *Parsifal*, which the critics swooningly called "without doubt the most perfect production ever made on the American lyric stage." This was followed by another American premiere—Donizetti's *L'Elisir d'Amore*, which revealed that Caruso had an unsuspected flair for comedy—and suddenly it was noticed that there never had been as many as two new operas introduced in a season. When it turned out that both the operas and the chief performers had been selected by Otto Kahn of Kuhn, Loeb & Company, the Diamond Horseshoe didn't know what to think. Neither, for that matter, did Wall Street.

Heinrich Conried would probably have stayed at the Met for many years if it had not been for three unrelated circumstances. There was, for one thing, the apparent great success of Oscar Hammerstein's Manhattan Opera, five blocks away. There was also the unfortunate publicity that attached itself to the Met when a New York woman accused Enrico Caruso of molesting her in Central Park. Finally there was Conried's health, which began to fail in 1907, the year that Kahn was elected chairman of the board of the Metropolitan Opera. Quietly Kahn set about to find a successor, and he soon became convinced that the man should be Giulio Gatti-Casazza, who, for the past ten years, had been general manager of La Scala in Milan.

When Kahn's first letter to Gatti-Casazza arrived in Milan, the impresario showed it to La Scala's conductor, Arturo Toscanini. Toscanini said he thought Gatti ought to accept and, furthermore, said that he would like to go with him to New York. A meeting between Kahn and Gatti was scheduled in Paris, and, after details of salary and contract

had been worked out, Gatti-Casazza delivered the following florid
acceptance speech (at least this was how he remembered it in his
autobiography):

> "Thank you, Mr. Kahn, for the faith you have shown in me. I am
> well aware that you are besieged and importuned by a large number
> of persons who aspire to Conried's place. I certainly will not importune
> you in any way, the more so since at the Scala in Milan I am very
> well situated in every respect. Nevertheless, if you and your col-
> leagues believe that I am the person suited for the Metropolitan, please
> let me know, and in that event I hope that we shall be able to come
> to an agreement, I should wish that in that case an offer should also
> be made to Maestro Toscanini."

It was of course a great coup for Kahn, who had managed to capture not
one but two of Europe's greatest musical figures for the Met. His opera
house, he had begun to say, would one day wear "the blue ribbon of the
opera world." In announcing that he had hired Gatti-Casazza and
Toscanini, Kahn, lest anyone think that the emphasis of the company
would be "too Italian," was careful to say that French, German, and
Italian operas would be performed with equal frequency.

There were to be other innovations. Kahn announced that, for the
first time in the Met's history, the entire management staff would be on
salary, and that Gatti-Casazza would not have to concern himself with
box-office receipts as previous impresarios had done. Any losses would
be absorbed by "the board of the Metropolitan Opera Company," which
pretty much meant Otto Kahn. The newspapers applauded the news as
"a change from the old order to the new. . . . Power has passed from
the older generation to the younger." Art and culture, it was said, were
at last coming to America, delivered by the Metropolitan Opera and
Otto Kahn.

All at once, he was very much a figure about town. His comings and
goings—to the theater, to the opera, to restaurants, to clubs—were
chronicled in the papers. One saw him on Fifth Avenue on Sunday
mornings, strolling with his dachshunds in his tall silk hat and silver-
handled cane. One marveled at the polished tips of his shoes below his
spats, the perfection of his mohair gloves, the inevitable large pearl
stickpin in his tie, placed just above the V in his velvet-collared Chester-
field. Few men of the day possessed quite such dash. He reminded many
people of Goethe's description of Kahn's home town, Mannheim:
"Friendly, serene, and symmetrical." There was, about his build, a
certain elegant frailness. Still, he always stood and walked with ramrod
straightness, a relic of his service with the Mainz Hussars, and there was
nothing indefinite about his large, blue, appraising eyes under their

heavy dark brows, nor anything accidental about his handlebar mustache, so perfectly shaped and brushed that it might have been a clever bit of *trompe l'oeil* painting. He was, in fact, a fashion plate of almost Renaissance proportions.

He also possessed a commodity that had been something of a rarity in New York's German Jewish crowd. He could smile. He smiled often and easily and well, and his smile served him particularly well in an era, and in a city, that was growing used to chilly and ill-mannered millionaires. He could also speak. Unlike Jacob Schiff, whose accent often made him difficult to understand, Kahn was admired for his "beautiful English accent," which was actually a style of speech called "Continental English"—clipped, flattened, undiphthonged. He was one of the first in the crowd to be often in demand as a public speaker. He was at home on the dais. He adored the spotlight.

Also, though he pretended to have a patrician disdain for personal publicity, he loved it, and his own public and press relations were nearly always perfect. Like Harriman and Jacob Schiff, he believed in personally inspecting railroads in which Kuhn, Loeb had an interest. Once, traveling to Denver to look over a new line, he had descended the steps of his private car to be interviewed by reporters who observed, with wonder, that the great Otto Kahn was "the most simply dressed man there." (He had had the good sense to omit tall silks, spats, and stickpins in the provinces.) At another time, speaking to a general audience, he had said that there should not be less government control of big business, but more—endearing himself to workingmen. At the Met he adopted the habit of strolling into the press room on opening nights and gathering the reviewers around him. Then he would lead them out into the street—to a nearby saloon for a drink or two, or to enjoy a few vaudeville acts at a nearby theater or, in the days of Minsky, to watch burlesque. He would then guide them back to the opera house, considerably cheered up, for the final aria. His mock-formal invitations—"Would any of you gentlemen perhaps care to accompany me for a few moments?"—became so familiar that the minute Kahn entered the press room the reviewers reached for their coats. Needless to say, Met performances were nearly always favorably reviewed.

He had begun collecting clippings about himself around 1901. From then on he was engaged in a long love affair with the press. He scanned the newspapers morning and night for mention of his name, and "The sight of his picture in the paper gave him more pleasure than the news that he had made several thousand dollars in a stock transaction," according to one biographer.* Eventually he employed the famous

* Mary Jane Matz, *The Many Lives of Otto Kahn* (Macmillan).

public-relations firm of Ivy Lee to see to it that the press was properly informed of his activities, and he kept all his press cuttings bound in expensive cloth-and-leather volumes of over a hundred pages each. In the end there were a dozen of these. Stamped in gold letters on the spine of each fat volume were the words "FROM THE PRESS," and on the title page were the tiny, extremely modest initials, "O.H.K."

These were the initials that signed his memoranda which set so many things in motion at the Metropolitan Opera Company, and one member of his staff commented that they really stood for "Opera House Kahn." His memos covered the most minute details of the Met and its operations—new lights for the vestibules, latches for the lobby doors, a wider door for the ladies' room, memos about scenery, costumes, makeup, and lights. In his tiny, European script O.H.K. wanted to know, "Why have the chimes for the temple scene in *Parsifal* not been sent to Philadelphia?" To Gatti-Casazza, he wrote: "President and Mrs. Taft will be at *Aida* on the 15th inst. in Box 35. Please decorate it with a flag and have a nice bouquet, I suggest orchids and lilies of the valley, placed in the box for Mrs. Taft, with the compliments of the Board of Directors." Next he was writing to an unknown opera goer who had complained about waiting in line for two hours only to find a sold-out house. He enclosed two free tickets.

To his Kuhn, Loeb partners, it was all very startling. They were not disapproving but merely mystified. It was hard for them to imagine how he could do his work at the office and still do so much for the Metropolitan Opera. It was even harder when they realized that he *was* the Metropolitan. Actually, Kahn, who said that his family's motto was "*Immer rastlos voran*"—"Ever restlessly forward"—worked as many as eighteen hours a day at his double job, and often was required to combine the two.

There was, for instance, Kahn's handling of the dispute between the Pennsylvania Railroad and the Delaware & Hudson, which is considered one of his greatest achievements. At the time, the main lines between New York and Chicago were four: the New York Central, the Pennsylvania, the B & O, and the Erie, in that order of importance. Mr. L. F. Loree of the Delaware & Hudson began to dream of building a "fifth system" to Chicago and, for that purpose, began secretly buying up large stock holdings in the Nickel Plate, the Wabash, the Western Maryland, and the Lehigh Valley, in hopes of consolidating these lines into a line competitive with the Pennsylvania.

When Kahn learned of Loree's plan, he was horrified. It sounded painfully like the great Union Pacific–Northern Pacific fight of 1901, which had been his memorable introduction to railroading warfare. This, however, was considerably worse. At least rival banking houses had been involved in the Hill-Harriman affair. But both the Pennsylvania and Loree were Kuhn, Loeb clients. There had, in fact, been no situation quite like it in the history of railroading *or* banking.

Kahn's strategy was to invite both Loree and Samuel Rea, president of the Pennsylvania, to meetings with him at the Kuhn, Loeb offices on a Saturday morning.* He placed Rea in one conference room and Loree in another. Kuhn, Loeb had held this sort of meeting before, with warring factions in adjoining rooms, but the problem had always been to keep the one unaware of the presence of the other. Kahn, however, decided to reverse this tactic. Separately, he told each man that his rival waited just beyond the door and that the door between them would not be opened until the terms of a peace had been agreed upon. Kahn's device produced a curious psychological effect: each man became aware of the importance of the moment, and of how much hung upon its outcome. It was a device borrowed from the theater, but it worked. Both Rea and Loree, who had arrived each determined to destroy the other, were suddenly in a mood to compromise.

Meanwhile, adding to the suspense and to Kahn's footwork was the fact that, in a third Kuhn, Loeb conference room, Signor Gatti-Casazza was waiting in one of his not-too-infrequent fits of temper. From the moment of his arrival in New York Gatti had complained about the Met. The stage was too short and too narrow; the storehouses for scenery were too far from the theater, and sets had to be stacked outside on the sidewalk. There were no rehearsal rooms for ballet, chorus, or orchestra. The house contained too many "blind" seats in side sections of the orchestra. And so on. Kahn had agreed with him, and had promised, "In two or three years a new Metropolitan Opera House will be built for you." That promise had been made many times since, and, sadly, Kahn's dream of a new opera house was one he was never able to push to fulfillment.

In a fourth conference room was a young tenor who had written to Kahn for an audition. (It was the sort of thing Gatti-Casazza disapproved of his doing.)

And so, that Saturday morning, Kahn moved nimbly up and down corridors, back and forth between four separate meetings.

Presently, the temper of Gatti-Casazza had cooled, and he had departed with a kiss on both cheeks for Kahn. The young man had sung an aria, been given a check, and had gone. Undisturbed by the singing nearby, the two railroad presidents had agreed to come to terms, and Kahn opened the intervening door and brought them together. Rea offered to buy Loree's railroad shares at a price so generous that Loree could hardly demur, and a major railroad war had been averted.

* Unlike his mentor, Jacob Schiff, Kahn nearly always worked on Saturdays.

For all Gatti-Casazza's splendid management, the Met was always running out of money, and Otto Kahn proved himself as adept at fundraising as he was at handling the press. He was particularly good at the "matching gift" technique which, of course, had been used successfully by Schiff. He would match every sizable gift with an equal one of his own. As early as 1909, barely a year after Gatti-Casazza had joined the Met, Kahn was able to write to the Met's board: "I am enclosing two checks of $50,000 each from Mr. Vanderbilt and myself," and a month later: "I am enclosing two checks from myself and Mr. Vanderbilt for $25,000 each." The following year he wrote: "I am enclosing my check for $43,375. . . ."

His gifts to the Metropolitan Opera began to amount to never less than $100,000 a year. In 1932 Kahn was asked bluntly by a young composer how much, all told, he had given to the Met, and he replied with his usual pleasant suavity, "For your personal and confidential information, I may say that my endeavors, in one way or another, to aid the cause of the Metropolitan Opera have cost me over two million dollars."

Fellow board members, however, have put the figure somewhat higher, at $2.5 million. And both they and Otto Kahn seem to forget two fairly important items: the million dollars-plus Kahn spent in his unsuccessful attempt to locate the company in a new opera house, and the $1.2 million which he paid to Oscar Hammerstein for the Manhattan Opera House, to remove the Met's competition.

In 1917 Otto Kahn was offered a box in the Diamond Horseshoe, an event which the New York *Herald* discreetly called "notable," considering Kahn's religion and which, by every sensible standard, was certainly long overdue. It was Box 14. Jacob Schiff, the *Herald* noted, for all his philanthropies, and though he had been an American citizen since 1870, had never been permitted to own a box, though he had been allowed to rent "Box 18 for certain performances."

With his characteristic aplomb and expert sense of public relations, Kahn did not refuse the offer of the box. He accepted it graciously. But he continued to sit in the Director's Box, where he had always sat. His new box, he explained, would be loaned to foreign dignitaries who visited the city.

It was probably the grandest gesture he could have made. It contained tolerance, wit, and just the right touch of derision. Somehow, this gesture made the banality of anti-Semitism all the more apparent, while at the same time it was clear that, as far as *some* Jews were concerned, some of the crusty social barriers that had been erected over the course of two generations were collapsing by going out of style.

40

THE "SINISTER TRANSMUTATION"

"Father, we must do this no longer," Frieda Schiff Warburg whispered to Jacob Schiff. It was the summer of 1915, and the family was in Bar Harbor. As she and her father strolled down the shaded street of the town, chatting, Frieda had noticed people giving the two of them odd and hostile looks. She realized it was because they had been speaking, as they always did, in German. From that afternoon on, the Schiffs and Warburgs never spoke German again in public.

World War I had a deep and unsettling effect on the German Jewish crowd, and provided, perhaps, the most serious test of their emotional mettle since the founding fathers had arrived on American shores. Among the most deeply torn was Jacob Schiff. He was sixty-eight now, and beginning to show his age. He had developed a corklike dryness, a rigidity and crustiness, and an unwillingness to change his ways. He had grown accustomed to taking the waters annually at Marienbad, and the thought of a war between his adopted country and the land of his birth dismayed him. In the beginning he seemed to regard the war as something that had been devised against him personally, to inconvenience him and alter his routine.

He had had to endure a good deal during the past few years. For one thing, his hearing had begun to fail, and since he was too proud to admit to his incapacity, several sad and embarrassing things had happened. He had, at one point, invited President Theodore Roosevelt to speak at a banquet for one of his philanthropies, and Roosevelt spoke of his 1906 appointment of Oscar Straus to his Cabinet, saying, "When this country conferred upon me the honor of making me President of the United States, I of course at once called my good friend Oscar Straus to my side, and asked him to serve as Secretary of Commerce. It was not a question of religion, of politics, or of catering to any specific group. It was simply a matter of the best man for the job."

Schiff, who had been able to hear none of this, then rose to his feet and said, "President Roosevelt has been so kind in the past as to honor me with his confidences, and it was a great thrill to me that, when he became President, he told me he wanted to have a representative Jew in his Cabinet. He asked me who might be the best candidate to represent our people. I had no hesitancy in at once saying that Oscar Straus was the ideal man, and I believe, as a result, he named Mr. Straus immediately as his Secretary of Commerce."

Poor Schiff, when he was told later what had happened, was furious, and denied that he had ever made such a statement, though of course there were hundreds of witnesses to the fact that he had.

And the first decade of the twentieth century had produced other problems. Panics were occurring with alarming frequency. In 1903 there was the so-called "rich man's panic," caused by manipulators in U.S. Steel stock, when Steel plunged from $58 to $8, taking most of the market with it. Then, four years later, the Panic of 1907 had threatened to wreck the whole fabric of Wall Street. These panics had naturally led to louder talk of the need for "banking reforms" and for a central reserve banking system.* In the noisy aftermath of the 1907 panic, it was all but forgotten that Jacob Schiff had for some time urged radical banking reform, and had called the American monetary system "a disgrace to a civilized community." Instead, as usually happened, since he was a banker, he emerged identified as one of the villains of the panic.

The Panic of 1907 led, rather belatedly, to the Monetary Trust

---

* In 1910 Paul Warburg and Nelson Aldrich together drafted the Aldrich Bill, the first to include central banking as an element of banking reform. Paul Warburg had, meanwhile, set up the National Citizen's League for Promotion of a Sound Banking System. The Federal Reserve Board Act, largely Warburg-designed, was passed in 1913, but the System was not operative until 1915. Warburg resigned from Kuhn, Loeb in 1917 to serve on the Board.

Investigation of 1912 by the Pujo Committee, named after its Senate Chairman. By now Wall Street was used to the pattern of panic, followed by an investigation, followed by tongue-clicking and head-shaking and muckraking in the press. But the Pujo Committee's intent was, on the surface, deadly serious. It was to find out whether there was indeed a "money trust" controlling *all* industrial and financial affairs in the United States—a national financial conspiracy, in other words—just as trusts had been accused of trying to control whole areas of industry. The committee fixed its attention on seven men. The only man not connected with the so-called "White Protestant banking group" was Jacob Schiff.

Though the committee didn't find the monstrous trust it was looking for, it did find an almost unravelable interlocking of directorships and controls involving both industry and banking—polarized around two main money groups, headed by Morgan and Rockefeller—and so complicated in its scheme that it seemed unlikely that even its principal men understood it. It was as though American financial affairs had a life of their own, and had woven their own strange and marvelous cocoon. The committee disclosed that Kuhn, Loeb, despite its excellent relationships with Morgan, had primarily been allied with the Rockefeller-controlled National City Bank, of which Jacob Schiff had long been a director, and therefore that Schiff seemed to enjoy the best of both worlds.

All major banks were hauled in before the Pujo Committee and asked to produce records of their transactions since 1900. These were pre-income tax days, and one can of course wonder whether records produced were full ones. But, in any case, Kuhn, Loeb seemed to be doing nicely. In the five years since 1907 the firm by itself had marketed over $500 million in securities, and in the ten years prior to 1907 over $800 million in cooperation with other houses. Schiff admitted that there was "some collusion" in setting prices asked and bid for issues. "It was not good form to create unreasonable interference or competition," he testified. "Good practices did not justify competition for security issues." But there was, nonetheless, "a sort of rivalry" between firms—and Schiff mentioned instances when Speyer & Company had occasionally, sneakily, tried to make a deal with a Kuhn, Loeb client. As an argument against a Wall Street money conspiracy, that one seemed rather weak.

The Pujo Committee, in other words, certainly revealed that, though there might be no formal "money trust" agreement, there was a great deal of cooperation among the major powers in Wall Street. The Morgan–Baker–First National Bank group and the Rockefeller–Stillman–National City Bank group formed the inner circle. The powers were Steel and Oil, each with its massive bank. And, contrary to what everyone had supposed, there was no rivalry revealed between these "rival" factions. Kuhn, Loeb, the committee decided somewhat vaguely, was "qualifiedly allied, only, with the inner group." While some people wondered what "qualifiedly allied, only" meant, others—particularly some members of the press—took it to mean that Jacob Schiff had an inside track to both the leading powers of Wall Street. Well, even he admitted that he did.

As usually happened after Congressional investigations, when the publicity died down, everybody went back to what he had been doing all along. No one was punished, or even scolded, and there were no immediate reforms. But still—and Jacob Schiff understood this—the Pujo Committee investigation of 1913 marked the end of an era. America's bankers had been building a kind of fortress from which they had dominated not only the financial but also the industrial scene. The first crack had appeared in that structure.

Now, in 1914, Europe was at war. Worried, Jacob Schiff had begun to talk of a "negotiated peace" with Germany, and in letters to his friend President Eliot of Harvard he outlined his proposals. When these letters were published, they were widely misinterpreted. Instead of a negotiated peace, it was inferred that Schiff wanted a German victory, and it was widely rumored in Wall Street and elsewhere that Kuhn, Loeb & Company was pro-German. It was an era of tension and suspicion, when anything out of the ordinary was considered subversive. Though Schiff dutifully stopped speaking German to his family in public, one of his own partners did not help matters when he was quoted as doubting "whether a native-born American could understand even half of what Schiff says, even when he is speaking in English."

From the outset of the war in 1914, Kuhn, Loeb had stopped financing any transactions, directly or indirectly, for Germany or any of her allies. Late in the summer of 1915, after the Schiffs had returned home from Bar Harbor, Britain's financial wizard, Lord Rufus Reading, arrived in New York as the head of the Anglo-French Commission, hoping to negotiate an Allied loan from Wall Street bankers. Both Otto Kahn and Morti Schiff thought this an excellent moment to dispel forever any notions that the firm had German sympathies, and to have Kuhn, Loeb come out strongly behind the Allied cause. Meeting with Lord Reading, Kahn and Morti assured the Briton that a loan for as much as $500 million could be obtained for France and England, and without collateral. The young men told Reading that, though they were in favor of Kuhn, Loeb handling the loan, the senior partner would of course have to be consulted before final arrangements could be made.

When Kahn and Morti approached Jacob Schiff, he reacted characteristically. He would approve the half-billion-dollar loan—on one condition. The Allies could have their money if the French and British finance ministers would give Jacob Schiff their assurance, in writing, that "not one cent of the proceeds of the loan would be given to Russia."

It was like Morti and the pool table all over again. Schiff's partners were aghast. One could not, in time of war, offer money of that size to one ally at the expense of another. Once again, Schiff's condition was impossible to fulfill. Lord Reading replied politely that, while he understood Mr. Schiff's motives, "no government could accept conditions which discriminated against one of its allies in war." When Reading's reply was received, a meeting was quickly called in the Kuhn, Loeb partners' room. Mr. Schiff rose majestically to say, "I cannot stultify myself by aiding those who in bitter enmity have tortured my people and will continue to do so, whatever fine professions they may make in their hour of need. I cannot sacrifice my profoundest convictions. This is a matter between me and my conscience."

Everyone who knew him knew what he meant. Again and again, he had refused to participate in loans involving Czarist Russia. He had predicted, in fact encouraged, a Russian revolution. He had helped assure that Russia lost its war with Japan. In protest against the massacre of Russian Jews at Odessa in 1905, he had gone to President Roosevelt, urging him to urge the Congress to act against the Czarist government and had succeeded in getting Roosevelt to write a personal letter to the Czar. After Jacob's speech, there was a short silence. He then offered to resign from Kuhn, Loeb rather than be connected with the loan. Needless to say, his resignation offer was immediately and unanimously rejected. To Lord Reading, the firm addressed a short note, asking to be excused from participation.

That evening, leaving the office, Otto Kahn said sorrowfully to Morti, "The old man was magnificent today, but wait till you see the papers in the morning." Sure enough, the headlines proclaimed:

KUHN, LOEB, GERMAN BANKERS, REFUSE TO AID ALLIES

It was as though a funeral wreath had been hung on Kuhn, Loeb's door. While reaction in New York was shocked and silent, reaction in London was angry and noisy. All at once, the Kuhn, Loeb name became unmentionable anywhere in the city. Doors on both sides of the Atlantic that had been open were suddenly closed.

It seemed to be up to Otto Kahn to do something about it. Certainly no one could sensibly call *him* pro-German. From as early as 1907 Kahn had been quoted as an expert on European affairs, and in speeches he had deplored a Germany being "possessed gradually by a demoniacal, obsessive worship of power and a will toward world dominion." The

German people, he had declared, were "misled, corrupted, and systematically poisoned by the Prussian ruling class, their very minds perverted
and their moral fiber rotted." He had seen as a young boy in Mannheim
the Prussian spirit "ruthlessly pulling down the old Germany, which was
dear to me, to which I was linked by ties of blood, fond memories and
cherished sentiments." On subsequent trips to Germany he had watched
what he called the "sinister transmutation" which Prussianism had
effected in Germany and which he felt was a threat to the entire world.
Kahn had read Schopenhauer and Nietzsche and understood better than
most Americans some of the doctrines—"the will to war, will to power
and will to overpower"—that were guiding German thought. In the fall
of 1914 he had told Gatti-Casazza to remove all German operas from
the repertory of the Metropolitan for the duration of the European war,
and his aim was mainly to stop performances of the works of Wagner,
which, he felt, "translated Nietzsche's *Übermensch* philosophy into a
language disturbingly understandable even to illiterates." This was not
easy for him to do, because Wagner's music was perhaps his greatest
love. And finally, of course, his own anti-German position was not an
easy one. Like Felix Warburg and many other German Americans who
were pro-Ally, Otto Kahn had friends and relatives in Germany, and in
the German Army.

His sister, for example, was married to a man named Felix Deutsch
who was head of one of the largest public utilities corporations in
Germany. In March, 1915, Kahn wrote his brother-in-law to say how
much he regretted Germany's declaration of war, that he felt Germany
had precipitated the war, and that the "rape of Belgium" made him
ashamed to be German-born. Deutsch replied curtly and disagreeably,
and this inspired Kahn to write Deutsch a twenty-three-page letter
pouring out all his sentiments. The letter, which took him four days to
write, reveals him as a stylist of particular power. He accuses Prussianism of

> throwing overboard everything that civilization and humanitarian prog-
> ress of centuries has accomplished toward lessening the cruelty, the
> hatred and the sufferings engendered by war and toward protecting
> non-combatants from its terrors . . . the violation of innocent Bel-
> gium, in defiance of solemn treaties, and unspeakable treatment inflicted
> on her people, the bombardment without warning of open places (which
> Germany was the first to practise), the destruction of great monu-
> ments of art which belong to all mankind, the *Lusitania* horror, the
> strewing of mines; the use of poison gases, causing death by torture
> or incurable disease; the taking of hostages—these are the facts that
> the noncombatant nations charge against Germany. . . . Such words
> and ideas are greeted with contempt by your spokesmen and scorn-

fully termed empty phrases and sentiment. If these are mere phrases, then the whole upward struggle of the world for endless years past has been founded on sentimentality.

Kahn's fat letter to Deutsch was spotted by a French censor, who, in a routine check, opened it to see what the great American financier was saying to the great German industrialist. He soon realized that he had something of possibly great importance. He copied the letter, sent the original on, and delivered the copy to the French Minister of Information. From there it made its way to England, and very soon a copy of Kahn's letter was in every Allied foreign office. Excerpted and reprinted in bulk, in its original German, it soon became a major item of Allied propaganda, and was being scattered over Germany from planes. Kahn, at first, was less than pleased at this development, since he had not intended his letter to his brother-in-law for use as an anti-German leaflet. However, soon after Jacob Schiff's refusal to participate in the Allied loan, Kahn, in an attempt to lift some of the pall that had fallen on Kuhn, Loeb, permitted his famous letter to be published in the *New York Times*.

He continued his work to bring the firm out of its unfortunate spot. Both he and Morti Schiff asked to make private contributions to the Allied loan—Kahn's was for $100,000—and this also helped. Kahn, who had always been an Anglophile and was still a British subject, had for several years kept a large house in London called St. Dunstan's, in Regent's Park, which had fourteen acres of gardens and grounds and was one of the English capital's great showplaces. At the time of Jacob Schiff's decision against the loan, "sods of earth" had been hurled at the windows of St. Dunstan's, and now Kahn decided to make a definite move to woo back England's public and financial community.

Presently the *Times* of London was announcing:

> The King and Queen are showing great interest in arrangements which have been completed to provide for the welfare of officers and men of both services who lose their sight in the war. The scheme is in the hands of the Blinded Soldiers' and Sailors' Committee, of which Mr. C. Arthur Pearson is chairman. . . .
>
> Mr. Otto Kahn has generously placed at the disposal of the Committee, for the purposes of a hostel, St. Dunstan's. . . . In the grounds will be installed an open-air club where those of the blind men who wish to live in the country will be taught poultry-culture, garden and farm work, way-finding, marketing, and sports and games.

By the fall of 1915 St. Dunstan's was serving 130 blind British veterans, and the congratulatory mail was pouring in to Otto Kahn. "You have certainly endeared yourself to all on this side of the water," said one.

"No single thing that has been done by an American has been such a conspicuous and effective help as the turning over of St. Dunstan's as a hospital and training place for the blind," said another.

In fairness it should be pointed out that not all Otto Kahn's public relations went that smoothly. As his wealth increased to Croesus proportions, Otto Kahn's love of stately mansions became overweening. In addition to St. Dunstan's, he had his Italian villa in Morristown, New Jersey, and no less than three houses in East Sixty-eighth Street. He was in the process of selling these three, however, and of building his huge house at 1100 Fifth Avenue, just down the street from the Warburgs, and, as though one country house weren't enough, he was building another in Cold Spring Harbor, Long Island. Jacob Schiff, who scolded the Warburgs for ostentation, gave up when it came to Kahn. Kahn's Long Island place would eventually take workmen and landscape gardeners two years to build. It was in the Norman style, H-shaped from the sky, and would require a staff of 125 servants. It was very nearly as big as the old Grand Union Hotel at Saratoga. The Georgian dining room would seat two hundred, and there were so many guest rooms, each with a sunken bath, that a little card rack (of sterling silver) was secured to each door so that servants could keep track of guests, and the guests could keep track of each other. There were miles of formal gardens and acres of hothouses. In a period of wartime belt-tightening, shortages, and general austerity, the Cold Spring Harbor house was widely criticized.

Meanwhile, his celebrated letter to Felix Deutsch had made Kahn in demand as an anti-German pamphleteer. He had wanted, as a boy, to be a playwright, and he took up his pen again with glee. He was best at invective, and his alliterative polemics talked of "perfidious plotters . . . architects of anarchy . . . violators of international Law." Germany, he wrote, was guilty of "crime heaped upon crime in hideous defiance of the laws of God and man." In Germany his attacks were reaching their mark, and presently there was a concerted German propaganda attack against Otto Kahn. He was called a "traitor . . . turncoat . . . betrayer and corrupter of German morale." And, inevitably, with these attacks came a wave of anti-Semitism, which, of course, swept poor Jacob Schiff along with it. He was now being vilified by both the United States and Germany. Men like Otto Kahn, the German Government announced, were no more qualified to speak for the Allied powers than Jacob Schiff was qualified to speak for Germany.* These men, said the Kaiser's spokesmen, were Jews—"outsiders, men without a country, empty of every sentiment except the love

---

* It was a subtle way to continue to hammer the point, with Americans and Britishers, that Schiff was pro-German—though he never was.

of money." Undaunted, Otto Kahn continued writing essays and making speeches.

While President Wilson continued to defend American neutrality, Kahn became convinced that intervention was inevitable and essential. He had, however, been hesitant to comment on American policy in any of his speeches or essays since he was not an American citizen. At the same time, he had been reluctant to give up his British citizenship for fear that such a move would lead to further criticism in England. In January, 1917, he reached his decision and, characteristically, announced it in the *New York Times.* He would become a naturalized American. He received his final papers on March 28, and had less than ten days to put forth his interventionist views. On April 6 America was in the war.

Now his speechmaking and propaganda campaign went into full swing. In one of his fieriest talks, called "The Accursed Spirit of Prussianism," first delivered at a Liberty Loan drive, he spoke of "an abominable spirit . . . and the German Government, obsessed with it, deserves to be called the enemy of the whole human race." His speeches were printed in newspapers across the country, and in Paris and London. Then, translated into German, they went to the U.S. Government Printing Office, from where, by the hundreds of thousands, they were scattered from the air over Germany. Kahn's specialty began to be his talks before German-American groups in which he urged them to see modern Germany in its true lights, and to "set their faces like flint against the monstrous doctrines and acts which robbed them of the Germany they loved, the Germany which had the affection and admiration of the entire world." He spoke to the German populations of Milwaukee and Minneapolis and, in Madison, Wisconsin, announced that he would turn over his entire income for war work and charities— "after deducting necessary expenses for myself and my family." This news made front-page copy in every city in America, and a joyous Kahn wrote: "What a glory to be an American! What a joy to be alive in these soul-stirring days!" Seldom had a banker enjoyed a war so much, and even more glorious moments were to come. As the German Army advanced toward the Marne, it encountered what it took to be an abandoned convoy of American supply trucks. The soldiers fell upon the trucks, tearing open the packages they contained, which the soldiers expected to be food, only to find bales of Otto Kahn's propaganda pamphlets. The German soldiers sat around reading what Kahn had to say, and that evening there were several desertions.

The Kaiser's anger, which had been only barely under control, boiled over when he heard of this incident. Newspapers in Berlin, Frankfurt, and Cologne launched massive attacks against Kahn and quoted the

Kaiser himself as saying that Otto Kahn and men like him were *"Schmutzfinken,"* or filthy pigs.

Undismayed by the Kaiser's nasty-name-calling, Kahn stepped up his pamphleteering. "I wear the vilification of the Boche and pro-Boche as a badge of honor!" he cried. "My name has been on the blackest page of the Black Book of the German Government for four years." He then announced his boldest move of all: he would go to Europe himself and "evaluate the situation." Once again he made the front pages.

It was April, 1918, and the North Atlantic was full of U-boats. Nevertheless, he sailed off for England, not at all sure how he would be received there. Renouncing his British citizenship had, as he expected, been criticized, and also the British had not forgotten Jacob Schiff's stand on the Allied loan. As recently as February of that year—nearly four years after Lord Reading's visit—the London *Times* had mentioned Schiff adversely, quoting him as having told a *Times* correspondent that he was "willing to help the Kaiser rather than the Allies." As Kahn sailed off for Europe, however, his anti-Kaiser position was helped considerably by a published report that Germany now considered Otto Kahn the number one enemy of the state. All submarines in the Atlantic, it was said, had received instructions to torpedo Kahn's boat, and to give this project top priority. The Kaiser was supposed to have said, "We would rather eliminate him than either the President or Pershing."*

Though Kahn later confessed to being "frightened" during the crossing, the voyage took place without incident, and Kahn was received respectfully in England, where he was known for St. Dunstan's, and where he was described as an example of "changed sentiment of Germans in the United States." He was a far greater success in France, where they remembered Otto Kahn for his work to place French operas in the repertory of the Metropolitan, and they gave him a hero's welcome. Speaking in French, announcing that he would give 10,000 francs to the French Society of Dramatic Writers, he called France *"la Terre Sainte de l'humanité,"* and the deafening applause is said to have continued for eighty minutes. He had dinner with Clemenceau, who called him "the greatest living American," and then, though the battle of the Aisne was raging, he paid a visit to the front and dined with General Pershing in a château which had been bombarded by shellfire an hour earlier.† He then went on to Spain and, perhaps, the most important of his contributions to the Allied war effort.

---

* It is wise to remember that Kahn, at this point, had employed the publicist Ivy Lee to handle his public relations. Though very possibly true, this story smacks of press agentry.

† In World War I bombardments often stopped conveniently for lunch.

In Madrid, after conferring with King Alfonso XIII, whom Kahn described as "very intelligent, exceedingly well posted and one of the most attractive men I have ever met," Kahn happened to overhear, at a diplomatic reception, a conversation between "a pair of swarthy fellows."

The men, speaking in Spanish, apparently assumed that Kahn, an American, could not understand what they were saying. They were wrong. Kahn found some of their remarks highly interesting. There was, one of them hinted, to be an uprising very soon of the Spartacus League in Brussels. The Spartacus League, sometimes called the German Leninists, eventually became the foundation of the German Communist party, and during the war the League had functioned as an underground group to stir up internal dissent and to undermine German unity. (Later, the League's chief, Karl Liebknecht, received a prison sentence for his anti-Junker activities during the war.)

Kahn was immediately aware of how important news of an underground revolution could be to the Allies. Quivering with the excitement of international intrigue, he hurried to the British Ambassador in Madrid. The Ambassador listened gravely to what Kahn had to say, and that evening placed Kahn's report in the diplomatic pouch to London. In London it went directly to Downing Street and into the hands of Lloyd George, who, reportedly, "could scarcely believe what he read. But knowing Kahn's reputation for scrupulous accuracy, he investigated the report and found it true."

Kahn's report persuaded the Allied strategists to move ahead strongly. "He did us great service by reporting on this affair," one of Lloyd George's ministers said later, and it has even been claimed that the final armistice would have been delayed by as much as six months if it hadn't been for the efforts of Secret Agent Otto Kahn.

By the end of the war Otto Kahn was being called "The King of New York." And, in the process, the sour reputation of Kuhn, Loeb & Company at the war's outset had sweetened considerably.

41

CALAMITIES
AND SOLUTIONS

After the reaction to his war loan stand, Jacob Schiff had little more to say about the war with Germany. One of his rare public statements about the war was made in the summer of 1918, just a few months before the Armistice, when he said, "Though I left Germany as a very young man and adopted this as my country fifty-three years ago, I believe I understand Prussian aspirations and Hohenzollern methods sufficiently to confirm my belief in the most forcible necessity for winning this war completely." Throughout the war he had concentrated on another, and to him equally crucial, matter.

He had always believed in the principle of *zedakah*, the charity which literally means "justice." During his youth in Germany, he recalled, "Kindliness was the keynote of the household and from the first ten-pfennig piece that was received as an allowance it was made our duty to put one-tenth aside for charity, according to the old Jewish tradition." He had continued this 10 percent tithing system throughout his life and, though he was called one of New York's foremost philanthropists, he insisted that only what he had given above and beyond this figure could be considered "philanthropy." He once startled a well-meaning woman who congratulated him on a particularly large gift by saying, somewhat abruptly, "That wasn't my money." He meant, of course, that the gift came from the one-tenth of his income that he felt *had* to be given away.

He had an individualistic approach to giving that would have dismayed a modern foundation executive. In addition to having invented the "matching gift" system, he also believed that a man's giving should be done in his lifetime and, most important, under his personal supervision. In his spare time, he visited the Lower East Side looking for worthy "cases" among immigrants. He personally headed his pet project, Montefiore Hospital—originally founded for Jewish "incurables," and later broadened at his insistence—and hired the staff as well as paid regular visits to all the patients. To raise money, he once organized and headed a benefit bazaar in Central Park which netted $160,000 for the hospital—much more than the most glittering charity ball can earn today. He also believed that self-help was an essential part of any charity, and frequently wrote personal letters to get immigrants jobs. For one young man who wanted to be a merchant he purchased a candy store; for a man who had cut hair in Europe he bought a barbershop. He rented any number of newsstands, and installed his cases behind them. He occasionally hired men directly into Kuhn, Loeb & Company, and his son-in-law, Felix Warburg, adopted his habit of hiring promising youngsters. (He once hired the hat boy at Savarin's restaurant and made him an office boy; he was George W. Bovenizer, later to become one of the firm's most important partners. Felix also hired his wife's milliner's son.) With J. P. Morgan, Seth Low, and James Speyer, Schiff developed a plan to found "a pawn shop on humanitarian principles," which became the Provident Loan Society. Each founder contributed $5,000 —and Schiff assessed each Kuhn, Loeb partner in that amount also— and the Society started with capital of $100,000. Soon, it was loaning out money at the rate of $34 million a year.

In 1912 the newspapers were full of gloomy talk about trusts and everyone was muttering about the abuses of great wealth. The *New York Times,* however, published an article about what it called "the New York public service trust," and the men whose charities most benefited the city. "It is impossible to consider," said the *Times,* "what New York's so-called public activities would do without these men. As we name things 'trusts,' here we have one—it is a trust of public spirit." Heading this list of leaders were Joseph Seligman's son, Isaac Newton Seligman, Felix Warburg, and Jacob Schiff. Conspicuously absent from the list was the name of Rockefeller.

The *Times* article distressed Schiff, who believed in the Talmudic principle that twice blessed is he who gives in secret. Though he gave a building to the Jewish Theological Seminary; two buildings to the Young Men's Hebrew Association; a social hall to Barnard College; the Semitic Museum building, and much of its contents, to Harvard; a large endowment to Frankfurt University in Germany; and the building which houses the Israel Institute of Technology in Haifa, he would never permit his name to be attached to any of these structures. His single exception to this rule was the Schiff Pavilion at his Montefiore Hospital. He would never discuss the size of his gifts and rebuffed reporters who asked him about his philanthropies. Because of Schiff's secrecy, the exact total amount of his giving is now impossible to calculate. It has been estimated at between $50 and $100 million.

In 1906 a small group of the most important men in the German Jewish banking crowd had met at Jacob Schiff's house to discuss a matter of some urgency. Their worry was anti-Semitism. The Dreyfus case had not yet been settled, and the coals from the Kishinev pogroms had not cooled. To Schiff, it had begun to seem as though all the gains which Jews had made over the past hundred years were being threatened and might soon be lost. Out of the meeting came the American Jewish Committee, an organization designed to protect the rights and better the condition of Jews throughout the world. In its way, it was something of an innovation, for the AJC proposed to combine traditional Jewish communal giving with the techniques of such American overseas philanthropies as the Red Cross.

The AJC was an organization sponsored, at the outset, by a mere handful of extremely rich men. It was really all in the family and "in the crowd," and it soon became clear that a less loosely structured, larger, and more formal and all-encompassing sort of organization would be required to do the task the AJC had set for itself. As 1914—"the comma in the twentieth century"—approached, the relief of Jews in Eastern Europe became a far more overpowering problem than that of Jews on the Lower East Side. In Russia and Rumania it had become clear government policy to force Jews to emigrate, but where would they go? The slums of New York and London were overcrowded and seemed incapable of holding any more, while millions clamored to be received. In the salons of Paris, Berlin, and Vienna, anti-Semitic chatter was becoming fashionable, and even certain politicians in Washington and London were making racist allusions with the caricature of the poor Eastern European Jew who had found his way to the Lower East Side or to Whitechapel as their target. Implications of what the Jews would have to face throughout the next half-century were beginning to dawn as, across the Continent of Europe, the lights began to go out.

During the war between 600,000 and 700,000 Jews fled eastward out of Poland and the Baltic countries, and another 100,000 from Galicia and Bukovina. Others escaped westward—half a million to Austria, perhaps 100,000 into Germany. The migrations were terrified and erratic, for no one knew where he was going or whether, or for how long, he would be allowed to stay. Some thirty thousand Jewish refugees camped, without shelter, in a Russian forest. When Turkey entered the war on the side of Germany, there was suddenly a desperate situation for Jewish communities in Palestine. Many Jews in the Holy Land had escaped from Czarist Russia, and they were now suspected as enemy aliens. At the end of August, 1914, Henry Morgenthau, who was United States Ambassador to Turkey, cabled Jacob Schiff asking for $50,000 in immediate aid. The American Jewish Committee contributed $25,000 of this figure, Schiff personally gave $12,500, and the Provisional Zionist Committee another $12,500. But as the war spread and hopes for an early peace vanished, it was obvious to Schiff that the relief work to be done in Europe was beyond the scope of the AJC.

American Jews were, of course, divided. The AJC was merely another symbol of that division. In a crisis that faced all the Jews, one could not have a factionalized solution. All Jews in America would have somehow to join in a consolidated effort.

There were, at the time, hundreds of Jewish charitable organizations in the United States. In October, 1914, Schiff asked representatives of forty of the largest to meet with his AJC. At that meeting, a committee consisting of Oscar S. Straus, Julian W. Mack, Louis D. Brandeis, Harry Fischel, and Meyer London, who "commanded the respect of every element," was asked to select one hundred leading American Jews to be the American Jewish Relief Committee. "All Jews," Schiff announced solemnly, "of every shade of thought, irrespective of the land of their birth, are admonished to contribute with the utmost generosity." Louis Marshall was to be president of this new organization, and Jacob Schiff the treasurer. Schiff, however, asked that this honor be given to his son-in-law, Felix Warburg.

Working closely with Schiff, Felix decided that the treasurer's chief job would be to set up a disbursing agency through which American funds could be sent on to Europe. For this purpose—which, at first, seemed simple but which later on became so staggeringly important that it completely eclipsed its parent organization—Felix held his first meeting of the Joint Distribution Committee of American Funds for the Relief of Jewish War Sufferers on November 27, 1914. This was the famous Joint Distribution Committee which, by the end of the war, was distributing an income of as much as $16.4 million a year.

The work of the Joint was based on a simple assumption: that Jews had a right either to live where they were or to emigrate; the Joint was devised to facilitate either of these alternatives. As Oscar Handlin has said, "The historic program of the Joint offered all Jews a basis for unity of action. Its American insistence on 'giving to all an equal opportunity for survival and creative life' was enriched by 'the Biblical concept of social obligation and mercy.' It could therefore rise above all factional divisions." Stefan Zweig said of the Joint, "Later, at some future date, we shall again gladly and passionately discuss whether Jews should be Zionists, revisionists, territorialists or assimilationists; we shall discuss the hair-splitting point of whether we are a nation, a religion, a people or a race. All of these time-consuming, theoretical discussions can wait. Now there is but one thing for us to do—to give help."

For the next fifty years, the Joint would continue to exert its unifying force upon the disputatious, splintered Jewry of America. While young Otto Kahn was stylishly aiding the war effort, Jacob Schiff in his twilight years was, in his quiet way, adding even more glory to his name.

The scope of what had been called Schiff's "complex Oriental nature" was becoming clear. Long before it was fashionable for American millionaires to have humanitarian instincts, he had spoken out for the Negro, for free public education, for the Child Labor Amendment, and for the rights of trade unions. He had an abiding, idealistic faith in the Fatherhood of God and the brotherhood of man. No wonder he always thought, right up to the time of his death, that the Joint was strictly a temporary organization. He always expected—and, in fact, anticipated —the day when the injustices the Joint was designed to solve would disappear, when the need for the Joint would vanish, and it could be disbanded.

42

THE RISE OF A HOUSE OF ISSUE

In 1900 Lehman Brothers, though it had been successful, was still considered essentially a commodity brokerage house. In prestige and importance it was ranked so far below Kuhn, Loeb that it was not even considered in the same business. The Lehmans had nothing of the social power of the Seligmans, and nothing approaching the wealth of the Schiffs, Warburgs, or Otto Kahn.

The Lehmans, however, were far from being needy. From cotton brokerage they had branched into commodities underground—particularly petroleum—and Mayer and Emanuel were mentioned in every list of the city's richest men. One of the most spectacular young men in the class of 1899 at Williams College was Herbert H. Lehman. Among the companies his father and uncle had bought into, along with P. A. B. Widener and John Jacob Astor, was the Electric Vehicle Company, an early automobile manufacturer, and the Rubber Tire Wheel Company of Springfield, Ohio, the first American maker of pneumatic tires. Young Herbert arrived on the Williams campus with not only his own car—in

329

itself a rarity—but his own chauffeur. Periodically, Herbert's driver painted the car's license plate with oil, causing dust from the road to obscure the numbers on the plate, thereby making the young dandy difficult to identify by police as he sped about the landscape. It was hard to believe that this high-living fellow would later become one of New York's most meticulous governors, so concerned with maintaining his personal dignity that, for years during his stay in Albany, he refused to dine at his favorite restaurant, Keeler's, for fear it would not "look right to have the Governor seen eating in a public restaurant," and who, at a Democratic function in New York, walked out when he felt he had not been seated properly at the banquet table.

On Wall Street the Age of the Trusts seemed about to pass the Lehmans by. Between 1898 and 1904 alone, over four billion dollars' worth of new securities in industrial combinations had been sold— through bankers—to investors. In 1893 there had been twelve large trusts with an aggregate capital of less than 2 billion dollars. By 1904 there were 318 such trusts, one of which was capitalized at almost a billion and a half. The trust system, which had been a brain child of John D. Rockefeller's lawyers, was to put the voting power of a group of companies into the hands of a group of trustees. Technically, the individual companies would remain independent, as far as their operations were concerned, and therefore they would not be liable to antitrust action. But central control of voting meant that no company could step very far out of line. (Jacob Schiff never approved of voting trusts and the kind of control they gave over company operations, but he sold their securities cheerfully enough.) The theory of the trust was that eliminating competition among the consolidated units would bring about immediate economies and therefore increased profits. It worked—sometimes.

The Age of Trusts was the age of the investment banker. Money needed to launch new enterprises and to put their securities on the market made bankers' contributions essential. Banking houses had had experience selling government and railroad bonds in Europe, and this stood them in good stead. Now they could sell the new corporate stocks—whose values might or might not be watered. As the twentieth century advanced, the European market for American securities became less important; there was a well-heeled investing public in America to consider.

There were companies who figured they could do without investment bankers. In 1902 the Pennsylvania Railroad came up with a plan to bring their line directly into New York City, through tunnels under the Hudson River, which would make the Pennsylvania competitive with the New York Central. There were powerful interests in both New York and

New Jersey opposing the plan, but Jacob Schiff, who had been the Pennsylvania's banker for over twenty years, went actively to work rallying support for it, writing a letter to his friend Isidor Straus of Macy's, pointing out the advantages to the city and its businesses and asking for his help.

The bond issue put out to finance the construction of the tunnels was reasonably priced and was considered a bargain, and so the railroad decided, to save the underwriter's fees, to bring the issue out itself. Schiff advised against this, and the Pennsylvania seems to have been in a rather ungrateful frame of mind, considering all Schiff's hard work. But Schiff accepted the decision in good grace. Soon, however, without the market support and stamp of approval provided by an investment banking house, the tunnel bonds were in trouble, and the price fell so disastrously that Kuhn, Loeb had to step in and perform a last-minute rescue operation. It was a dramatic example to industry of the importance of a banking house and its abilities to find and "sell" a market. It was also the last time a company would ever attempt to offer securities to the public without the backing of a "house of issue."

The investment banks sold securities to the public in any one of, or in any combination of, three basic ways. They might *underwrite*—or, simply speaking, guarantee the success of an issue which they would actually sell. In return for the greater risk the underwriter took, he was given the say on the price the issue could be sold at, to whom it should be sold, where, and by what means. Or a banker might sell securities on the market under a *negotiated* system—selling a company's stocks on a commission basis while, at the same time, lending the company money for its operating, development, or expansion expenses. Ideally, the banker makes money in two ways in such an operation. (This was Joseph Seligman's favorite banking technique with railroads; he, of course, often lost.) The third method was *contracting,* where an investment house bought up an entire issue outright, and then either parceled it out to other houses or sold it exclusively. This was Kuhn, Loeb's favorite way of operating, and to the outsider it might seem to involve the greatest risk. Actually, contracting was seldom done unless an issue was considered a sure bet.

Little of this lucrative business had been done by the house of Lehman Brothers by the turn of the century. In fact, in the first fifty years of its existence, the Lehmans underwrote only one issue—in 1899, for something called the International Steam Pump Company, a pump trust consisting of five pump manufacturers. The combine did not work out well and, to conform with antitrust laws, it was reorganized as the Worthington Pump & Machinery Corporation. Once bitten, the Lehmans dropped out of underwriting for several years. They continued with commodities—cotton, coffee, and petroleum futures—and, for their own portfolios, bought issues of the day.*

But when Emanuel Lehman died, control of the firm was fully in the hands of the second generation—a group of restless, eager, ambitious boys: Philip, Sigmund, Arthur, Meyer H., and Herbert. Particularly ingenious when it came to banking was Philip, Emanuel's son, and it is Philip Lehman's wizardry—along with the strength of his will and the assertiveness of his personality ("At anything he did, Philip *had* to win," says a member of the family)—that has established the Emanuel Lehman branch of the family as the dominant one in the firm's affairs.†
In an era when no self-respecting private banker would deign to back retail stores, textile manufacturers, clothing or cigarette makers—to say nothing of the indignity of mail-order houses and five-and-ten operations —Philip Lehman led his cousins directly into such businesses with quickly profitable results. Very early, Lehman Brothers helped finance and develop the American Potash and Chemical Corporation—and continued to back it until it was sold, for a nice figure indeed, to the Standard Oil Company of New Jersey.

It was Philip Lehman's generation that first married into the elite of New York's German Jewry. He and his cousins married, variously, Strauses, Altschuls, Lewisohns, Lauers, Limburgs, Fatmans, Goodharts, and—in the case of his cousin Sigmund—first-cousin Lehmans, thereby aligning the Lehmans with other fortunes and banking houses. The marriage of Arthur Lehman to Adolph Lewisohn's daughter was of prime importance, for it brought the Lewisohn mining enterprises under the Lehman wing.

It was at Philip Lehman's insistence that the firm first began to venture into underwriting, the step that would lead Lehman Brothers into investment banking. He had often discussed it with his best friend, Henry Goldman.

Henry's father, Marcus Goldman, had died a few years before Philip's, and the proceeds of the business old Marcus had carried in the lining of his hat had left his heirs more than comfortably off. Henry, too, was ambitious and eager to move into something beyond commercial paper sales—in which Goldman, Sachs had become the leading dealers in New York. Business mergers were not so fashionable in those days as they have become, and so the two friends did not consider this. But they

* When young Herbert Lehman became a partner in 1908, he was startled to see how many "speculative" and "cat-and-dog" stocks his father, Mayer, and his Uncle Emanuel had bought for the firm. There was a large block of stock in the Electric Boat Company—soon to be filling the Atlantic with submarines—plus 1,000 shares of something called the Bethlehem Steel Company.

† While the Mayer branch, which produced Herbert, has become known for public service.

did toy with the idea of forming an underwriting firm of their own, Goldman & Lehman. But the pressures, both practical and sentimental, not to abandon their respective family firms were strong, and so at last they decided to collaborate in underwriting as a side line. Each house would continue with its specialty—Lehman with commodities, Goldman, Sachs with commercial paper—and the two friends would go in as partners in underwriting ventures, splitting the profits fifty-fifty.

Goldman, Sachs, like Lehman Brothers, was a firm tied together with tight matrimonial knots. Two of Henry Goldman's sisters were married to two Sachs brothers. In 1906 Henry Goldman's brother-in-law's sister, Emelia, married a man named Samuel Hammerslough.* Hammerslough's older sister, Augusta, was married to a man named Samuel Rosenwald, and their son, Julius Rosenwald, who nobody thought would amount to anything, had gone to Chicago at a tender age and bought up a mail-order house called Sears, Roebuck & Company. The relationship may have been tenuous, but when Julius Rosenwald wanted money he approached his "cousin," Henry Goldman. Julius wanted to expand Sears, Roebuck, and he asked Goldman for a loan of five million dollars.

Goldman introduced Rosenwald to Philip Lehman, and the two bankers offered Rosenwald a better suggestion. Why not make a public offering of Sears stock—and make ten million dollars? It was a fairly daring notion, because there had never before been a mail-order security on the market. There was no way of telling how the stock-buying public would react to Sears. Rosenwald agreed, and the foundation of a gigantic mail-order house was laid. Few Sears, Roebuck shareholders today regret Philip Lehman's and Henry Goldman's idea.

Lehman and Goldman went on to cooperate in other issues, nearly all of them for Goldman, Sachs clients. They became specialists in helping privately owned companies "go public," an operation that has always been heavy with risk. In 1910 they underwrote an issue for the Underwood Corporation; in 1911 they introduced Studebaker. A year later the friends put the first shares of a variety chain store on the market; it was the F. W. Woolworth Company. The following year they presented the Continental Can Company. In all, the two men collaborated in fourteen major securities issues, and were considered Wall Street's hottest young underwriting team, when the guns of August were fired in 1914.

Henry Goldman's brother-in-law, Sam Sachs, had returned from a trip to England just after the war's outbreak. While there, he had

---

* A former peddler who had migrated to Springfield, Illinois, and gone into the men's clothing business. Hammerslough always liked to recall the extra-long trousers he cut for one of his best customers, Abraham Lincoln.

assured Goldman, Sachs's correspondent firm in London, Kleinwort, that Goldman, Sachs stood firmly behind Great Britain. In New York, however, to his dismay, he learned that Henry Goldman had already made several pro-German speeches.

When the Anglo-French loan had been turned down by Kuhn, Loeb, it had gone to J. P. Morgan, and most leading Wall Street firms were asking Morgan for participations. However, Henry Goldman, one of Goldman, Sachs's most important partners, had announced that he wanted nothing to do with the loan, and for outspokenly pro-Germans reasons. There was, furthermore, a rule at Goldman, Sachs that the firm could sponsor no issue unless all partners agreed unanimously. An intense, high-strung, didactic man, when Henry's partners and sisters begged him to modify, or at least conceal, his feelings, he refused and his public utterances became more frequent and startling. The Prussianism that Otto Kahn deplored, Henry Goldman admired. He quoted Nietzsche to anyone who would listen. Sam and Harry Sachs, meanwhile, went directly to Morgan as Otto Kahn and Morti Schiff had done, to take personal subscriptions in the loan in an attempt to save the day. But Goldman's damage had been done, and Goldman, Sachs was another German firm to fall under a heavy pall.

Even the United States' entry into the war in 1917 did nothing to curb Henry Goldman's tongue. A situation which the family has called "painful"—and which must have been a great deal more than that—had begun to exist on both a business and domestic level. While Henry Goldman ranted, his nephew Howard Sachs was on active duty with the 26th Division; Sam Sachs's son Paul, another nephew, was with the Red Cross in France; other members of the joint families were selling Liberty Bonds, winding bandages, and appearing at rallies to "bury the Kaiser."

The Kleinwort bank in London cabled New York to say that Goldman, Sachs was in danger of being blacklisted in England. At that point Goldman himself realized what was happening and came to his partners to say that he guessed he was "out of step." They heartily agreed, and his resignation was accepted.

For several months, though no longer a partner, Goldman kept his office at Goldman, Sachs. But as the wartime atmosphere grew more heated, this became an impossible arrangement. He departed to a midtown office of his own. With Henry Goldman went his share of the firm's funds, which was sizable. This fact did the firm even more damage than his pro-Germanism had done, and since Goldman, Sachs was not so fortunate as to have a crusading patriot like Otto Kahn working for it, the firm fell upon lean times from which it did not emerge until after the war. This did little to endear Henry Goldman to the rest of his family. Henry Goldman and Samuel Sachs never spoke again. Neither did Henry and his sister Louise, who was Sam Sachs's wife. The hostilities continued in the next generation, and to this day there are hardly any Goldmans who are on speaking terms with any Sachses.

In the early 1930's Henry Goldman traveled to his beloved Germany with the idea of settling there permanently. With Hitler rising to power, this was certainly a mistake. Goldman was seized and searched and was subjected to "many other humiliations," according to the family. He returned to New York, a defeated and disillusioned man, and died there, a victim of his own dream of Nietzschean power.

Philip Lehman, meanwhile, was as surprised and distressed about his old friend's feelings as Goldman's partners were. After an initial meeting on the subject, the two men parted angrily. When Goldman left Goldman, Sachs, the break between the friends was final. Lehman Brothers and Goldman, Sachs continued to try to collaborate on underwriting issues, but the relationship between the two firms was not what it had been. There were frequent arguments. Why, the Lehmans demanded, did Goldman, Sachs take all the credit, with their name showily at the top of the ads, for ventures for which Lehmans had supplied the money? Goldman, Sachs, in turn, asked why the Lehmans expected half the profits on deals originated by Goldman, Sachs. The arguments frequently disintegrated into angry name-calling. "They were both too ambitious," one banker has said, "to stay married." But there was more to it than that.

Henry Goldman's replacement at Goldman, Sachs was a suave and polished Southerner named Waddill Catchings, whose background was in the iron and steel industry. Presently Catchings was attracting national attention with a series of books, written in collaboration with William T. Foster, which expanded grandly, and with a certain literary style, on the increasingly rosy future of America's postwar economy. The Lehmans, however, distrusted the flamboyant Catchings. Philip Lehman felt Catchings "lacked balance," was "too ambitious and aggressive" and "too optimistic." (Events a decade later, in 1929, proved the Lehmans right and caught Catchings unaware.) At the same time, a Brooklyn youngster just out of P.S. 13 named Sidney Weinberg had been looking across the harbor to the towering financial district of Manhattan and decided that was where the money was. He had gone, by his own account, "to the top of the tallest building" in the district, which was then 43 Exchange Place, and started working his way down, asking for a job at each floor. He made it all the way to the second floor before he found Goldman, Sachs and was hired as an office boy. Catchings had taken Weinberg under his wing, and the Lehmans thought Weinberg had promise.* But Weinberg was impatient with the Lehman connection and wanted to break it. The relationship between the two firms grew steadily more bitter until, at last, a formal memorandum of separation was drafted.

The memorandum listed sixty different corporations that the Lehmans and Goldman, Sachs had jointly underwritten, and these firms were then divided according to which firm had "prime interest." Goldman, Sachs got forty-one companies, and the Lehmans were granted the remaining nineteen. Sears, needless to say, went to Goldman, Sachs. Each banking house agreed not to invade the territory of the other.

Hard feelings continued to exist between the two firms until as late as 1956, when Sears, Roebuck decided to set up a sales-acceptance subsidiary. At that point Sidney Weinberg called on Robert Lehman, Philip Lehman's son, and asked Lehman Brothers to resume its historic place in Sears financing.

In the long run the split benefited both firms, but Lehman Brothers most of all. It forced Philip Lehman to go into investment banking on his own, without depending on the crutch of Goldman, Sachs. As one investment banker has said, "I think it's the best thing that ever happened to Lehman because they took off their coats, rolled up their sleeves, and went out to get some business. Lehman always had a lot of money, but that's different from being aggressive to get business. After the dispute they became real go-getters."

What the Lehmans got, among other things, was the solitary elegance of Number One William Street—the structure, first built by the Seligmans, which makes Lehman Brothers the only investment banking house in Wall Street to occupy a building of its own. (And quite a building it is, with its own eighth-floor dining room and its own gymnasium.) The Lehmans have continued Philip's policy—backing issues which, at the outset at least, seemed too "undignified" for other bankers to handle. Among these were early stocks in airlines, electronics, motion picture and liquor companies, all of which have helped the Lehmans become what *Fortune* calls "one of the biggest profit makers—many believe the biggest—in the business." Today Lehman partners sit on boards of dozens of U.S. corporations, guide several billion dollars' worth of investment funds, including the assets of the Lehman Corporation—itself a half-billion-dollar affair.

The Lehmans like to describe themselves as "merchants of money," intermediaries between men who want to produce goods and men looking for something to do with surplus funds. They can also—thanks to continuing family control—call themselves "the oldest partnership"

---

* He is now the senior partner at Goldman, Sachs, and one of the half-dozen most powerful men in Wall Street.

among U.S. investment houses. But they are still interested in what Philip Lehman first described as "trying to buy something for a dollar, and selling it for two."

Socially, from Philip Lehman's generation on, the Lehmans have also done well, though they have been called, as a family, "dull," and "cut-and-dried," and "bankerish." Another friend says, "The women in the Lehman family have all been charming, but a lot of the Lehman men are rough—real horse-traders, like Philip." Certainly the Lehmans, as a family and as a banking firm, have, in the long run, been vastly aided by Herbert Lehman. Though certain members of the family, particularly from the Philip Lehman branch, remain to this day scandalized by the political career and affiliation of Herbert, and by his retirement from Lehman Brothers, which some considered a breach of family trust, most admit that he lifted the family name to a position of national importance, and that his reputation for integrity and efficiency, first as Governor, then as Senator, cannot but have helped the bank.

Though he was a creditable Governor of New York, it was as a United States Senator, in his seventies, that he had his finest hour and displayed the spunk and grit for which the family is known. The Senator from Wisconsin, Joseph R. McCarthy, brandishing one of his usually bogus sheets of paper, stood up in 1950 to claim it was a photostat of a letter by Owen Lattimore to the Office of War Information urging that the OWI hire men sympathetic to the cause of Communist China. Senator Charles Tobey of New Hampshire asked McCarthy why he did not offer the letter for publication in the *Congressional Record*. He could not, McCarthy explained, because the letter was marked "secret." Then why, Tobey asked, was McCarthy revealing its contents on the Senate floor? McCarthy's evasive reply to this was that the letter was accompanied by documents attesting to "unusual personal habits" of persons high in government.

This was too much for Herbert Lehman. He stood up to ask if he could be allowed to read the letter.

"Does the Senator care to step over?" McCarthy shouted, and, with that, Herbert Lehman strode across the Senate aisle and said to Mc-Carthy, "May I see the letter?" He held out his hand for it.

McCarthy, shaken, answered, "The Senator may step to my desk and read the letter."

"I am here to read the letter," said Lehman. "Will the Senator from Wisconsin let me see the letter?"

Clutching his sheaf of papers to his bosom, his voice rising shrilly, McCarthy whined, "Does the Senator wish to come close enough to read it?"

Lehman stared at him contemptuously for a dramatic moment, still holding out his hand. Then he turned on his heel and walked back to his seat.

The letter, when eventually published, turned out to be harmless, as Lehman had suspected. And in the meantime his brothers and partners back home in South William Street must have realized that Herbert, "dirty Democrat" though he might be, "wild-eyed friends" like Roosevelt, Al Smith, and Jim Farley though he might have, was nonetheless showering even further glory upon the House of Lehman.

43

"PFLICHT UND

ARBEIT"

In a way, there was almost a logical *rightness* in the moment Jacob Schiff chose to die. Though he was a more sophisticated financier than Joseph Seligman, he was nonetheless a financier from the nineteenth century. In a sense he was a bridge between the Seligmans and modern banking. He would not have fit, furthermore, into the new decade that was under way. In his old-fashioned white ascot ties and his frock coats, he would not have belonged in the 1920's.

The summer of 1920 passed as all the others had. There was the same rigorous schedule. After winter in the city, June and July were spent at the house on Rumson Road in Elberon. August was passed at Bar Harbor. While there, having failed with his children, Jacob tried to instill his love of hiking and mountain climbing in his grandchildren; they disliked it even more than Morti and Frieda had, but, since he expected them to, they went along with him. Always a believer in exercise, he had taken up cycling. On Sundays in Bar Harbor, the family cycled—the younger children speeding on ahead, then stopping to wait until their elderly grandparent, pedaling slowly, made his way up to them. To his grandchildren, he was "Grandpa"; to his servants, "the old gentleman." There were only a few changes in his ways. One was his sudden habit of reaching down to pick up a baby grandchild and cuddle it against his whiskered chin, letting it sniff the fresh rose in his buttonhole. Every morning at Rumson Road he would walk in the garden, saying his prayers. Then he would pick a red rose for each lady in the house. These were little gestures of pleasure and love which he had never permitted himself before.

In September the family came back to Rumson Road. There was only one difference. Though he would not admit it, and would let no one speak of it, Jacob Schiff, now seventy-three, was unwell. On the Day of Atonement, though Therese and his servants begged him to relax his rule, he insisted on fasting, saying, finally, that if he was going to die he would prefer to do so observing the strictures of his faith. He was reminded that the Scriptures do not require an ill person to fast; nonetheless, he replied, he wished to. The next day, very much weaker, he announced one of his rare changes in plan: he wished to return to New York right away, instead of waiting until the end of the month. It was September 23. Wordlessly, the family packed to move back to the city.

No. 965 Fifth Avenue was a considerably more tasteful house than the old "house full of horrors" at 932. Schiff's friend Sir Ernest Cassel had become his artistic mentor, and the lighted drawing-room cabinets displayed the beautiful collection of majolica and one of antique porcelain which the London financier himself had given to the Schiffs. Sir Ernest had helped Schiff to assemble a good collection of paintings of the nineteenth-century French School—"Stick to a *school,* stick to a *school,*" Sir Ernest had reminded him—and a splendid collection of Oriental jades and crystals. The only relics of the old house were the portraits of Jacob and Therese Schiff, and the bronze bas-relief by Augustus Saint-Gaudens of the two Schiff children, the one for which Frieda and Morti had been made to pose through an entire Christmas holiday.* Sir Ernest had not effected these changes in the Schiffs' style easily. Repeatedly, Jacob had complained about "extravagance" and "too much luxury," and had refused to spend money on this or that article Sir Ernest had wanted him to buy.

Jacob, too, had been right about Morti's tendencies toward extravagance; for all his father's efforts to bend the twig toward frugality, Morti had become a bit of a spender. After becoming a Kuhn, Loeb partner at the age of twenty-three, Morti became very social, joining what was becoming known in the postwar years as "the International Set." Though colorblind, Morti had an insatiable love of paintings and was the despair of dealers, who said they could never show Morti Schiff a second-rate

* A copy hangs in the Metropolitan Museum of Art.

piece of work and convince him it was a masterpiece. Morti had started a collection of art, books, bindings, and furniture that would eventually be declared worth nearly a million dollars. He had built a huge house on hundreds of acres of ground at Oyster Bay, Long Island, where Otto Kahn soon became a neighbor, and had rebuilt another old house in Paris. His days of bicycles, new or secondhand, were long gone by. In fact, to Jacob Schiff's distress, Sir Ernest was stimulating Morti's prodigality. "You know," Sir Ernest once said to Frieda, "I rather encouraged Morti's spending money because I believe a man must learn how to spend gracefully, but not showily. Your father, you know, didn't always hold with my ideas."

Now the children and the grandchildren were summoned to the great Fifth Avenue house to await what they were certain was the inevitable. Waiting, they whispered the story of the old gentleman's insistence on his Yom Kippur fast, two days before. The fasting of the man who, as a boy, had climbed down a drain pipe to avoid a Hebrew lesson, seemed to give the end of Jacob Schiff's life, which came quietly on September 25, a kind of pious logic, too. In silence, the family filed past, saying good-bye. The next morning the *New York Times* devoted its lead story and its entire second page to his career.

The funeral was an extraordinary affair, not for its pomp and grandeur, though there was plenty of that, and not for the weight of the testimonials that poured in from heads of state, government officials, public, and the press, though there was plenty of that, too. It was remarkable for the sheer power of the emotion that gripped the thousands of mourners through the ceremony. Jewish survivors of the pogroms of Russia felt they owed their lives directly to him. To millions who had never laid eyes on him, who knew him only as the founder of the American Jewish Committee and the guiding spirit behind the Joint Distribution Committee, his name stood for salvation. Outside Temple Emanu-El, on both sides of Fifth Avenue, people stood, many in beards and *shaitels.* Jews from the Lower East Side, whom Schiff had made it a point to visit on foot, had now made it a point to come, on foot, to bid him good-bye. The crowds stood in silence, reverentially; a few wept; many knelt in prayer. Rich and poor alike were gripped by a shared sense of loss, and when the bier made its slow progress down the temple steps, the whole corner of the city seemed to grow silent.

There was the usual speculation in the press about the size of his estate. Estimates ranged from fifty to two hundred million. Actually, his estate amounted to some forty million dollars. It was clear that he had given away much more than that amount in his lifetime.

As the twenties progressed, it began to seem as though Jacob Schiff had been one of the last pious Jews in the German Jewish upper crust. It was almost as though, with Schiff gone, everyone could unbend a bit and, without fear of his displeasure, convert. The 1920's saw the conversions of a number of Seligmans, who became, variously, Methodists, Unitarians, Episcopalians, Christian Scientists, and Roman Catholics. Otto Kahn, who had begun to say privately that "St. Paul, St. Francis, and Jesus were the three greatest figures of history," was toying with the idea of becoming a Catholic and had begun to "play down" his Jewish background. (A story, possibly apocryphal, which for years circulated within the crowd, has it that Otto Kahn's two daughters, Margaret and Maude, were carefully shielded from the fact that they were Jewish; when a mischievous French governess broke the news to them, the two little girls threw their breakfast trays on the floor and cried in their room for hours.) Mixed marriages were suddenly fashionable, and when they occurred, it was usually the Jewish partner who converted—though at least one non-Jewish young lady, marrying a Seligman, became Jewish after being given a "rabbinical bath."

Instead of Jacob Schiff's great pride in his faith, a certain ambivalent attitude began to reveal itself among upper-class Jews toward their religious heritage. At times, it was possible to believe that they were Jews in one breath and non-Jews in the next—that whether to be Jewish or not was rather like selecting the right fork for the right course at dinner. Even those who had converted felt it wrong, really, to deny that they were Jewish, leaving the impression that they regarded Jewishness as a racial as well as a religious matter. At the same time, they did not believe in "making a point" of being Jewish, regarding it as a "personal" thing, implying that Jewishness is purely a religious affair after all.

For the Jew, living in two communities was always something of a strain. When the edges between these communities began to blur, certain confusions of feelings and loyalties were inevitable, and never was this more apparent than when the third generation of the German Jewish crowd grew to maturity. Young Will Guggenheim was not the only man to harbor an illusion that he was not really Jewish. Adolph Lewisohn's son, Julius, cherished the same fantasy, as did Joseph Seligman's grandson, Joseph, II.* In Germany the oldest Warburg boy—Felix's brother Aby—had, after boldly marrying a gentile girl, begun to disintegrate. Was it the pressures of trying to conform to both communities that made a man like Aby an alien in each? For religion, Aby Warburg began to substitute astrology. He became obsessive about his personal enthusiasms, which included the study of primitive cultures. He became a compulsive book collector and writer of articles on such divergent subjects as tapestries, postage stamps "as symbols of political power,"

---

* Whose tragic solution was to commit suicide, as his cousin, Washington Seligman, had done in 1912.

Indian snake dances, primitive religions and superstitions, paintings, and theatrical drawings. His library eventually grew to contain some sixty thousand volumes plus twenty thousand photographs, mostly bearing on the revival of Greek antiquity. He also assembled a remarkable collection of photographs dealing with the persistence of symbolism through the ages, which is strangely like Sigmund Freud's studies which were being carried on at about the same time.

For all this squirrel-like collecting, Aby was dissatisfied, troubled. During World War I he had a nervous breakdown from which he never fully recovered, and he developed, according to the family, a number of "phobias," one of which was other Warburgs. He blamed the Warburgs for the fact that he was Jewish—a sensible enough conclusion—and became convinced that his two American brothers, Felix and Paul, who had become so rich by way of marrying Loebs and Schiffs, were dealing unfairly with him in a financial sense. He spent whatever time was left over from collecting writing long and bitter letters to his family, outlining his grievances. There were times when the mention of his brothers could send him into an uncontrollable fury, and at times like these only the gentle-natured Felix, whom he loved, seemed able to calm him. "It was as though," says one of the family thoughtfully, trying to puzzle poor Aby out, "he hated *being* a Warburg and yet, at the same time, couldn't escape the fact that he *was* a Warburg." Aby died in Hamburg in 1929. His wife, Mary, managed to hold up her side of the mixed marriage somewhat better. Watching Hitler's rise to power, she began quietly organizing the removal of her husband's collections elsewhere. Working through the American Consul in Berlin, Aby's nephew, Eric Warburg, arranged to have the material shipped to England. It took 535 crates on two small steamers, the *Hermia* and the *Jessica,* to get Aby's collections down the Elbe, across the North Sea, into the Thames, where they now form the basis of the library at the Warburg Institute of London University. While the shipment was being loaded, Aby's widow, Mary, served tea and sandwiches on the dock to the packers, who were anti-Nazis.

Another mixed-married gentleman was Jimmie Speyer, the inheritor, in New York, of his Uncle Philip's Speyer & Company. Like Aby Warburg, Jimmie Speyer could never seem to decide—to his own satisfaction, at least—just how Jewish he was. Speyer was a small, dapper, starch-collared, and rather prickly man. He was so proud of his name that he would never allow his firm to take a lower position than anyone else's in the floating of a loan, and this Speyer vanity had, by the 1920's, meant that the firm had declined somewhat in power. Nonetheless he occupied a high-ceilinged, Old World office in a Pine Street building modeled after the Palazzo Pandolfini in Florence, from which

he operated a patrician, one-man banking house. Mr. Speyer's personal
bearing was so Old World itself, so Continental, as to have seemed
downright exotic. He was so distinctly European that it seemed unlikely
that he would have been interested in things American at all. Yet he was
the guiding spirit behind the Museum of the City of New York, the
handsome colonial structure on upper Fifth Avenue which houses the
city's most delightful collection of Americana. He was a director of
Mount Sinai Hospital, a steady donor to Jewish charities, and an
outstanding critic of clubs and schools that practiced racial or religious
discrimination. Yet he was a member of the Racquet Club, where other
Jews were not even welcomed as guests of members. His pride in his
Speyer name had caused him to have created, by royal decree, some
artificial Speyers. Once, lunching with the old Kaiser Wilhelm (*that* was
how Old World Jimmie Speyer could be), Mr. Speyer mentioned his
sorrow at having no sons to carry on. "But surely there are some
Speyers left in Frankfurt," said the Kaiser. "None," said Speyer sadly.
"This will never do," said the Kaiser. "There must *always* be a Speyer in
Frankfurt!" And so the Kaiser conferred a title upon Speyer's brother-in-
law, Eduard Beit, authorizing Eduard to add "von Speyer" to his name.
It was an ennobling "von" that even such favored "court" Jews as
Albert Ballin did not have.

Jimmie Speyer's country house on the Hudson was called "Wald-
heim," but he married a gentile girl named Ellin Prince whose ancestry
traced back to colonial days. He was so proud of his wife's antecedents
that, in his listing in *Who's Who,* he included her parents' names
(including her mother's *maiden* name). Yet his own parents' names,
Eduard Gumpertz and Sophie Rubino Speyer, he omitted.

While some members of the crowd seemed uncertain whether or not
to claim their Jewish antecedents, others were quite definite about it.
One such was Howard Goodhart, Mrs. Hattie Lehman Goodhart's son.
He, at one point, evolved a theory that he was directly descended from
Philo Judaeus, the Greco-Judean philosopher of 20 B.C. Goodhart's
reason for thinking so was simple. He believed that, as generations
passed—among Jews, at least—certain names kept reappearing, though
with their spellings slightly changed. The fact that his father's name was
Philip J. Goodhart was enough to convince Howard that it all must have
started with Philo Judaeus. To reinforce his connection with Philo, if
not quite to prove it, Goodhart hired, at some expense, Professor
Goodenough at Yale to write a book about Philo. Though the book was
not a great best-seller, Mr. Goodhart liked it, and gave it to all his
friends.

"The golf," as it was fashionable to call it, was beginning to dominate
the upper-class sporting scene. With the golf came the country club, and

soon the Harmonie Club was relinquishing its title as the most fashionable Jewish club to the Century Country Club in White Plains. For years the Century was an almost exclusively German club, with an unwritten rule against "Orientals." It was, furthermore, almost exclusively Wall Street, with, as it was said, a few "token Gimbels" from the world of common trade. Only recently has the social cast of the Century begun to change, but a distinction is still drawn between the Jews of the Century and those of the Sunningdale Golf Club in Scarsdale, which is considered by many German Jews to be somewhat *arriviste*.

There were, as the twenties progressed, certain families of the crowd who wished to expand their social horizons somewhat and who were impatient with Jewish country clubs. Morti Schiff, for instance, was much fonder of the Piping Rock Club, one of Long Island's most elegant gentile clubs. He hardly ever appeared at the Century. Other families got themselves in odd situations. Lehmans, Warburgs, Strooks, Ittlesons, Stralems, and Seligmans began, in the twenties, to winter at Palm Beach (needless to say the crowd vigorously eschewed the Jewish mecca, Miami Beach), where they mingled comfortably in gentile circles, without ever being invited to join the elite Christian Everglades Club. At the same time, though not admitted to the Everglades, Henry Seligman was, from his summer home in Elberon, invited to join the equally elite and equally Christian Deal Golf Club, leading to the observation that Henry was a "seasonal Jew." On Long Island the glossy Maidstone Club and the more modest Devon Yacht Club are considered gentile clubs. Yet a New York family, blackballed by the Century, changed their name, applied to the Maidstone, and were taken in, doing much better in alien corn.

Otto Kahn's Morristown estate adjoined the grounds of the super-upper-class (and gentile) Morristown Club, which Kahn had not been invited to join. At one point, the club wished to enlarge its golf course and inquired of Kahn whether he would be willing to sell a few hundred acres. Kahn, with his perfect sense of public relations and his love of the grand gesture, said that he would gladly *give* the club any land it needed. Overwhelmed, the club accepted—and then guiltily decided that it had better ask Mr. Kahn to join. It did, and Otto Kahn accepted with pleasure—though one of the members commented later, "He was a gentleman. He never came around."

It was at about this time that Adolph Lewisohn's daughter Adele, who had married Mayer Lehman's son Arthur, had her name inserted in the New York *Social Register*.

It began to seem as though the devout and pious Jewishness of Jacob Schiff had had a point. What would he have thought of these carryings on? With his philosophy of *Pflicht und Arbeit*—duty and work—he had been the conscience of the German Jewish crowd. But he was gone.

PART V

NEW YORK
21, N.Y.

44

THE END OF
A LINE

J & W. Seligman & Company, though it had been first eclipsed by Kuhn, Loeb and, next, by the Lehmans—to whom the Seligmans sold their building—still managed to produce moments of fiscal excitement. In 1910 Joseph Seligman's ancient rival, J. P. Morgan, was an old man who increasingly allowed others to make his decisions and handle his affairs, and one of these was George W. Perkins, who laughed out loud when a "visionary nitwit" named Will Durant told him that there would one day be as many as fifty thousand automobiles on the roads of America. Shouting, "Impossible!" Perkins threw Durant out of the office. This was too bad for Morgan, because Durant lowered his sights a notch and approached the Seligmans.

Durant's burgeoning General Motors Corporation had already absorbed a number of individual companies—Buick, Oldsmobile, Cadillac, and some twenty others. But even the Seligmans, perhaps because they knew they had a Morgan reject, were initially wary. They agreed to take on Durant, but on staggeringly stiff terms. In return for underwrit-

ing $15 million worth of Durant's GM notes,* the bankers demanded
that Durant put up *all* his company's assets as security, in addition to
giving control of his board to the Seligman group. Durant also wanted
$2.5 million in cash, and for this the Seligmans made him put up $4
million worth of stock as security, and charged him 6 percent interest
for five years. As an indication of how shaky a venture Durant's was
considered to be, the lawyers who drew up the papers on the deal cut
their normal fee to less than one-half, in order to get cash and not stock
as their fee.

This was in 1910. Three years later, Albert Strauss, who, with his
brother Frederick,† had been one of the first nonfamily Seligman partners and who had gone on the board of General Motors, was offered
$30 a share for his General Motors common stock. Strauss declined to
sell, and the Seligmans held on to theirs. By the war's end, in 1919, the
original GM common was selling for $850 a share.

The House of Morgan's less than clairvoyant appraisal of the auto-
motive industry is often given as the reason why the Ford Motor
Company for so many years refused to go public. Motor stocks of the
period were considered so speculative that "Only the Jewish banks will
handle them," and this would not have suited Henry Ford, Sr., a virulent
anti-Semite. Nevertheless, the leading gentile banker, Morgan, would
not see Ford. It was in the Dearborn, Michigan, *Independent,* which
Ford controlled, that he caused to be published for the first time in
America the *Protocols of the Learned Elders of Zion,* the spurious
document purportedly prepared by an international conference of Jews
and Freemasons, outlining their plans to take over the world. (A proven
fake, it was traced to an anti-Semitic Russian writer in Kishinev at the
time of the pogroms.) As a result of this, it was many years before most
Jews would buy a Ford car.

And yet, after Henry Ford's death, it was a Jewish bank, Goldman,
Sachs & Company, which first brought out Ford stock and, under the
guiding genius of Sidney Weinberg, devised the intricate construction of
the Ford Foundation. Today Weinberg is the chief financial adviser to
Henry Ford II, and is on the board of directors of the Ford Motor
Company. The ironies of high finance never cease. Where great money is
to be made, much can be forgiven.

The individual members of the Seligman family, meanwhile, who had
always referred to Mrs. Astor and *her* crowd as "the butterflies," were
beginning to display some oddly butterfly-like characteristics of their
own. The men of the family seemed definitely to prefer being gentlemen

---

* In cooperation with Lee, Higginson and the Central Trust Company.
† No kin to the single-"s" Strauses.

of leisure to working, and a number of the ladies were devoting themselves as assiduously as Mrs. Astor had to being hostesses. There was,
for instance, Mrs. Henry Seligman, the wife of the original Jesse's son.
Formerly Addie Walter, she was a double Seligman, having married,
first, Joseph's son David, and, upon his death, his first cousin. All
through the twenties her parties, in her houses in Elberon, Palm Beach,
and in East Fifty-sixth Street, were celebrated. She had a butler, De Witt
(not to be confused with De Witt Seligman, another cousin of her
husband's), who she liked to say "set the standard for a whole generation" of German Jewish families. He was stationed at the foot of the
stairs, and arriving guests learned to fear his look of icy disapproval.
When Addie Seligman died—at the depth of the depression in 1934 and
at the height of her entertaining career—her dinner plates alone, not
including cups, saucers, or soup bowls, brought $2,660.92 at auction.
De Witt, a millionaire from tips he had received from guests, retired.

But for all the good times, there were some members of the family
who noticed some disturbing Seligman symptoms. Joseph's grandson,
George Hellman, was alarmed at what was happening to the Seligman
birth rate. At the procreative rate of the original David and Fanny
Seligman—who produced eight sons and three daughters—there should
have been, Mr. Hellman computed, some 1,536 Seligman boys in New
York in his own generation. Yet the opposite was the case. Early
Seligmans had the knack of producing mostly boys; later generations
produced female children or none at all. The Seligman name, in barely
three generations' time, was dying out.

It was a genetic fact that other families of the crowd were having to
face. It was almost as though, as the families grew rich and the need to
produce sons grew less acute, fewer sons were born.

Needless to say, the number of Seligman-named partners downtown
at J. & W. Seligman & Company was diminishing at a similar rate.
During the 1920's the firm's seat on the New York Stock Exchange was
held in the name of Jefferson Seligman, the fruit-and-ginger and dresses-
from-Klein's-distributing partner. At the time of the stock market crash
of 1929, Jeff Seligman was there, doing his bit. According to one
partner, "In October, 1929, when the panic was a day or two old, Jeff
appeared on the floor of the Exchange for the first time in years. He
hadn't done a stroke of work since anyone could remember. I don't
think he executed any orders—he simply appeared, wearing a flower in
the buttonhole of his Prince Albert. One of the afternoon papers
commented on the calming effect induced by the appearance of 'the well-
known international banker.' "

Calming effect or no, Jeff Seligman did nothing to improve the
Seligman birth rate. He died in 1937 at the age of seventy-eight, leaving,

according to Geoffrey T. Hellman, "a somewhat diminished estate, which consisted, in part, of a rather large remainder of ginger and Klein's dresses," and without issue.

The Seligmans had become very family-conscious and family-proud and, at one point, hired a designer and a printer to prepare an elaborate *Seligman Family Register*. Bound and published in a limited edition of one hundred copies, it is printed on heavy vellum and contains the names of 255 people, plus portraits of the original eleven Seligman children from Baiersdorf. Through the *Register,* it is possible to trace the Seligman family's weblike interconnection with other families of the crowd—the Beers, Walters, Goodharts, Guggenheims, Lewisohns, Wassermanns, Nathans, Lilienthals, Lehmans, Wolffs, and Loebs. The Seligmans become the true anchor family of the crowd. It is possible to see how the Seligmans can—and do, with a reasonable degree of accuracy—get themselves connected with the royal House of Windsor, and be able to speak of "our cousin, Princess Margaret." ("Do you suppose," suggests one member of the crowd slyly, "that Princess Margaret ever speaks of 'My cousins, the Seligmans'?") The connection works this way: Isaac Seligman, in London, married, in 1869, a Miss Lina Messel. A later member of the Messel family was Sir Oliver Messel, who is related to a young man named Antony Armstrong-Jones, now Lord Snowden. The Seligmans could also boast a British knight of their very own, Isaac's son, who became Sir Charles Seligman.

But, for all its luster and what George Hellman somewhat wistfully calls the "slight haze of social prestige" that still clings to the Seligman name, it is presently the responsibility of just two small boys, both great-great-grandsons of Joseph, to see to it that it is carried on.

45

THE FALL, AND
AFTER

Felix Warburg's brother Paul had had an unhappy childhood, picked on
by his older brothers Aby and Max, who called him ugly and weak. Even
his mother seemed not to understand him. By the time he had reached
young manhood, he had developed a distinct inferiority complex, and was
forever apologizing for himself. He had a habit of prefacing his remarks
with "You won't like what I'm going to say, but . . ." Still, he was
possibly the most brilliant and versatile of all the Warburgs and, for
years, was a sort of itinerant Kuhn, Loeb partner, spending half of each
year in New York and the other half with the Warburg bank in
Germany, serving as a financial liaison between the two countries. He
had always considered American banking primitive and haphazard. He
had met secretly with Senator Nelson Aldrich at Sea Island, Georgia,
and had worked out the Federal Reserve System, and yet when Aldrich
tried to give Paul Warburg full credit, Paul, typically, refused to take
any credit whatever. He was offered the post of Chairman of the Federal
Reserve Board but, insisting that he was unworthy, refused any position

higher than Vice Chairman. As anti-German feeling mounted during World War I, and as Kuhn, Loeb became the target of much of this, Paul felt it deeply. In 1918 he wrote to President Wilson saying, in his customary self-effacing way, that he felt a naturalized citizen ought not to have such a high post with the Board. Secretly he hoped Wilson would not accept his offer to resign, but, to his discouragement and dismay, Wilson did. Even sadder, Paul Warburg returned to New York from Washington, and became chairman of the board of the Bank of Manhattan. In his spare time, he wrote a monumental history of the Federal Reserve System, and a number of sad, introspective poems.

He was, as it turned out, a Cassandra, and, since prophets of doom do not usually find a sympathetic audience, Paul Warburg was made even more unhappy. As the 1920's progressed, he began saying that the prosperity was false and could not last, that the bubble would burst. For this sort of talk, he was soon the most unpopular man on Wall Street. "Here comes old Gloomy Gus!" someone shouted in 1928, when Paul Warburg entered the Century Club, and he was hissed and booed at a directors' meeting. He went right on, though. Early in 1929 in an annual report of the International Acceptance Bank, Paul stated flatly that climbing prices of stocks were "in the majority of cases quite unrelated to respective increases in plant, property, or earning power," and he also predicted that if "orgies of unrestrained speculation" were not curbed and controlled, "the ultimate collapse is certain not only to affect the speculators themselves but also to bring about a general depression involving the entire country." There were more boos and hisses. This statement was issued in March. The "ultimate collapse" came barely six months later. How right Paul Warburg was need hardly be mentioned, but when he tried to say, "I told you so," in 1930, he was even more enthusiastically disliked.

Meanwhile, there were other problems—disturbing political developments in Germany. Paul and Felix Warburg both felt that the future boded ill for Jewish banks in Germany, and wanted to liquidate M. M. Warburg & Company. But brother Max, head of the Hamburg house, was stubborn. He could, he insisted, "make a deal" with this man Hitler.

The great stock market crash of 1929 affected each banker differently, but those few who had taken Paul Warburg's advice found themselves considerably better off. One of these was Paul's brother-in-law, Morti Schiff. Poor Morti. For all his attempts to move with the International Set, most of his life had been spent squarely under his father's thumb. Now he was to have only a little over ten years of freedom. He died, suddenly, in 1931, after having a pleasant dinner with his daughter, Dorothy. Paul Warburg had warned Morti to "get out of the market" in 1929 and to put his funds into cash. When Morti's estate was appraised, he was found to have left $28,718,213 in securities, plus property in France worth around a million dollars, a book, binding, painting, and furniture collection worth £153,427, and—thanks to Paul Warburg—$7,683,527 in cash. Between the time of the estate's appraisal and its distribution to his heirs, the value of Morti's securities dropped 54 percent. If it hadn't been for all that cash, things would have been difficult. As it was, Morti's heirs were very proud of him. For all Jacob Schiff's worries about Morti's extravagance, Morti had managed to put aside a tidy sum.

Goldman, Sachs was less fortunate in the crash. Under the influence of optimistic Waddill Catchings, the firm had, in 1928, somewhat belatedly decided to get into the investment-trust field—in which a banking house formed a trust, made investments, sold shares to the public, and hopefully kept a fat share for itself. Catchings' idea was to form the Goldman, Sachs Trading Corporation, capitalized at $100 million, and to sell 90 percent of its shares to the public, keeping 10 percent for itself. The firm then merged this interest with the Financial and Industrial Corporation, which in turn had stock control of the Manufacturers Trust Company. All this might have put Goldman, Sachs in an enviable position if it had been done in 1923 instead of 1928. As it was, the interlacings were so complicated that it took ten years of legal wrangling to straighten out who owed what and to whom after the crash. Catchings, meanwhile, had withdrawn from the firm and had gone to California to be a radio producer.

The market collapse found others in embarrassing positions. Otto Kahn's older daughter Maude had married Major General Sir John Marriott, and had moved to England, and, sometime before the crash, Kahn had sold Maude large blocks of five different securities. All five, by 1930, were nearly worthless when Maude gave them back to him, so that he could sell them at a convenient market loss of $117,000. Or so it seemed to the Pecora Investigating Committee in 1933, looking into "under-the-counter" dealings such as this one in an attempt to fix the blame for 1929. Otto Kahn, with his customary urbanity, denied that there had been anything "peculiar" about this intrafamily transaction. When it also turned out that Kahn had paid no income taxes for the years 1930, 1931, and 1932,* Kahn politely explained that, "apparently," he had suffered such heavy losses that he had had no income to declare. When pressed, he admitted that he simply could not explain why he had paid no income taxes. He was, he said, "abysmally ignorant of income tax returns," which were handled entirely by an accountant "in whom I have the deepest trust." As usual in these investigations, no

* Neither, for the same period, had J. P. Morgan, Jr.

one on Wall Street was really hurt, but the Pecora Investigation did result in a tightening of banking and investment rules, in the creation of the Securities and Exchange Commission, and in the end of unrestrained finance.

In those parlous early days of the Great Depression, even families who had come through the crash intact felt it not only wise but fitting to reduce their scale of living. Mrs. Henry Seligman, whose fortune had undergone only small damage, kept De Witt but, to trim expenses for appearances' sake, dismissed her footman, John.

Not so Adolph Lewisohn. While everyone else instituted small economies here and there, he went right on living like a potentate, spending as much as, if not more than, ever. He kept his four houses—at 881 Fifth Avenue, at Elberon, at Prospect Point on Upper Saranac Lake, and "Heatherdale Farm," at Ardsley-on-Hudson in Westchester County. At the Ardsley place he had, in addition to magnificent hothouses that grew exotic plants of every order, a miniature railroad and his own private blacksmith shop. His wife had died at an early age, and from that point onward, to his family's distress, Adolph kicked up his heels. He became incorrigible. Wringing his hands, his son Sam came to him and cried, "Father! You're spending your capital!" "Who made it?" Adolph Lewisohn replied.

He had always loved music, and had never been able to forget the days when he had been a choirboy in the Hamburg Synagogue. Now, in his seventies, he suddenly took up singing again. He hired a number of singing teachers, including the then well-known J. Bertram Fox. Whenever Adolph entertained—which was often—he required his guests to listen as, in a thin and quavery voice, he sang German *lieder,* a repertory of songs by Schumann, Schubert, Mozart, and Brahms. To the family, it seemed undignified, but, as if the singing weren't bad enough, at the age of eighty he took up tap dancing. Adolph argued that he enjoyed these pastimes. He said that tap dancing was good exercise, and that singing helped him in public speaking.

He loved to take excursions, by motor or by train. Throughout the depression, he moved grandly about, back and forth to Europe and between his various residences. With him, in a long procession of chauffeur-driven automobiles (or private railroad cars, or roped-off sections of first class) went his retinue—his personal secretary (male), stenographer (female), valet, chef, singing teachers, dancing teachers, a French instructor, and his personal barber, Gustav Purmann. (Purmann's salary was only $300 a month, but Lewisohn also tipped him regularly with $500 checks, Impressionist paintings, eggs and chickens from "Heatherdale Farm," and, on at least two occasions, Buick automobiles.) Then there were his friends.

The boy who had enjoyed reading the *Fremdenliste* now liked to surround himself with people of every variety. Perhaps because of his family's hostile attitude toward his spending, Adolph Lewisohn's personal *mishpoche* was composed of guests and *onhengers*. In return for their board and keep and traveling expenses, he asked only that they keep him pleasant company.

He preferred creative people (some jealous souls said that he also preferred gentiles)—writers, painters, singers, dancers, actors. He favored "unknowns," whose talents he could discover and help promote. (Basil Rathbone was an early member of the Lewisohn entourage whose promise was fulfilled.) Also, since he was such a merry widower, he had no objection to young ladies who joined his parties and whose function was mostly decorative. Members of the *mishpoche* were always welcome at any and all of the Lewisohn houses, and at times the troupe of followers grew so large that if a friend didn't keep careful track of his host's next-day plans, it was easy to get left behind.

As a host Adolph insisted on a few prerogatives. Though he was more a listener than a talker, he did, whenever he had anything to say, demand that everyone else in the room be silent. He enjoyed playing bridge, but had a highly individual approach to the game. The following is a typical Lewisohn bridge contract:

Lewisohn (dealer): "One club."

West: "Two diamonds."

North: "Two spades."

East: "Five diamonds."

Lewisohn: "One club."

The hand was played at one club.

In his gold-and-white ballroom at 881 Fifth Avenue he held, for years, his famous New Year's Eve parties. As originally conceived, they were thrown for a specific list of guests, including all the German Jewish upper crust. But the parties became so popular, and gate-crashers became so numerous, that they became, in effect, great open houses for all New York. One New Yorker, who grew up in the 1930's, recalls that he never knew there was any other way to pass New Year's Eve than to dress up in white tie and tails and go to Adolph Lewisohn's. It was understood that there was only one rule at these parties: No guest was to remove more than a single bottle of liquor, which could be concealed under a coat.

Looking back, it seems a miracle that no more was ever stolen. But only occasionally did a Lewisohn party get out of hand. Mr. Lewisohn's chief steward always stationed himself at the foot of the marble basement stairs, to keep an eye on the collection of precious stones and jewels that were displayed there in lighted glass cases—many of the stones uncovered during the Lewisohns' mining adventures. And, at one party, an unidentified man in an oversize overcoat appeared, swaying, at the top of the stairs. He shouted once, "Down with the filthy capitalists!" Then he lurched and fell all the way down the stairs amid the exploding champagne bottles that had been concealed about his person.

But under ordinary circumstances the highlight of the evening was when the round-faced little host—looking, indeed, like an elderly choirboy—got to his feet and began to sing.

In New York and Europe he had begun to buy paintings of the Barbizon School—Dupré, Daubigny, Jacque, and Français—which was then "fashionable." Few people had bought Impressionists in any quantity. But on the advice of a woman friend who had told him that it was more fashionable to be unfashionable, he sold his Barbizon pictures at the top of their market and bought, canvas for canvas, an equal collection of Impressionists at the bottom of their market, turning a tidy profit in the transaction. People thought he was crazy, and giggled about the "cheap paintings" silly Adolph was hanging on his walls—by such painters as Renoir, Cézanne, Monet, Degas, Gauguin, and a youngster named Picasso. One little Monet cost him only three hundred dollars in 1919. By the late twenties Adolph was saying proudly, "That little canvas is worth ten thousand dollars!" Today it might bring a hundred thousand.

As he grew older and began to realize his dream of great wealth, he began to cherish another ambition—not only to be "a rich man," as he put it, but to be loved as "a citizen." He wanted to be identified with his city and with his country, and he rankled, as did so many others of the crowd, at being labeled "a leading Jew." As the thirties progressed, and news from his native Germany grew more distressing, this became increasingly important to him.

In his efforts to be a friend to mankind, he began a long program of giving away lordly sums to worthwhile causes and institutions. Many of his philanthropies are well known—the Lewisohn Stadium, the Pathological Laboratory Building at Mount Sinai Hospital, the School of Mining at Columbia, the Orphanage of the Hebrew Sheltering Guardian Society in Pleasantville, New York. But of other deeds less has been written, such as his work in the cause of prison reform. He once confided to a friend that as a child in Hamburg after his mother's death and his father's remarriage he had often felt like a prisoner in his father's house. His youth, he said, had given him an unhappy taste of what men in confinement suffered. He labored and gave money to improve conditions in prisons, to establish agencies that would help former prisoners find jobs after their release, and dreamed of a day when prisons could be done away with altogether. He was much ahead of his time in this, and was also a regular "prison visitor"—a charitable activity that has never been popular in this country, though it is in England. He used to speak proudly of the time he had dinner with a convicted murderer.

But somehow, for all his work and all his philanthropies, some mysterious ingredient that it took to be loved always eluded him. He never seemed to achieve Jacob Schiff's prestige. For all his entertaining, he never matched the Seligmans' social status, and, when his son Sam married Joseph Seligman's granddaughter, Margaret Seligman, the Seligmans sniffed their disapproval.

He used to say, "I wouldn't mind losing all my money. I don't have to live the way I do—I could live very simply. But I'd hate to be thought a *fool.*" More than anything, he dreaded appearing ridiculous. And yet— with his round little figure, his polished bald head, his nearsighted eyes peering through their comically thick spectacles, in his spotless gray spats and his vests aglitter with shining black buttons; throwing his increasingly unwieldy parties, surrounded by his fawning retinue of "friends"—he did, at times, seem the butt of all jokes. He was a Jewish Great Gatsby in the wrong decade, and, as a result, he always seemed a little inappropriate.

As an old man, he began to dictate his autobiography which he titled, significantly, "The Citizenship of Adolph Lewisohn." It was never published, and it is a fascinating—and also, in some ways, baffling— document. He mentions his marriage to Emma Cahn of New York in 1878, but never mentions her by her first name again. A few references to her follow—always as "my wife" or "Mrs. Lewisohn." He took her to England on their wedding trip aboard the Cunarder *Russia*. She complained about their stateroom, which was next to the coal chutes, but nothing could be done about it. It was also a business trip for Adolph, and he wrote: "We could not always be together, for in London I had to be at the office while my wife went out to see the sights." He added: "I suppose that generally it would be considered a hardship to have to attend to business while travelling, especially on a wedding trip; but, with the right spirit, business with its interesting contacts not only is a constant education but becomes a splendid pastime." Adolph's wife then drops from the pages completely.

The rest of the book concerns itself with Adolph's many successes in the copper industry. He does not mention his wife's death in 1916. He never mentions the five children she bore him, or his grandchildren. He seems to have been a man consumed, early in life, by himself.

But his son Sam always stuck by him and, in Adolph's later years, seemed to have been the only one who truly loved him. Sam was a witty, intelligent, and charming man. But even with Sam, Adolph was distant and reserved, too locked in his private grief and loneliness to be father. When Sam married Margaret Seligman, he brought his young bride to live in his father's house. They had their own apartment on an upper floor, but they always took their evening meal with the old gentleman. Their four daughters were born and raised there.

One granddaughter, Joan Lewisohn Simon, wrote an admittedly autobiographical novel called *Portrait of a Father,* in which she has harsh things to say about both her father and grandfather, the latter of whom she describes as looking like "a turtle standing on its hind legs."

The little girls would dine with their nurse and governess upstairs, and each evening at precisely three minutes past six, just as the liveried butler was removing the service plates, they would hear the creak and rattle of the elevator ascending. Then the gate would clank open and shut, and their grandfather's footsteps would shuffle across the thick carpet toward the dining room. The servants would stiffen and eye the little girls warningly. "Best manners!" hissed the governess as their grandfather walked to the head of the table and removed a little black book from his vest pocket. He would then proceed to read to them, in a thick accent which they couldn't understand, from the book. The girls and the servants would sit in numbed silence until he finished this ritual. Then he would bow slightly, turn, and depart.

The little girls interpreted it as a kind of blessing. It wasn't until years later that they discovered that the black book was his engagement book. He had been reading to them, every night, his list of his week's appointments.

Joan Simon remembers being eighteen in the Fifth Avenue house and "sitting downstairs, waiting nervously for an evening date, on a stiff wooden chair adjoining a long formal table that in a club would have been arrayed with magazines," and hearing, to her "dismay," the elevator landing. It was her grandfather, and he came into the room and sat in another stiff chair—her chair's twin—a table length away from her to wait for his chauffeur to pick him up for a dinner engagement. There they sat, "two occupants of the same house for eighteen years," and could find nothing to say to each other. Finally they spoke of the weather, then "recoiled into silence."

It was even harder for Margaret Seligman Lewisohn, a beautiful and intelligent woman herself. Joan Simon has spoken of how awkward her mother used to feel in the house while the great New Year's Eve parties were going on—parties of which she was officially the hostess, and yet not really. In his ninetieth year—his last—Adolph Lewisohn sang and danced at his New Year's Eve party until 3 A.M.

The disappointing size of his estate was the cause of many bitter scenes. His heirs, who in 1930 had expected thirty million dollars to divide between them, found, eight years later, only three millions. (Today his descendants rather wistfully say that at one point he was worth two hundred million.) Though he left, among other things, a priceless collection of paintings, two of his granddaughters found themselves quarreling over possession of a Grand Rapids telephone stand.

One granddaughter, who did not live in the same house with him, remembers him kindly. "He had," says Mrs. Richard Bernhard vigorously, "the most wonderful knack of coming out with the punch line, putting the capstone on every argument. You could talk to him, and you wouldn't believe he was even listening to you—then out it would come." Once, she recalls, when her late husband, a partner in Wertheim & Company, had been offered a particularly tempting new job in England in the late twenties, they took the question to Mr. Lewisohn, the family patriarch. He listened in silence to all the younger man's arguments for going back to England—or perhaps he wasn't listening. Then suddenly he raised his head and said, "Your forefathers came to America because it was the land of promise." That was all. Mr. Bernhard stayed in New York.

As a boy in Hamburg, Adolph had taken long, solitary walks in the woods outside the city, picking wildflowers. He had once created his own little herbarium which he kept flourishing in his window overlooking the canal. In his great Ardsley estate, he had fabulous gardens and huge hothouses filled with growing plants. He used to like to take his friends and various tutors on walks through his gardens, and at times he would stoop and talk tenderly to the flowers.

Toward the end of his autobiography, he makes this haunting statement: "As I sit here in the comfort and leisure of my home, dictating from time to time these random memories of a long life, I feel that I am talking, not to the public, but to a kindly indulgent company of my friends . . . but the distance between human hearts seems greater than in the old days."

It was. But he never knew why.

46

THE END
OF A DREAM

In the early 1930's there suddenly appeared a fictitious Warburg. He was, or so he signed himself, Sidney Warburg, and he made his appearance as the author of a pamphlet titled *The Resources of National Socialism: Three Conversations with Hitler.* In a preface to this apologia, this Warburg claimed to be the son of Felix Warburg. Felix had four sons—Frederick, Gerald, Paul, and Edward—but no Sidney. Sidney Warburg was a hoax. No Warburg ever had a conversation with Hitler. But one, Paul's and Felix's brother Max, came close.

Max Warburg, head of M. M. Warburg & Company in Germany, was, as the family used to say, "not a typical Warburg." Typical Warburgs were dark and flashing-eyed, with wide foreheads and prominent noses. Max, however, looked like his mother's family, the Oppenheims, with blue eyes, fair hair, and a small nose. These physiological details are important since during Hitler's rise it was often helpful for a Jew not to "look Jewish."

Max Warburg joined the German Army as a young man, and chose the smart Hussars. He loved his uniform and was such a good soldier that, as a special favor, he was permitted to attend Officers Corps meetings, even though he knew that as a Jew he could never receive a commission. Nonetheless, in his early twenties he had written to Grossvater Warburg saying that he wanted to make the German Army his career. Grossvater was flabbergasted, and wrote back saying that he didn't know which was worse—having a son who would turn his back on the family bank in favor of the army or tolerating the humiliation of a son who would never be more than a noncommissioned officer. At last Max gave in and returned to Hamburg to learn banking.

Max was something of a tufthunter. As part of his training, he was sent to England for a year, where he worked for the House of Rothschild. He was a familiar figure at West End parties and, to keep the various members of the English aristocracy straightened out, sat up at nights memorizing Burke's *Peerage* and Debrett. He was remarkably adaptable, and, according to the family, by the end of that year in London Max was "more British than the British," with an impeccable Etonian accent. Returning to Germany, he became a close friend of Albert Ballin, the famous court Jewish friend of the Kaiser, who headed the enormously prosperous Hamburg-America Line, which was one of the greatest factors in German life, not just as a business but also as Germany's most powerful advertisement of itself to the world at large.

Though court life in Germany was strict and rule-ridden—the rule that Jews were not received was one of the most unshakable—suddenly Max Warburg, along with Ballin, was a familiar figure on the Kaiser's yacht. As the century moved into its third decade, the Hamburg-America Line became notably Hitlerian in its stance, and Max Warburg had become a member of the Hamburg-America's executive committee.

In retrospect, there were many ironies in Max Warburg's life. Certainly his special treatment began to convince him that he was somehow specially equipped to handle "the Jewish question," as it was being called in Germany. During World War I Max was financial adviser to the Imperial Government of Germany, and at the war's end he was appointed to a special committee to assist the German peace delegation at Versailles. He was so devotedly German that, when he saw the "humiliating" terms of the treaty submitted by the Allied Powers, he promptly resigned from his committee post and had demanded that all the other members resign as well. But poisonous myths were being created—that the German Army had never been defeated but had been stabbed in the back by "the November criminals"—the Republicans, the Socialists, and the Jews. Soon "the Jew Max Warburg" was being named among those responsible for the Versailles Treaty, and, as the false rumors spread, he was called the infamous treaty's architect. An attempt on his life was planned, and for several months after Versailles Max was forced to hide in the country outside Hamburg. It was during this period that his brothers in America, given the perspective that distance provides, began urging Max to leave Germany.

But Max was too much of a German. When the German Republic was coming into being, Max was offered his choice of two posts: Minister of Finance or Ambassador to the United States. To everybody's surprise, he turned them both down—for reasons that revealed a certain ambivalence in his nature. He would rather not accept the post of Minister of Finance, he said, because he considered the job "too big and too important," because the problems facing the young Republic were "very grave," and because "any mistake which I might make would reflect on all German Jewry." He turned down the ambassadorship saying that, as head of M. M. Warburg for many years, he was "more accustomed to command than to obey." He added that "An ambassador is nothing more than a glorified messenger boy."

For all this loftiness, even arrogance, of tone, it is quite clear that by 1930 Max Warburg was a seriously frightened man. His main concern became saving, if at all possible, the Warburg bank and properties in Germany. To do so, he used his old connections with the Kaiser and the imperial court to become a close friend of the prominent Nazi, Hjalmar Schacht, president of the Reichsbank, the German Federal Bank.* Schacht often turned to Max for advice in financial matters, and continued doing so for several years after Hitler came to power. Through Schacht, Max became convinced that the Warburg bank would never be seized and that he himself might be to Hitler what Albert Ballin had been to the Kaiser, the court Jew. Alas, as the months marched relentlessly onward, this possibility seemed less than remote, particularly to Max's despairing brothers in New York. A law of April, 1933, decreed that all Jews be dismissed from government service and the universities, and they were also barred from the professions. Yet a week later, Max Warburg was dining with his friend, the Nazi Schacht. In September, 1935, marriages between Jews and persons of "German blood" were forbidden, and Jews were deprived of virtually all their remaining rights.

Yet Max Warburg still hung on to the family bank and, that winter, submitted to Schacht the Warburg Plan—a system designed to facilitate the emigration of Jews out of Germany. The Warburg Plan would help *other* German Jews to escape; Max himself still seems to have believed he would be spared. Schacht spent several months going over the Warburg Plan, submitted it to a number of committees and "experts" on the "Jewish question," and the plan is said to have rested for several days on the desk of the *Führer* himself. However, though Max made

* Schacht was later tried, and acquitted, as a war criminal.

several inquiries about the status of his plan, very little seemed to have been done about it. The Warburg Plan was still passing from desk to desk in the Nazi regime in the autumn of 1937 when Max Warburg, still harboring a hopeless hope that his plan would save the Jews of Germany, sailed for New York from Hamburg to find supporters in America. He was still in New York in 1938 when word reached him of the burning of the shops and synagogues, and it was only then that he saw the futility of returning to Germany. Shortly afterward, the 140-year-old bank was taken forcibly away from the Warburgs. Max, an old and broken man, asked his son Eric, already a citizen, to help him get his American citizenship.

In the United States Max began to write his memoirs, in which he spoke candidly of what it was like to be an important Jew surviving under Hitler until as late as 1937–1938. The manuscript, in the early 1940's, was accepted by the Macmillan Company for publication, and an advance was paid. But the Warburg family, now that the United States was in the war, became fearful that "the moment was not right" for such a document. Perhaps, all things considered, it wasn't. Too many terrible fires were already burning. Max withdrew the manuscript and returned the advance, and now, when much that it may have contained could be enlightening, both of the Nazis he knew and of his own complex character, it has disappeared. Max Warburg became an American citizen in 1944, at the age of seventy-seven, and died two years later.

Eric Warburg, who had considerably more foresight than his father and who was the first of the German Warburgs to become a United States citizen, enlisted in the U.S. Army early in the war, becoming one of the few German-born officers in the American forces. In the customary Warburg way, with great *élan,* Eric was able to avenge his father's treatment in Germany, and to even the Warburg score with the Nazis. In the African campaign, as a Lieutenant Colonel in Air Force Intelligence, Eric's knowledge of the language enabled him to interrogate shot-down German soldiers. He took part in the Normandy invasion and, when Hermann Göring was captured, was Göring's chief U.S. interrogator. The interrogation lasted forty-eight hours, and, though grueling, the session was conducted with perfect Warburg aplomb.

Eric usually had the last, sardonic word. Once, when he was escorting a captured German general to the billet in a farmhouse that had been assigned to him, the general protested the accommodations violently, shouting, *"Ich bin doch ein General vom Wehrmacht!"* Eric Warburg, with splendidly quiet tact, replied, *"Ja, aber leider haben wir Sie nicht erwartet."* ("Yes, but unfortunately we weren't expecting you.")

After the war it was Eric who persuaded the Allies to let the family bank in Hamburg resume operations, and he is now the senior partner in the Hamburg office, though both he and his young son, Max II, remain U.S. citizens.*

The war drew families together as randomly as it flung them apart, and in New York the effect of Hitler's policies toward Jews was most profound. It was the end of a dream. The dream had managed to survive, almost intact, the First World War. That war had been easy to blame, as Otto Kahn had done, on "the Prussian ruling class." Part of the dream had involved romantic associations with the homeland and sentimental nostalgia for "the old Germany" which, in the mind's eye, had always been green and springlike:

> Denk ich am Deutschland in der Nacht
> So bin ich um en Schlaf Gebracht. . . .

But an even more important part of the dream had been the German Jew's notion, in Germany and America, of his "specialness." When the German Jew thought of himself, he tended to do so in terms of the poetry of Heine and the music of Mendelssohn, and the many Jewish contributions, which every good German Jew could recite, to German science, education, and industry. As all these were systematically erased in Germany, New York's German Jewish families looked at one another in horror, reappraising all the things—their German culture and language, their German steamships, their German wines—from which they had once drawn a sense of importance and superiority. With a heavy feeling of loss, they took up the task of gathering scattered members of their families in from the flames of Europe.

The Lehmans, for instance, were among the families who established special trust funds to help relatives abroad, and how delicate and painful a problem this could be is clear from a letter written by Herbert Lehman, by then Governor of New York, to his niece, Dorothy Lehman Bernhard whom the family had placed in charge of this trust, in 1939. When it came to who was a "relative" and who was not, Mrs. Bernhard had found it difficult to draw the line, and the governor was not of much assistance:

> I have taken note of the very long list of people who have written asking for help but to whom you felt we could not give assistance because their relationship could not be proved, or because they were too old, or undesirable for emigration. While many of these cases are undoubtedly worthy or very pathetic, I think you will have to main-

* Since the war the Warburg bank has been called Brinckmann, Wirtz & Company, but it is the private hope of the Warburgs that the historic name will soon be restored to it.

tain the position you have already taken. . . . I think that we have assumed all the responsibility that we dare to undertake, and those people who are not related or not connected will have to be helped through general funds. The list for whom we have already issued affidavits is really a staggering one, and I believe we now must simply permit those who wish to emigrate to work through usual channels. I hate to take this position because I know of the urgency of the situation. . . .

The letter closes on this dismally prophetic note: "I think, however, that these people who have written us are in no different position from the thousands of people who need assistance and must be helped, if at all, through general funds."

Therese Loeb Schiff worried about her half-brother, Jim Loeb, who still lived on a forest estate outside Murnau, Germany. After many years he had married a woman named Toni Hambuchen who had been his nurse and companion through some of his worst periods of depression. Working on his collection of rare books, the two had become virtual recluses, and rarely ventured outside their house. Still, the citizens of Murnau had grown fond of their mysterious and lonely neighbors, and on James Loeb's sixtieth birthday they had given him the Freedom of the City. He accepted the honor shyly, and withdrew to his house. Soon afterward, Therese Schiff received word that both James Loeb and his wife had died, quietly, within a few weeks of one another. This was in 1933, but poor Jim Loeb's struggle with Nazi Germany was not yet over.

Soon Murnau extended the Freedom of the City to Adolf Hitler. James Loeb had died without direct heirs, but he had become attached to his stepson, Joseph Hambuchen, Toni's son by a previous marriage. The bulk of the Loeb estate went to Joseph—which was fortunate, since Joseph had American citizenship through his stepfather and, as a result, escaped having his property seized by the Nazis. The collection of books was hastily shipped to England, where it was stored throughout the duration of one war. He had bequeathed his art collection to the Munich Museum, where it still is, though since Hitler James Loeb's name has never been mentioned in connection with it. Jim Loeb had been concerned about his mental health, and about his brother Morris, the chemist, who was certainly "peculiar," and about his sister Guta, Mrs. Isaac Newton Seligman, who was in a New York State sanitarium. And so Jim Loeb had given several large sums of money for the foundation of a neurological and psychiatric research center in Munich under Dr. Binswanger, who had treated him. The research center was a project that excited him even more than his library, and plans for it had filled the last months of his life. But Loeb's building, taken over by the

Nazis soon after his death, was turned into a center for experiment of race-superiority theories, and his name was scratched from the stone.

In 1947 Felix Warburg's son Paul was making a tour of inspection of the American Zone in Germany with Ambassador Lewis Douglas, and the two men stopped at an American Army guest house in Murnau, outside Munich. The first thing young Warburg saw upon opening the door was a portrait of his great-grandfather, Solomon Loeb. With a start, he realized that this was his Great-Uncle James Loeb's house, and that the kindly, worried, dyspeptic founder of Kuhn, Loeb & Company, one of New York's greatest Jewish banking houses, had gazed dispassionately upon a German drawing room throughout the rise and fall of Hitler's Third Reich.

The ironies go on and on. In the early 1930's Otto Kahn, in his sixties, had suddenly been smitten with a longing to return to Germany. Writing of the cities of his youth, Mannheim and Bemberg, he said: "How lovely those places are! What a romantic spell attaches to them! The older I get the more I develop a regular sentimental 'Heimweh' in the spring. . . . *Mein Herz ist nicht hier.*"

In Mannheim, where Kahn's homesick *Herz* lay, his father had founded a reading room for workers, and Kahn had continued to support it. In 1932 Otto Kahn sent his contribution of a thousand marks to the Bernhard Kahn *Lesehalle* of the Mannheim *Volkhochsschule,* saying, as he did so, that he couldn't continue his support "with self-respect as a Jew if, after the lapse of another year, the Hitler party continues to be by far the strongest and most popular party in Germany." In much less than a year the Nazis had closed the library, fired the director, confiscated the books, and that dream was over. Sadly, Kahn declined an invitation to attend a dinner of the Academy of Political Science when he heard that the German Ambassador to Washington would be there. He advised his steward, also, to serve no more Moselle and Rhine wines at the Kahn table, and all future orders from his wine merchant in Frankfurt were canceled.

Finally—the most painful decision of all—Otto Kahn discontinued plans, which had been quietly undertaken for some time, to convert to Roman Catholicism. He simply could not bring himself to desert his people at a moment when they faced their greatest crisis. As he said, at a banquet for the Joint Distribution Committee, "This is the time for every one of us to heed the call of the blood which courses in his veins and loyally and proudly to stand up and be counted with his fellow Jews." Yet we can almost hear him add, *"Mein Herz ist nicht hier."*

Other Jews, who had accused Otto Kahn of being a passive anti-Semite, and who never realized that he was merely indifferent to

Judaism, were jubilant. "At last Otto Kahn is *bar mitzvah!*" they cried. In the winter of 1934 he went, as usual, to Palm Beach, returning to New York at the end of March. On March 29 he went to his office, and there, rising from luncheon in the Kuhn, Loeb private dining room, he fell forward, dead. Everyone was sure he would have been pleased that he looked so well—his beautiful mustache brushed, his Savile Row suit immaculate, a fresh carnation in his buttonhole, and his English shoes from Peel's, under his spotless spats, boned and rubbed to a fine, soft gleam.

In the same year a dream ended for the Seligmans, too. They had founded, long before the First World War, an orphanage in their native village of Baiersdorf, and had continued to support it. It was a nonsectarian institution, and, indeed, it had always cared for more Gentile children than Jewish. Nonetheless, it was closed. And, in the process, Henry Seligmanstrasse changed its name to Adolf Hitlerstrasse.

"This man," Otto Kahn once said, "is the enemy of humanity. But he attacks each of us in such an intensely *personal* way."

47

WHERE ARE THEY NOW?

As the German Jewish crowd composed itself after the agony of the Second World War, it attempted, without ever so saying, to impose a sort of order on itself, a scheme of values, and a system for dealing with the problems which it had begun to see as inevitable. It was decided, for example, that the proper moment for "telling" a boy that he was Jewish, and therefore "different," was on the eve of his departure for boarding school. In the drawing room the little conference was called, with Mother, Father, Grandmother, and Grandfather present in, often, a very solemn circle. Thereupon what might be called the Facts of Faith were presented. One young man, raised to consider himself a "free-thinker," recalls such a moment shortly before he was to leave for Taft, and remembers asking, in awe, "Does that mean that I'm related to people like Albert Einstein, and Otto Kahn, and Robert Moses?" He was told yes, that this was true, but that there were also certain difficulties inherent in being Jewish, and that, somehow or other, these had to be faced and handled. As a result of these revelations, young Jewish boys

370

have often set off for Taft, Middlesex, Hotchkiss, Kent, and Exeter in a high state of nervousness, and, since the teens can be a heartless age, many have encountered the predicted troubles.

James Warburg was only in the seventh grade when he made the unsettling discovery. His parents, Paul and Nina Warburg, had become "twice-a-year Jews," attending the synagogue only on the Jewish New Year's Day and the Day of Atonement, and of his parents' faith young James only knew that "I felt warmly about Grandfather Warburg's Friday evenings and loved the sound of Hebrew. On the other hand, I was repelled by the proselytizing religiosity of my New York uncle, Jacob Schiff." At Miss Bovee's Elementary School in New York, which James attended, it was the practice for each student to put his initials in the upper corner of each school paper before passing it forward. As Warburg remembers in his autobiography, *The Long Road Home,* "A slightly older boy whom I rather liked used to insert an E between the letters JW with which I initialed my papers until I put a stop to it by signing myself JPW. Apparently the word 'Jew' could be a term of opprobrium; and apparently there were some, or perhaps even many, people who disliked Jews and looked down upon them. My mother confirmed that such was indeed the case. She said that because of this a Jewish boy should always be very careful not to push himself forward. This puzzled me. It seemed like accepting some sort of second-class status."

It goes without saying that a boy brought up in a strict orthodoxy, or even with the emphasis on ritual that Jacob Schiff had recommended, would suffer no such confusion. James Warburg continues, "I gathered the impression from both of my parents that, no matter what other people might feel, to be a Jew was something of which to be proud. Why this should be so remained unclear. Evidently, my parents wanted their son to feel that he had fallen heir to a precious heritage, but neither of them could or would explain just what remained of this heritage if the Jewish religion were shucked off. It seemed to me that nothing more remained than a disbelief in the divinity of Jesus Christ."

Faced with these uncertainties, and with parents who—as the joke went in the crowd—were "just a little bit Jewish," James Warburg reacted the way several of his generation did. He decided that if he was going to be a Jew "and suffer whatever social or other disadvantages this might entail" he would be "a *real* Jew," like his Grandfather Warburg. He announced at the age of ten that he wished to study Hebrew, to learn Jewish religious history, and to be *bar mitzvah.* He also revealed that he intended to become a rabbi, at which piece of news "My parents were rather surprised—whether pleased or displeased I could not tell." (One can rather imagine, however.)

That the rabbinate did not gain James Warburg, and that his religious

zeal was short-lived, can be blamed on his Uncle Felix, who had, from
the beginning, an unfailing instinct for what made an upper-class
American. He had made sure that his own children learned all the
proper upper-class things—that they played tennis, rode well, and could
handle a sailboat. He had made it a tradition for Warburg boys to go to
Middlesex, one of the most socially impeccable New England schools,
with a socially impeccable headmaster, Frederick Winsor, whose wife
was "a Boston Paine," and where daily and Sunday chapel—Episcopal
—were compulsory.

Paul Warburg was never certain how he felt about New England
boarding schools—so many boys seemed to emerge from them having
lost their Jewishness altogether—but Felix insisted that Middlesex was
just the thing for the aspiring rabbi, James. Four years later James
Warburg graduated from Middlesex not even so much as a twice-a-year
Jew; he was, he said, a "Jeffersonian deist." He added, furthermore, that
he was "never aware of the slightest trace of anti-Semitism among the
teachers or the boys"—nor was there, of course, any anti-Jefferson-
ianism.

Other sons of the crowd, however, have encountered anti-Semitism,
both subtle and overt, at otherwise fine boys' schools where "Jew-baiting"
continues to be a popular sport. Perhaps the sport persists because the
young Jew is so well prepared for it—defensive, edgy, quick at times
to sense aspersions where, perhaps, none were intended. But often they
are intended. At the Hotchkiss School, not too many years ago, the son
of one of New York's most prominent Jewish families, a bright, active,
and well-liked boy, was considered a promising sculptor and was given a
one-man show. His show included a number of handsome heads molded
of soft modeling clay. One morning it was discovered that someone, in
the night, had defaced each of the heads by giving it a large Semitic nose.
The desecration outraged Headmaster George Van Santvoord, who made
it the basis of a stirring chapel sermon. Most interesting was the attitude
of the young sculptor himself, who had begged that the matter be forgotten and was so embarrassed at being the subject of a sermon that he
became sick to his stomach.

At Williams College, meanwhile, a nephew of Governor Herbert
Lehman was taken into the Governor's fraternity, Phi Gamma Delta,
and then politely told that he would be "the last of your family. We
can't take in too many of you, you know." This young man, however,
decided to stay in the fraternity, though since then fraternities themselves have disappeared from the Williams campus.

Though anti-Semitism did not end with Hitler, it has been said that
the Second World War did much to eliminate hard feelings between
German Jews and the later arrivals from Eastern Europe. "World War

II Made One of American Jewry," an item in the Jewish press announced not long ago. This, however, is open to some debate. When the oldest daughter of Mrs. John D. Gordan (who is a Goodhart, a Walter, and a great-granddaughter of Mayer Lehman) was considering colleges, she settled upon Barnard, "largely because of the high percentage of Jewish girls." But when Miss Gordan arrived at Barnard, and revealed her family's connection with the Lehmans, Goodharts, Walters, and with Temple Emanu-El, "All the other girls," says her mother, "immediately assumed that she was the worst sort of snob."

And, in the careless reaches of Fire Island in a recent summer, a situation developed between two neighboring families—let us call them the A's and the B's—that split the community for several weeks. It began when Mrs. A's little boy—call him Billy—appeared outside Mrs. B's large front window and, for reasons that are uncertain, made unpleasant faces and spat on the glass. Mrs. B, who saw the deed, was incensed. She charged out of her house, seized young Billy, and spanked him so soundly that Billy ran wailing home saying that Mrs. B had "beaten" him. Mrs. A, outraged, went to her telephone and harsh words flew back and forth between the two women. The feud then escalated to the point where both families consulted their lawyers, and the A's instigated a suit against the B's for Mrs. B's abusive treatment of Billy. At the height of the furor, one neighbor remarked half-seriously, "Well, at least nobody can say that anti-Semitism enters into it"—since both the A's and the B's were Jewish. "Oh, but you're entirely wrong!" cried a friend. "That's what's at the *heart* of it. Didn't you know? The A's are *white* Jews."

There continues to be that question of class. The old differentiation between the German "uptown" Jew and the Russian of the "Lower East Side" has become a difference between the "quiet, cultivated Wall Street type" and the "noisy, pushy, Seventh Avenue type"—who do not mix any more easily than oil and water. And out of all this has come the impression that Jews "dominate" both these fields in the city.

A *Fortune* survey in 1936, however, looking into the billowing anti-Semitism in both Europe and America, pointed out that the Jewish community had not at all monopolized industry, as was often claimed, though Jews had tended to gravitate toward certain segments of it. There were then, as there continue to be, few Jews in important positions in the insurance business. Yet the liquor business, which traditionally was the prerogative of Jews in Poland (for one reason because they did not drink), is heavily in Jewish (non-German) hands in the United States, accounting for about half of the distillers. Advertising is essentially a "white, Anglo-Saxon Protestant" business in New York, yet broadcasting, which is so closely allied to it, might be said to be the opposite, since two major networks are headed by Jews. There have been few Jews, if any, in automobile manufacturing, though there are many in dealerships and the car-rental business; there are few in heavy industry, hardly any in transportation or utilities. The magazine remarked on a "tendency to crowd together [and a] pronounced psychological trait: clannishness, tribal inclinations," and said that the Jewish influence and position were "to be found in those reaches of industry where manufacturer and merchant meet, hence the dominance in retailing."

The survey took notice of the historical accidents that tended to move Jewish businessmen from one area to another—from the theater into the motion picture industry, from the junk business, which was such an easy start for a penniless immigrant, to the scrap-metal business. The magazine added: "Wherever Jews may be, industrially or culturally or professionally or merely geographically, they are always present in numbers and almost always present as Jews." But note was also taken that many German Jews, who had got their start in dry goods and the clothing trade—and who had provided employment for many later-arriving Eastern Jews—considered themselves as having "graduated" into banking, and having "turned over" the garment industry to the rude Easterners.

Yet even in finance the Jewish position was limited to certain types of banking. In the 1930's, of 420 directors of the New York Clearing House, only thirty were Jews. There were practically no Jewish employees in the largest commercial banks, nor are there today. In investment banking Jews occupied a strong but not overwhelming position. Kuhn, Loeb had become the largest Jewish house, followed by the Seligmans, Speyers, Ladenburg-Thalmann, and Lehman Brothers, but none of these was as large as the House of Morgan, and, collectively, they were easily outweighed by non-Jewish houses, including Dillon, Read, which might be termed a semi-Jewish house.* In foreign loans, Morgan did 20 percent of the business, followed by the National City Bank and Dillon, Read, with 12 percent apiece. In domestic activity, however, Kuhn, Loeb and Morgan were nearly neck and neck—putting the lie, somewhat, to notions of the "international" aspect of Jewish banking. Of 252 members of the New York Stock Exchange, only forty-six were Jewish.

With the creation of the Securities and Exchange Commission and the network of laws controlling the stock market, Wall Street banking lost

* Dillon of Dillon, Read was originally named Lapowski before joining the gentile firm of William Read & Company, which grew to prominence in the early 1920's. Though Jewish, as *Fortune* discreetly put it, Mr. Dillon was never "identified" with the Jewish bankers or the Jewish community of New York.

much of its old raffishness and, to many people's way of thinking, much of its romance and all its fun. In place of its old free-wheeling excitement—the noise and hubbub, sights and sounds that had first appealed to the early Seligman brothers—Wall Street assumed a new sobriety; the daredevil days were over, and in their place had come a new mood of caution, a new emphasis on conformity and routine. The handshaken agreement—as well as the double-cross—became less popular in an age of adding machines, paperwork, and lawyers. Investment banking and stockbrokerage had become, according to one Wall Street man, "less of a game and more of a business." At the same time, any essential differences between the operations of the German Jewish bankers, who had once relied heavily on ties of friendship and kinship, and their gentile counterparts began to blur and disappear. And, ironically, as Wall Street, that notorious painted lady, became respectable, the third- and fourth-generation German Jews had, in many cases, turned to more "respectable" operations than banking—to teaching, medicine, law, publishing. Soon there was not a single one of the so-called "Jewish houses" which did not have a number of non-Jewish partners, and only a few today are headed by members of the founding families. Among them are Kuhn, Loeb, whose senior partners today include John M. Schiff and Frederick M. Warburg, both great-grandsons of Solomon Loeb, and Gilbert W. Kahn, Otto Kahn's son who, through his mother, is a grandson of another founder, Abraham Wolff. Lehman Brothers, too, is headed by Emanuel Lehman's grandson, Robert Lehman. But others, such as Goldman, Sachs and J. & W. Seligman & Company, have passed "out of the crowd."

There is one young Jewish house which has demonstrated that much can be accomplished in the old-time way—through a judicious mixture of marriages, sons, mergers, and money. Carl Morris Loeb was born in Frankfurt, the son of a dry-goods merchant, and, in what was becoming a time-honored way, ran away from the family retailing business as a youth to work as an office boy for one of Germany's leading metal-fabricating firms, Metallgesellschaft. In 1892, when Loeb was seventeen, the firm sent the young man to work in the St. Louis office of its United States subsidiary, the American Metal Company. He had an uncanny "feel" for commodity values, and within three years was manager of the St. Louis office.

At this point, young Loeb came to the attention of American Metal's president, Jacob Langeloth. But even more important, from the standpoint of his future career, was Carl Loeb's choice of a wife. She was Adeline Moses, the daughter of Alfred Huger Moses, the head of one of the most prominent Jewish families in the South.* The Moses family had been merchant bankers in Montgomery, and, though Adeline's father had experienced hard times in the post-Civil War South—which explained his presence in St. Louis in the real-estate business—he had other important qualifications. The original Lehman brothers, Mayer and Emanuel, had been his best friends in Montgomery.

Jacob Langeloth brought Carl Loeb to New York, at the age of thirty, to be a vice president of American Metal, and there—though, as everyone pointed out, they were not "real" Loebs—Adeline's connection with the Lehmans proved socially helpful. The new Loebs became fixtures of the German Jewish crowd, and ten years later Carl M. Loeb was president of the American Metal Company. This was his fortunate position when, during World War I, American Metal became separated from its German parent, Metallgesellschaft, and, in one of the shortest success stories on record, Carl Loeb found himself in control of the American company.

Soon however, Carl Loeb was quarreling with his board of directors, who considered their president too dictatorial. In the summer of 1929 Loeb offered his resignation, and it was accepted. Once again, he had chosen, uncannily, the most auspicious moment. Part of the separation agreement was that he sell back some eighty thousand shares of American Metal that he owned at the stock's considerably inflated market price. He did so, and six months later American Metal had dropped 50 percent in the great crash. In 1930 Carl Loeb was out of a job, but very rich.

He was a handsome, imperious man, whose wife never called him anything but a respectful "Mr. Loeb." In New York the couple occupied what has been described as a "His and Hers apartment," a vast affair spread out across a building so large that their respective bedrooms were exactly a block apart. Mr. Loeb's favorite means of communication throughout this large territory was the handwritten memorandum signed "C.M.L." He liked to entertain opulently, and, before an important dinner party, he liked to stage a full dress rehearsal of the forthcoming dinner one night ahead of the actual affair, complete in every detail including substitute guests who stood in for the guests expected the following night.† Sometimes, as is so often the case in show business, the rehearsals went better than the actual performances —as happened when Loeb entertained a visiting Belgian financier whom

---

* Through Adeline Moses Loeb, her grandchildren today can trace remote cousinships to such people as Mrs. Randolph Churchill, Mrs. William A. M. Burden, Jr., and the Duchess of Norfolk.

† The substitutes were culled from Loeb's "B-List" of friends. One woman says, "I'd been going to lovely dinners at the Loebs' for years before I discovered that I was one of his guinea pigs—that if I was asked for a Wednesday, the *real* party would be Thursday."

he particularly wanted to impress. The dinner was disastrous. Mrs. Loeb had retired to her bedroom afterward, when she heard her husband's footsteps approaching down the long corridor that separated the two apartments. Waiting breathlessly for his angry knock, she saw instead a memorandum slipped beneath her door. It said: "Fire the cook. C.M.L."

Adeline Loeb was the crowd's Mrs. Malaprop, beloved for her slips of the tongue and, at times, what seemed like slips of the entire mind. Meeting Otto Kahn for the first time, she is said to have gushed, "I know your father, the Aga!" When told the story of how Oscar Levant, whose ex-wife married Arthur Loew, had wickedly telephoned the newlyweds on their wedding night to ask, "What's playing at Loew's State?" Mrs. Loeb waited patiently for a punch line and, when none came, asked, "Well, what was?" On another occasion, when one of her sons got into a fight at the Century Country Club and she reproached him, he said, "But Mother, he called me a son of a bitch!" Mrs. Loeb replied, "That's funny. He doesn't even know me."

For a while after his retirement from American Metal, Carl Loeb busied himself as a gentleman of leisure, and he and his wife took a world cruise. But he was a restless, ambitious man, and soon Adeline Loeb was turning to her son John to say, "Do something about your father. I'd do anything to get him out of the house." John Loeb's solution was simple and direct. He suggested to his father that they buy a seat on the New York Stock Exchange. Carl asked his son one question: "Do you think you can run an investment banking house?"

John replied that he thought he could. He had already learned certain lessons from previous generations of bankers in the crowd, and among them was the importance of marrying well. Just as the Lehmans had secured their position by marrying Goodharts and Lewisohns, so John L. Loeb secured his by marrying a Lehman—the youngest daughter of the Arthur Lehmans, Frances, who is always called "Peter" because, some say, she bore a childhood resemblance to Peter Rabbit. Others say her father, in his Old World way, had always wanted a boy. When John and Peter Loeb were married, it was said that he was an adventurer and had married her for her money, even though the great fortune she *might* have inherited from her grandfather, Adolph Lewisohn, failed to materialize, thanks to the latter's industrious spending. What she had more than money was social position and, of course, banking connections. One sister was married to Richard Bernhard, a partner at Wertheim & Company. Another married Benjamin Buttenwieser, still one of the most important partners at Kuhn, Loeb.

John Loeb's new firm opened its doors in January, 1931. Six years later, through a merger with Rhoades & Company, an old gentile firm that needed money, the Loebs' firm, which needed a prestige name,

became Carl M. Loeb, Rhoades & Company. Like his banking prede-
cessors, John Loeb has kept his house tightly "in the family," employ-
ing, among others, his son, John Loeb, Jr., a nephew, Thomas Kempner,
and, until his recent death, a son-in-law, Richard Beaty, as Loeb,
Rhoades partners. There has never been any doubt, however, about who
is in charge. Today, John L. Loeb (the L. stands for Langeloth) heads a
firm whose partners decorate the boards of directors of sixty American
corporations; which manages investment funds totaling over $500 mil-
lion; which has brokerage income alone of $27 million a year; which has
fourteen offices and more than a thousand employees of its own,
plus twenty-two correspondent firms in 140 cities in the United States
and Canada. The firm's $12.5 million in stated capital places it among
the top firms in Wall Street. It need hardly be added that John Loeb,
since he is married to one, enjoys excellent relations with the still larger
and more prestigious House of Lehman.

John Loeb has inherited his father's astonishing sense of timing.
Thanks to antennae around the world that amount to something very
like a private CIA, he completed the sale of the firm's major Cuban
sugar holdings the day before Fidel Castro took over. In 1945 the Loeb
and Lehman millions received a new infusion of wealth when Clifford
W. Michel joined Loeb, Rhoades. Michel was married to the former
Barbara Richards, one of the granddaughters of Julius Bache, and
therefore related to the Cahns and the Sheftels and, by marriage at least,
to the Lewisohns (to whom the Lehmans, of course, were already
related). Another Bache granddaughter was Mrs. F. Warren Pershing,
wife of the son of the World War I General, and head of Pershing &
Company, a rich brokerage house. Then, in 1953, John Loeb's daughter, Ann, married Edgar Bronfman, elder son of Samuel Bronfman, the
founder and chief executive of Distillers Corporation–Seagrams, Ltd.,
undoubtedly the richest man in Canada and among the wealthiest in the
world. Bronfman money is not formally a part of Loeb, Rhoades
capital, but one of the firm's partners has said, "He's a kind of partner
who is awfully important." (At the Loeb-Bronfman wedding, Mr. Loeb
was overheard to say, "Now I know what it feels like to be a poor
relation.") The Bronfman millions, however, have joined Loeb-Lehman
and Bache holdings to make up the largest single holding of stock in
New York's Empire Trust Company, which has assets of some $300
million. Edgar Bronfman, now in his middle thirties and head of his
father's American subsidiary, Joseph E. Seagram & Sons, joined the
board of directors of the Empire Trust Company in 1963. The young
Bronfmans occupy a New York apartment with its own gymnasium, an
air-conditioned estate in Westchester built in the Georgian style, and a
4,480-acre hideaway in Florida called, appropriately, the V.O. Ranch.

At sixty-four, John Loeb, a governor of the New York Stock Exchange, is held in almost dreadful awe in Wall Street. A tall, slender, handsome, and immaculately tailored man with jet-black hair and dark, beetling brows, he looks half his age. In the Salvador Dali portrait of him that hangs in his house in Westchester, an armored knight on horseback prances in the middle distance; one suspects that this romantic dash and flair were what the artist saw in John L. Loeb. He is a firm believer in rigid exercise, which accounts for his youthful looks and splendid physique.

He has been called an overpowering father, and a tough-minded, high-handed, even ruthless businessman. "Whenever I approach my father," says one of his sons half-seriously, "I automatically begin to say, 'I'm sorry.'" One of Loeb's favorite tactics, when an associate is ushered into his office, is to work busily at some item on his desk for a moment or two, and then look up and inquire, "What time is it?" Recently a visitor was so dismayed by this approach that he replied, "Whatever time you say it is, Mr. Loeb!" Another habit is to receive petitioners— who come, as a rule, with elaborate presentations explaining why Loeb, Rhoades should help finance their companies—to listen to their arguments patiently, to smile and nod sympathetically as they talk, and then, when they finish, to stand up and say, "No." "It's discouraging," says one man, "because you never know at which point he might have been willing to bargain or negotiate."

John Loeb believes that a deal, when set, "is set in concrete," according to a friend. Not long ago, when a major corporation had sought out Loeb, Rhoades for a major underwriting venture, the president of the company at the last moment began demanding further concessions. John Loeb turned abruptly to his partners and, suggesting that their time could be better spent on other matters, led them out of the meeting. The next few hours were tense ones at Loeb, Rhoades, for most members of the firm were certain that they had lost an important account. John Loeb, however, had suspected that the corporation needed Loeb, Rhoades money and, sure enough, the president telephoned later in the day to say that he was ready to sign—on Loeb's original terms.

Because of his personal power, to say nothing of the vast financial power he now wields, one approaches John Loeb's special chair under the ormolu chandelier in the Loeb, Rhoades private dining room on tiptoe, always certain of the importance of what one has to say. He has, in other words, the kind of influence and presence that has not been seen on Wall Street since the days of Jacob Schiff.

In many ways, John Loeb is like his friend and contemporary, Robert Lehman, Philip's son and the present head of Lehman Brothers, who has been called "the last of the imperiously rich men" and "the aristocrat of the autocrats." Robert Lehman's power in the money market is as vast as Loeb's, perhaps even vaster, and the phrase, "Bobby wants to speak to you," strikes terror in the breast of all at One South William Street. His office in the building is small—many junior partners have larger space—but it gives him a psychological advantage. "When you go into that little office, you really feel crowded out by him," says one man. He himself, also slight of stature, seems to fill the room.

Lehman, however, in recent years has turned his attention increasingly to his art collection. Started by his father, who bought paintings more for an investment than out of a love of beauty, the Lehman Collection has been so enormously added to by Robert that it is now the largest, and possibly the finest, private art collection in America. The paintings range from thirteenth-century Italian to twentieth-century French, and include Goya's famous *The Countess of Altamira and Her Daughter,* El Greco's *Saint Jerome as Cardinal,* Botticelli's *Annunciation,* and *The Legend of Saints Eligius and Godeberta* by Petrus Christus, plus literally scores of others that are just as fine. The collection also includes Persian and Chinese ceramics, Renaissance medallions and enamels, and the largest assemblage of medieval aquaemanales (water pitchers) outside Nürnberg. The collection—guided by Robert Lehman's straightforward philosophy, which is, "If I see something I like, I buy it"—hangs in the offices of Lehman Brothers downtown, and also on the walls of Robert Lehman's eighteen-room Park Avenue apartment. But the bulk of it is contained in the late Philip Lehman's town house in Fifty-fourth Street, which his son maintains as a private museum and which outsiders—art scholars only—may see by appointment. Here, heavily guarded, behind gold doors and in rooms covered with deep Persian rugs and hung with gold-fringed red plush, are most of the old masters, the Gothic tapestries, the Renaissance furniture, the Italian majolica, and the other *objets d'art.* Often at night the collector himself visits the house, sometimes with his curator, sometimes alone, and prowls the great, silent rooms like a solitary Croesus contemplating all that he has amassed.

It was once supposed that Robert Lehman, being a banker, would buy art more with an eye to the dollar than with discrimination or taste. There is a concentration, in the collection, on Sienese primitives, which are painted with a great deal of gold leaf, and Lehman's public-relations man, Benjamin Sonnenberg, once commented, "What other kind of paintings would a banker buy than Sienese, with all that gold in them?" At the same time, when some three hundred items from the Lehman Collection were sent for exhibit at the Orangerie of the Louvre in Paris in the summer of 1956, one French critic wrote; "We would like the purchases of our museums to be inspired by a taste as severe as that of which M. Robert Lehman today gives us dazzling evidence." The exhibition was the talk of Paris, waiting lines formed outside the Orangerie, and over seventeen thousand people saw the show in the first two weeks alone—statistics which gratified the banker in Robert Lehman.

Today Bobby Lehman is seventy-four, and the collection continues to grow. Its total value is now impossible to calculate, and, inheritance taxes being what they are, it is unlikely that Lehman's son or any of his other heirs will be able to maintain the Lehman Collection intact and in the family. The future of the town house in Fifty-fourth Street is uncertain, and the subject of much speculation in the art world. Benjamin Sonnenberg, however, has an answer. He says of his friend and client, "To begin with, Bobby isn't *going* to die. He's firmly convinced he's immortal. And furthermore, if he should turn out to be wrong, being a Lehman he'll figure out some way to take it all with him."

Robert Lehman himself is quite aware that his death and the disposition of his collection are often discussed, and he is able to view his situation with a certain humor. Not long ago he visited the Sterling and Francine Clark Institute in Williamstown, Massachusetts, where twin tombs for the museum's founders flank the entrance to the building that houses *their* art collection. Starting up the museum's steps, he paused to gaze solemnly at the marble plaques bearing the names of Mr. and Mrs. Clark. He whispered softly, "What a way to go!"

48

"FAMILIENGEFÜHL"
. . . AND NO BARE
FEET AT DINNER

After Jacob Schiff's death, Therese Loeb Schiff began to blossom. Under the dominance of her husband, she had always seemed a meek little thing whose most effective form of protest was to burst into tears. Now she began to assert herself. She seemed, of all things, to have a personality. She became, as her husband had been, a person to be reckoned with.

She announced, for one thing, that she had no intention of leaving the big Fifth Avenue house, as her family suggested, and moving to an apartment or, as several widows in the crowd had done, to the Plaza. She would continue to live in the style Jacob Schiff had set, tended to by Joseph, her major-domo. She continued her Tuesdays "at home." She developed projects for herself. One was her practice of giving each grandson—there were five—a raccoon coat when he entered college. Morti's son, John Schiff, and Frieda's son, Paul Warburg, reached college age at the same time. John was accepted at Yale, but Paul failed his exams. John got his coat, but Paul did not. John's coat was stolen in the middle of his freshman year, whereupon Therese bought him another. This outraged Paul; John had had *two* coats, and he had had none. Therese was adamant, but Paul took his case to Joseph, who, the boys knew, was one of the few people who had any influence over Mrs. Schiff. He got his coat.

Young Paul Warburg was a great deal like his father, Felix—a prankster, a playboy, a charmer. At the age of twelve he was asked, "What did you do today?" and he airily replied, "I had lunch at Mr. and Mrs. Henry Morgenthau's. Mrs. Morgenthau thinks I'm very well read. We discussed Wells's *Outline of History* and Strachey's *Queen Victoria*." He had read neither book. He never did go to college. On a summer trip to Paris, after an all-night outing with Jack Straus and two young ladies, Paul wandered back to the Ritz at dawn and, somehow, got into the wrong room. Seeing "something large" on the bed, he flung his black ebony cane at it. It was his mother, who sat up in bed and said with perfect poise, "You father will speak to you about this in the morning."

There had been few divorces in the crowd until Paul's generation. He divorced his first two wives. His brother Gerald divorced his first wife. His cousin Jimmy Warburg divorced *his* first two wives. His cousin Renata divorced her first husband, and his brother Edward married a divorcee. For a while, Paul Warburg worked in the bond department of the International Acceptance Bank. One of his jokes was to say, as he entered the office each day, "Good morning, Mr. Carlton," to the clerk who adjusted the Western Union ticker tape. (The joke was that Newcomb Carlton was chairman of the board of Western Union.) Once a visiting partner from M. M. Warburg in Germany found the ticker out of order and, remembering Paul's greeting, picked up the phone and demanded to speak to Mr. Carlton. He was put through to Newcomb Carlton and said, "Get your tools and get right over here. Our ticker's broken." Carlton telephoned the bank's president to say, "There are a lot of things I'll do for your bank, but I won't come over and fix your ticker." Shortly thereafter, Paul Warburg took an office at Carl M. Loeb, Rhoades and, as the family puts it, "began to settle down."

Paul's nickname was "Piggy," and his brother Edward's was "Peep" or "Peeper." This was because his old German nurse had said he was like a little *peepmatz,* or peeping sparrow. (For a while, his brothers called him "Matz," but Grandmother Schiff objected.) Edward was interested in art, and wanted to teach. He approached Georgianna Goddard King, head of the art department at Bryn Mawr, who said she would like to hire him but had no budget for another instructor. Edward offered to work without pay, but Miss King said no one was permitted to do so. "But if I were to receive a check from some anonymous donor for a thousand dollars, that could go for your salary." Edward Warburg said, "Shall I write the check now?" Miss King replied, "There's no hurry." Edward's course was a great success, and soon Edward was able to approach Miss King and ask, "Don't you think I should give myself a raise?" Later, Edward Warburg helped organize the film library at the Museum of Modern Art and, with Lincoln Kirstein and George Balanchine, launched the School of American Ballet.

On Edward's twenty-first birthday Felix Warburg had written to his son:

> For men like you who have to describe—and want to teach—the impressions which works of beauty make or ought to make on people at large, it is unavoidable to ask yourself "How does that strike me?" But otherwise I have found too much feeling of one's pulse a weakening process, and I would rather watch others' reactions and try to be helpful than self-indulgent or, what is the worst quality, self-pitying. Avoid that always—but pity others with all the noblesse oblige that station requires . . . remain a gentleman . . . and you will make people happy by your company, your sympathy, your understanding. The world is full of beauty and some kindly people—find them and be as happy and as lucky as has been so far your
>
> Old devoted Father

He was an unusual father in that he encouraged each of his sons' enthusiasms, and did not insist that any of them go into banking. Gerald became a cellist of some note, and later formed the Stradivarius Quartet, named for the four instruments his father had collected. Only Frederick became a fourth-generation Kuhn, Loeb partner. But of course Felix himself had begun to say, a little sadly, "I was never born to be a banker. I've buried nine partners, and now end up as the sole survivor of this big firm, with nothing but young people around me."

In summer all the scattered Warburgs liked to gather at Woodlands in White Plains, where both Felix and Paul had houses, and where the children had been given parcels of property and, in some cases, houses of their own. Felix bought two hundred acres adjacent to Woodlands which he called Meadow Farm, and this became Therese Loeb Schiff's summer home. Even though it belonged to the Warburgs, Meadow Farm was always called "Mrs. Schiff's house," and she grew quite possessive about it. No one, she announced, was to use her bedroom while she was away—except, she added, "Felix may use it if he wishes." Even long after Therese's death in 1933 at the age of eighty—on her last Tuesday "at home"—Meadow Farm was still "Mrs. Schiff's house," and the couple who cared for it would allow no changes, always saying, "Mrs. Schiff liked it this way."

The house at Meadow Farm was considerably more modest than the huge old place at Woodlands, and, after Felix Warburg's death in 1937, Frieda moved to Meadow Farm for her summers. Here she worked on dispersing items from her husband's estate—the art collection to museums in Washington, Boston, Springfield, Brooklyn, and New York, as well as to Harvard, Vassar, Princeton, New York University, and the David Mannes School of Music. She also busied herself with the Felix and Frieda Schiff Warburg Foundation, which aids a number of Jewish causes as well as the Visiting Nurse Service, the Central Institute for the Deaf in St. Louis, New York University, the Planned Parenthood Federation, the National Urban League, Tuskegee Institute, the Museum of Modern Art, the Metropolitan Museum of Art, the Lewisohn Stadium Concerts and—hard though it may be to believe—a long list of other charities.

After Felix's death, Frieda herself established a separate foundation for settling immigrants in Israel. By 1955 it had built over a thousand homes. In winter Frieda traveled to her house on Eden Road at Palm Beach, where in her twilight years her afternoons were filled with bridge and canasta and visits with old friends. Adele Lewisohn Lehman had a place nearby, and so did the Henry Ittlesons, the Sol Strooks, and Edithe Neustadt Stralem, whose sister had married Frieda's brother Morti. In all three places—New York, Palm Beach, and Westchester— there were plenty of family around. Still, whenever she had a free moment, Frieda dictated her reminiscences into a recording gadget, as her family had urged her to. "They say I am a link with the past," she said.

She wrote: "To me, and to all our family, it has always been of the utmost importance to know one's past and to live up to it with pride and a true sense of responsibility." Her memoirs gently took to task certain members of the family—her brother Morti's branch—who, she felt, did not always "live up to" the past. Of Morti Schiff himself she wrote: "I loved him dearly, even though I might criticize his 'society' kind of life, which I knew was a sort of escape for him."

Of Morti's daughter, the four-times married Dorothy Schiff, publisher of the New York *Post,* Frieda said: "Many of her ventures, matrimonial and otherwise, have left some time-gaps when it was not easy for us to maintain contact. To me, she is disarmingly amusing and charming, even if her enthusiasms at times seem to carry her beyond her depth. . . . I am always tremendously amused by her giggly anecdotes and her youthful exuberances concerning the passing scene." Of Morti's son, the polo-playing Kuhn, Loeb partner, John Schiff, who married the George

F. Baker, Jr.'s' daughter Edith and who went sailing into the *Social Register,* the Piping Rock Club, the Turf and Field, the Creek, the Grolier, the River, the National Golf Links, the Meadow Brook, the Pilgrims, and the Metropolitan Club of Washington, his aunt commented: "Like his father he has a way of making abrupt, short, assertive statements which sound brusque until the shy grin that follows gives him away. He was brought up in the tradition of the Long Island gentleman, which sometimes comes into amusing conflict with his underlying German-Jewish inheritance."

Outside the winter house on Eden Road, there nested a pair of cardinals—wintering also—whom Frieda named "Spellman" and "Mrs. Spellman." Frieda wrote:

> I like to think that the birds, like myself, have not only derived warmth from the sun but from the surroundings in which we have found ourselves. It is pleasant to realize that these good things have been and will be a part of my life always. . . . There have been times when I yearned for the ability to lose myself in deep religious faith, and, although I have observed many of these forms, I must admit that the most meaningful experience to me has been the sense of family (*Familiengefühl*) which has grown and flourished in our household.

Familiengefühl had become the crowd's most powerful religion. It was why family holidays and anniversaries had become far more important than the Sabbath or the Jewish holy days. For the Seligmans, at one point, there were 243 days out of every calendar year that marked a family anniversary of some sort, and nearly every one of these was given some sort of observance. Lives revolved around family days. Had not young Felix and Frieda Warburg chosen a family birthday— Frederick's—to move into their new house at 1109 Fifth Avenue? It was *Familiengefühl* that warmed Margaret Seligman Lewisohn's debut party, held at the Warburgs' house. Congreve, the Warburgs' steward-butler, had, as his somewhat unusual hobby, been raising chickens from an incubator in the Warburg basement. It was probably the only chicken hatchery on upper Fifth Avenue, and no one in the family was entirely sure whether it was a good idea. But when Congreve incorporated his project into the family debut, everyone forgave him. He designed a centerpiece for the party consisting of three-day-old baby chicks "coming out" of a brooder, with a low white picket fence all around it. The chicks chirped all through the party.

Since the family was still the business, a little *Geschaftengefühl* mixed with the *Familiengefühl* was not inappropriate. And, on the eve of his daughter's marriage, Felix Warburg could write to his son Gerald to say:

Carola's wedding presents are coming in, and as she reports to me, business is good. Do not get too fat, because the house will be crowded on the 27th, for with 280 people who insist on seeing Carola married, and about 900 who will come afterward to shake her poor hand off, there will not be any rugs left in the house, and anything that is eatable, drinkable or smokable will disappear very fast. Dr. Magnes will officiate and I am quite sure he will say the right thing at the right time.

For Jacob Schiff's sixtieth birthday, a huge family party had been held at 1109. A stage and screen were erected in the second-floor music room, and at the height of the evening the lights dimmed and Gerald Warburg, dressed as Mercury, appeared from behind a curtain and pointed dramatically to an enormous photograph of the Rock of Gibraltar that appeared on the screen. The lights dimmed once more and, with a thunderous roll of drums from offstage, a photograph of the twenty-two-story Kuhn, Loeb building was superimposed upon the Rock.

But perhaps the gathering with the most *Familiengefühl* of all was Frieda Schiff Warburg's own sixtieth-birthday party, planned as a surprise for her by the children and grandchildren. Her sons Frederick and Edward devised a skit which showed that religion *was* the family. It was their version of the Seder ceremony, reinterpreting the Exodus from Egypt. But Egypt, in the Warburg version, was southern Germany, and the Lost Tribes of Israel—Solomon Loeb and his brothers—were given a Baedeker but managed to get themselves even more lost; instead of turning right at the Nile, they turned left and found themselves in Cincinnati. There, Frederick declared, the family's business was "buying feathers from the Indians and selling them at football games." Next, Edward gave an illustrated lecture on Frieda's life, using slides of various works of art to represent its various phases: a hectic cubist painting to show her frame of mind after her morning telephone calls; a plump Lachaise sculpture to show her girth before visiting Elizabeth Arden's Maine Chance Farm, and a Pavlova figure by Malvina Hoffman to show the "new" Frieda Schiff, after Arden. As a finale, her sons delivered a poem they had written for the occasion. It asked a long series of questions about who did what in the Warburg family, and the chanted answer, at the end of each stanza, was: "The boys, the boys."

Frieda and Felix Warburg's only daughter, Carola, has a summer home in Katonah, in upper Westchester, a large, rambling old place at the end of a long, shaded lane, and the house stands on a little rise under huge old trees, surrounded by rolling lawns, a garden, and a tennis court. Carola Warburg is the widow of Walter N. Rothschild—of "the Brooklyn branch," as he used to say, of the European House of

Rothschild—head of the Abraham & Straus department store, and a well-known yachtsman who, among other benefactions, presented his fifty-five-foot yawl, the *Avanti,* to the United States Naval Academy and once gave an elephant to the Prospect Park Zoo. Mrs. Rothschild is a tall, handsome, silver-haired woman who nearly always wears blue— "It's the only color I seem to see"—and whose main charitable interests are hospitals and the American Girl Scouts, of which she was national vice president. She is on the boards of Montefiore Hospital, of the Brearley School, of the Ellin Prince Speyer Animal Medical Center— Mrs. Rothschild lives surrounded by dogs—of the Maternal Center, and is active in the Federation of Jewish Philanthropies. When asked, however, if she is a practicing Jew, she answers, "Well, I was married by a rabbi," and one gathers that this is one of the few concessions she has made to her religious heritage. She is, of course, Jacob Schiff's granddaughter, and the great-granddaughter of Solomon Loeb and Fanny Kuhn; her cousins, near and remote, are named Lewisohn and Seligman; in her dining room, amidst some of her own paintings, many of which are of fruit—"I had a fruit period"—hangs the Anders Zorn portrait of Frieda Schiff Warburg, painted in the pink dress she wore the night she first met Felix. One might expect Carola Warburg Rothschild to encapsulate all the values of her forebears. In many ways, she does.

Of her father, she says, "Fizzie taught them all how to do it. They all learned from him. The Schiffs were never strong on humor. The Warburgs were. We had a certain graciousness of living, and a sense of *noblesse oblige. That's* what we had—and discipline. We had discipline."

As her mother and grandmother did before her, Mrs. Rothschild spends much of her Katonah summers surrounded by small grandchildren—she has thirteen—who have such names as Peters and Bradford (her three children all married non-Jews). Meals in her dining room are nowhere near as formal as they were in her grandfather's day, but, of course, they are still served by a white-coated butler, and one day one of the children sat down at the dinner table in his bare feet. "I looked at him," says Mrs. Rothschild, "and I said, 'No bare feet at the dinner table.' He said to me, 'Is that a rule, Grandma?' and I said, 'Well, I hadn't really thought about it. But yes. It's a rule.' He said, 'Okay, if it's a rule.' It's that simple. If you tell a child it's a rule, he obeys it. It's discipline again. That's what's been omitted from so many of these young people's lives—discipline. You can't give a horse its head without using the rein. You have to rein to be under control. You have to accept rules and limitations in order to cope with things. If you have discipline, then you can always rise to occasions."

Index